MANU SAMHITA

MANU SAMHITA:

ENGLISH TRANSLATION

MANMATHA NATH DUTT

GYAN

Published by

Gyan Publishing House
5, Ansari Road
Daryaganj, New Delhi-110002
Phone: 011-47034999, 9811692060
E-mail: books@gyanbooks.com

Distribution Network
gyanbooks.com
India, USA, Canada, UK, Australia

ISBN: 978-93-6920-247-8 (PB)

First Published, 1909

2nd Impression 2025

Printed at: Gyan Press, Delhi.

MANU SAMHITA
Author : MANMATHA NATH DUTT

MANU SAMHITA.

[English Translation]

PUBLISHED FOR

THE SOCIETY FOR THE RESUSCITATION OF
INDIAN LITERATURE.

FOUNDED BY

MANMATHA NATH DUTT, (Shastri), M.A.,

Rector, Keshub Academy,

Author of the English Translations of the Rāmāyanam, Mahā-Bhāratam, Srimadbhāgavatam, Mahánirvána-Tantram, Harivaṁs'a, Agni Purānam, Mārkandéya Purānam, &c., &c.

3, FURRIAPUKUR STREET, P. O., SHAMBAZAR.

CALCUTTA

PRINTED AND PUBLISHED BY H. C. DAS, ELYSIUM PRESS,
3, FURRIAPUKUR STREET.

1909.

MANU SAMHITA'.

CHAPTER I.

(UNTO) Manu,* blissfully seated with his mind abstracted from the world of the senses, came the great sages. Having worshipped him, they, conformably to reason and propriety,† interrogated him in the following manner. (1)

Kulluka substantiates his statement regarding the highest authority of the Institutes of *Manu* among the *Dharma S'àstras* of ancient India by making quotations from the *Chhândogya Bràhmana, Brihaspati*, and the *Mahàbhàratam*.

Whatever Manu said is medicine to those, who need medication (for their impiety)

Chhândogya Bràhmana.

The superiority of *Manu* lies in its being founded on the true import of the *Vedas*. The Smriti, which is contradictory to the teachings of *Manu*, is no *Smriti* at all. So long does the science of reasoning or Grammar shine as long as Manu, the preceptor in matters of virtue and salvation, does not appear in the field.

Brihaspati.

The Purânas, the Institutes of *Manu*, the Vedas with their allied sciences, and the A'yurveda are the four (branches of study), which are, by themselves, authoritative, and which should not be destroyed by means of sophisticated reasoning (like that of the Buddhists).

Mahàbhàratam.

* The first couplet begins with the term "Manu" in accordance with an established precept of Sanskrit Rhetoric, that "all literary undertakings must begin with a term of auspicious import, or signifying Deity," Manu being the name of Agni (fire-god), or of Prajâpati (creator according to others).—*Kulluka.*

† The text has *Yathâ-nyâyam*.—In conformity with the rules of Logic or propriety, to ask an absurd or improper question being interdicted by the rules of our *Dharma S'àstras*.—*Kulluka.*

Be pleased, O thou, who art possessed of the six kinds of opulence, to expound to us, in due order,* the duties of all the (four) social orders, as well as those of the members of the mixed castes.† (2)

Thou alone art cognisant, O lord, of the imports and regulations of the self-origined Vedas, incomprehensible in (their meaning) and innumerable (in their ramifications), as well as of the rites (enjoined to be (performed), and truths inculcated, (therein.)‡ (3)

He§ of imponderable prowess, being thus interrogated by the magnanimous Rishis, replied, hear, O ye great sages. (4)

---

* *Anupurvas'ah* :—In due order, that is, commencing with the rite of *Jâta Karma* (post-natal rite) and, after that, dealing with the successive rites in the order in which they are celebrated in life.—*Kulluka.*

† *Antara-Prabhavanâncha* *i. e.*, sons begotten by members of superior castes on wives of inferior castes, and *vice versa*, as well as those who are the offspring of unions with foreign women.—*Kulluka.*

‡ *Kàrya-tattvàrtha-vit* :—MEDHA'TITHI, a bigoted advocate of the Vedic rites, explains the passage as "cognisant of the meanings of the principles of Vedic rites and sacrifices" We, however, have thought fit to follow KULLUKA BHATTA in our translation, inasmuch as MEDHA'TITHI's construction of the text excludes many a cardinal point of the Vedic doctrine, such as the knowledge of Brahma, etc., narrows the general scope of the Vedas, and restricts the enquiry to the discussion of a single topic —*Tr.*

§ The use of the pronoun in the third person, singular, in the present couplet, strongly raises the presumption that the Manu Samhitâ, as we have it now, is not what it was originally written by its author *Manu* but is merely a recension of the original work by a disciple of that great patriarch, most probably by Bhrigu. The probability amounts almost to a certainty when we think that it might have been quite within the province of Bhrigu, who revised the old Vedic system of Astronomy, to recast and revise the Vedic codes of Ethics and Laws, which were collated

(Originally) was* this universe enveloped in darkness,† invisible to the sight, without any sign to indicate

---

and codified by Manu. Others, on the contrary, assert that, it was a common practice with our ancient masters to mention their names in the third person instead of saying "I so and so shall now discourse on such and such a topic," and quote an aphorism of Jaimini in support of their statement.

Manu's description of the creation of the universe in answer to the query of the Rishis regarding the Laws of virtue and good conduct, etc, should not be regarded as unseasonable or out of place. MEDHA'TITHI holds that the description of the evolution of the universe has been here introduced to show that the different forms of existence, from the lowest animalculum to the most exalted Brahmâ, are but the effects of different degrees of piety. Hence, this topic has a distinct and special bearing upon the main thesis of the Samhitâ, inasmuch as it unfolds the successive stages of evolution of the individualised self (*Jiva*) and marks the order in which it works up its progression upward, or is constrained to descend into the lower planes of life. GOVINDA RAJA (another commentator of the Samhita) subscribes to the same opinion, and says that, the description of this evolution of the universe is for the ascertainment of Brahma, the real cause of the universe, the knowledge of Brahma being held as the *Summum bonum* of life, and its acquisition, imperatively obligatory on all, as so unequivocally enjoined by the holy *Yàjnavalkya*, *Vàdaràyana*, and the author of the *Mahàbhàratam*. Nor are the *S'rutis* silent on the point, but rather they inculcate the knowledge of Brahma as the highest virtue in man—*Kulluka.*

* (*A'sid*)—From the unknowable and invisible nature of the universe, enveloped in primordial gloom, it must not be presumed that nothing existed prior to it, that it was evolved out of pure Nothingness. *Chhàndogya Upanishad* has an express text on the subject, "O beloved, there was the only Real (*Brahma*) in the beginning."

† *Tamobhutam* :—The gloom of Primal Nature, *Prakriti*, resulting from the latent or potential existence of all ideas in her body, the state of equipose among the qualities of *Sattva*, *Rajas* and *Tamas*.

its existence, unknowable,* and beyond the inference of reasoning or logic—as if hushed all round in one universal sleep.† (5)

After that, the self-origined Deity, though unmanifest himself, caused this universe to be gradually manifested, by transmuting his energy to the twenty-four categories such as, the primordial elements of indomitable prowess—etc., and gave the first impetus to Nature to be evolved out.‡ (6)

---

* Unknowable even by means of inference (*Arthàpatti*)—DHARANIDHARA.

† *Prasuptam* :—Lulled in sleep, as opposed to death, indicating in its midst the potential existence of life, awaiting progressive evolution and manifestation.

‡ By dint of his will, the Supreme Brahma, the underlying substratum or reality of the universe, 'gave the first impetus to Nature to shake off her state of primal equipose, and to be gradually and successively evolved out in those categories and elements, which were necessary for the constitution of the present universe. Nature alone, in the absence of a guiding, controlling Will to shape her course and destiny, might not have been sufficient to evoke a universe into being. The fortuitous congregates of atoms could never have got themselves weighed and arranged in different groups and measures for the formation of different objects without the preconcerted scheme of a devising Genius. The mad whirl-gig of molecular combines would never have been timed with such majestic rythm of motion and harmony as we find in the marches of the stars without the control of a master Harmonist. Inertia, and a few other forms of physical force may account for the perpetual motion we see everywhere in the universe, but who gave the first impetus to motion is a question which cannot be answered without admitting the existence of another reality behind the universe.

The Indian Rishis were fully aware of the absurdity of creating a system of philosophy, which tries to account for the evolution of the universe without the intervention of this unknown reality, endeavours to dethrone God from His throne, and

He, who is beyond the cognisance of the senses, subtile, unmanifest, eternal, and imponderable, and who runs through all created things, originated by himself (7)

He, wishing to create various kinds of creatures from out of his own body,* first created water,† and cast his seed therein. (8)

That egg had a golden colour, resplendent like the (aggregative) effulgence of a thousand suns :—In that (egg) Brahmâ‡ himself was born—Brahmâ, the grandfather (progenitor) of all creatures and regions. (9)

---

places Nature on it in His stead. The *Bhagavad Gità* lends its authority to this interpretation of KULLUKA when it says,

"Through my agency Nature gives birth to the mobile and the immobile."

Both GOVINDARAJA and MEDHATHITHI explain the term *Tamonudu* as dispeller of gloom, we have followed KULLUKA's interpretation "*Prakriti-Pravartaka*."

* The immaculate or unmodified Prakriti (Nature), before the commencement of the process of evolution, pregnant with the potential seeds of the five material elements, the five cognitive senses, the five operative senses, the mind, life (vitality) acts, knowledge and desire, etc, is called the body of Brahma in the parlance of Vedantism, and, as such, not having a separate existence from that of Brahma It is through the workings of the innate forces of his Self that Brahma is transformed in the shape of the universe —*Kulluka*.

† The first material element evolved out after Mahat, Egoism, and the five *Tanmàtras* (subtle sensibles) etc.

‡ In the previous cycle of evolution of the universe, Brahma contemplated himself as *Hiranyagaybha*, who was both identical with, and separate from, him. The astral body of this Hiranyagarbha, which survived the dissolution of the universe as a thought-form in Brahma, was reanimated, when Brahmâ again entered it in the form of life in the beginning of the evolution of our present Universe.—*Kulluka*.

The water is called Nára, inasmuch as it is the first offspring of Nara (the supreme self),* and inasmuch as water was the first receptacle of the Supreme Self, manifested as Brahmâ, the Supreme Self is called *Nârâyana* (10)

That which is primal, unmanifest, eternal (principle), encompassing both the real and the phenomenal, the individual created by that principle is called *Brahmâ*. (11)

In that egg that divinity, having lived for one (Brâhma) year, thought, "let the egg be broken in halves," and the egg was so divided. (12)

Out of those two parts he created the heaven and the earth, and in their midst he eternally placed the sky and the eight quarters, and the seas all around. (13)

He recovered the mind, which partakes of the nature of the Supreme Self, and embraceth both the character of the noumenon and the phenomenon. Prior to the evolution of the mind, (he recovered) the principle of Egoism, the real incentive to all works. (14)

Prior to the evolution of the principle of Egoism, was evolved the principle of Mahat (principle of apprehension). All these categories (products of evolution) are possessed of the three qualities (of *Sattwa*, *Rajas* and *Tamas*). Gradually he created (caused to be

---

The astral bodies or immutable thought-forms exist in the eternal consciousness of Brahma, and they become re-animated or re-deceased according to the influx or out-flow of life into, or from, them, according to the exigencies of the evolution or involution of Prakriti, or to express it in the language of every day life, at the creation or dissolution of the universe.

* The text has *Nara-Sunava*, the offspring of Nara, the supreme Self, the term *Nàra*, water being derived from "Nara" coupled with the affix "an" denoting filialty.

evolved out) the five cognitive senses, the recipients of the sound, light, taste, and smell.* (15)

By combining the subtlest parts of the principle of Egoism, and the five Tanmâtras, with their modifications, the senses, and the five material elements, he created all creatures. (16)

Inasmuch as the subtle particles of these six prinples (Egoism and the five Tanmâtras), which contrive to compose the body of Brahma, enfolded by *Prakriti* (Nature), are connected with the five elements as their effect, the wise call the person of Brahma as his body (*S'ariram*), from the fact of its being composed of these six (*shat*) principles. (17)

From Brahma, manifested in the form of the five *Tanmâtras,* were produced the great (material) elements, together with their functions ;† (and) the deathless Mind, which is the procreating cause of all creations, together with its subtle functions of inclination, antipathy, etc. was produced from Brahma, evolved out as the principle of Egoism. (18)

From the subtle particles of these seven Purushalike‡ prineiples of irrepressible energy *vis.*, the principles of *Mahat*, Egoism and the five *Tanmâtras* has originated this universe. From the real has proceeded the phenomenal. (19)

---

* The particle "cha" includes the five operative senses and the five *Tanmàtras* as well.—*Kulluka.*

† The function of A'kâs'a (ether) is space-giving, that of Vâyu is motion or arrangement, that of fire is transformation (lit heating or cooking); that of water, aggregation or mass-making, and that of Earth is receptivity.—*Kulluka*

‡ Because the Purusha was transformed into them at the outset.

Of these elements, each successive one partakes of the virtues of the preceding element, or in other words, the virtues of an element is corresponding to the number which is placed against it in the list.* (20)

The names and functions and professions of all creatures he (Hiranyagarbha) separately created† according to the directions of the Vedas. (21)

The Lord created the Devas, who formed the limbs (as it were) of the religious rites,‡ and the Devas possessed of life, the hosts of subtle *Devas*, the *Sádhyas*, and the eternal sacrifice. (22)

The three Vedas, distinguished by the names of *Rik, Yayush* and *Sâman*, he milched from the Fire, air and the sun for the performances of religious sacrifices. (23)

---

* Ether or *A'kas'a*, which stands first in the list, has only the one property of sound ; air which occupies the second place in the list has two properties *vis* , sound and touch ; the third element (fire) has three properties, *viz.*, sound, touch and sight, (colour), the fourth element water has the four properties of sound, touch, sight (colour) and taste, while the earth, which stands fifth in the list, has the five properties of sound, touch, sight (colour), taste and smell.—*Kulluka.*

† The Vedas, which eternally exist, are merged in Brahma at the time of the dissolution of the universe only to be patent in the beginning of the next cycle of its evolution, furnishing Hiranyagarbha (the spirit of the burning egg or globe of primal cosmic matter) with forms and patterns of a former cycle for the guidance of his work of universal creation.

The priority of the Vedas to the birth of the universe is also asserted in the *S'aviraka Sutram.*

S'abda iti Chennátah Prabhavát Pratakshánu mánábhyám.

‡ He created two classes of divinities, animate such as Indra and others, and inanimate such as (ladles) etc., the utensils which are employed in the course of a Vedic sacrifice and are invested with a kind of divinity — *Kulluka.*

He created Time, the divisions of Time, the stars, the planets, the rivers, the seas, the mountains, the plains, and the uneven grounds. (24)

Contemplation (*Tapas*), speech, satisfaction of the mind, desire and anger. Wishing to create these creatures, he thus created this creation. (25)

For the classification of acts, he distinguished virtue from vice, and connected the creatures with the pairs of opposite, such as pleasure and pain, (heat and cold), etc. (26)

With the five subtile and transforming *Tanmātras*, he created this universe, in due order, (from the subtile to the gross, and from the gross to the grosser, and so on). (27)

To the work, for which he, the lord, ordained a creature in the beginning, it spontaneously reverted in its successive incarnations. (28)

To acts of love or cruelty, of mildness or ferocity, or of virtue or vice, it should spontaneously revert, which he ordained for it in the beginning. (29)

As the characteristic features of a season of the year appear at the advent of that season, so the acts of embodied creatures spontaneously assail them (in the proper time). (30)

For the furtherance of the (good of the) world, he created Brāhmana, Kshatriya, Vais'ya, and S'udra from his mouth, arms, thighs, and legs.* (31)

* The division of castes, according to the social economists of ancient India, has its basis, on the four broad, distinctive functions in the economy of the divine organism. The cogitative, the protective, the sustentative and the operative functions, which are so vitally essential to the continuance of each individual organism, the living envelop of each individual Self or *Jiva*, must have their prototypes in similar functions of the divine body

of *Bramhà*, the direct motive principle of universal Evolution. A man, or a being, inorder to live, must think, and reason, and desire. He must have some faculty within him which might help him to anticipate his wants, to profit by the lessons of the past, to co-ordinate his innumerable relations with his environments, and to develop the deeper possibilities of his nature; and to this function or principle, which is governed by the Laws of his prototype's being, the ancient *A'chàryyas* gave the name of *Bràmhana*. Similarly, there must be in man some function exclusively set apart for combating the hidden foes of his organism, to help and accelerate a cure in the case of disease; another function, to store up and manufacture energy from the ingredients of ingested food, or from the physical elements of Nature, and another function to ungrudgingly and unremittingly serve the other three functions in the discharge of their works, *i. e.*, to be at the the beck and call of Ideation (*Brahmana*), Protectiveness (*Kshatriya*,) and sustentative function (*Vais'ya*). They respectively gave them the names of *Kshatriya* (soldier), *Vais'ya* (merchant or farmer) and *S'udra* (artisan or servant). *S'udravtam* is held identical with *Karmatvam*, (work, action, or service. Originally a S'udra meant an evangelist of service to mankind, although by an unfortunate degeneration of its meaning, it subsequently came to be synonymous with something low or vile.

As in the body, so in the body politic; as in the body politic, so in the universal body politic, and hence the ancient *A'chàryyas* came to look upon these relations of Bráhmana, Kshatriya, Vais'ya and S'udra, this classification of the units of society for the furtherance of the common weal, like the classification of functions in the divine organism of which they are the exponents, to be eternally existing in the social economy of man, whenever and wherever occurring.

These distinctions of castes have nothing of the hatered and the sense of inequality, which prompted many a civilized society of modern times to lay down an arbitrary barrier between man and man, to create an artificial gulf between the classes and the masses, only on the basis of money qualification. The framers of the ancient Samhitâs recognised the inevitable necessity of organizing a division of labour among the several orders of the society. The caste system had its origin in the principle of co

Having divided his body into two parts, He, the lord (Brahmá), became male by means of the (one. half,

---

operation and reciprocal help, and not in contempt and spitefulness as it is now erroneously believed in certain quarters. A good S'udra (an artisan) was as much free and as much honourable as any Kshatriya, or any Vais'ya, or even any Brahmana in ancient India. The Rishis took them under their own spiritual clanship (*Pravara*), and sages like the holy Kás'yapa, Angirasa, Pálakyapa (*vide* the Agnipuranam) wrote books on sculpture, architecture, veterenary medicine and other branches of art entirely for the training and guidance of the S'udras of their age. In the caste system the Rishis solved once for all the problem of capital and labour, which so badly threatens the modern industries of the West It was not the out-come of monopolies or vested interests for in the primitive societies of communistic enjoyment man had the instinctive wisdom to exclude all exclusiveness, either in acquisition or possession, for the mere continuance of his race and being, if for nothing else. It was not based on the superior rights of conquest, for a S'udra, if not otherwise morally disqualified, used to enjoy all the civic rights and privileges in common with a member of the twice-born order. It was not established with the imprecations and anathemas of a crafty priesthood, for some of the authors of the ancient Samhitás (Vishnu Ch. 57, V. 16) authorised the Bráhmanas to partake of boiled rice cooked by the S'údras. For reasons stated above, the Rishis advised the society to protect the interests of its different orders with certain limitations. Unqualified equality is impossible in society, and the Rishis, as the best possible alternative, promulgated general equality in civic rights among individuals, and specific limitations of privileges, as of a class against class. The Rishis honestly believed that there can be no society without such distinctions, and they did not err in their belief.

Kulluka subscribes to this view when he says that, Bráhmanas etc, arose out of the divisions of the divine energy (Daivyás'chá S'aktyá) as expressed by his different organs such as, the face, etc., (*Mukhádibhyah*) and quotes a *S'ruti* ; the Bráhmana was in his mouth.

and female by means of the other,* and on that female he begat Viraj.† (32)

* He begat *Vairaj i.e.* by means of sexual reproduction—*Kulluka*.

† We can not sufficiently bring home to the minds of our readers the fact that these couplets (32—34) reflect a knowledge of Embryology and the principle of sexual diamorphism in our ancient masters, which amounts almost to the superhuman, when we read these verses in the light of modern science, and with the help of the kinder light of the Ayurveda. Bramhá, the prototype of all creating agents in this world, first divided his body into two equal parts, of which the one was endued with the male and the other with the female sexual virtues. Then by uniting these two parts or principles he progenerated Viraj. Thus we find the three modes of reproduction *i.e.*, reproduction (by fission or division), sexual reproduction as in hermaphrodistic creatures, and sexual reproduction by the union of parents of distinct sexual characters plainly contemplated in the lines of the couplet. It is indeed a far cry from the birth of Vairaj to the evolution of distinct sexual characters in man and woman. Professors Geddes and Thompson in their excellent work on the "Evolution of sex" have delineated for general readers the long series of animal existence through which the distinct sexual characters of our species have been evolved out, and the many attempts of Nature to take a retrograde step towards a lost type, but we can not but contemplate the fact with the greatest complacence that it is Manu, who first promulgated the doctrine that the distinct sexual characters have evolved out of a state of original hermaphrodism, as now demonstrated by the savants of modern science.

The Vishuupurânam fills up the deficiency in the statement by explicitly saying that the left part was endued with the female sexual characteristics and the right half with the male ones, and these two opposite polarities of life, the Pitrikâs'akti and the Mátrikás'akti, according to the Ayurveda, predominate in the right and left halves of the body of each man and

Having practised *Tapas*, whom the Virat-Individual himself created, him, O ye, foremost of the twice-born ones, know to be Manu, my (humble) self, the (second) or immediate creator of all (things and beings). (33)

I, having wished to progenerate creatures, practised the most austere *Tapas*, and at first created the ten great Rishis, the lords of creatures, (named as) Marichi, Atri, Angirasa, Pulasta, Pulaha, Kratu, Prachétas, Vas'istha, Bhrigu and Nárada.* (34—35)

These (Rishis) of indomitable prowess created, in their turn, seven other Manus,† and divinities other than those whom Brahmá had created, together with their celestial abodes, and great sages of irresistible prowess. (36)

[And] Yakshas, Rakshas, Pis'áchas, Gandharvas, Apsarasas, Asuras, Nágas, serpents, birds (such as Garuda) and the several classes of Pitris. (37)

* A'NANDA GIRI in his commentary on the *Brihad A'ranyaka Upanishad* [Ch. I.—Bráhmana (Udgitha)—S. VII.] explained the term *Angirasa* as a compound of *Anga* meaning members, causes and effects, and *Rasa* meaning essence, substance; the whole meaning is therefore the substance on which the cause and effects depend.

Marichih is light, *Pulasta* is dimensiveness, *Pulaha* is contractibility, *Kratuh* is moral laws, *Prachetas* is self-consciousness, *Vas'istha* is conformability to Law, *Bhrigu* is buoyancy or supportiveness (Gravitation ?), *Nárada* is water giving or vitalising principle.

The ten Prajápatis then are the ten fundamental principles of the material universe.

† The term Manu here indicates the office of Manu; each Manu takes his birth in the cycle of time he is intended to preside over.—*K*

Lightnings, thunders, clouds, shafts of varied coloured light,* rainbows, falling meteors, meteoric claps or reports,† luminous bodies with trailing banners of light,‡ and other luminous bodies.§ (38)

Kinnaras, monkeys, fish, various species of birds, beasts, deer, men, and beasts with two rows of teeth. (39)

Insects, worms, flees, lice, parasites, all kinds of gnats and stinging flies, and the different kinds of trees and climbing plants. (40)

Thus these (Manus), through the merit of the *Tapas* they had practised, and in conformity with my ordination, created all the mobile and immobile things, each in the womb, best suited to it in consideration of the mission of its life.|| (41)

Now I shall relate to you the work and the nature of origin of each of these creatures, as narrated [by the masters of old.] (42)

Quadrupeds, deer, wild beasts, those provided with two rows of teeth, Râkshasas, Pis'achas and men, who are viviparous (placental) in their origin. (43)

All birds, serpents, alligators, turtles, and fish and

---

* The text has *Rohita*, KULLUKA explains it as shafts of refracted light of prismatic colours.

† *Nirghâta* :- which literally means the report of any disturbing physical phenomenon occurring in the earth or heaven such as, that of a meteor or earthquake.—*Kulluka.*

‡ *Ketumscha* :—Trailing light of any falling heavenly body such as a meteor, etc.

§ *Jyotimshi* :—KULLUKA explains it as *Dhruvâdin*, the pole star, etc.

|| *Yathâ-Karma Tapo Yogât* :—The nature of the work a creature is intended to perform in life.—*Kulluka.*

their like, whether amphibious or aquatic in their habits, are oviparous. (44)

Gnats, Mosquitos, lice, flees, and such other insects, which originate from heat (decomposed matter) are called *Svedaja*. (45)

All vegetables, which sprout from seeds or graftings, are called *Udbhit* (*lit.* bursting out of the earth), while those (plants), which die as their fruit (corns) are ripe and bear a large number of flowers and ears, are called *Oshadhis* (cereals). (46)

Those trees, which bear fruit without blossoming, are called *Vanaspatis*, while those which bear both fruits and flowers are called *Vrikshas*. (47)

There are various kinds of shrubs and bushy plants, and various kinds of weeds and grass, creepers and trailing plants, some of which grow from seeds and others from grafts. (48)

Variously enshrouded by the quality of Tamas, (Ignorance, or Non-consciousness), the effects of their own acts, they retain their consciousness inward, susceptible to pleasure and pain. (49) *

* Even the most cursory reader of this *Samhita* can not but be impressed with the deep insight of its author into the nature of things, which strongly favours the hypothesis that the truths the Rishis preached were clear perceptive truths and not mere deductions from empirical knowledge. Huxley has demonstrated the fact that the "difference between the vegetable and animal life is one of quantity, and not of quality" (THREE ESSAYS) and Professor J C. Bose Response in the Living and Non-Living has startled the world by his epoch-making discovery that the tissues of plants give almost the same response under pressure or stimulus.

Thus (I have) related the origin of all forms of existence from Brahmâ downward, which occur in this miserable world of constant change, tossing with its waves of birth and death. (50.*

---

* These fifty couplets from the beginning represent the accepted, orthodox view of Bráhmanism regarding the evolution of the universe, and as the view of *Manu* on the subject is regarded as the reconciliation between the two opposite schools of *Brâhmanic* thought, *viz.*, the *Sânkhya* and the *Vedanta*, it will not be amiss if we try to undersand here the real significations of the terms or concepts occurring in the text, divested of their metaphors and allegories

A'NANDA GIRI in his commentary on the (*Brihad A'ranyaka Upanishad, Brahmana*, III. S IX.) says that, creation pre-supposes non-creation and hence the manifest creator entails the necessity of admitting the existence of a non-produced creator, as the "five produced fires" necessarily indicate a non-produced one from which they have originated. This unmanifest spirit, from which Hiranyagarbha or I'svara (supreme ruler, the first produced, or manifest seed of the universe) originated, is called *Brahma* from the all-pervading Nature of its Self This Brahma, or unmanifest, absolute spirituality is the receptacle of *Prakriti* or Universal *Nescience*. *Prakriti* is inherent in *Brahma*, the absolute consciousness, as "my sleep" is inherent in "my consciousness." They are not two separate entities, but united co-relatives, perfect *Science* and absolute *Nescience*. When that *Brahma* rouses up from sleep state of quiescience after the involution of the Universal Nature, that Nescience, or that unconsciousness of sleep of the non-manifest Spirit is naturally transformed into the principle of Apprehension (*Mahat Tattvam*). Now the human mind is so constructed that it cannot think of any apprehension without referring it to a Self or Ego. "I feel," "I think," "I perceive." As there must be the factor of "I" or mineness in all acts of perception or cognition, the principle of Mahat was transformed into *Ahankâra* the principle of mine-ness. With the sense of Egoism arises the necessity of perception, and so from *Ahankâra* originated the five subtile *Tan-Mâtras*, the atoms of perception, if we may be warranted to use such a term. With perception there arose the necessity of intellection, and the next category we find in the list is the ***Manah*** or mind, from which the *Indriyas* or the senses originated. As thinking implies action, and action means the contact with the non-self (the external world), the five *Tan-mâtras*, in their turn, were transformed into the gross elements of ether, air, light, water and earth, to supply the *Indriyas* with their respective objects. Hitherto we do not find any creator or creation, these categories of *Mahat*, *Ahankàra*, *Pancha-tanmàtras*, the ***Mind***, the senses and the elements being the modifications of ***Prakriti***, or the universal *Nescience*

Then what are these? A'nanda Giri in his commentary on the *Brihad Aranyaka Upanishad (Brâhmana, III.)* says that "whatever is in the effect must also be in the cause." Now, according to the *Vedànta*, the individual soul or self is encased in a subtile body consisting of four sheaths or *Koshas viz.*, the *Vijnànamaya Kosha* (Intellectual Sheath), the *Manomaya Kosha* (the Mental Sheath), the *Prânamaya Kosha* (the Sheath of Vital airs) and the *Annamaya Kosha* (the Sheath of nutriment). The first is composed of intellect and the five intellectual senses. The second is formed by the mind and the five organs of action or operation, the third consists of the five vital airs governing the processes of inspiration, respiration, circulation, etc. The fourth is formed by the gross matter. In the same manner the principles of *Mahat* (apprehension), *Ahankàra* (mineness), the *Tan-màtras* and the mind, etc., formed the body of Brahma on the eve of the evolution of the universe. The Sheaths or the subtile organism of the individual self is inseparable from it as long as it has to undergo transmigrations; the subtile organism (S'ariram) of the universal self is inseparable from it as long it has to undergo transformations in the form of Hiranyagarbha (the first embodied self) etc., the *Ahankàra* in either case being transformed into three distinct kinds such as, the *Vaikàrika* (phenomenal, the creator of mind), the *Taijasa* (thermic, the creator of the senses) and the *Bhutàdi* (the creator of gross matter).

In the next stage of Evolution we find that *Apa* (*lit* water), whose property is mass-making, has been created, and on it the

N. B. For "under pressure or stimulus." (p. 15, l. 31.) read under "pressure or stimulus as the tissues of animals."

seed or egg of Brahma, resplendent with the aggregative effulgence of a thousand suns, is lying afloat. We need hardly say that this egg, the conglomeration of Paramânus (atoms) of the *Vais'eshika* philosophy, is the globe of the first cosmic matter from which the worlds and systems of the universe have subsequently evolved out, and we need not wonder at the statement that the material atoms have come into being out of the immaterial components of the body of Brahma, if we consider the modern Scientific definition of atoms, "as projections of units of consciousness into space." (*Maxwell.*)

These twenty four categories then were the body of Brahma, or in which Brahma (the universal substance) was successively transformed immediately before this material universe was called into existence, as Jayâditya has expressed it in his work. We need hardly say that, the *Sânkhya* philosophy starts with this unmodified Prakriti as the prime cause of this universe; and the *Vais'eshika,* with this resplendent egg of Hiranyagarbha, the conglomeration of atoms (*Paramânupunja*) as the first condition of creation, though with the difference of meanings of these two terms. The *Mula Prakriti* of the *Sànkhyas* and the primeval gloom of Manu, which enveloped the supreme Self before the creation, are both negative entities. But the *Mula Prakriti,* the state of quiescience of the three qualities of *Sattwa, Rajas* and *Tamas* (knowledge, desire and Ignorance) is an original entity, self-existing and eternal. The *Sânkhya* dismisses all further enquiries into the final cause by saying, it is impossible to ask the origin of that which is original (*Mule Mulâbhàvàt Amulam Mulam)* and supplies that starting place to the human mind without which it can not exercise its reasoning about cause and effect. The *Vais'eshikas,* on the other hand, say that, the atoms are eternal, and their combinations and conglomerations as the only mediate condition of the evolution of the universe, are effected through the agency of an unseen cause (*Adrishta*), which is unknown and unknowable, and which, like the final cause of all agnostic philosophies, partakes of the nature of "fate" or "Necessity." Beyond this stage there is no material difference of opinion among the exponents of the different schools of Brahmanic philosophy as regards the process and order of the evolution of the universe.

Now to return to the Samhitâ: From out of the body of Brahma, the unconditioned Self, was produced *Apa* (lit, water) and in that he cast his seeds which were formed into an egg, bright as a thousand suns Then by dint of contemplation, Bramhá transformed himself into *Hiranyagarbha*, the first embodied soul, and in that egg *Hiranyagarbha* or Brahmà was born. (See note ‡ p. 5.)

Now let us examine what did the Rishi mean by Nára (water); we learn from the Samhitâ that it is a kind of principle, which emanated from the body of Narà, the universal substance whose function is fluidity and mass-making (*Samhati*), and in that principle, the first material force (*Sakti-rupma-Kulluka*) he cast his seed. His seed developed itself into an egg resplendent as a thousand suns, the primal globe of burning cosmic matter. Brahmá (*Prajapati* of the *upanishads*) by means of his objective mental qualities entered that egg and was born in it as Brahmá or *Hiranyagarbha*. The passage of the text elucidates that life was inherent in the primal cosmic matter, or as *Anandagiri* in his commentary of the *Brihad Aranyaka Upanishad* (*Brahmana* III. S. 21) expresses it, "this is likeness (identity) of life. This identity is not merely found in the different bodies in proportion to their size, because life has no shape and is everywhere."

Why this seed was called an egg? Because, like the impregnated ovum, it was divided simultaneously with the commencement of its evolutien, and was subjected to the influences of two polarities of life, motion or vibration, the *Upasarpani* and the *Apasarpuni* of the Vais'eshika philosophy, the centrifugal and centripetal forces in the material plane. The universal egg was divided and broken in parts with which the first embodied soul created the stars and the solar systems, etc. The text here is only a poetic representation of the doctrine of the *Vaiseshika*, the atomic theory of ancient India, in which connection it may be said that *Kanàda*, the founder of the *Vais'eshika*, by pouring a few drops of oil in a basin of water and by stirring it with a stick, first demonstrated the origin of the worlds out of a primal globe of cosmic matter. Perhaps the term "*Apa*" (water) in the text, the vehicle of the primordial atoms, is so named after the water of *Kanada's* experiment-basin.

The notion of *Viraj*, dividing his own substance into male and female, occurs in more than one Purána. But the Manu Samhitâ

Having thus created me and all (the universe), He of imponderable prowess vanished in Himself, by oppressing (destroying) the time (of evolution) with the time of Dissolution. (51)

When that effulgent Being awakes, the universe is animated; when He of reposeful mind sleeps, the universe is folded up (vanishes). (52)

When he reposes in himself, the self-conscious, embodied selves, with their bodies, the fruits of their acts, cease their respective activities, and the mind,* divested of its functions, reposes languid. (53)

When the all (whole universe) is simultaneously merged in it, then this universal spirit, divested of all its works, happily sleeps the dreamless sleep.† (54)

The individualised Self, with its senses, long continues in a state of unconsciousness, ceases to perform any act, then it passes over from its former body in its true appearance.‡ (55)

---

makes *Viraj* to be the issue of such a separation of persons and Manu himself to be his offspring. The *Brihad Aranyaka Upanishad* relates the allegory of an incestuous marriage and intercourse of the first Manu with his daughter S'atarupá (*B. A. Upanishad. Brahmana* IV, S. 4.

* The text has *Manas* which means the mind with all its functions and the senses and their faculties.—*Kulluka.*

† *Nrivitah* :—Devoid of the states of wakening or sleep It may be questioned that how can there be any such thing as dreamless sleep in the supreme Self, whose nature is perfect knowledge and felicity. The answer is that this is merely an analogy based upon the functions of animal life (anthropomorphism, *Jiva dharma.*)—*Kulluka.*

‡ Acts (*Karma*)—acts of respiration and such like bodily functions. The astral body of the individual leaves and goes out of its former gross body and the life (vitality) and the senses follow and overtake it in its next rebirth, as stated in the *Brihad A'ranyaka* :

When being extremely attenuated (subtile) in form, the individual Self *(jiva)*, in combination with the (eight categories),* enters into the seed of a mobile or immobile being, then it is said to assume a gross form. (56)

And thus he (Brahmá), though himself deathless, by his wakening and sleep, is constantly vitalising and killing all the mobile and immobile (creatures). (57)

Having framed this, (code) at the beginning of creation, he (Brahmá) taught it to me in conformity with the rites laid down in the S'âstras; and I, in my turn, communicated it to Marichi and other Munis.† (58)

This Sage Bhrigu will narrate to you the code, inasmuch as he has learnt it in entirety from my own self. (59)

"Him going out (leaping over, follows life, and the flying life do the senses follow."—*Kulluka.*

* *Samsrishta*—In combination with the eight categories of the five subtile elements, the senses, the mind, the intellect, desire, Vayus, acts and the Nescience. The astral body (*Linga S'arira*) goes out in company of these.—*Kulluka.*

† MEDHATITHI asks how is it that, the authorship of this code, which was actually framed by Brahmâ himself, came to be attributed to Manu? He answers the question by explaining the term *S'âstram* as "injunctions and prohibitions as disclosed by the true meaning of the code." Hence these injunctions and prohibitions were ordained by Brahmâ and Manu subsequently wrote a Code of Laws based on those ordinations, etc., in verse. *Kulluka* subscribes to the same opinion and says that hence it is no contradiction to say that, "Brahmâ originally composed a *Samhitá* containing a hundred thousand couplets and taught it to Manu, who, in his turn, summarised the work and wrote it out again in his own language." Hence it is not at all contradictory to the couplet of Nárada,

He recollected this code composed of a hundred thousand

Having been thus commanded by him (Manu), the great sage Bhrigu complacently told them all, hear, O ye Rishis. 60)

In the line of this Manu, the son of the self-begotten one (Brahmá), six other Manus* were born; those magnanimous Manus) of great prowess procreated their respective progenies.† (61)

Svarochisha, Auttami, Támasa, Raivata, Châkshusa of great energy, and the son of Vivasvân (Vaivasvat) [these are the six Manus.] (62)

These seven Manus of great prowess, beginning with Sváyambhuva, in their respective cycles, created all this universe (*lit.*) mobile and immobile things.) (63)

Eighteen *Nimeshas*† (twinkles of the eye) make one *Káshthá*, thirty *Kásthás* make one *Kalá*, thirty *Kalás* make one *Muhurta* (forty-eight minutes), and thirty *Muhurtas* make one day and night. 64)

The sun divided the day and night of the Devas and men. The night is for the sleep of creatures, and the day is for the performance of works. (65)

One month of men makes one day and night of the *Pitris*, each fortnight of men being equal to a day or a night of theirs. The dark fortnight of men is the working time (day) of the *Pitris*, the light fortnight is the time for their sleep (night of the manes). (66)

One full year of men makes one day and night of the Devas. The Northern solstice is their day, the Southern solstice is their night. (67)

* *Svah Svah Prajáh*—Their own progenies in their respective times, *i.e.*, cycles of time over which they respectively ruled.

Kulluka.

† The time taken by spontaneously opening and closing the eye-lid is called *Nimesha.*—*Kulluka.*

The duration of one day and night of Brahmâ, as well as that of each cycle of time such as the Satyam, etc., now hear me briefly narrate in succession. (68)

The *Krita Yuga* consists of four thousand years (of the Devas); four hundred such years form the *Sandhyâ** (dawn) of that cycle, and four hundred such years form its *Sandhyâms'a*† (eve). (69)

Of the remaining *yugas*, the duration of each succeeding *yuga* and its *Sandhyâ* and *Sandhyâms'a*, are respectively less than those of its predecessor by one thousand and one hundred years.‡ (70)

Twelve thousands of such four *Yugas*, as computed before in their order of enumeration, count as one *yuga* of the Devas. (71)

A thousand *yugas* of the Devas count as one day of Brahmâ and his night is of a similar duration. (72)

[The wise], who know such a thousand *yugas* to be a day of Brahmâ and another such a thousand *yugas* to be his night, are called the knowers of true day and night. (73)

* *Sandhyà* here means the forepart of a cycle of time; and *Sandhyàms'a* its closing part.—*Kulluka*.

† A period of as many hundred years is its Sandhyâ and a similar period is its *Sandhyams'a* and the period that intervenes between the *Sandhyà* and *Sandhyàms'a* is called the *yuga*.

Vishnupuranam.

‡ The text has *Ekapâyena Vartante*—the amplification of its meaning would be that the *Treta Yuga* consists of three thousand (divine years, its *Sandhyà* and *Sandhyàms'a* being respectively composed of three hundred years The *Dvàpara Yuga* consists of two thousand (divine) years and its *Sandhyà* and *Sandhyàms'a* being composed of two hundred years each. The *Kali Yuga* is composed of one thousand (divine) years, its *Sandhyà* and *Sandhyàms'a* respectively consisting of a hundred such years.

At the expiry of his day and night, he wakes up from his sleep, and awake, creates the mind, which partakes of the nature of both the real and the phenomenal.* (74)

Impelled by (its) desire of creation, the mind (or *Mahat* creates (begins the work of creation), and the A'kás'a (ether) is created therefrom (in the order described before)† whose property is sound. (75)

From the modification of the ether is born the pure, mighty air, the carrier of all kinds of smell, and whose property is touch. (76)

From the modification of the air is born the illuminant, gloom-dispelling, effulgent light, whose property is sight. (77)

From the modification of light (heat) was born the water, whose property is taste, (and) from the water was born the Earth whose property is smell. This was the creation at the out-set.‡ (78

---

* The text has *Srijati Manah* which being literally translated means created the mind. KULLUKA says, that by the term *Srijati* (creates) is meant that he engaged his mind in creating the three regions of *Bhu, Bhuba* and *Sva*, and quotes a Pauranic text in support of his statement.

Manah Srisikshayà-yuktam Sargàya Nidadhe Punah.

Again he engaged his mind, teeming with the desire of creation, in the act of creating.

Manah here is identical with the principle of Mahat (apprehension) into which the energy of the Supreme Brahma was transformed after the dissolution of the Universe; what Mahat is to Brahma in the first cycle of unspecified creation, the *Manah* is to Brahma in respect of the subsequent specific creations.

† In the order of Egoism or Mineness (*Ahankàra*), the five *tanmàtras* and so on.—*Kulluka.*

‡ *Srishtiràditah.* Creation of material elements in the beginning of creation, *i.e.*, after the dissolution of the Universe) and

Seventy-one of such Divine *yugas*, each consisting of twelve thousand years as mentioned before, constitute the period of a *Manvantara* (the ruling time of a Manu). (79)

Innumerable such *Manvantaras*, innumerable creations and dissolutions of the universe,* the Supreme† Being makes out of sport.‡ (80)

Virtue was four-footed,§ and Truth, in special, was entire in the *Krita Yuga*. [In that age] men did not earn anything by vicious means.|| (81)

In the other *Yugas*, Virtue, on account of the foulness¶ of means by which money or knowledge was acquired in them, became successively divested of its

---

with these elements the various worlds or regions were subsequently created.—*Kulluka.*

* Though only fourteen *Manvantaras* have been enumerated in the Puranam, in fact there had been innumerable *Manvantaras*, and innumerable times the universe had been created and destroyed.—*Kulluka.*

† The text has *Paramehsthi*. *lit.*, he, who is not qualified by any name, form, or attributes (*Anávritta-Lakshane tisthati iti Parameshkthi*).—*Kulluka.*

‡ This is another instance of the anthropomorphic virtues being attributed to Brahma, which in fact have no room in his real nature, *Lokavattu Lilá Kaivalyam* (Human-like is his sport, (creation) and emancipation (dissolution of the universe), *S'áriraka Sutram.*

§ Virtue is represented as a bull in the *A'gamas*, its four feet respectively consisting of Tapas (contemplation), knowledge, celebration of sacrifice (*Yajna*), and gift-making (Dânam).—*Kulluka.*

|| *Nádharmenágama*—KULLUKA explains *Adharmena* as "by means not sanctioned by the *Vedas*."

¶ *A'gamát* :—Vicious or dishonest means—KULLUKA. MEDHATITHI and GOVINDARAJ explain it with " *Vedát*," (from the *Vedas*, the whole meaning, according to them, being the virtue, which is earned by living in conformity with the teachings of the *Vedas*.

one foot in each. On account of theft, untruthfulness and dissimulation, the virtue, which is earned by pursuing an honest profession, successively became less by a quarter [in each *Yuga*.] (82)

In the *Krita Yuga* (golden age) men knew no disease, and used to witness the realisation of all their desires.* The duration of human life was four hundred years.† In each of the [three succeeding ages] such as the *Tretâ*, etc., the life-duration of man respectively became less by a quarter. (83)

The duration of human life, the fruits of acts done by the mortals,‡ and the energies (moral force) of embodied creatures§ are proportionate (to the ethical forces) of each age. (84)

Of one kind is the virtue in the *Krita Yuga*, different is it in the *Tretâ*. Of one kind is it in the *Dvâpara* and different is it in the *Kali Yuga*, successively and proportionately decreasing according (to the spirit of) each age. (85)

The practice of *Tapas* (divine contemplation and communion) was the greatest virtue in the age of *Krita*; knowledge (of Self) was the highest virtue in the age of *Tretá* (the age of three-quarter virtue); performance

---

* *Sarva-Siddhârthâh* :—Successful in all their undertakings. They knew no failure as vice, which wards off and opposes all success, was absent in that age.—*Kulluka.*

† *S'atàyu Và Purusha* (the duration of human life is a hundred years) is the *S'ruti*, which lays down, according to KULLUKA, the extent of human longevity in the present *Kaliyuga*; or *S'atam* (a hundred) is here indefinitely used for a large number. Hence the text is not at all contradictory to the *S'ruti*.

‡ *A's'ishas'chaib Karmanàm*—Fruits of Vedic rites performed for the fruition of any desire.—*Kulluka.*

§ *Prabhàvas'cha S'areerinàm*—Capacity of Brahmanas to make their imprecations or benedictions effective.—*Kulluka.*

of religious sacrifices was the highest virtue in the *Dvápara* (age of two-quarter virtue), and gift-making or charity is the highest virtue in the *Kali-Yuga*. (86)

For the preservation* of all this creation, He of great effulgence, laid down separate duties for those originated from his mouth (Brâhmanas), from His arms (Kshatriyas), from His thighs (Vais'yas), and from His legs (S'udras). (87)

Study (of the *Vedas*), teaching, performance of sacrifices, officiating as priests at other men's sacrifices, gift-making, and acceptance of gifts are the duties of Bráhmaṇas. (88)

Protection of the people, gift-making, performance of sacrifices, study of the *Vedas*, and abstention from luxury† are, in general, the duties of Kshatriyas. (89)

Rearing of cattle (sheep, etc.,) gift-making, performance of sacrifices, study (of the *Vedas*), merchandise, money-lending and agriculture are the duties of Vaisyas. (90)

Only one work did the lord ordain for S'udras, *viz.*, to ungrudgingly serve the three above-said social orders. (91)

Sacred is the whole person of a man, more sacred is the part of his body, which lies above his navel, and

---

* *Guptyartham*—Each contributing to the well-being of all, and all jointly contributing to the welfare of each in the manner of libations of clarified butter cast in the fire by the celebrant of a sacrifice (*Agnau Prás'tàhutih*). The vapours of clarified butter cast in the sacrificial fire ascend the sun god. The sun god, thus propitiated, sends down the rain. The rain greatly favours the growth of food-crops, and food gives sustenance to the living creatures.—*Kulluka*.

† *Vishayeshvaprasaktis'cha* :—Non-attachment to music, women, dancing and articles of luxury.—*Kulluka*.

most sacred is his face (head); this is what the self-origined (Brahmâ) has said. (92)

From the fact of his having originated from the mouth, for the reason of his being the eldest born (of Brahmá), for the reason of his being the repository of the *Vedas*, Bráhmaṇa is the ruler of all the creation, in asmuch as he lays down the duties [of all the social orders.] (93)

Him, the self-origined one, having practised *Tapas*, created from out of his mouth, for the preservation of creation, and in order that the *Pitris* (manes) and the *Devas* (celestials) might obtain their (portions of the sacrificial) oblation. (94).

Through the mouth of this (Brâhmaṇa), the celestials eat their *Havyas* (oblations), and the manes, their *Kavyas* (oblations.)* (95)

Of the created things the animate creatures are the highest; of the animate creatures the intelligent ones are the highest, of the intelligent creatures men are the highest, and among men the Bráhmanas are the highest. (96)

Among Bráhmaṇas the erudite ones are the highest, among the erudite Brâhmaṇas those, who think it their duty to perform the *S'astric* rites,† are the highest, among the latter those, who perform such rites, are the highest, and among the performers of rites the knowers of Brahma are the highest. (97)

* *Havya*: oblations offered unto the deities are called *Havyas*, while those offered unto the manes are called *Kavyas*.—*Kulluka*.

† *Krita-Buddhayah*—those, who have the notion (*Buddhi*) of duty *i. e.*, those who are aware of the imperatively obligatory nature of the performance of Vedic rites.—*Kulluka*.

The Brâhmana has originated as the eternal embodiment of virtue. His origin is for the furtherance of virtue ; he becomes of the essence of Brahma. (98)

Born as a Bráhmaṇa, he wields the supremacy of the world, the ruler of all creatures, the custodian of the treasure of virtue.* (99)

Whatever property (wealth) is in this world belongs to the Bráhmaṇa. For the fact of his being the eldest born (of the creator),† all wealth legitimately belongs to the Bráhmaṇa. (100)

Whatever does a Bráhmaṇa eat, whatever does a Bráhmaṇa wear, whatever does a Bráhmaṇa receive, is his own property, even if it belongs to another, in asmuch as it is through the kindness of Bráhmaṇas do the other castes) enjoy. (101)

For the classification of the works (duties) of the Bráhmaṇa and other castes of society in the order of their enumeration, the wise Manu, the grandson of the self-origined one,‡ framed this code. (102)

This code should be diligently read and taught in its entirety to his pupils by an erudite Brâhmaṇa, and not by (a member of) any other (caste).§ (103)

---

* *Dharma-Koshasya Guptaye*—The Brâhmana is virtually the ruler of all the other social orders, inasmuch as it is he who formulates the duties of men and teaches them of God and religion.—*Kulluka.*

† *S'raisthenàbhijanena* : for the reason of his being prior to the Kshatriya, Vais'ya, and S'udra in respect of time,

‡ Svâyambhuba, or the Manu of the first *Manvantar*, the grandson of the self-origined Brahmá.

§ KULLUKA interprets the passage to mean that, all the twice-born orders are competent to read this *Samhità*, and says that it authorises only a Bráhmana to teach it to his pupils, condemning the interpretation of *Medhatithi* who holds the concluding part

A Bráhmaṇa, who, while observing the vow of self-control, continence, etc., reads this code, is not tainted by the daily acts of iniquity done by his mind, speech and body. (104)

He sanctifies the row (*pankti*)* and the seven generations of his ancestors and descendants. He is fit to be honoured even with the gift of the whole earth. (105)

This code (*i.e.*, the reading of this code) is the greatest of all auspicious rites.† It improves the intellect (of its reader), imparts fame and longevity, and is superlatively auspicious. (106)

In this (code) are (described) virtues (duties) in their entirety, merits and demerits of acts, and the eternal rules of conduct, which govern the four social orders. (107)

Conduct is the highest virtue, as inculcated by the *Smriti* and the *S'ruti* (*Vedas*). Hence, a Bráhmaṇa, with his senses under control, shall always conform to rules of conduct. (108)

---

of the couplet to be an intentional repitition, specically disqualifying the other three castes (Kshatriya, Vais'ya and Sudra) to read the *Samhità*, or to use his own language it is a mere *Anuvàda* (*i.e.* an explanatory repetition or reference to what is already mentioned, and which illustrates or explains a *Vidhi* or direction previously laid down, but does not itself lay down any direction.)

* *Pankti*:—means the row of Bráhmanas with whom he may chance to sit down to a *S'ràddha* repast.

† The text has *Svastyayanam* which literally means a rite or an undertaking in which lies (*Yayanam*) the continued enjoyment or non-destruction of a wished for object. Mutterings of *Mantras Homas* (burnt offerings), etc., are usually included within the *Svastyayanam* (benedictory rites) in as much as they are calculated to oppose the advent of evil and to ensure the continuance of a blessing already received and enjoyed.—*Kulluka.*

Devoid of conduct,* a Bráhmaṇa does not obtain the merit of reading the *Vedas.* Possessed of (good) conduct, he reaps the entire fruit (of such study). (109)

Having thus observed the origin of virtue from (good) conduct, the sages accepted conduct as the basis of all austerities.† (110)

The origin of the universe (*Jagat*),‡ the sacramental rites (*Samskâras*),§ the performance of vows (*Vratas*) and the rules of ceremonial ablutions.|| (111)

Rules as to visiting one's wife, conditions and forms of marriage, the mode of performing the great sacrifices (*Maha-yajnas*),¶ and the eternal *S'ráddha.* (112)

* The text has *Achàràdvichyutah,* which literally means "fallen from conduct."

† The text has *Tapasa* which here includes not only contemplation in the manner of *Yoga* but austere penances, and expiatory rites such as, the *Chàndràyanam,* etc.—*Kulluka.*

‡ The term *Jagat* (universe) emphatically demonstrates the fact that the Rishis, who first used the term, were fully cognisant of the perpetually moving, changing character of every thing included within it. The motion of our earth, which was known to the Acharyas, at least two or three centuries before the Christian era, is but a necessary corrolary deduced from the denotation of the term *Jagat.*

§ Such as the rites of tonsure, post-natal purification, etc. —*Kulluka.*

|| Such as the vow of celibacy (*Brahmacharyayam* etc.) —*Kulluka.*

Snánasya Paramam Vidhim—The mode of performing the ceremony of ablution by a student after returning from his preceptor's house.—*Kulluka.*

¶ *Maha-Yajnas,* the five daily sacrifices of the householder such as the *Vais'vadeva,* etc.—*Kulluka.*

Descriptions of professions, the vows of *Snâtakas*, *articles which ought or ought not to be eaten, purification of articles.* (113)

Means by which females can earn virtue, penitential austerities, emancipation of the Self, asceticism, duties of kings, and laws relating to money-debts. (114)

The mode of examining witnesses, duties of wives and husbands, divisions of shares, laws of gambling, and the punishment of thieves, etc. (115)

The specific duties (works) of Vais'yas and S'udras, as well as those of the members of mixed castes, duties in times of distress, and the mode of performing expiatory penances. (116)

Re-births according to the merits of three kinds of works,† means of self-emancipation, and the ascertainment of goodness and badness of acts. (117)

The duties of citizenship, duties peculiar to one's caste, and the eternal family-duties, and the duties of *Pâshandas*—these are the subjects lord Manu described in this code.‡ ((118)

The Code, as Manu, interrogated by me, first narrated, that you shall hear from me to-day. (119)

---

* Subjects included within asterisks are treated in the fourth chapter.

† *Trividham Karma-Sambhavam* :—According to the merit of any of the three kinds of acts such as good, middling and bad. —*Kulluka.*

‡ *Pâshandas*—Men, who follow scriptures other than the *Vedas*; and do forbidden acts.—*Kulluka.*

CHAPTER II.

THE virtue, which pious men, well read (in the *Vedas*)* and free from attachment and aversion,† have followed from time immemorial, (for the reason of its being based on the *Vedas*, the eternal repository of truth), and as to the truth or falsity of which the dictates of the heart are the concluding proof :‡ now hear me describe that virtue. (1)

What is virtue? KanÂda, the founder of the *Vais'eshika* system of philosophy, answers, that, which gives prosperity (cessation of wants) in this life and the highest success (Self-emancipation) hereafter, is called virtue (*Yatobhyudayo Nis'reyasa Siddhi Sa dharma iti.*)

HA'RITA says :—Now I shall discourse on Virtue. That which is sanctioned by the S'rutis (Scriptures, both *Vaidic* and *Tântrik*) is virtue (*S'ruti Pramânaka Dharma.*)

JAIMINI says :—The object indicated (as good) by a Scriptural Commandment is Virtue (*Chodanâ-lakshanortho Dharma, iti*).

The *Bhavishya Puranam* observes, "virtute is synonymous with *good (S'reya)*, and "good" denotes prosperity. There are five kinds of the eternal virtue which has its basis in the Vedas.

* The text has *Vidvatbhih*, KULLUKA explains it by *Vedavidbhi*, men well-versed in the *Vedas*.

† The text has *Arâgibhih*,—which means that it should not be pursued out of any desire or greed. Virtue is the offspring of an unsullied soul and should be pursued with an unstained heart, and for its own sake only.

‡ The text has *Hridayenâbhyunujnato* :—KULLUKA explains it by "which the mind, as charmed by its sweetness, freely approves."

GOVINDARAJ explains it as "that about which the mind does not entertain any doubt."

That, by pursuing which the mind, free from all doubt and scepticism, naturally enjoys a state of self-complacency, is called *Dharma* or Virtue.

Not commendable is the spirit of desire in man, nor the total absence of such a spirit (in him) is detected in this world. The study of the *Vedas* and the performance of the *Vaidic* rites and sacrifices fall within the boundary of acts with a desire.* (2)

Desire is based on volition or determination,† and the religious sacrifices are based on solemn determinations. All vows, Niyamas (self-control), and religious duties‡ are said to be born of desire or determination. (3)

No action is found, in this world, of a man without

MEDHA'TITHI explains "*Hridayam*" (heart) by "notions derived from perusing the *Vedas*, the whole meaning, according to him, being that to which the mind, pregnant with notions originated from the study of the *Vedas*, gives its unstinted sanction.

The true meaning of the couplet, we venture to suggest, is that "Virtue which does not spring up from the passions of the mind, which, like the religion founded by a false, designing prophet, does not live only an ephemeral existence, which, for the reason of its being based on the teachings of the eternal *Vedas*, pious men have been pursuing from time immemorial, which the pious ritualists, with minds, purified by the teachings of the *Vedas*, and equipped with testimonies and evidences of its truth, have been adoring ever since the birth of creation, and about the truth of which the dictates of the heart furnish the conclusive proof, now hear me discourse on that virtue."

* Acts performed for the fruition of a desire cannot be commended, in asmuch as it is these acts which bind the Self of a man to the necessary chain of re-births, while daily *(Nitya)* and accidental *(Naimittika)* religious rites lead to salvation by illumining self-knowledge.—*Kulluka.*

† The text has *Samkalpa* which means volition or desire, as well as a solem vow to perform a religious ceremony.

‡ Such as the duties of *Snàtakas*, etc, described in the fourth Chapter of this *Samhità.*—*Kulluka.*

desire. Whatever act a person does is but the effort of his desire. (4)

A man, by properly doing the acts enjoined to be performed in the *Vedas*,* attains to the state of Brahma;† even in this world he may obtain all his wished-for objects.‡ (5)

The entire *Vedas*,§ the law codes framed by men, well versed in the *Vedas*, from their recollections,|| as well as the rules of life observed by them,¶ the

* The desire or greed for the fruit of a virtuous act is here condemned, but not the desire or wish to perform such an act without an eye to its merit.

† The text has *Amaralokatàm* (*lit.* state of the immortals)—KULLUKA explains it by *Brahma-bhàvam*, the state of Brahma.

‡ As in the *Chhàndogya*," when he wishes to attain to the region of the manes, the manes appear unto him simultaneously with his desire (*Sa Yadâ Pitriloka-kâmo Bhavati, Samkalpâdevâsya Pitarah Samuttishthanti.*)

§ The *Rik*, *Sama*, *Yajus*, and *Atharva Vedas*, as containing all precepts (*Vidhis*), explanatory remarks recommending a precept by stating the merit arising from its proper observance (*Arthavàda*) and *Mantras*.—*Kulluka*.

|| *Smriti S'ile Cha Tadvidàm*. The recollections of Sages well-versed in the *Vedas*, as recorded in the Law Codes bearing their names, and which are collectively called the *Smriti* (things remembered).

¶ *S'ilam*—Observance of rules of life such as *Bràhmanism*, etc. —*Kulluka*.

HA'RITA observes that, there are thirteen kinds of *S'ilam* such as, devotion to the gods and manes, amiability, non-aggressiveness, non-maliciousness, mildness, smoothness (of temper), friendliness, sweet-speaking, gratitude, protectiveness, kindness, and contentment.

GOVINDARAJ explains *S'ilam* by absence of attachment and aversion, etc.

costumes* etc., of the pious, and the feeling of self-complacency† are the proofs of virtue. (6)

The duties, which Manu has described as obligatory on any particular person, have been so ordained in the *Vedas*, for he (Manu) is omniscient.‡ (7)

Having observed all the S'âstras,§ allied with the *Vedas* with the eye of knowledge, the erudite one shall perform the duties (peculiar to his order) in conformity with the proofs of the *S'ruti*. (8)

By practising pieties inculcated in the *S'ruti* and the *Smriti*, a person acquires fame in this life and excellent happiness in the next. (9)

The *Veda* is called the *S'ruti*, and the Dharma S'âstra is called the *Smriti*. Their teachings should not be put to the test of logic,|| for virtue has emanated from these two. (10)

The Brâhmana, who by dint of logic, tries to bring these S'âstras into disrepute, shall be excommunicated

---

* *A'châra*, costumes, etc., of the ascetics such as the blankets, barks of trees, etc.

† The text has *Atmanastushti* satisfaction of the mind in cases of alternatives (*Vikalpa*). As for instance, there is a regulation that burnt offerings may be made either at sunrise or at sunset. The satisfaction of the mind which the offerer derives by making such offerings either at morning or evening is the satisfactory evidence that the offering has been rightly made. GARGA says that, in such cases of alternatives Self-satisfaction is the test (*Vaikalpike Atmatushtis'cha.*)

‡ *Sarvajnânamayo hi sah.* GOVINDARAJ parses it as an adjective to *Veda*, explaining it by "inasmuch as the *Veda* is the repository of all knowledge."

§ Such as the Grammar, Mimânsa, etc.—*Kulluka*.

|| Their imports should not be misconstrued by sophistry (Kutarka.)—*Kulluka*.

from the society, as a heretical* calumniator of the *Vedas*. (11)

The *Vedas*, the *Smriti*, good conduct, and self-complacency of one's own, the wise call these four as the positive proofs of virtue. (12)

The sense of virtue germinates in those, who are non-attached to desire and wealth. To all enquirers of virtue the *S'ruti* is the highest (conclusive) proof. (13)

In a case of two conflicting *S'rutis*, both of which are equally authoritative, the wise have called both of them as virtues of equal authority.† (14)

[As for example, there are two] *Vaidic S'rutis* that, Homas should be performed before sunrise, and Homas should be performed after sunrise. These two times are different, but Homas may be performed at either of them [according to the privilege of the offerer and the nature of the deity to whom the libations are offered]. (15)

He, whose all life, from the rite of *Nisheka* to that of funeral, is governed by the regulations of the S'âstras, is alone competent to read, or to hear this S'âstra, and no other. (16)

The tract of country, which lies between the *Sarasvati*, and the *Drishadvati*, the two celestial rivers, that god-built country is called *Brahmavartam*. (17)

The conduct of life, as it obtains from generation to generation in that country among the twice-born

* *Nâstika* is the term which occurs in the text; literally it means an athiest, although it is often used in the sense of sceptic, agnostic, etc.

† In the conflict of two *Srutis* of equal authority either of them may be followed as an alternative.—*Gautama*.

and the mixed castes, is called *Saddchdr* (good conduct) (18)

Kurukshetra, Matsya, Pánchâla and Surasenaka are called the land of the *Brahmarshis*, they are inferior to *Brahmavartam* (in respect of sanctity).* (19)

From a Brâhmana, born in this country, every one in this world should learn his own proper duties. (20)

The tract of land, which extends between the Vindhya and the Himalaya, and lies to the east of Vinas'ana† and west of Prayâga,‡ is called *Madhya-Des'a* (central country). (21)

The tract of land, lying between the eastern and the western seas and included between the Vindhya and the Himâlaya, is called *A'ryavarta* (the country of the A'ryans) by the wise. (22)

The country, in which black antelopes are found to roam about in nature, should be understood as a sacrificial country, the rest is the country of the *Mlechchhas*.§ (23)

These countries, the twice-born ones shall be careful to make their home ; a S'udra, in quest of a living, may adopt any country as his own. (24)

* *Kurukshetra*—an extensive tract of land near Delhi extending from the south of the *Sarasvati* to the north of the *Drishadvati.*

Matsya is the name of a country lying to the west of modern Dholpur. Its capital *Virat* is probably same as Bairat, forty miles north of Jeypur.

Panchala, the modern Gangetic Doab.

Surasenaka is the country around Muttra.

† *Vinas'ana,* the country in which the river *Sarasvati* is lost in the desert.

‡ *Prayàga* is modern Allahabad.

§ *Yajniya Deshah i.e.,* land in which religious sacrifices may be performed and celebrated.—*Kulluka.*

Thus has been briefly described the source of virtue,* as well as the origin of all (the universe). Now hear me describe the respective duties of the different social orders. (25)

With the auspicious Vedic rites, the purification of the bodies of twice-born ones shall be effected, as (examplified in) the rites of *Garbhâdhânam*, etc. These Vedic rites are purifying both in this life and the next. (26)

By means of the Vedic rites of consecration of the womb, post-natal purification, tonsure, and initiation with the thread, the sin of the twice-born ones, pertaining to the seed and womb (of their parents), is absolved. (27)

The study of the three *Vedas*, Vows,† burnt offerings‡ *Ijâs*,§ sons, the great sacrifices,‖ and sacrifices¶ make the soul of a man** competent to attain to Brahma. (28)

---

* The text has *Dharmasya Yoni*,—KULLUKA explains it as the revealer of virtue, *i e.*, the *Vedas*, as disclosed by the counplet *Vedokhila Dharma Mulam*,—GOVINDARAJ explains it by "origin of virtue, *i.e.*, the different acts of piety such as, the rites of *S'ràddhas, Ashtakàs*, etc, as contemplated by the first verse of this chapter.

† *Vratas* or vows of forswearing meat, wine, etc.

‡ *Homas* or burnt offerings known as the *Sàvitri Homa, Charu Homa*, etc., as well as those daily offered at morning and evening.

§ *Ijas*—rites of propitiating the gods, Rishis and manes with libations of water by a student (*Brahmachàrin*); a man is debtor to the *Devas* by the *Vedic* study, to the Rishis by sacrifice, and to the manes by the son.

‖ The great sacrifices are the five *Brahma Yajnas*.

¶ *Yajnas* or sacrifices such as the *Jyotistoma*, etc.

** The text has *Tanu*, which literally means body,—KULLUKA explains it by "embodied soul."

The rite of *Játakarma* (post-natal purification) shall be done unto a male child before the cutting of its umbilical cord; and at that time, it should be fed with honey, clarified butter, and gold-leaf. (29)

The rite of nomenclature shall be done unto it, in the tenth or twelfth month, on a day marked by an auspicious star, or by an auspicious phase of the moon, or by a good *Muhurta*. (30)

The name of a Bráhmaṇa shall be a term of blissful import, that of a Kshatriya shall be one denoting strength, that of a Vais'ya shall be one connected with a term denoting wealth, (and) the name of a S'udra shall be a term implying vileness. (31)

The name of a Brâhmaṇa shall be prefixed to "S'arman," that of a Kshatriya shall be coupled with a term denoting protection, the name of a Vais'ya shall be prefixed to a term denoting prosperity, and that of a S'udra shall be a term prefixed to one denoting service. (32)

Of women, the names shall be terms which can be easily pronounced, not of any cruel import, explicit in their meanings, sweet, of auspicious significations, ending in long sounds, and coupled with terms implying bliss or benediction. (33)

In the fourth month* shall be done the rite of showing the child to the sun; in the sixth month. the rite of feeding the child with boiled rice, or according to the custom obtaining in the family. (34)

For virtue, the rite of tousure, in respect of all

* In the third month according to *Yama*, the name of the rite (*Niscràmanam*) literally means taking the child out of the room.

the twice-born orders, shall be done unto the child in its first or third year,* as ordained by the *S'ruti.* (35)

The rite of initiation with the thread shall be done unto a Brâhmaṇa boy in his eighth year, unto a Kshatriya boy in his eleventh year, and unto a Vais'ya boy in his twelfth year, counted from the day of conception. (36)

Wishing† the energy of Brahma,‡ a Bráhmaṇa (boy) should be initiated with the thread in his fifth year; wishing strength,§ a Kshatriya boy should be so initiated in his sixth year; and wishing wealth, a Vais'ya boy should be initiated with the thread in his eighth year. (37)

The time for initiation with the thread (*Sâvitri*) in respect of a Bráhmaṇa lasts till his sixteenth year;|| that of a Kshatriya, till his twenty-second year; and that of a Vais'ya, till his twenty-fourth year. (38)

Henceforth (beyond these age-limits) these three twice born ones, not duly initiated with the thread,

* In the third year the rite of tonsure, or according to the family custom—*A's'vâlayana's Grihya suttam.*

† Though such a desire on the part of the child is impossible, its father is supposed to cherish them in his heart.—*Kulluka.*

‡ *Brahma Varchasam*—The spiritual force or energy which is derived from the study and right understanding of the *Vedas*—*Kulluka.*

§ *Balârthinah*—*i.e.*, strength of kingdom, and that derived from the possession of horses, elephants, etc.

|| The text has A'-S'odashât; the prefix A' in this instance, according to KULLUKA, has the force of "till the completion (of" the sixteenth year). Others, on the contrary, relying on the opinion of YAMA, "after his fifteenth year, a Brâhmana, not initiated with the thread, becomes degraded," say that, the force of the prefix A' in A'S'odashát is "up to the limit of." We, however, have followed KULLUKA in our translation.

become *Vrâtyas* (of broken vows), and are degraded from the society of the Aryans. (39)

A Bráhmana, even in the time of distress, must not hold any connection with these *Vrâtyas*, not duly expiated according to the regulation, either by marriage, or by (Vedic) study. (40)

The *Brahmachârins* (of the three social orders) shall respectively wear hempen, silken, and woolen cloths, and put on upper sheets (*uttaríyas*) respectively made of the skins of the antelope, *Ruru* (a species of deer) and goat.* (41)

The girdle of a Bráhmana (student) shall be made of three strings of *Munjá* grass, evenly and smoothly tied, that of a Kshatriya shall be made of *Murvá* fibres tied in the shape of a bow-string, and that of a Vais'ya shall be made of hemp-twists. (42)

In the absence of *Munjâ* grass, etc., the girdles of (Bráhmanas, Kshatriyas and Vais'yas) shall be respectively made of the fibres of *Kusa*, *Ashmantuka* and *Valvaja*, consisting of one, three, or five ties, (according to the family-custom, each tie being tied with three strings of such fibre-thread. (43)

The holy thread of a Bráhmana shall be made with three strings† of cotton thread, that of a Kshatriya

* A Bráhmana student shall wear a cloth made of hemp twists and put on an antelope-skin as his upper sheet. A Kshatriya *Brahmachârin* shall put on a silk-cloth and an upper sheet made of the skin of a *Ruru* deer, and a Vais'ya *Brahmachàrin* shall put on a woolen cloth and an upper sheet made of the goat's skin —*Kulluka*.

† *Trivit* (*lit*, thrice rounded) is the term that occurs in the text. But although Manu ordains that the holy thread of a twice born one, whether Brâhmana, Kshatriya or Vais'ya, must

with three strings of hempen thread, and that of a Vais'ya with three strings of woolen thread, suspended from the upper (part of the body). (44)

For virtue, a Bráhmana shall carry a staff made of the *Vilva* or the *Palás'a* wood;* a Kshatriya, one made of the *Vata* or the Catechu wood; and a Vais'ya, one made of the *Pilu* or the *Audumvara* wood. (45)

The staff of a Bráhmana (religious student) shall be made of a height so as to reach to the hair of his head, that of a Kshatriya (student) shall of a height so as to reach his forehead, while that of a Vais'ya (student) shall be of a height so as to reach up to the tip of his nose. (46)

The staff shall be straight, whole-barked, not eaten into by worms (*lit.* unulcerated), beautiful to look at, unburnt, and uncreative of terror to any person.† (47)

With such a desirable staff in his hand, and having worshipped the sun and thrice circumambulated the fire, he (a religious student) shall go forth asking for alms, as laid down in the regulation. (48)

The foremost of the twice-born ones (a Bráhmana student), duly initiated with the thread, shall beg alms

of three strings of thread, yet in practice it is made to consist of nine strings, each three of them being fastened with a knot or *Granthi* on the authority of the *Chhándogya Paris'ishtam*.

DEVALA too says that the holy thread must consist of nine strings (*yajnopavitam kurvita sutràni nava tantavah*).

* The text has *Vilva* and *Palàsa* staffs. But here only either of these staffs should be carried as stated in the Vasishtha, *Vailva Pàlàs'o và Danda* (a staff either of the *Vilva* or the *Palàs'a* wood)

† *An-udvega-karà Nrinàm*—with which he must not threaten any.

by pronouncing the term "*Bhavat*" in the first part,* a Kshatriya, by uttering it in the middle part, and a Vais'ya, by uttering it at the end, (of his begging formula). (49)

He shall beg alms first of his own mother, or sister, or mother's sister,† or of any other woman, who might not insult him with a refusal. (50)

Having collected so much alms as necessary and undeceitfully made over the same to his preceptor, he shall sip water: and pure in body, he shall eat his meal, sitting with his face towards the east. (51)

He, who eats his meal with his face towards the east, acquires longevity; by eating his meal with his face towards the south, a person acquires fame. He, who eats his meal with his face towards the west, acquires opulence; by eating with his face towards the north, he acquires truthfulness. (52)

Having sipped water, a twice-born one shall eat his meal, each day, self-controlled; having eaten, he shall again sip water and touch the external orifices of his organs‡ with water. (53)

Each day, having worshipped it, and without speaking ill of it, he shall eat his food. Let him rejoice at

---

* The formula for a Bráhmana is *Bhaban Vikshàm dehi*, you (be pleased) to give me alms, that for a Kshatriya student is *Vikshàm Bhaban dehi* (alms you be pleased to give), and that for a Vais'ya student is *Vikshám dehi Bhavan*, give me alms, O thou revered one.

† In the absence of his mother, he shall beg of his sister; in the absence of a sister he shall beg of his mother's sister; in the absence of a mother's sister he shall beg of a woman, who might not refuse him the alms, —*Kulluka*

‡ The text has *Khàni*, which means the external orifices of the organs. The mouth, the eyes, the nostrils, and the ducts of the ears are what is here contemplated.—*Kulluka.*

the sight of his entire food (*Lit*, boiled-rice), and propitiate it, and pray it to be available, each day.* (54)

Food, daily worshipped, gives strength and vitality. Unworshipped food destroys both the worlds of its partaker.† (55)

Let him not eat the leaving of any body's (food),‡ nor take a (third) meal during the interval of his morning and evening ones § Let him avoid over-eating. He must not go any where without washing his mouth after eating. (56)

Over-eating brings on ill-health, shortens the duration of life, proves hostile to acts (sacrifices) which lead to heaven, is sinful and condemned by men. Hence, let him avoid over-eating. (57)

Always shall a Brâhmana sip water with the *Brahma-tirtham*, with the *Kâya*, or with the *Daiva-tirtham*, but never with the *Pitri-tirtham*. (58)

The region about the ball of the thumb is called the *Brahma-tirtham*, the *Kaya-tirtham* lies at the root

---

* As it is said in the A'DIPURA'NAM, "in as much as it is in the *S'ruti* that food is Vishnu himself, let a person, seeking vitality, constantly meditate upon me, worship me, eat me with joy, rejoice at my sight, propitiate me, pray me to be available each day, and renounce, at my sight, his grief from whatsoever cause arisen.

† Both MEDHA'TITHI and GOVINDARA'JA observe that, this worship is daily obligatory like the rites of *Sandhyâ*, and as it is a daily obligatory duty (*Nitya Karma*), its violation entails sin, although its performance does not give any merit. This enumeration of benefits of the worshipped food is a praise of the food, a mere *Arthavâda* and is not here introduced to rouse up the desire of the partaker for securing those fruits or benefits in the manner of a *Kâmya Karma* (act for the fruition of a desire).

‡ Hereby the giving of leavings even to a S'udra is prohibited.

§ For the purposes of the vow of a

of the small finger, the *Daivam-tirtham* lies at the tips of the fingers, and the *Pitri-tirtham* (sacred to the manes) lies between the middle parts of the index and the small fingers (59)

First, let him thrice sip water, and then twice rub his closed lips with the tip of his wet thumb. After that, let him touch his organs, chest,* and head with water. (60)

A person, conversant with virtue, and seeking purification, shall sit in a lonely place, facing towards the east or the north, and constantly do the rite of *A'chamanam* (sipping water) with cool,† frothless water by the aid of the (above-said) *Tirthas*. (61)

[In connection with the rite of *A'chamanam*] a Bráhmaṇa is purified by sipping water, enough to reach down to (the region of) his heart; a Kshatriya, by sipping water enough to moisten his throat; a Vais'ya, by sipping enough water to moisten his mouth; and a S'udra, by sipping a quantity sufficient to moisten his lips and the tip of his tongue. (62)

A twice-born one is said to be *upaviti* (wearing the holy thread in the usual way) when the holy thread or the upper sheet lies suspended from his left shoulder on his right hip, leaving the right arm untouched and (free). Similarly, when the same lies suspended from his left shoulder, he is called *Prâchinâviti*, when

---

* The text has *A'tmânam* which means Self. Self or the soul, according to the Upanishads, is located in the heart; hence it is the practice to touch the chest with water in an act of *A'chamanam*.

† According to *A'pastambha* hot or boiled water may be used by a sick or diseased person.

it hangs round his neck (like a necklace), he is called *Niviti.* (63.*

A torn girdle (*Mekhalâ*), antelope-skin (*Ajina*), or holy thread, as well as a broken staff, or ewer should be cast in the water, and a new one should be taken by consecrating it with the *Mantra.* (64)

The rite of *Kes'ânta** should be done unto a Bráhmana in his sixteenth year, unto a Kshatriya in his twenty-second year, and unto a Vais'ya in his twenty-fourth year. (65)

For the purification of their persons, these rites, excepting that of initiation with the thread, shall be done unto women, in due time and in due order, without any *Vaidic Mantras.* (66)

The sacrament of marriage is to a female, what initiation with the thread is to a male. The service of the husband is to the wife, what his residence in the preceptor's house, as a religious student, is to the husband; the household duty is to a woman, what the making of burnt offerings is to a man. (67)

Thus is described the regulation of initiation with the thread in respect of the twice-born ones, the sacred initiation which is as a second birth unto them. Now hear me describe the acts and duties (*Karma-Yoga*) which are obligatory on them, after initiation. (68)

Having initiated a pupil, let the preceptor teach him the rules of purification and good conduct, as well as the mode of doing burnt offerings and *Sandhyâs*, (69)

For the end of studying the *Vedas*, let a student, self-controlled, clad in a light garment, and looking

---

* This stanza is but a paraphrase of the opinion of *Gobhila* on the subject.

towards the north,* do the rite of *A'chamanam*, and unite his palms in the manner of a *Brahmânjali*,† after which, lessons shall be given to him. (70)

At the commencement and at the close of his *Vedic* study, a student shall catch hold of the feet of his preceptor. He shall read with the palms of his hands united. This is called *Brahmânjali* (the united palms of Brahma or *Vedic* study.) (71)

With his arms parallelly outstretched, he shall make obeisance unto his preceptor, by touching his (preceptor's) right-foot with the right, and his left-foot with the left hand of his own.‡ (72)

Let the preceptor, free from laziness, address his pupil, at the time of teaching, as "O, do you read now," and end his (day's) lesson by saying, "let there be a stop here." (73)

Let a Brâhmana utter *Pranava* at the commencement and at the end of his study. *Pranava*, not uttered at the commencement, leads to the destruction of the reading; not pronounced at the close, it kills the remembrance of the studied subject. (74)

Seated on a (mattress) of *Kus'a* grass, with their tops directed towards the east, and purified by taking hold of the *Kus'a* blades in his hands, let him purify

* On his right hand side the pupil, looking towards the east or the north.—*Gautama.*

† *Brahmânjali* :—Drawing up the hands a little in a flexed posture and then by uniting the palms—this is called *Brahmânjali*.—*Kulluka.*

‡ Laying the palms of his outstretched hands on their back on the ground, let him catch hold of his preceptor's right foot with his right hand and his left foot with his left hand.—*Paithanemi.*

himself by practising three *Prânâyâmas,** after which he shall become competent to utter the *Pranava.* (75)

Akâra (A), *Ukâra* (U) and *Makâra* (M), (the component letters of the *Mantra, Om*), *Prajâpati,* (the creator of the universe), milched from the three *Vedas,* together with the (*Vyâhriti Mantras*) *Bhurbhuvah* and *Svah.*† (76)

* *Prànàyàma*—Regulation of the breath in a particular manner. 'He shall purify his body by three *Prànàyàmas,* consisting of fifteen *Màtràs* (*i. e.,* lasting for a time necessary to utter fifteen short vowels).—*Gautama.*

† We find both in the *Upanishads* and the *Puranas* that, this material, phenomenal universe, with its life and living inmates, has evolved out of the eternal "*Om,*" the exponent of vibrations of the primordial ether. The inspired rhapsodists of the *Rik Veda* chant that, there is only one substance in the world, and the *Tàntrikas* and *Tattvavàdins* (knowers of *Tattvas*) aver that, the different forms of matter have originated from that one substance through the variations of atomic vibrations, or to express it in their own terms, through the action of the different Matrix sounds (*Màtrikà Varnas*). Sound is the first expression of a thought or idea, and therefore the Matrix sounds were the first realisation of the idea of universal evolution.

Now the component sounds of "Om" (A + U + M) represent all the sounds, both vowel and consonant, of the Sanskrit Alphabet, and hence they are the matrix sounds or vibrations that ushered into being all forms of existence. A (अ) is the first vowel sound as well as the first letter of the Alphabet, and U (उ) is the middle vowel sound; or in other words, the rest of the vowel sounds are but the modifications of A (अ) and U (उ). M (म) is the last consonant sound, the last letter of the five *Vargas* or groups of principal consonants, the remaining consonants being only auxiliary or intermediate sounds (*Antasthas* and *Ayogavàhas*). Thus we see that the components of Om represent the three whole gamuts of existence, the *Vyâhritis,* or the *Bhur bhuva* and *Svah* (the spheres of being, becoming and Self). *Prajàpati* milched this Om, with the three *Vyàhritis*, from the three *Vedas, i.e.*, he

Prajâpati, the inmate of the supreme sphere, recovered each (of the three feet of the) *Gâyatri*, consisting of the *Riks*, running as *Tad*, etc., from the three *Vedas*. (77)

The *Veda*-knowing Bráhmaṇà, who mutters this three-footed *(Tripâda) Gâyatri*, preceded by the *Pranava** and the *Vyàhriti Mantras*, at meetings of the day and night, becomes associated with (obtains) the merit of reading the entire *Vedas*. (78)

A twice-born one, who mutters these three Riks a thousand times, each day, is able to cast off all sin within a month, as a snake casts off its slough. (79)

A Bráhmana, Kshatriya, or a Vais'ya, who becomes dissociated with this *Rich* (*Gâyatri*), or deviates from performing his religious duties in proper times, is condemned by the virtuous. (80)

The three great eternal *Vyáhritis*, appended to the *Omkâra*, and the three-footed *Gâyatri* form the mouth of *Brahma*.‡ (81)

He, who unremittingly mutters these *Mantras* for three years in succession, attains to the Supreme Brahma, becoming all-coursing like the air, and unaffected and all-embracing like the universal expanse of ether. (82)

The single-lettered (*Mantra*, *Om*) is the Supreme

recovered this knowledge of the eternal economy of things from the three *Vedas*, the repository of eternal knowledge.

* *Pranava* is same as the "*Om* or *Omkàra*."

† *Vyàhritis*, the three *Vyàhritis*, such as, the *Bhuh*, *Bhuvah* and *Svah*.

‡ Bráhmana-mukham (*lit.* mouth of Brahma), KULLUKA explains it by "the chief means of attaining to *Brahma*, or the mouth of the *Vedas*. *i. e.*, to be muttered before commencing the study of the *Vedas*.

Brahmá, *Pránàyamas** are the highest austerity, there is nothing greater than the *Sávitri* (*Gáyatri*) *Mantra*, and truthfulness is greater than silence. (83)

All the *Vaidic* rites such as, the *Japas*, *Homas*, etc., do perish in time,† but eternal (*lit.* decayless) is the *Pranava*, since *Pranava* is identical with *Brahma-Prajápati*. (84)

A *Japa-yajna* (muttering of a *Mantra*) is ten times more meritorious than a *Vidhi-yajna* (Ritualistic sacrifice). The muttering of a *Mantra* in a low or inaudible tone (*Upâms'u Japa*) is a hundred times, and a *Mánasa Japa* (mental repetition of a *Mantra*) is a thousand times as much meritorious. (85)

The four *Pâka-yajnas*,‡ if added to the *Vidhi-yajnas*,§ cannot count a sixteenth part of a *Japa-yajna* in respect of merit. (86)

Undoubtedly by means of *Japa* alone, a Bráhmaṇa achieves success (becomes liberated), no matter whether he performs any other *Vaidic* sacrifice or not; since a Bráhmaṇa is said to be a friend|| of *Brahma*. (87)

---

* *Dharanidhara* reads the text as *Ekàkshara-param Brahma*, *Prànàyàma-param Tapah*, meaning *Brahma* is symbolised by the single lettered *Mantra* (*Om*). *Tapas* essentially consists in practising *Prànàyamas*. We have adopted KULLUKA's reading who has followed MEDHA'TITHI

† Perish aften their fruits are exhausted.—*Kulluka*.

‡ The four *Pàka-yajnas* (*lit*, sacrifices in which rice is cooked) other than the one known as the *Brahma yajna* (study of the *Vedas*) are the *Vais'vadevas*, *Homas*, *Vali-karmas*, daily *Sr'àddhas* and *Atithi-puja* (hospitality to *Atithis*).

§ Such as *Darsa-Paurnamàsi* and the like sacrifices —*Kulluka*.

|| The text has *Maitro Bràhmana Uchyate*—KULLUKA explains it by *Brahmanah Sambandhi* related to *Brahma i. e.*, he is merged in the supreme self, as narrated in the *A'gamas*.

The senses, spontaneously running towards their attractive objects of gratification, the erudite one shall control, as a charioteer controls his (harnessed) horses. (88)

Of the eleven senses, enumerated by the sages of yore, I shall discourse on each of them in detail and in due order. (89)

The ears, the skin, the eyes, the tongue, the nose which is the fifth, the anus, the reproductive organ, the hands, the legs, and the speech which is the tenth, (these are the ten senses). (90)

The first five, in due succession, commencing with the ears, are called the cognitive senses (*Buddhindriyâni*), the (second) five, commencing with the anus, are called the operative senses (*Karmendriyâni.*) (91)

The mind is known as the eleventh (sense), which partakes of the nature of both the cognitive and the operative senses, and by conquering which, one is enabled to conquer the (other) ten (senses). (92)

(A person), through the contact of his senses (sense organs) with their objects of gratification, undoubtedly acquires sin.* Hence, by controlling them, one achieves success (obtains liberation.) (93)

Never is desire extinguished by enjoying the objects of desire; like the fire fed with libations, of clarified butter, it doubly burns up.† (94)

* Compare *S'ankara's* commentary on the *Brihad A'ranyaka Upanishad* Ch. I. Bráhmana III. (Udgithá). For by contact, which is their connection with the special work, which they well performed, they were allied with the sin of the demons.

† Compare the saying of *Yayáti* in the *Vishnu-purânam*. Food grain, gold, animals, and women that exist in this world, desire even in respect of a single one of these objects of enjoyment is never satiated, hence let a man renounce inordinate desire. With

Of one who has obtained all the objects of his desire and the other who has renounced all the objects of desire, the man of renunciation is superior to him of enjoyment. (95)

These senses, attached to their respective objects, cannot be so effectively controlled by means of inanition (*i.e.*, by withholding them from their objects) as by the cultivation of knowledge.* (96)

The study of the (*Vedas*), renunciation, the performance of religious sacrifices, self-control and devotional austerities, made by him, O Brâhmana, who is wicked at heart, can never be successful.† (97)

The man, who, having heard, touched, seen, eaten or smelled anything (whether good or bad), does not feel pleasure or pain, is said to have conquered his senses. (98)

Of all the senses (of a man), if only one sense manages to leak out, thereby all his wisdom leaks out, like the water of a water-bladder (through its only outlet.) (99)

Having controlled the concourse of (the external) sense organs and, having subdued the mind, let him work out all his ends, averting the pain of the body by means of *Yoga*. (100)

During the morning *Sandhyâ*, he (the votary) shall

---

the mind attached to objects of the senses, I have lived a thousand years complete, still my thirst does not abate—*Vishnu Puranam.*

* *Jnânena* :—by constantly thinking of the unstable character of prosperity, the transitoriness of human life, and the obnoxous nature of the human body which is a bag of bones and muscles, etc.—*Kulluka.*

† The text has *Dushta-bhàvasya*, which literally means of a man of bad or sullied feelings and ideas. KULLUKA explains it as whose mind is tainted by the object of the senses.

mutter the *Sâvitri* (*Mantra*), standing, until the sun is seen (on the horizon). During the evening *Sandhyá* he shall mutter the *Mantra*, in a sitting posture, until the stars do appear (in the heaven).* (101)

By muttering the *Mantra* in a standing position during the rite of morning *Sandhyâ*, one is absolved of the sin accumulated in the night. By muttering it in a sitting posture in the evening,† one is absolved of the sin acquired during the day.‡ (102)

He, who does not stand by his morning *Sandhyâ*, nor worships in the evening, shall be disqualified from performing all Brahmanic rites, like unto a S'udra. (103)

Incapable of reading a large portion of the *Vedas*, he, conforming to the regulation of daily reading the *Vedas*, shall mutter, self-controlled, and with undivided attention, the *Sâvitri Mantra*, coupled with the *Vyâhritis*, on the shore of a river or pool in a lonely forest. (104)

There is no prohibition in respect of reading the allied branches of the *Vedic* study (such as, the Prosody, Grammar, rules of pronounciation, etc.,) or in respect of the *Homa Mantras*, or in respect of that portion of the *Veda* which should be read each day (*i.e.*, the *Sandhyâ Mantras*), during the period in which the study of the *Vedas* is ordinarily interdicted. (105)

---

* MEDHA'TITHI gives prominence to the postures taken by the votary during the performance of the *Sandhyà* prayer as the primary factor in imparting merit :

† *Sandhyà*, according to *Yàjna-Valkya*, lasts for a *Mahurta* (forty-eight minutes) at either meeting of the day and the night.

‡ Compare *Yàjna-Valkya* ; the sin unknowingly committed by a man, either in the day or night, is expiated by thrice performing *Sandhyà*, each day.

This prohibition does not extend to the daily rites of (*Japas*, *Homas*, etc.), in asmuch as they are called the *Brahma Satram** (the sacrifice of Brahma); the offering of *Vaidic* recitation, made during the continuance of the period of non-study, which is symbolised by the *Mantra*, *Vashat*,† produces auspicious fruits. (106):

Unto him, who, pure and self-controlled, studies the *Vedas*, according to the regulation, continuously for a year, (the study) sheds, milk, milk-curd, clarified butter and honey,‡ each day. (107)

A *Vaidic* student (*Brahmachârin*), until he returns to his father's house, shall kindle the fire at morning and evening, beg alms, lie on the bare ground, and do what is conducive to the good of his preceptor,† each day. (108)

The son of the preceptor, one who is devoted to service, a virtuous person, one who is pure, a relation, one who is capable of comprehending the (meaning of the *Vedas*), an honest youth, a son, and a paying student, these ten are fit to be taught. (109)

Without being asked, one must not speak anything

---

* KULLUKA amplifies the term *Brahma Satram* as *Brahma* (Veda) *eva Satram*, *i. e*, the sacrifice of *Brahma*, the preposition "of" having an appositive sense in this instance.

† *Vashat* is the term that is uttered at the close of a *Vaidic* lesson. Hence the term is here figuratively used for the suspense of *Vedic* study, or in other words it is here used to denote the period during which the study of the *Vedas* is forbidden.

‡ The text has *Payo-dadhi-ghritam Madhu* (milk, curd, clarified butter and honey) which, according to the technicalities of the *Hindu Sàstra*, means the satisfaction of the gods and the manes. Compare *Yàjna-valkya*, the twice born one, who reads the *Rig-Veda*, every day, is said to satisfy the gods with milk and honey, and the manes with honey and clarified butter.

to any person,* nor should he speak if any question is put to him without decorum. In such cases, the intelligent one shall behave like a dumb person.* (110)

He, who puts an improper question, or he who answers an improper one, either of them meets his doom, or incurs the enmity of the either. (111)

Where there is no virtue or gain, or where there is no prospect of a counter-balancing service, there knowledge should not be imparted, like a good seed in a barren soil. (112)

Even in the absence of a means of livelihood, rather let a *Vedic* preceptor die with his knowledge than impart it to an unworthy recipient (pupil) (113)

The presiding deity of knowledge† came to a Bráhmaṇa and said, "preserve me, I am thy highest treasure. Do not impart me to a malicious person, thereby my potency will be kept unimpugned.† (114)

To him, whom thou shalt know to be pure, perfectly continent, and free from the follies of the world, to that Bráhmaṇa, to that custodian of the treasure of knowledge, shalt thou impart me." (115)

He, who acquires the knowledge of the *Vedas* (lessons in the *Vedas*) from a studying pupil, or from a teaching preceptor, without his permission, stands guilty of the theft of Brahma and goes to hell for his crime. (116)

---

* The text has *Jadavat*, which literally means like a fool or an idiot. KULLUKA explains it by *Muka-iva*, like a dumb person.

† The text has *vidyá*, the presiding goddess of knowledge. Compare Vaistha Ch. II, vs. 2—5.

Him, from whom one has acquired any secular, *Vaidic*, or spiritual knowledge,* he shall reverentially accost without waiting to be first spoken to. (117)

A Brâhmaṇa, who, knowing only the *Gâyatri Mantra*, conforms to the rules of conduct as laid down in the Ordinance, is superior to a Brâhmaṇa, who, although well-versed in the three *Vedas*, eats forbidden food and sells things which ought not to be sold.† (118)

He, who sits on a bed or a cushion on which his preceptor (or superior) is used to sit, shall find no good (prosperity) in this world. Happening to sit on a bed or cushion (at the time), he shall stand up, leaving his bed or cushion, and accost his preceptor at his advent. (119)

At the advent of an old man, old in years and wisdom), the vital airs of a youth heave up and attempt to leap over to him; they are restored to their normal condition by his rising up from his seat and duly welcoming him in. (120)

The duration of life, fame, and bodily strength, these four (things) of him, who sits in the assembly of the old‡ and serves them faithfully, each day, are found to increase. (121)

Having accosted an elderly person, a Brâhmaṇa,

---

* A spiritual teacher is more venerable than a *Vaidic* preceptor, and a *Vaidic* preceptor is more venerable than an imparter of secular knowledge.—*Kulluka*.

† The text has *Sarvâs'i* and *Sarva-Vikrayi* which literally means eater of all kinds of food and seller of all articles of sale. KULLUKA explains it by *Nishiddha-bhojana-s'ila* and *Pratishiddha Vikretâ* which we have adpoted in our translation.

‡ In the assembly of preceptors or superiors —*Kulluka*.

after the accosting, shall enumerate his own name as, I am that so and so who accost you.* (122)

If the person, accosted, chances not to know Sanskrit (the usual language of accosting), then the accoster shall address him as, I am so and so; likewise ladies in general should be thus accosted. (123)

At the time of accosting one shall utter the term "Bho" (O) at the end of his name, inasmuch as that term, in common with the name of a person, signifies the fact of addressing. (124)

A Brâhmaṇa accoster shall be re-accosted as, "be long-lived, O you, handsome-looking one," and the last vowel sound of his name, in the event of its ending in a vowel sound, shall be pronounced in a *Pluta* voice.† (125)

A Bráhmaṇa, who, having been accosted, does not know how to return it (*i.e.*, does not know the formula of re-accosting), shall not be accosted at all by the erudite. He is like unto a S'udra. (126)

In meeting a Bráhmaṇa, his spiritual good will be the first thing that shall be enquired; similarly, the worldly peace of a Kshatriya, the opulence of a Vais'ya, and

---

* Both Medhátithi and GOVINDARAJA hold that, the accoster shall couple his own name with the term of accosting or welcome.

Let him accost (a superior) by mentioning his own name as, I am so and so that accost you.—*Gautama.*

O, I am that so and so, let him thus mention his own name.—*Sámkhyáyana.*

† The final vowel of the name of a Brahmana (*As'udra*), or if it does not terminate in a vowel sound, the one immediately preceding the last letter of the name should be uttered in a thrice prolated or protracted manner at the time of addressing or accosting a Brahmana (*Teh pluta Udàtta-Pànini*).

the good health* of a S'udra are the things that shall be asked after the first meeting. (127)

A virtuous man shall not address a person, engaged in celebrating a sacrifice, although his younger in years, by his own name. He shall address him as, "Bho" (O), "Bhabat" (revered one), etc. (128)

One shall address another man's wife, not related to him by marriage, as Bhabati (revered lady), etc., he shall address his younger sister as, O thou fortunate one (*Subhage*). (129)

One shall stand up in the presence of one's uncles, father-in-law, maternal uncles, priests *(Rittviks)* and preceptors, although younger than him in years, and welcome them as, I am that so and so, etc., (that accost you). (130)

A mother's sister, the wife of a maternal uncle, or a father's sister shall be revered as the wife of a *Guru*. All these are equally venerable as the preceptor's wife. (131)

One shall accost a wife of his elder brother, belonging to his own caste, by clasping her feet, on returning from a distant country; one shall accost his aunt and mother-in-law by clasping their feet. (132)

One shall behave unto his elder sister, mother's sister, or father's sister as his own mother; but his mother is the most venerable of them all. (133)

* A'PASTAMVA says that these forms of addressing may be used in accosting one's junior or equal in age. GOVINDARAJA says that, in as much as these terms (*Kshema*, etc.) are synonymous, what is contemplated here is that, these different terms should be used in accosting persons of different castes.

Among inmates of the same village or town, persons* younger than one another even by ten years are equal; among professional dancers and musicians, persons younger than one another even by five years are equal. Among Bráhmanas well-versed in the *Vedas*, even three years' youngers shall be treated as equals. Among blood-relations it is only a small desparity of age that makes one entitled to respect and veneration. (134

A Bráhmana, ten years old, and a Kshatriya of a hundred years of age, shall be considered as a father and a son; the Brâhmana shall be treated as the father of the Kshatriya. (135)

Wealth (honestly acquired) friends (relations), age, work, and erudition (knowledge) which forms the fifth, these are the sources of honour, each succeeding one being more honourable than the one preceding it in the (order of enumeration.) (136)

Among members of the three castes, he, who has the best of the five abovesaid qualifications, is entitled to the highest honour. Even a S'udra of ninety years complete† shall be respected by the twice-born ones. (137)

[On the road] one must give way to a carter, to a man of more than ninety years of age, to a sick folk,

---

* An educated man living in the same town or village with an illeterate person, older than him even by ten years, shall not show any special marks of respect to him for his years, as he is bound to do to an equally uneducated fellow citizen of his, older than him by more than ten years.—*Kulluka.*

† The text has *Das'amimgatah* which literally means" in his nineties." *Kulluka.*

to a carrier of weights, to a woman, to a *Snátaka,** to the king, and to a bridegroom.† (138)

When all these meet together (on the road), greatest preference shall be shown to the king and the *Snâtaka*. Of a king and a *Snâtaka*, the first shall give way (show respect) to the last. (139)

A Bráhmaṇa, who having initiated a pupil with the thread teaches him the *Vedas* with all its mysteries‡ and ceremonials, is said to be an *A'châryaya* unto that pupil. (140)

He, who, in consideration of fees, teaches a portion of the *Vedas* and any of the *Vedángas* (allied branches of *Vaidic* study) to a pupul, is said to be the *Upâdhyâya* of the latter. (141)

He, who does the (consecrating) rites of *Nisheka* etc., unto a child according to the ordinance, and maintains him with food (and raiment), is said to be his Guru (father). (142)

A Bráhmana, who, being appointed by another, does for him the religious sacrifices, called the *Agnyâdheyam*§

---

* The text has *Snàtaka*, which means a Bráhmana religious student returning from his preceptor's house after finishing his student's career.

† *Vara* here means a bridgroom on his way to, or from the bride's house before, or after the marriage is formally solemnized —*Kulluka*.

‡ The text has *Sakalpam Sarahasyamcha*. *Kalpa* means the branch of *Vaidic* literature which deals with ceremonials and the celebration of religious sacrifices. *Rahasyam* (lit mysteries) is the transcendental truths inculcated in the Upanishads.—*Kulluka*.

§ The rite of first kindling the sacred fire in which oblations, or libations of melted butter are fit to be offered—*Kulluka*.

Páka-yajna, *Agni-Stoma*, etc., is said to be his *Rittvik* (priest).* (143)

He, who fills the ears of a person with the eternal truths of the *Vaidic Mantras*, is said to be his father and mother; against him he shall not rebel. (144)

An *A'chàryaya* excels ten *Upàdhyàyas*, a father excels a hundred *A'cháryayas*, and a mother excels a thousand fathers, in respect of veneration.† (145)

---

* A *Rittvik*, otherwise devoid of the qualifications of a *Brahmachàrin* (such as the vow of continence, etc.) should be revered as a *Brahmachàrin*—*Kulluka*.

† An A'cháryaya is more venerable than ten Upâdhyâyas; a father is more venerable than a hundred A'châryayas, and a mother is more venerable than a thousand fathers.—*Kulluka*.

It is held by certain western Scholars that, the sentiment expressed in this couplet dates from the time when the sanctity and obligations of marriage, as a social institution, were but very partially observed and discharged by men, or when but a very crude form of marriage was adopted in society. After the days of promiscuity, the first attempt at forming a domestic economy must necessarily be a (government by the mother). The mother was the queen, the protectrix, the food-earning agent in the first house of man. In the days of promiscuous intercourse the mothers of men, like the mothers of beasts, had to take the sole care of the child; and hence with the arduous nature of the maternal duties there arose the sense of the child's obligation to its mother. In that stage of society it was natural for the primitive man to look upon his father as a mere progenitor whom perhaps he had very little chance of seeing in his life, and to consider the mother as a thousand times more necessary and valuable for the rearing of his life, from the days of his helpless infancy to those of his resourceful adolescence. But the *Tàntriks*, on the other hand, relying solely on their admirable embryology hold that, the function of the paternal element is only to call the life force latent in the impregnated ovum into being, and that the maternal element is the real manufucturer of life. Beyond this evoking of life

Of one's own progenitor and imparter (teacher) of the *Vedas*, he, who teaches him the *Vedas*, is superior to his progenitor, since the birth of a Bráhmaṇa through the *Vedas* is his eternal existence both in this world and the next. (146)

The birth of a man through the lustful meeting of his parents in his mother's womb is the birth which he has in common with the beasts. (147)

The birth, which the *A'cháryaya*, well-conversant with the *Vedas*, procreates for him through the *Sàvitri* initiation, according to the Regulation, is his real, decay-less, immortal birth (*i.e.*, birth in immortality). (148

Him, who benefits a man by imparting to him a lesser or greater amouut of *Vaidic* knowledge, let that man revere as his preceptor (*Guru*), on account of imparting that much knowledge of the *Vedas*. (149)

A Bráhmaṇa, who, although of a tender age, causes the initiation of an old man in the *Vedas*, and teaches him his religious duties (by explaining their true import), him such an old man is in duty bound to venerate as his own father. (150)

Even the infant son of Angirâ, whose vision extended far into the depths of the unseen mysteries,* taught his own fathers† and used to address them as sons. (151)

---

force in the ovum the paternal element is perfectly inoperative and hence they decree that a mother is a thousand times more venerable than a father.

* The text has *Kavi*. *Sâyana* explains it in his renowned *Scholia* to the *Rigveda* by *Kränta-darshi* "of a far-reaching vision."

† The text has *Pitrin*, *Kulluka* explains by *Pitrivyàn*, *Pitrivya putràn*, paternal uncles and sons of paternal uncles.

Having been thus addressed by A'ngirasa, they, mad with rage, demanded its reason of the Devas, and the assembled Devas said unto them, "the boy has not spoken indecorum." (152)

An ignoramus* is veritably a boy, the imparter of the *Mantras*† is like unto a father, for since the ancient time it has been the practice to a call an ignoramus a boy and an imparter of the *Mantras* a father. (153)

Neither by years (age) nor by grey hairs, neither by wealth nor by friends (relations) does one become great. The Rishis made a compact of yore that, "he of us who will study the entire *Veda* with the allied branches of study‡ will be called great. (154)

(Elderliness) among the Bráhmaṇas is according to knowledge, that among the Kshatriyas is proportionate to prowess, that among the Vais'yas is proportionate to wealth,§ and that among the S'udras is proportionate to age (*lit* date of birth.) (155)

Grey hairs do not make an old man; a young man, who has studied, the Devas designate him as really old. (156)

---

* The text has *Ajna*, which literally means "an ignoramus" Kulluka explains it by "one ignorant of the *Vedas*.'

† *Mantràda* is the term that occurs in the text, its literal meaning being the imparter of the *Mantra*. *Kulluka* explains it by teacher of the *Vedas*.

* The text has *Anuchànah*. *Kulluka* explains it by *Sànga Vedàdheyatà*, the reader of all the *Vedas* with the allied branches of knowledge, such as the prosody, grammar, rules of ceremonials, rules of pronounciation, astronomy and *Mimànsa* (exigetic dissertations on the Vedas)

§ The text has *Dhana-dhanyatah i.e.* according to one's possession of food grains, animals etc.

Like unto a wooden elephant or a leathern deer, a Bráhmaṇa, who has not studied, bears only the name of a Bráhmaṇa. (157)

As a eunuch is (sexually) fruitless (unsuccessful) in respect of a woman, as (sexually) fruitless is the meeting of two cows, as fruitless is the gift to an ignoramus,* so fruitless (is the life of a) Bráhmaṇa who has not studied the *Riks* (*i.e.*, the *Vedas*). (158)

The good of creatures should be effected with kind and sympathetic means;† desiring virtue, one shall use sweet and gentle words under the circumstances. (159)

He, whose speech and mind are always pure‡ and fully restrained,§ derives all the benefits enumerated in the *Vedânta*.‖ (160)

Persecuted or oppressed, one must not hurt the feelings of others. Let him wish or do no injury to any body. Let him not use a harsh word, that bars the gate of heaven, to any body. (161)

Let a Bráhmaṇa shun worldly honours, like a poison,

---

* The text has *Ajna* which means an ignorant person; certain commentators explain it by "a mad person."

† The text has *Bhutànàm* * * *S'reyo'nus'âsanam*, the literal rendering of which has been given above. KULLUKA explains *Bhutânâm* by "*S'iskyânâm* (of pupils)," and *S'reyo*, by "instruction," the whole meaning, according to him, is that instructions should be given with the help of compassionate means.

‡ The text has *S'uddhi* (pure). KULLUKA explains it as speech, unsullied by untruthfulness, and mind, free from desire, aversion, hatred, etc.

§ The text has *Samyag gupte*, KULLUKA explains it as mind restrained from walking in forbidden paths.

‖ *Vedântopagatam phalam. i e*, lordliness of the universe, and emancipation of Self, etc., described in the *Vedànta*, as the result of practising its tenets.

throughout his life. Desiring immortality, let him court humiliation all through his days. (162)

He, who habituates himself to bear humiliation, happily sleeps, happily wakes (from sleep) and travels in the path of duty.* The humiliator suffers a double death.† (163)

Let a duly initiated Bráhmaṇa, by dint of gradual practice, acquire, while residing in the house of his preceptor, this *Tapas* (penitential austerity), which would enable him to fully comprehend the import of the *Vedas.*‡ (164)

By means of special austerities and various (other) vows practised according to the Regulation, a twice-born one (Bráhmaṇa) shall master all the *Vedas* with

---

* The discomfiture, which a man suffers for having had to bear with humiliations, ceases to torment the person, who, from his very childhood, learns to look upon honour and dishonour with equal indifference, and thus robs humiliation of its sting. In the armoury of the petty vexations of life there is no dart keen enough to hurt him under his mail of healthy contempt for littleness. There is nothing in this world to disturb his night's repose, or to cloud the gladness of life which returns to him, each day, with the morning song and sunshine. With his head touching the stars in the conscious glory of a larger manhood, he treads triumphant in the path of duty, without casting a look at the shady by-paths of life, or lending his ears to the siren-songs of pleasure. The glory of this world, at its best worth, is but a mist, a vapour, and the commercial success of life may, in reality, be the very opposite of success.

† The text has *Vinas'yati*, KULLUKA explains it by "doubly dies out of self-reproach."

‡ The text has *Brahmàdhigamikam tapah* which may also mean penitential austerity that enables one to attain to *Brahma*. KULLUKA has explained *Brahma* by *Veda*, and we have adopted KULLUKA's interpretation.

their *Rahasyas* (*i.e.*, the mystic transcendentalism as inculcated in the *Upanishads*). (165)

Let the foremost of the twice-born ones (Bráhmaṇas) constantly commit the *Vedas* to memory, inasmuch as the study (recitation) of the *Vedas* is said to be the highest *Tapasyâ** for a Bráhmaṇa. (166)

Even he, who indulges in such articles of luxury as, the garland of flowers, etc., by studying the *Vedas*, each day, according to his might, acquires such an efficiency in *Tapas* that its (energy) surcharges his whole body from the tips of his finger-nails to the crown of his head. (167)

A Bráhmaṇa, who not having studied the *Vedas*, tries to acquire other forms of (secular) learning,† is degraded to the status of a S'udra with all his progeny, even in his life-time. (168)

The first birth of a Brâhmaṇa is in the womb of his mother, his second birth is through his initiation with the holy thread, and his third birth lies through his initiation in the *Vaidic* sacrifices (*Jyotishtoma*, etc.) as ordained by the *S'ruti*.‡ (169)

In respect of the birth of a Bráhmaṇa in *Brahma*, of which the wearing of the holy girdle (*Mekhalá*) is the symbol, the *Sávitri* (*Gâyatri Mantra*) is his mother and the preceptor (*A'cháryaya*) is his father. (170)

* *Tapas* means austerity with communion with the supreme Self.

† The text has *Anyatra Kurute S'ramam*. KULLUKA explains it by "forms of learning other than the *Smriti* and *Vedàngas*." Compare *Sankha*, "Before the studying the *Vedas*, let him not study any other subject of study."

‡ Which the priests (*Riṭtviḳs*) perform to make him competent for the celebration of the *Vaidic* sacrifices, to make him initiated in the sacrifice; through that he takes birth again.—*S'ruti*.

Before his initiation with the thread, a Bráhmaṇa is not competent to perform any kind of religious rites;* hence, for the fact that, the *A'cháryaya* imparts to him the knowledge of the *Vedas*, the *A'cháryaya* is his called father. (171)

A Bráhmaṇa, until he is again born in the *Vedas*, continues like unto a S'udra. Let him not utter any *Vaidic Mantras* except those of the *S'râddha*,† before his initiation with the thread. (172)

To a Brâhmaṇa, duly initiated with the thread, shall be given instructions, regarding the practice of vows,‡ gradually and in conformity with the Regulation; he shall be made to get by heart the (different portions§ of the) *Vedas*. (173)

The kinds of skin, thread, staff and girdle, which have been ordained for a (*Brahmachârin*) at the time of initiation with the thread, shall be likewise used by him in connection with practising a vow.|| (174)

---

* The text has *Karma*, KULLUKA explains it by *Srauta* or *S'màrta Karma*, *i. e.*, acts enjoined to be performed in the *S'ruti* (*Vedas*) and *Smriti*.

† *Svadhà* is the term that occurs in the text. *Svadhà* is the word which is uttered at the time of offering oblations to the manes. Here it figuratively stands for the *S'ràddha Mantras*. KULLUKA explains it by "*Mantras* which are recited during the celebration of a first (*Nava*) *S'ràddha* ceremony."

‡ The text has *Vratàdes'àn*, KULLUKA explains it by "commandments to practise the vows which he promised to undertake at the time of initiation, *viz.*, I will collect fuel for the sacrificial fire, I will not sleep in the day, etc.

§ *Brahmana*, the successive portions of the *Vedas* such as, the *Mantra Bràhmanas*, etc.—*Kulluka*.

|| Such as the penances of *Govarta*, *Chàndràyanam*, etc.

A *Brahmachárin*, while residing with his preceptor, shall control his senses and observe these rules of conduct for the augmentation of his psychic power. (175)

Let him be pure, let him bathe each day,* propitiate the gods and manes with libations of water, worship the deities, and cast sacrificial twigs (*Samidh*) in the fire, each morning and evening. (176)

Let him forswear the use of honey, meat, scents, garlands of flowers, and articles of sweet taste which acquire an acid flavour when stale. Let him refrain from visiting women and killing animals. (177)

Let him forswear the use of anointments (unguents), collyriums, shoes, and umbrella; let him renounce lust, anger, greed, dancing, singing and music: (178)

Gambling with dice, idle gossips, scandal, falsehood, embracing, and casting lustful eyes on females, and doing injury to others. (179)

He must sleep always alone, and let him not cast his seed (by any unnatural means.) A lustful casting of seed kills one's vow. (180)

A Bráhmana religious student, who has unintentionally spent himself in sleep, shall bathe and worship the sun and thrice mutter the *Rik* running as *Punarmâm*. (181)

He shall fetch pitchers-ful of water, flowers, cow-dung, clay and *Kus'a* grass asmuch as his preceptor might require, and beg alms, every day. (182)

---

* Morning and evening, let him bathe each day.—*Vishnu.*

Though daily baths are forbidden by *Gautama* in respect of *Brahmachàrins*, this prohibition extends only to wanton bathing, as *Baudhàyana* expresses it. Let him not bathe (many times) out of a spirit of bravado.—*Baudhàyana.*

Of house-holders, who celebrate the *Vaidic* sacrifices and complacently perform the duties peculiar to their order, a *Brahmachârin*, pure in body and spirit, shall beg alms, each day. (183)

He shall not beg alms of his preceptor's family, nor of his cognates and relations. In the absence of any other house-holder, he shall beg alms, leaving each preceding one of these persons. (184)

In the absence of (fit persons of whom the *Vedas* gives a *Brahmachârin* the sanction to beg alms), let him, silent and self-controlled, beg alms of the whole village (*i. e.*, of all the four castes) without repeating the proper formula of begging. (185)

Let him collect fuels (*Samid*) for the sacrificial fire from a distant forest* and place them in the open; with them he must punctually offer the burnt offerings, morning and evening, each day. (186)

In health, if a *Brahmachârin* fails to beg alms, or to kindle the sacrificial fire with the fuel of *Samid* twigs, for seven days in succession, he must do the penance of an *Avakirni* (of broken vow). (187)

A *Brahmachârin*, having been invited to a repast given in connection with a *S'râddha* offered to the deities, may take to his satisfaction (articles of food) which do not soil the vow) of a vowist ;† invited to a repast in connection with a *S'râddha* offered to the manes, he may take to his satisfaction such food, which

---

* The dry twigs of trees which have been mentioned in the *Vedas* as holy and fit to be used with the burnt offerings. They should be collected from a distance as it is evident from the use of the term *Durât* in the text.

† The text has *Vratabat*, *i. e*, all articles of food excepting meat, honey, etc., *Madhu Mâmsa-Varjam*.—*Kulluka.*

a *Rishi* may eat* without impugnity, even if without incurring the sin of eating the food given by one and the same person ; thereby his vow is not nullified. (188—89)

Wise men have ordained alms-begging as equally obligatory on *Brahmachârins* of all the twice-born castes (Brâhmaṇa, Kshatriya, and Vais'ya), but a Kshatriya or a Vais'ya *Brahmachârin* is not authorised to partake of a *S'râddha* repast given by a single person. (190)

Goaded by his preceptor or not, he shall take special care of his lessons and evince a special interest in things conducive to his preceptor's benefit, each day. (191)

Controlling his body (physical propulsions), speech, intellect, senses and mind, let him sit with the palms of his hands, united together, looking at the face of his preceptor. (192)

Covering his body with the upper sheet (of garment in a manner so as to leave) the right arm free and uncovered, let him sit, meek and self-controlled, each day, in the front of his preceptor, after being told by him, "sit down here." (193)

By the side of his preceptor he shall eat food and wear garments inferior to those of his preceptor. After him he shall go to, and prior to him he shall leave his bed. (194)

Comfortably lying in bed or seated on a cushion, or with his face turned back, he must not hear his preceptor's order, nor speak to him. (195)

If his preceptor orders him for any thing when he is seated, he shall rise up ; if he does that standing, he

---

* *Rishivat, i e., Nivâra* grains and such like food-stuff which a holy sage usually eats in his hermitage.—*Kulluka.*

shall advance a few steps towards him; if he does that while strolling, he shall follow him; and if he does that while going away, he shall run after him and receive that order or speak to him. (196)

The preceptor happening to look at any other side, be shall stand in front of him; the preceptor happening to be at a little distance, he shall go unto him; and his preceptor happening to be in bed or seated, he shall hung down his head and receive his order and speak unto him. (197)

By the side of his preceptor he shall always occupy a lower bed or seat; within the sight of his preceptor he must not sit in an easy or careless posture. (198)

He shall not utter his preceptor's name even at his back. He must not mimick his gait, speech or voice. (199)

Let him shut up the ducts of his ears in a place where his preceptor is calumnised or spoken ill of, or he must go elsewhere from that place. (200)

A calumniator of his *Guru* shall be born as an ass, and a vilifier of his *Guru* shall be a dog, in his next birth. For having wrongfully enjoyed the property of his *Guru*, he shall be born as a worm; one envious of his *Guru's* excellence shall take birth as an insect in his next incarnation. (201)

He shall not worship his *Guru* (with garlands of flowers, sandal-pastes, etc,) from a distance,* nor when angry or in the company of ladies. Happening to meet his *Guru* from a car or from (raised, seat, he shall get down and pay him respect. (202)

---

* He shall not send such offerings of flowers, etc, to his *Guru* through a third person from a distance.—*Kulluka.*

He must not sit with his *Guru* when the wind will be blowing from his direction to that of his *Guru*,* or the contrary; while in his company, he must not say anything which is inaudible to his *Guru*. (203)

In a bullock cart, in a cart drawn by a horse or a camel, on the terrace of a buiiding, in a courtyard, on a large mattress of reeds, on a stone-slab, in a boat he may sit by the side of his preceptor (*Guru*). (204)

In the event of the (preceptor) of his preceptor being near, he must behave unto him as unto his own preceptor; while residing in his preceptor's house, he (the pupil) shall not accost even his own parents without first having obtained the preceptor's permission. (205)

Unto his preceptor, (teacher) and superior relations such as uncles, etc.), unto counsellors of good, and unto those who dissuade him from evil ways, he shall always thus behave. (206)

As well as unto his elders in virtue and wisdom: likewise unto his preceptor's sons and friends and relations thus he shall constantly behave. (207)

A preceptor's son, if he be his younger or equal in age, or if he be a disciple of his in respect of the celebration of a religious sacrifice, he (the pupil) shall respect as his own preceptor, in the event of that (son) having taught him the *Vedas*. (208)

He shall not rub the person of his preceptor's son,

---

* The text has *Prativàte Anuvàte*. The wind is said to be *Prativâta* when it blows from the direction of the *Guru* to that of the pupil, and *Anuvâta* when it blows from the direction of the pupil to that of the preceptor. A pupil is forbidden to sit by his *Guru*, when the wind blows from either of these directions, lest the particles of saliva, etc., from his mouth, while speaking, might not fall upon his preceptor's body.

nor help him in bathing, nor eat the leaving of his food, (as he shall do in the case of his preceptor). (209)

The wives of a preceptor of his own caste shall be revered (by a pupil) as the preceptor himself. His wives of different castes shall be honoured with mere accosting and by rising from the seat. (210)

A pupil shall not anoint the person of his preceptor's wife, nor help her in her bath, nor rub her person, nor comb her hair. (211)

A pupil, twenty years old, (or) who has attained the age of discretion, shall not accost his preceptor's wife, if she be a youthful one, by clasping her feet. (212)

To defile men is the nature of women, hence the wise are never infatuated nor un-circumspect about them. (213)

Man, by nature, is subject to lust and anger; women are quite competent to lead even the wise men astray, not to speak of fools, (their easy victims). (214)

One shall not reside in a solitary place even with his own mother, sister or daughter. Powerful are the passions (lit senses) of a man, and they sometimes over-whelmn even the wise. (215)

If desired, the young pupil may accost a youthful wife of his preceptor, according to the Regulation,* by mentioning his name as I am so and so (that accost you). (216)

Having returned from a distant country, he, bearing in mind the rules of good couduct, shall accost (an elderly) wife of his *Guru* by clasping her feet, on the first day; on all subsequent days, he shall simply accost her without clasping her feet.) (217).

---

* That is without clasping her feet.—*Kulluka.*

As by digging (the earth) with a digging instrument, one gets water, so by faithfully serving him, a pupil acquires (all) the knowledge which is contained in his *Guru* (preceptor). (218)

A *Brahmachárin*, whose head is clean shaved, or who wears clotted hair, or grows a single tuft of clotted hair on his crown, let not the rising or setting sun find within the precincts of a village.* (219)

If the sun rises, seeing him asleep, out of wilful laziness, or goes down finding him resting in bed out of ignorance, let him mutter the *Gâyatri Mantra* and fast for a whole day. (220)

A sleeping (*brahmachárin*), roused up from his sleep by the sun, if he fails to do this penance, is associated with a great sin. (221)

Both in the morning and evening, let him, pure and self-controlled, mutter the *Gâyatri*, and pray, sitting in a holy place, as laid down in the Regulation. (222)

Even if a woman or a S'udra advises him to do any good act, let him do that, or whatever his mind approves of, (if that is not hostile to the *S'âstra*.) (223)

Some say that virtue and wealth are the only good in life, others aver that wealth and desire are the highest good, some hold that virtue is the only good, others say that wealth is the only good in life : virtue wealth and desire combinedly form the good in life. This is the conclusion. (224)

The preceptor is the living image of *Brahma*, the father is that of *Prajâpati* (creator) ; the mother is the living image of the earth, and the uterine brother is one's own image (second self.) (225)

* He must be in his forest-home before the sun sets, nor quit it for a village before he rises in the morning.

Hence, a man, and specially a Bráhmaṇa, even being hardly oppressed by them, shall not insult a father, a mother, or an elder brother. (226)

Even in the course of a hundred years, a son can not repay the trouble which his parents have undergone for the purpose of bringing him up. (227)

Let him constantly do what is good to his parents, and specially what conduces to the comfort of his preceptor. The satisfaction of these three is the consummation of all *Tapas* (penitential austerities) (228)

Serving these three constitutes the highest *Tapas*; without their permission, let him not practise any other piety. (229)

These three represent the three Regions,* the three orders of the society. They are the three *Vedas*, they are the three fires. (230)

The father is the household fire, the mother is the southern fire, and the preceptor is the sacrificial fire. These three fires are the most glorious in the world. (231)

A house-holder, who does not commit any folly in respect of these, conquers the three regions; effulgent as a god, he, even in his mortal frame, is enabled to enjoy the felicity of heaven. (232)

By means of devotion to his mother one conquers this world, by devotion to his father he conquers the middle world (firmament), and by devotion to his preceptor he attains to the region of *Brahma*. (233)

He adores all the virtues, who adores all these three; He, who belittles these three, belittles all the virtues. (234)

---

* *Trayo Lokàh*, the earth, the firmament, and the heaven.

Trayo As'ramàh the order of *Brahmachàrin* (the religious student), the order of the house-holder, and the order of hermits.

So long as these three live, let him not practise any other virtue (piety) ; let him tenderly serve them and always do whatever is good and pleasant to them. (235)

Whatever other virtues does he practise by mind, speech and acts, for his good in the other world, he shall inform them thereof. (236)

To serve them tenderly is the highest and most manifest consummation of his duty, all other pieties* are minor virtues. (237)

Respectful, let him acquire an auspicious knowledge† even from a S'udra ; the highest virtue,‡ even from a man of vile caste ; and a good wife,§ even from a bad family. (238)

Ambrosia may be taken even out of poison ; a good word, even from an infant ; a good conduct, even from an enemy ;‖ and gold, even from an unhallowed person. (239)

Women (wives), gems, knowledge, virtue, purity, good words (counsels), and the various kinds of art may be acquired from anywhere. (240)

In times of distress, a Bráhmaṇa student may take

---

* *Apadharma* is the term that occurs in the text, KULLUKA explains it by *Vaidic* sacrifices such as the *Agnishtoma*, etc.

† *S'ubhám Vidyám*—knowledge of manifest, or tested power and potency, such as the *Gàrudi Vidyá* (drugs and incantations for the cure of a snake-bite).—*Kulluka.*

‡ *Param Dharmam*, means liberation of the soul.—*Kulluka.*

§ The text has *Stri-ratnam* which literally means "a gem of a woman."

‖ *Amitràdapi Sadvrittam i.e.*, even the good conduct of one's enemy should be imitated.—*Kulluka.*

his lessons from a non-Bráhmaṇa* preceptor, and he shall serve his *Guru* (teacher) only so long as he shall actually study.† (241)

Wishing the most exalted existence (*i.e.*, liberation of self), after death, let not a Brâhmaṇa student live for good in the house of a non-Bráhmaṇa preceptor, or in the house of a Bráhmaṇa who has foresworn good conduct, and renounced his function of a *Vaidic* teacher. (242)

A (ritualistic) *Brahmachârin*, if he desires to live for good in the house of his preceptor, must render him services to the last day of his life. (243)

A Brâhmaṇa, who, to the last day of his life, thus serves his preceptor, attains by his own spiritual energy to the eternal abode of *Brahma*. (244)

Let not a virtuous *Vaidic* student pay any (money) to his preceptor ere he returns from his house after finishing his career. After having bathed‡ with the permission of his *Guru*, he must pay him a honorarium according to his pecuniary circumstances. (245)

* The text has *Abràhmanàt* which literally means from a non-Bráhmana. KULLUKA explains it by "in the absence of a Bráhmana, he may study under a Kshatriya; and in the absence of a Kshatriya, under a Vais'ya preceptor."

† Render all other services except that of washing his feet and eating the leaving of his food, etc.—*Kulluka*.

Brâhmana students shall serve a Kshatriya imparter of the *Mantra* (teacher of the *Vedas*) by such acts as following him etc. A Brâhmana even who has acquired knowledge from him shall be regarded by a (Kshatriya) as his *Guru*.—*Vyas'a*.

‡ Ablution at the close of his student's career, which formed, as it were, a signal for quitting the preceptor's roof for that of his paternal home.

A plot of land, gold, a cow, a horse, an umbrella, a pair of shoes, paddy, vegetables,* clothes, or whatever he is capable of giving him, with that he shall evoke the pleasure of his preceptor. (246)

On the death of his preceptor, unto a qualified son of his, or unto his (widowed) wife, or unto a cognate of his he shall behave as his preceptor. (247)

In the absence of all these three, let him, making use of his preceptor's seat and cushion, offer burnt offerings, (morning and evening, each day), and thereby make his Self competent to attain to *Brahma*. (248)

A Bráhmaṇa, who thus undeviatingly practises the vow of a ritualistic *Brahmachárin*, obtains an excellent status,‡ after death, and stands not under the necessity of reverting to human existence. (249)

* In return of the knowledge acquired from him, he shall give unto his preceptor a few vegetables even if his wordly circumstances do not admit of his giving any other thing. A gift however precious or costly is no adequate return for the benefit which a preceptor accords to his pupil. Compare,

There is no such thing in this world, by giving which a pupil can discharge his debt to a preceptor, who has taught him, no more than a single letter of the alphabet.—*Laghu Hàrita*.

† In the absence of a qualified son of his *Guru* he shall behave unto (render services) to his widowed wife as his preceptor, and even in the absence of such a widowed wife he shall extend the same differential treatment to a surviving cognate of his (such as an uncle, etc.—*Kulluka*.

‡ The text has, *Uttamam Sthànam*, KULLUKA explains it by "he goes to the vicinity of *Brahma*."

CHAPTER III.

In his preceptor's house, a *Brahmachârin*, having practised the vow of (studying) the three *Vedas** for thirty-six years, or for a half or a quarter of that period,† or for a period necessary to fully comprehend them. ; (1)

Or having studied (all) the *Vedas*, or two *Vedas*, or a single *Veda*† in the proper order of *Mantra*, Bráhmaṇas‡ etc., without the least deviation from his vows,§ shall enter the order of the householder.|| (2)

A (youthful) *Brahmachârin*, renowned for the completion of his vow of a *Vaidic* study, and who has studied the *Vedas* from his father or preceptor, and is about to enter the order of the house-holder,¶ shall be

---

* *Traivedikam Vratam*, literally means the "vow of three *Vedas*;" but although the three *Vedas* (*Rik*, *Sàman* and *Yajus*) have been here specifically mentioned, we shall have to understand the four *Vedas* (*viz.*, the *Rik*, *Sàman*, *Yajus*, and *Atharvan*) by the term *Traivedikam*, the *Atharvan* being included within the *Rig Veda*. Hence we find in the *Vishnu Puranam*, "The allied branches of *Vaidic* study and the four *Vedas* (*Angàni Vedás'chatvàrah*, etc).

† Compare *Yajnavalkya* —The vow of a *Brahmacharin* for twelve or five years in respect of (studying) each *Veda* (*Prativedam Brahmacharyayam Dvàdas'àvdam Pancha vâ.*)

‡ According to the *Sàkha (school)* of the *Vedas* he belongs to.—*Kulluka*.

§ *Mantras*, Bràhmanas are the different divisions of the *Vedas*.

|| The vow of perfect continence and abstinence from honey, meat, etc.

¶ The text has *Gàrhasthyas'rama* (the order of the householder) *i. e.*, he shall impose upon himself the obligations of matrimony and discharge the duties of married life, marriage, being the first step to house-keeping.—*Kulluka*.

presented with a cow, and a cup of honey,* when he, decorated with garlands of flowers, will be found seated in his bed. (3)

Having bathed with the permission of his *Guru* at the termination of his vow, a Bráhmaṇa shall marry a wife of his own caste, possessed of auspicious signs. (4)

For the purposes of marriage and sexual intercourse, a girl, not related to his mother by the tie of *Sapinda*† relationship, nor to his father as a *Sagotra*‡ (cognate), is as well recommended in respect of a Brâhmaṇa. (5)

However great (illustrious), or opulent with (the possession of kine, goats, sheep, money and paddy), they might be, (the following) ten families should be avoided in respect of taking a bride from (any of) them. (6)

---

* The father or the preceptor shall thus worship (offer) him with a cow and a cup of honey (*Madhu-parkam*).

† *Sapinda*-relationship is extinguished in the seventh degree of descent.

‡ *Sagotra* means persons belonging to the same spiritual clanship, or descendants from a common ancestor.

According to the *Dharma Sàstra* one cannot marry a female *Sapinda* relation of his mother, though he can marry a female *Sagotra* relation of hers.

The particle "cha," includes father's sisters and their daughters who are not his *Sagotras*. *Vyàsa*, on the other hand, forbids the marriage with a mother's *Sagotra* girl.

Some desire not marriage with a mother's *sagotra* girl. In a case when the name of the girl's family is not known, one can marry her without the least hesitation.—*Vyàsa*.

Having married a daughter of his maternal uncle, or a girl belonging to his mother's *Sagotra*, or a girl belonging to the same *Gotra* or *Pravara* (spiritual clanship) with his father, or having gifted a girl in such a marriage, a *Brahmana* shall do a *Chàndràyana* penance by way of expiation.—*Vasistha*.

A family of doers of mean acts, a family in which no male child is born, a family of men devoid of Vaidic knowledge, a family of hairy men and women, and a family in which consumptive, epileptic, leprous or leucodermic members are born, these are the ten families in which one is forbidden to marry. (7)

Let him not marry a girl of brown complexion, or one with a limb in less or excess, or one who is a pronounced invalid, or a hairy one, or one devoid of hairs on her body, or a garrullous one, or one whose eye-balls are brown or yellow. (8)

Nor a girl who has a name implying a star, tree, river, mountain, bird, serpent or servilence, nor one whose name denotes a dreadful object. (9)

A well-formed girl, without hairs on her limbs, and having a sweet name and a gait resembling that of a swan or an elephant, slender, with small pearly teeth, and a crown of thin, silky hair, he shall take for his wife. (10)

A girl, who has no uterine brother of her own, or* whose father's name is unknown, shall not be married out of the apprehension of a *Putrikâ*† compact. (11)

* A girl married on the express condition that the son of her womb will be a son unto her father; or given in marriage with such an intention is called a *Putrikâ*. *Abhisandhi-mâtrât Putrikà* —*Gautama*.

† GOVINDARAJA explains the verse by referring the term *Putrikà dharma Sankayà* to both the clauses, "who has no uterine brother" and "whose father's name is not known." We have adopted KULLUKA'S interpretation as being more consistent with reason. KULLUKA says that the prohibition as regards marrying a girl of unknown parentage is for the apprehension lest she might be a foundling or an illegitimate one.

A girl belonging to his own caste is recommended to a Bráhmaṇa for holy wedlock ; for desire, a wife he may take from any of the three remaining castes, her precedence being according to her caste. (12)

A S'udra woman is the wife of a S'udra ; a Vais'ya can marry a S'udra or a Vais'ya wife, a Kshatriya can take a S'udra, a Vais'ya or a Kshatriya wife ; and a Brâhmaṇa can marry a S'udra, Vais'ya, Kshatriya or a Brâhmaṇa wife. (13)

In no history or chronicles can be found that, even in the time of distress, a Brâhmaṇa or a Kshatriya has (lawfully) married a S'udra wife. (14)

By marrying a low caste woman through the intoxication of desire (passion), a twice-born one* degrades himself, with the nine generations of his progeny, to the status of a S'udra. (15)

He, who marries a S'udra woman, becomes degraded. This is the opinion of *Atri* and of (*Gautama*,) the son of *Utathya*. By visiting a S'udra wife† for the purpose of begetting offspring on her, a twice-born one becomes degraded ; this is the opinion of *S'anaka*. The fathership of his S'udra children degrades a twice-born one. This is the opinion of *Bhrigu*. (16)

* Whether a Brahmana, or a Kshatriya, or a Vais'ya.—*Kulluka.*

† The text has (*Sutotpattyà* (by procreating children) and *Tad-apatyatayà* (on account of his having *i. e.*, begetting Sudra children). Both MEDHATITHI and GOVINDARAJA explain the first (*Sutopattyà*) by "visiting a S'udra wife, accidentally married out of ignorance, on the fourth day of her menses for the purpose of procreating a child as enjoined in the *Sàstra*, even if there be no offspring of that union, and the second (*Tadapatyatayà*) by "wilfully and knowingly begetting children on a S'udra wife.

By lying with a S'udra woman in his bed, a Brâhmaṇa falls into a degraded existence; by begetting a child on her, he stands divested of his Brahmanism. (17)

The oblations, offered by a twice-born one who is assisted by a S'udra woman in the capacity of his principal married wife in the rite of a *Pitri* or *Daiva S'râddha* ceremony, neither the manes, nor the divinities partake of. Even by practising hospitality to *Atithis*,* he cannot ascend to heaven, after death. (18)

By sucking the lips of a S'udra wife, by inhaling her breath, or by begetting children on her person, a twice-born one can never find any succour. (19)

Now hear me discourse on the eight forms of marriage, which contribute to the good, or to the evil of the four castes of men in the next world. (20)

They are known as the *Bráhma*, *Daiva, A'rsha, Prâjápatya, A'sura, Gándharva, Râkshasa* and *Pais'âcha,* which forms the eighth. (21)

Now I shall discuss all the forms of marriage which are proper for each of the social orders, the merit and demerit which appertain to each such form, and the benefit or otherwise which the offspring of each form can accord (to its parents). (22)

The six forms (of marriage) commencing with the first one (*Bráhma*) are proper for Brâhmaṇas; the four forms counted from the end (*Pais'âcha*) are not sinful for Kshatriyas, and the same set excepting that of *Râkshasa* shall be regarded as proper for Vais'yas. and S'udras. (23)

The four forms (of Marriage) the seers have ordained as proper for Brâhmaṇas; only the Râkshasa form as

Atithis i. e., chance guests or chance arrivals at his house.

proper for Kshatriyas, and the A'sura form as proper for Vais'yas and S'udras.* (24)

Thus out of these five forms† of marriage, three‡ are lawful, and two are sinful (unlawful). Let a man never marry a wife either in the Pis'âcha or in the A'sura form, since these two forms are prohibited. (25)

A marriage, whether effected in the pure Gândharva, or in the pure Râkshasa form, as described before, or in a mode which is a combination of both of them,§ is (primarily) lawful for a Kshatriya. (26)

The form (of marriage) in which a well-attired bride, decorated with ornaments, is given in marriage to an erudite, good-charactered bridegroom, especially invited by the bride's father himself to receive her, is called Brâhma. (27)

* These are the forms of marriage which a Brahmana, a triya, a Vais'ya and a Sudra shall respectively consider as the most approved forms of taking a wife, and think of marrying in any other fashion wheu the marriage cannot be effected in any of these modes.—*Kulluka.*

† The five forms of marriage referred to in the text the *Pràjàpatya,* the *A'sura*, the *Gàndharva*, the *Ràkshasa*, and the *Pisàcha.*

‡ The three lawful forms are the *Pràjàpatya*, *the Gàndharva*, and the *Ràkshasa,* the *Prajapàtyà* form is lawful for Brahmanas; the *Gandharva*, for members of all the four social orders; and the *Râkshasa*, for Vais'yas and Sudras.—*Kulluka.*

§ The text has *Mis'ram* (mixed) the form of marriage in which the bridegroom, conscious of his well-returned or well-requitted love, carries away the bride by force or conquest, is called Mis'ra or Gândharva-Râkshasa.—*Kulluka.*

The marriage of Dushmanta and S'akuntalá furnishes the illustration of a pure Gândharva form of marriage; that of Vichitravirja and Ambicâ, of a Râkshasa form, and that of Arjuna and Subhadrâ, of a mixed Gándharva and Râkshasa form.—

The form of marriage in which the bride is gifted (*i e.*, given in marriage) to the person duly officiating as a priest at a *Vaidic* sacrifice, which is being celebrated, is called *Daiva* by the holy sages. (28)

The lawful form (of marriage) in which a bride, on the receipt of an ox and a cow, or of two oxen and two kine for the performance of religious sacrifices, is duly given in marriage to the bridegroom, according to the ordinance, is called *A'rsha* (by the wise.) (29)

The form, in which after having worshipped the bridegroom, the bride is given to him in marriage with the injunction, "let both of you jointly discharge the duties of a house-holder, is called *Prâjâpatya.* (30)

The form, in which the bridegroom, on paying money to her father and to herself, out of the promptings of his own desire,* receives the bride in marriage, is called A'sura.* (31)

* The text has *Svàchchh-andyàt,* which means out of his own selfish wish, in direct contravention of the provisions of the *S'àstra.* It may be set down to the credit of our ancient Rishis that, they were the first to condemn, and to rule out of court, this commercial element of the matrimonial compact. In all primitive societies, the father had absolute proprietary rights in his sons and daughters, and accordingly he missed no opportunity to make a good capital out of his daughters, by selling them to the highest bidders in the matrimonial market. Thus in the very nature of things the daughters came to be looked upon as excellent marketable commodities, and the dearest purchasers of their charms and favour as the most eligible bridegrooms. No wonder then that husbands, in their turn, learnt to look upon their wives as a kind of moveable property, a class of slaves whom they had to purchase for money or its equivalent. Thus we see in the earliar societies of the Roman empire, for any encroachment on the conjugal rights of a husband, the trespasser had to pay a fine to him just in common with an ordinary trespasser on land or on any other

The form, in which, for the reason of a reciprocal marriage of hearts, the bridegroom is mated with the bride, is called Gândharva. It originates from a couple's passionate desire of being united with each other.* (32)

The form of marriage, in which the bridegroom, by killing or hurting the guardians or relations of the bride, and by forcing open the door of her house, forcibly carries her away, weaping and screaming, is called Râkshasa. (33)

The form in which the bride, when alone, asleep, senseless, intoxicated, or delirious with wine, is ravished by the bridegroom, is called Pis'ácha, the eighth and the most sinful form of marriage. (34)

The marriage of a Brâhmaṇa must be preceded by the rite of water-gifting, the marriage of a member of any other caste may be preceded by (negotiated with) a formal betrothal, if the parties mutually desire it so. (35)

O Brâhmaṇas, now hear me fully describe the virtues (merits) of these different forms of marriage as narrated by Manu of yore. (36)

---

civic rights of his neighbour. But the Rishis in their perfect wisdom foresaw the evils of this form of legal marriage, which is but a modified form of slave-trade, and restricted it to Vaisyas (Merchants) and Sudras (artisans) alone whose compulsary stays in foreign or distant countries many times left it the only form of marriage, open to them among strangers From its name we can legitimately presume that this form of marriage was in vogue among the Assyrians (*Asuras*), and more so, when we consider that in ancient Chaldea and Babylon it was quite honourable for a girl to earn her marriage-dowry even by selling her favours.

* The consummation of marriage by the lovers, even before it is formally solemnized, is not condemned in the *Gàndharva* form of marriage.

The male offspring of a *Bráhma* form of marriage, if he does good works, succours his own self, as well as his ten ancestors* and ten descendants† from (the effects of) sin. (37)

The male offspring of a *Daiva* form of marriage succours (his own self and) his seven ancestors and seven descendants; and that of an *A'rsha* form of marriage succours (his own self) and his three ancestors and three descendants, while that of a *Prájápatya* form of marriage succours (his own self) and his six ancestors and six descendants, (from the effects of) sin. (38)

Sons born of the four forms of marriage, consecutively counted from the *Bráhma* form, become possessed of the energy of *Brahma*† and are recognised (as well-born) by honest men. (39)

Handsome looking, wealthy, renowned, possessed of fortitude and good qualities, virtuous and amply provided with all the objects of enjoyment, these sons‡ live for a hundred years. (40)

Sons of the remaining (four) low (forms of marriage) are born cruel, untruthful, and hostile to the religion of *Brahma* (*i.e.*, to the *Vedas*). (41)

Sons begotten on commendable wives§ are born with commendable traits (in their character); sons, the

---

* *Das'a Purvàn*—Ten ancestors such as the father, the grand-father, the great-grand-father, etc., and *Das'a Paràn* means ten descendants such as the son, the grandson, the great grandson, etc.

† Qualities which mark the spirit of a union (*i.e.*, form of marriage) are inherited by its offspring.—*Kulluka*.

‡ Offspring of these four forms of marriage, *viz*, *Bràhma, Daiva. A'rshah* and *Prajápatyah*.

§ Good wives married in any of the four preceding commendable forms of marriage.

offspring of unions with condemnable wives, are born with condemnable traits in their character. Hence, let a man avoid a vile form of matrimony. (42)

In a marriage between a man and a woman of the same caste they shall join their hands, while in the one contracted between a bride and a bridegroom of different castes the following rules should be observed. (43)

In her marriage with a Bráhmaṇa, a Kshatriya girl shall clasp a shaft; a Vais'ya girl, a goading stick;* and a S'udrá, the frill of his cloth with her hand, during the ceremony. (44)

Always faithful to her, for sexual pleasures, let him visit† his wife during her menstrual period, avoiding the days of the *Parva*,‡ and when not observing a vow.§ (45)

---

* The text has *Pratoda* which means a stick, or a rod used by a cow-herd in goading the kine of his flock

The brides shall respectively clasp an arrow, a goading-stick, etc., carried by the bridegroom in his hand during the ceremony.—*Kulluka.*

† This regulation is for one who has not procreated a son, the procreation of a son being obligatory on every one for discharging his debt to the manes.

Cf. By his birth a Bráhmana is a debtor by three debts.

By sacrifice he discharges his debt to the deities, by procreating a son he discharges his debt to the manes, and by studying the *Vedas* he discharges his debt to the *Rishis.*—*S'ruti.*

Also compare.—He who visits not his wife after she has bathed (on the fourth day of her menses,) commits the sin of fœticide.—*Paràsara*

For the end of begetting a male child he shall visit his wife on the even days during her menstrual period.—*Sushruta.*

‡ *Parvas,* such as the day of the full or new moon, etc

§ A vowist, as well as one who has begotten a son, stands not under the obligation of visiting his wife during her menstrual period.

The menstrual period of a woman naturally lasts for sixteen nights (days) inclusive of the four days of flow, which are condemned by the wise.* (46)

Of these (sixteen days), the first four, and the eleventh and the thirteenth are condemned by the wise for sexual purposes, the rest ten days are commended. (47)

Sons are born on the even days and daughters on the odd ones (of the menstrual period.) Hence, one, desiring the birth of a son, shall visit his wife on an even day. (48)

Even on an odd day, a comparative excess† of the paternal element gives rise to the birth of a male child, a comparative excess of the maternal element gives rise to the birth of a daughter. A sexless child, or a twin (a son and a daughter) is born when the paternal element is equal to the maternal one. (49)

Leaving these (six condemned days) and eight days out of the commended ten days, a person, to whatsoever order he might belong, who visits his wife on these two days alone, shall be regarded as a *Brahmachárin*.† (50)

An erudite father of a girl shall not take any thing by way of *S'ulka* from her bridegroom. By taking

* The first four days of the flow.

† The "*S'ukra-bàhulyam*" or *A'rtava-bàhulyam* of the text denotes the preponderance of the Katabolic (*Pitrikà S'akti*) or Anabolic energy (*Mátrikà S'akti*) in the impregnated ovum through the greater intensity of the father's or mother's desire at the time.

† MEDHA'TITHI holds that two days are allowed to a man, belonging to any order of the society whatsoever, for the enjoyment of conjugal pleasures, and says that, thereby his vow of continence is not broken. GOVINDARAJA holds that the license is given to a man after the death of his only son.

a dowry out of greed, he becomes the seller of his offspring. (51)

The friends and relations of a woman,* who, out of folly or avarice, live upon the property belonging to her,† or the wicked ones who oust her of the enjoyment of her own belongings‡ such as cloth, etc.,§ go to hell, (after death). (52)

Even the acceptance of a bovine pair (by the father of the bride from the bridegroom) is designated as a dowry by certain authorities, (the acceptance of) a dowry be it costly, or be it of insignificant value, constitutes the sale of the girl.|| (53)

* *Bàndhaváh* (friends and relations) is the term that occurs in the text. *Kulluka* explains it by "*Pati-Pitràdaya,*" father, husband, etc.

† The text has *S'tridhanam* (woman's property) which consists of dowries given to her by her friends and relations at the time of marriage, or on such-like occasions.—*Kulluka.*

‡ *Vàri yànáni* is the term that occurs in the text, KULLÙKA explains it by "horses, slave girls, etc."

§ *Vastram* (cloth). It lays down that it is sinful to dispossess her even of her most insignificant belonings such as, a cloth or a garment.—*Kulluka.*

|| GOVINDARAJA, grounding his statement on the view expressed in the preceding couplet, opines that, the verse 29 of this chapter, which authorises the bride's father to take a dowry of a bull and a cow from the bridegroom, does not reflect the opinion of Manu on the subject, but is merely an extract from another Code, quoted to be subsequently discussed and refuted. The acceptance of a dowry, however small and inexpensive, by the bride's father, or by the father of the bridegroom, spells as the price paid for the hands of the bride or of the bridegroom, and gives a commercial aspect to the transaction, transforming it into a veritable contract of buy and sale.

MEDHATITHI is evidently puzzled by this apparent contradiction and retires without being able to satisfactorily account for it.

A marriage in which the bride's relations do accept* the dowry (voluntarily presented by the bridegroom's father, etc.,) is no sale (of the bride), since such a present is but an adoration of the bride, done out of love or affection.† (54)

Seeking many a blessing (*i.e.*, God's gifts) in life, her father, mother, husband, or husband's younger brother shall maintain a bride with† a respectful love,‡ and give her ornaments for the decoration of her person. (55)

[The deities smile on the family] where the females are honoured (held in respect); fruitless are the acts§ (in the family) where they are dishonoured. (56)

KULLUKA says that, there is no contradiction at all between these two verses. In the *A'rsha* form of marriage although the bride's father is authorised to take a bull and a cow in the shape of a dowry from the bridegroom, the dowry is accepted to help the married couple to celebrate religious sacrifices (*Dharmatah*) and not for any specific gain or benefit of the bride. Under these circumstances it is no dowry at all, inasmuch as it is misnomer to call a benefit benefit that is not actually derived or enjoyed. Marriage, according to the Rishis, is a holy sacrament, a kind of psychic transformation, the two parties to it being blended together in spirit, and for all eternity, the two parties to it being transformed into that "human centaur" which is called man and wife. To turn it into a mere social or commercial contract is to transform Psyche into a shop-girl.

* *Nàdadate* i. e. do not appropriate it to their own use, or derive any benefit from it.

† The text has *Anris'amsyancha* which literally means "out of compassion."

‡ *Pujyáh* literally means to be adored or worshipped, KULLUKA explains it by "shall be respectfully supported with delectable articles of fare. etc.

§ *Viphalá Kriyá* The religious rites, even duly performed, fail to bear their fruits.

Prosperity reigns supreme in the family where females do not grieve; the family, in which they grieve, suffers a speedy destruction.* (57)

Like a fiend-cursed† home, utterly perisheth the house, which its daughters,‡ through suffering mortifications, do but (sadly) imprecate. (58)

Hence they should be satisfied with presents of food, raiments, ornaments, etc., by men seeking prosperity, on festive and ceremonial§ occasions. (59)

In the family where the husband is contended with the wife, and the wife with the husband, steadfast is the blessing of the deity. (60)

If even with garments and ornaments the wife fails to be attractive, or if the husband does not find any pleasure in her, no progeny of the husband is possible on account of the lack of that pleasure. (61)

A charming wife lends her charm to every thing and makes the whole world look attractive to her husband, a charmless|| wife robs the world of its charm. (62)

---

* The text has *Jàmaya.* Both MEDHA'TITHI and GOVINDARA'JA explain the term by newly married daughters in law, daughters, etc. (*Duhitri Navodà Snushàdaya.*)

† *Krityàhatàni*:—*Krityà* is a kind of female fiend evoked by murderous incantations.

‡ *Jàmaya*, daughters, sisters, daughters-in-law described in the preceding stanza.

§ *Satkàreshu*:—Such as the festivities of *Kaumadi* (night of the full moon in the month of *A's'vina*,) etc.—*Kulluka.*

|| The text has *Arochamànà* which leterally means charmless, *Kulluka* explains it by *Bhartri-Vidveshatayà Naràntara Samparkàt Màlinàm* a wife who through her hostility to the husband and her intrigue with another man makes the house gloomy.

By a bad marriage, by the extinction of religious ceremonies, by the non-study of the *Vedas*, and by insulting a Brâhmaṇa, the prestige of a good family is annihilated.* (63)

By pursuing handy craft* or agriculture, by begetting children on a S'udra wife, by trafficking in cows, horses, or carts, by entering the king's service, by officiating as a priest at the sacrifice of one who ought not to be so served, by living in open hostility to the *Vedas*, and by their non-study, men (Brâhmaṇas) degrade their families.† (64—65)

Families, rich in the opulence of *Vaidic* studies and in the performance of *Vaidic* sacrifices, even if they be poor in the riches of the world, are counted among the illustrious families (of the land) in point of renown and dignity. (66)

In the nuptial fire‡ a house-holder shall perform, according to the ordinance, all the house-hold rites,§ as well as the five great sacrifices;|| likewise over that fire shall be cooked the (daily) food of the household. (67)

---

* The text has *Kulànya kulàni Jànti*—which literally means families become no families. *Kulluka* says that a bad marriage, extinction of the religious ceremonies, neglect of Vaidic studies and a wilful affront to a Brahmana are the factors, which, being done in a family, kill its good name and position in the society.

† The text has *Nàstikyena* which literally meens by living the life of an athiest. We have adopted *Kulluka's* explanation.

‡ The text has *Bibahike'gnau* i. e. in the sacred fire kindled on the occasion of his nuptial ceremony as opposed to the *A'havaniya* (sacrificial) fire.

§ *Grihyam Karma*—the burnt offerings offered, each morning and evening, as well as the rites of *Ashtakà S'ràddhas* (to be described later on).——*Kulluka*

|| *Pancha-yajnas*—the five daily sacrificial rites such as, the offerings to the *Visvadevas* (i. e to all the duties) etc.——*Kulluka.*

A householder has five places where animal lives are destroyed; they are the hearth, the grinding stone, the broom-stick, the pestle and mortar, and the stool for the water-pitcher. These five, when performing their proper functions, kill animal-life. (68)

For the expiation of the sin committed by him in each of these five places, the great sages have ordained that, the householder-celebrants of sacrifices (*i.e.*, householders) shall daily perform the five great sacrifices (*Pancha-Yajnas*). (69)

The sacrifice of *Brahma* consists in teaching the *Vedas*, offering oblations or libations to the manes is called a *Pitri-yajna*, burnt offerings to the deities constitute a *Daiva-yajna*; offering oblations (food) to the animals is called a *Bhuta-yajna*, while hospitality to chance-guests is called a *Nri-yajna*. (70)

By not suffering the daily performance of these five sacrifices to be omitted, a householder, even living in his house, is not associated with the sin committed in the five life-killing places in the household (*Pancha-suná*.) (71)

He who does not feed the deities, the chance-guests, the beasts, the manes, and his own self, each day, by performing the five great sacrifices, is a dead man, even though he breathes. (72)

The five great sacrifices are called *Ahutam, Hutam, Prahutam,, Brahma-hutam* and *Prásitam*. (73)

A *Brahma-yajna* or muttering of *Mantras* is called *Ahutam*; offering oblations (food) to the beasts is called *Prahutam*; hospitality to men, chance-guests and Bràhmaṇas, in special, is called *Bràhma-hutam*, and offering oblations to the manes (in connection with the daily *S'ràddàs*) is called *Pràsitam*. (74)

[In the event of his incapacity of practising hospitality to chance-guests, etc.], let him be constantly engaged in studying the *Vedas*, and in making burnt offerings to the divinities. He, who constantly engages himself in doing the works of the deities, supports all the universe. (75)

Libations of clarified butter duly cast in the sacrificial fire ascend to the sun; from the sun originates the rain; from the rain, do the provisions; and from the provisions, the creatures. (76)

As all creatures live by taking recourse to the air, so all the different orders (of mendicants, forest-dwellers and anchorites) depend upon the householder for their existence. (77)

As the three orders of ascetics are maintained by the householder with the gifts of food and knowledge of the eternal *Vedas*, the householder is the foremost of all the four orders. (78)

Desiring eternal heaven, and happiness in this life, one shall assiduously discharge the duties of a householder. A weak mind and the uncontrolled senses are the barriers against the proper discharge of these duties. (79)

The *Rishis*, manes, animals, guests and relations expectantly look upon the householder (for maintenance, etc.) Hence, a wise householder shall properly discharge the duties he owes to them. (80)

Let him satisfy the *Rishis* with his Vaidic studies; the deities with the proper burnt offerings; the manes, with the *S'râddha* offerings; the guests, with food; and the animals, with oblations offered unto them. (81)

Let him constantly celebrate the (*Pârvana*) *S'râddha* ceremonies by offering fruit, (edible) roots, boiled rice, water and vegetables, etc., unto his manes, and evoke their satisfaction in special. (82)

In connection with the celebration of a *S'raddha* ceremony included within the five daily sacrifices, let him feed a single Brâhmaṇa; he need not feed any Brâhmaṇa in connection with the celebration of a *Vais'vadeva* sacrifice. (83)

Let a Bráhmaṇa offer, each day, oblations of consecrated boiled rice, cooked over the household fire, unto the following deities according to the Regulation, (*viz.* (84)

Unto Agni, unto Soma, unto Agni and Soma combined, unto all the deities, unto Dhanvantari, unto Kuhu, unto Anumati, unto Prajâpati, unto the earth and firmament, and unto Svistakrit at the end. (85—86)

Having thus duly offered oblations unto each of these deities, he shall circumambulate them from the east by the south and west to the north as follows:— Obeisance to Indra and obeisance to the attendants of Indra in the east, obeisance to Yama and obeisance to the attendants of Yama in the south, obeisance to Varuṇa and obeisance to the attendants of Varuṇa in the west, and obeisance to Soma and obeisance to the attendants of Soma in the north. (87)

Then at the threshold of the sacrificial chamber he shall offer oblations unto the Maruts, unto the "water" in the water, and unto the Vanaspatis (lords of the forest) in the pestle and mortar. (88)

On the head of the *Vastupurusha* he shall offer oblations unto the goddess S'ri, by saying, "obeisance unto S'ri, at his foot to the goddess Bhadrakâli, by saying "obeisance unto Bhadrakâli," unto Brahma inside the chamber, by saying, "obeisance unto Brahma," and finally unto the presiding deity of the household, by saying, "obeisance unto *Vâstudevatâ.*" (89)

Unto all the deities, unto ghosts that are abroad by day, and unto those that roam about in the night he shall offer oblations in the sky. (90)

On the ground, at his back, he shall offer oblations unto all the ghosts, by saying, "oblations unto all the spirits," and the residue of the food (boiled rice, thus offered unto the ghosts) he shall collect, and offer to the manes in the south, by saying, "obeisance to the manes." (91)

Unto dogs, unto the degraded, unto *Chandâlas** and persons afflicted with diseases which are the out-come of sin,† and unto crows and worms he shall offer oblations of boiled rice on the ground, taking care that they may not be soiled with dust. (92)

A Brâhmana, who thus daily worships all creatures with food, assumes a resplendent body, and goes by the straightest road to the abode of supreme bliss.‡ (93)

After offering these oblations, a householder shall first feed the *Atithi* guests arrived at his house, and then dole out alms§ to *Brahmachârins* and mendicants (94)

A Brâhmana householder obtains the same merit

* The text has "*S'vapachas*" which literally means cookers or eaters of dog's flesh.

† The text has *Pâpa-roginâm i. e.* persons afflicted with leprosy, phthisis, and kindred affections.——*Kulluka.*

‡ The text has *Sa Gachchhati Param Sthânam. Kulluka* explains it by "he is merged in the supreme *Brahma.*

§ The text has *Bhikshà*, which means a morsel of grain given to a poor man as alms.

Gràsamàtra Bhavet Bhikshà (A morsel of food is the quantity that shall be given as alms to a beggar)—*S'àtàtapa.*

by giving alms to beggars as a *Brahmachârin* does by making the gift of a cow to his preceptor in conformity with the ordinance. (95)

Let alms, or pitchers, full of water, be gifted to a Bráhmaṇa, thoroughly conversant with the meanings of the *Vedas,* by one duly worshipping him, and muttering words of benediction. (96)

Oblations offered unto the manes and deities by men, who, ignorant of the true spirit of gift-making, make gift unto burnt out* Brâhmaṇas, certainly do perish. (97)

Oblations cast in the mouth-fire of a Bráhmaṇa, kindled with the energy of *Vaidic* study and penitential austerities, succour one from great danger and from great sin as well. (98)

Let a householder give a cushion, and water for washing his feet unto an *Atithi,* arrived at his house (without invitation), and duly offer him cooked rice with curries etc., according to his might. (99)

A Bráhmaṇa guest, happening to remain unfed and unattended to even in the house of a householder, who daily lives upon the pickings of the field, or worships the five fires,† carries away the merit of all his pious acts. (100)

* The text has *Bhasmibhuta* which literally means burnt down to ashes. Kulluka explains it by "Brahmanas who are devoid of *Vaidic* studies and do not offer oblations to the manes and deities, and hence are like unto the extinguished charcoal.

† The text has *Panchàgninapi Juhvatah* : The worshipper of the five fires, *i.e.*, an extremely indigent Brahman. The five fires are the Tretâgni (the triad of fires), the *Avasakhyàagni* and the *Sabhya*, *Sabhya* being the fire which one uses in warming himself (in want of clothes.)—*Kulluka.*

Hays,* ground,† water, and a sweet word, which forms the fourth (in the list), are never wanting in the houses of the good. (101)

A Brâhmana, who resides for a single night in the house (of another), is called an *Atithi* (chance guest); since there is no certainty of his staying (there, the next day) he is called an *Atithi*.‡ (102)

A Brâhmana living in the same village with him, or one who lives on his wits, even if he calls at the house of a man living with his wife and (sacred) fire therein, must not be called an *Atithi*. (103)

Householders, who, ignorant of the demerit of eating food given by others, stroll about in a village other than his own, out of a greed for sharing other men's hospitalities, become the domestic beasts of those whose hospitalities they then partake of. (104)

An *Atithi* arrived after sunset§ at the house must not be discarded under any circumstances. An *Atithi* (guest), whether arrived at the house in the proper or improper time, must not be kept unfed.|| (105)

* The text has *Trinâni* (hays) *i.e.* hays for a bed.—*Kulluka*.

† The text has *Bhumi*, ground. KULLUKA explains it by *A'sanam*, a cushion.

‡ *Atithi* is derived from "A," without and "Sthiti," stay *i.e.*, one whose stay in the house is uncertain for more than one night.

§ The text has *Suryodhàh*, literally carried or borne by the sun.

|| In the proper time *i.e.* at the time of the performance of the *Vais'vadeva vali* (offerings to all the deites.)

GOVINDARAJA holds that it is a special provision for hospitalities to *Atithis* discarded on the score of not arriving at the time of the *Vais'vadeva* offering or of arriving at night fall.

Cf. O king, the sin of discarding an *Atithi* after sunset is eight times greater than what is incurred by not practising hospitality to an *Atithi* in the day.—*Vis.*

Let not (a householder) eat that himself which his *Atithi* has not partaken of; hospitality to an *Atithi* brings on wealth, fame, and longevity, and ensures heaven to him who practises it. (106)

Cushions, bedsteads. beddings, following* and worship should differ according to the stations of *Atithis*. Better cushions, etc., should be given to *Atithis* of superior status, ordinary ones to *Atithis* of equal rank with the host, and inferior ones to *Atithis* of inferior ranks (in life). (107)

If a guest (*Atithi*) arrives at his house after the completion of the *Vais'vadeva* offering, and after another guest has previously arrived, he shall duly cook and offer food (boiled rice) to the second *Atithi*, but there is no need of making a second offering to the *Vais'vadevas*.† (108)

Let not a Brâhmaṇa mention his own name and family for enjoying one's hospitality; he, who eats by giving out the name of his own self and family, eats egesta. (109)

A Kshatriya, Vais'ya, or S'udra guest in the house of a Brâhmaṇa, as well as a preceptor or a relation, happening to call at his house, is not called an *Atithi*. (110)

But even if a Kshatriya calls (at the house of a Brâhmaṇa) as an *Atithi*,‡ the master of the house shall

---

* The text has *Anuvrajyâm* which means an act of respectfully following a revered guest at the time of his departure.—*Kulluka*

† In connection with the sacred act of hospitality it is enjoined in the *S'âstra* that offerings should be made to all the deities (*Vis'vadevas*) before feeding the *Atithi*.

‡ The text has *Atithi-Dharmena* which means a Kshatriya, a resident of a distant or different village, seeking the hospitality of the house for the day.—*Kulluka*.

feed him sumptuously after the Brâhmaṇa *Atithis* have been repasted. (111)

If Vais'yas and S'udras arrive at his (Brâhmaṇa's) house as *Atithis*, he, out of compassion, shall feed them in the company of his own servants.* (112)

His friends and relations happening to be guests in his house out of love or affection, he (Brâhmaṇa) shall feed them with cooked food, as his circumstances would admit of, in the company of his own wife.† (113)

Newly married daughters and daughters-in-law,‡ infants, sick folks and pregnant women in the house he shall unhesitatingly feed before§ feeding the *Atithis*. (114)

He, who without having fed the abovenamed persons and the *Atithis* in the house, first eats anything himself, does not know that, his body will be devoured by dogs and vultures, after death. (115)

Let the master and mistress of the house eat what

---

* The text has *Kutumva* which literally means dependants. KULLUKA explains it by "in the company of the servants of the house after the Kshatriya *Atithis* have been fed and before the master and mistress of the house have taken their repast. 112

† The text has *Saha Bhâryayâ* i e. in the company of his wife. KULLUKA says that it is only another mode of saying that at the time when the master of the house will eat his meal, for it is laid down in the *S'âstra* that the meal time of the master is the same with that of the mistress of the house. 113

‡ The text has *Suvâsinih* which literally means well clad girls. We have adopted *Kulluka's* explanation.

§ MEDHATITHI reads the line as *Atithibhyonvagevaitân*, simultaneously with feeding the *Atithis* (guests.) We have however adopted KULLUKA's reading and explanation in our rendering of the text. 114

remains after feeding the Brâhmaṇas (guests), relations and servants. (116)

After worshipping the deities, Rishis, guests, manes and the household divinities* with oblations of boiled rice, let a householder eat his food at the end. (117)

He, who cooks food for his own sole use,† eats sin; food, which is the residue of sacrificial oblations, is recommended by the virtuous. (118)

One's King,‡ *Rittvika*, *Snâtaka*,§ preceptor, son-in-law,|| father-in-law or maternal uncle, happening to call at his house after the lapse of a year,¶ he shall well come by first offering him a cup of honey (*Madhuparkam*). (119)

A king or a *Snâtaka*, happening to call at his house even within a year (of the last visit) on the occasion of a sacrificial ceremony, he shall welcome in the method of *Madhuparkam*, and not otherwise; this is the conclusion. (120)

Each evening, the housewife shall offer oblations of cooked rice, without muttering any *Mantras*, to the

---

* The text has *Grihyâs'cha Devatâh* KULLUKA says that the *Bhuta-Yajna* (offering oblations to beasts) is also included within the meaning of the term.

† *Cf. Kevalâgho Bhavati Kevalàdah* (he who eats alone becomes associated with sin.)—*S'ruti.*

‡ A duly crowned Kshatriya.—*Kulluka.*

§ He who observes the vow of ceremonial ablution simply as a vowist or for studying the *Veas.*—*Kulluka.*

|| The text has *Priya*. KULLUKA explains it by "*Jàmàta*, a son-in-law.

¶ The text has *Parsimvatasarât*; after the expiry of a year. The prefix *Pari* in this instance has, according to Jayâditya, the sense of "leaving aside."

MEDHA'TITHI reads it as *Parisamvatsarân*, *i.e.*, those who have come back after the lapse of a year.

Vais'vedevas, inasmuch as such offerings are enjoined to be made, each) morning and evening. (121)

Let a Bràhmaṇa, who is a keeper of (the sacred) fire, offer a *Pinda S'râddha* to his manes on the day of the new moon, and after that perform the *Pindânvahâryakam S'ráddha* from month to month. (122)

Monthly *S'ráddhas* offered by men to their manes are called *Anvahâryam* by the wise; commendable meat-offerings should be made to them on these occasions. (123)

O ye foremost of Bràhmaṇas, now I shall fully describe who shall be invited to, and who shall be avoided in, a *S'râddha* repast, as well as the number (of Brâhmaṇas) to be invited and the nature of food with which they are to be fed. (124)

Two Brâhmaṇas shall be fed on the occasion of a *Daiva S'raddha* ceremony; and three, on the occasion of a *Pitri S'ráddha*; or one Brâhmaṇa on each such occasion. Even prosperous enough to feed many Brâhmaṇas, he shall not exceed the number, (fixed) (125)

In cases of feeding a large number of (Brâhmaṇas), proper attendance to them, and ascertainment of their purity, impurity, and the place and time of repasting (invitation) are the five factors that are destroyed (apt to suffer). (126)

This rite (of offering oblations to the manes) on each new moon* day is said to be conducive to the

---

* The text has *Vidhu-kshaye* (*i. e.* on the last day of the moon's wane) which is the reading adopted by KULLUKA, KANDARAJA and MEDHA'TITHI. GOVINDARAJA reads it as *Vidhi-kshaye* and explains it as this is the rule (*Vidhi*) on the last days of the moon's wane (*Kshaye*), *i. e.*, such *S'ráddhas* s ould be offered to the manes on the day of the new moon, each month. We have adopted

benefit of the manes. He, who is constantly engaged in performing this *Smárta** rite, acquires opulence.† (127)

Givers shall give unto Brâhmaṇas, well-read in the *Vedas*, the oblations of food they have offered to the manes and deities; given to the most deserving recipients (Brâhmaṇas), they bear great fruits. (128)

A Brâhmaṇa shall feed a single Brâhmaṇa, conversant with the *Vedas*, on the occasion of a *S'raddha* offered to the manes or deities; great is the merit which he shall acquire by feeding such a single (Brâhmaṇa), there being no merit in feeding a large number of Brâhmaṇas who are ignorant of *Vaidic Mantras*. (129)

The parentage,‡ etc., of a *Veda*-knowing Brâhmaṇa should be far enquired into; *Vaidic* Brâhmaṇas, sons of anscestors who had been well conversant with the *Vedas*, are the vehicles§ for conveying the oblations to the manes and deities. Gifts made unto such Brâhmaṇas are as meritorious as gifts made unto *Atithis*.‖ (130)

In the *S'râddha* where thousands of Bráhmaṇas, ignorant of the *Vedas*, are fed; if a single *Veda*-know-

---

KULLUKA's reading as being identical with those of the ancient commentators of the Samhitâ.

* The text has *Laukiki*, KULLUKA explains it by *Smarta, i.e.*, a rite enjoined to be performed in the *Smriti*.

† The text has *Preta-Krityá*, KULLUKA explains it by *Pitropakárartham, i.e.*, conducive to the benefit of the manes, and hence imparting wealth, good progeny etc. to the performer by way of reward.

‡ *Durâdeva Pariksheta*, the parentage, piety, erudition of these Bráhmanas and their remote ancestors should be enquired so as to determine whether they have acquired their excellence by heredity or not.

§ *Tirthas: Lit.* landing places.

‖ The same merit which one acquires by practising hospitality and making gifts to *Atithis*.

ing Bráhmaṇa therein is satisfied with the *S'ráddha* repast, the merit of feeding such thousands on the occasion is acquired by feeding that Brâhmaṇa alone. (131)

Oblations offered to the manes and deities should be given to Bráhmaṇas who are the most excellent in respect of knowledge; blood-stained hands are not washed pure with blood. (132)

A Bráhmaṇa, ignorant of the *Vedas*, shall have to eat as many morsels of burning spear-heads, after death, as he eats of the *S'rádaha* oblations to the manes and deities, in life. (133)

Some Bráhmaṇas are devoted to (the cultivation of) self knowledge, others are devoted to the practice of penitential austerities; some there are who are devoted to the study of the *Vedas* and to penitential austerities, while others are devoted to work. (134)

Oblations offered to the manes shall be given to Bráhmàṇas devoted to the knowledge of self to eat, oblations offered to the deities should be duly given to all these four classes of Bráhmaṇas. (135)

Of a Brâhmaṇa who is well-versed in the *Vedas* and whose father was ignorant of the *Vedas*, and one who is himself ignorant of the *Vedas* but whose father was well-versed in them, the ignorant son of the *Veda*-knowing father should be regarded as a worthier guest (in respect of a *S'ráddha* repast); but since adorable are the *Mantras* of the *Vedas*, a *Veda*-knowing son of a father, ignorant of the *Vedas*, should be as well-honoured (with an invitation to a *S'raddha* repast. (136—137)

No one, out of friendship, should be invited to a *S'ráddha* repast, friendship should be shown with other acts and monetary (presents). Let him invite a Brâhmaṇa to the *S'râddha* repast whom he neither knows to be his friend or foe. (138)

A *S'raddha*,* offered by a person to his manes or to the deities, in connection with which it is mainly his friends that are repasted, fails to bear any fruit in the next world. (139)

A person (Brâhmana), who, out of ignorance, tries to make friendship through the instrumentality of a *Sráddha* repast, that worst of Bráhmanas, for acquiring such *Srâddha* friends, falls from heaven.† (140)

A *Srâddha* repast, given to one's friends and relations, is called a fiendish repast by the *Rishis*. Like blind cows huddled together in one pen such a repast may contribute to cement friendship in this world, but gives no benefit in the next. (141).

As a sower, by sowing seeds in an alkaline soil, reaps no harvest, so a giver, by giving oblations (*i e.*, feeding) to a Brâhmana, ignorant of the Vedas, (in connexion with a *S'ráddha*), derives no benefit. (142).

A honorarium, duly given to an erudite (Veda-knowing) Brâhmana, makes its giver and recipient

* GOVINDARAJA asserts that feeding Bráhmanas is the essential factor of a *S'ráddha* ceremony, the offering of *Pindas* being only its minor and accessory feature. KULLUKA, following *A'pastambha* and others, asserts that the offering of oblations or offerings to the manes and the subsequent acceptance of those offerings by the Brâhmanas, present, form what is called a *S'ráddha*.

† The heaven-giving merit of a *S'râddha* is described by *Yâjnavalkya*.

Longevity, progeny, opulence, erudition, heaven, salvation, happiness and kingdom, do the manes, satisfied with *S'râddha* offerings, impart.

entitled to religious merits* both in this world and the next. (143)

[In the absence of a qualified Brâhmana], better it is to feed a friend or a relation than to feed an erudite foe on the occasion of a *S'râddha* ceremony, as oblations offered to a foe fail to bear any fruits in the next world. (144)

On the occasion of a *S'râddha* repast, let him carefully feed a Brâhmana who has studied the *Rik*, *Yajus*, or the *Sama Veda* with all its sub-divisions (such as the *Mantras*, *Brâhmanas*, etc). (145)

The satisfaction, which the seven generations of his ancestors who feeds any such Brâhmana (on the occasion of a *S'râddha* ceremony) derive from the act; lasts for all eternity. (146)

The aforesaid Veda-knowing Brâhmanas (*S'rotriyas*) should be regarded as the worthiest recipients of *S'râddha* oblations, offered by a man to the manes or deities, the following are their substitutes whom the wise shall feed when such *S'rotriyas* would be unavailable. (147)

One's mother's father, mother's brother, sister's son, father-in-law, preceptor, daughter's son, son-in-law, and sons of mother's or father's sisters priest, and dis-

---

* The text has *Phalabhâginah* * * * *Pretyachchacha*. Both MEDHATITHI and GOVINDARAJA explain it by "honorarium duly given to a Veda-knowing Bráhmana accords spiritual benefit to the donor in the next, and fame and good name etc., in this world. KULLUKA explains that such a gift accords fame etc., to the donor in this world and salvation, etc., in the next, as described by *Yàjnavalkya*, and the recipient of the donation, by celebrating religious sacrifices therewith, acquires spiritual benefit and the fame of earning honest money in this world, as a sacrifice celebrated with ill-gotten gain fails to bear any fruits.

ciples should be fed on the occasion of a *S'râddha* repast in the absence of (the ten aforesaid *S'rotriyas*). (148)

Fitness, erudition, etc. of Brâhmaṇas, to be fed on the occasion of a *Daiva S'râddha* ceremony, must not be tested, which shall be carefully done in respect of those to be fed on the occasion of a *S'râddha* offering to the manes. (142)

Those Brâhmaṇas, who are gold-stealers, degraded, sexless, or athiests must not be invited on the occasion of a *Srâddha*, offered to the manes, or to the deities, this is the dictum of Manu. (150)

Brahmachârins who wear clotted hairs,* or who are ignorant of the *Vedas*, Brâhmanas who are afflicted with skin diseases† or are gamblers, or officiate as priests at many men's sacrifices must not be fed on the occasion of a *S'râddha* ceremony. (151)

Brâhmaṇas, who are professional physicians, or live by worshipping divine images, or are meat-sellers, or carry on any kind of trade, should be avoided on the occasion of a *S'râddha*, offered to the manes, or to the deities. (152)

Servants of the king or of a village community, those afflicted with bad nail, black toothed ones, those who are hostile to their preceptors, and those (Brâhmaṇas) who have renounced their sacred fires and religious rites (enjoined to be performed in) the *Vedas* and *Smriti*, or live by usury. (153)

---

* The text has *Jatilam*, KULLUKA explains it as *Brahmachârins* who wear clotted hair or clearly shave their heads.

† The text has *Durbalam*, weak. KULLUKA explains it by Bráhmanas suffering from cutaneous affections.

Brâhmaṇas suffering from phthisis, those who rear cattle for livelihood, or marry before their elder brothers have been married, or have renounced the performance of the five (daily house-hold) sacrifices, or are inimically disposed towards the Brâhmaṇas, or suffer their younger brothers to marry before them, or are incumbents upon endowments (whether money or monasteries) made by others for the public weal. (154)

A Bráhmaṇa, who is a professional dancer, a *Yati* or a Brahmachárin whose vow of continency has been soiled by the contact of a woman, the (Brâhmaṇa) husband of a S'udra woman, one begotten on a re-married widow,* the son of a woman born before her marriage, and one who lives with a faithless wife. (155)

He who teaches the *Vedas* for money, as well as he who learns them from him, he who has got S'udra disciples or teaches S'udra students, a harsh tongued (Bráhmaṇa), and sons born in adultery during the life-time or after the death of their mother's husband. (156)

One who has wrongfully deserted his parents, or preceptor, as well as those who are associated either in *Vedaic* study or through marriage with those who have been degraded in life. (157)

One who is guilty of poisoning or of incendiarism, one who sells the Soma plant, one who partakes of the food of a man born in adultery,† a sea-faring

---

* The text has *Punarbhava*. It may also mean the son of a woman born in adultery after the demise of her husband.

† The text has *Kundah*, a son born in adultery during the life-time of her mother's lawful husband. KULLUKA holds that the two kinds of incestuous offspring mentioned in the preceding couplet are here contemplated by the term *Kundah*, which includes both *Kundah* and *Golakah*.

Brâhmaṇa, a professional eulogist, an oilman, and a forger of documents or a falsifier of weights. (158)

One who quarrels with his father,* a deceitful one,† a drunkard,‡ one afflicted with a (foul) sinful disease or under an imprecation, an arrogant (Brâhmaṇa), as well as the one who deals in any kind of sweet sap such as, (sugarcane juice, etc.) (159)

A (Brâhmaṇa) who constructs bows and arrows, one who marries a girl with an unmarried elder sister, one who injures his friends, one who lives by gambling with dice, and he who has learnt the *Vedas* from his son. (160)

One afflicted with epilepsy, scrofula, or leucoderma, or one who is wicked, insane, or blind, or speaks evil of the *Vedas*. (161)

A trainer of cows, horses, camels or elephants, a professional astrologer, a tamer of beasts and one teaches the science of war. (162)

One who obstructs a water course or diverts it in another channel, a professional mason or architect, one who plants trees, or goes on errands for money. (163)

A dog-player, one who lives by training falcons, a defiler of girls, one who kills animals, one who is in the service of a S'udra, and one who serves all classes of society as a priest. (164)

One who does not observe the rules of good conduct, a sexless (Brâhmaṇa), one who daily begs, or lives

---

* The text has *Pitrà Vivàdamânâh*, KULLUKA explains it, one who quarrels with his father whether for arguing a point of *S'astra* or for any worldly object.

† Several editions read *Kekarah*, squint-eyed.

‡ *Madyapa i.e.*, one who drinks any form of intoxicating liquor other than *Surà*

by agriculture, one afflicted with elephantisis of the legs, and one condemned by honest men. (165)

A Brâhmana who rears sheep or buffalloes for a living, one who has married a girl previously wedded to another, and one who carries corpses for money, all these Brâhmaṇas should be studiously avoided on the occasion of a *S'râddha* ceremony. (166)

A good and erudite Brâhmaṇa must avoid all these (*i e.*, the aforesaid) vile and condemnable Brâhmaṇas, who disgrace the row of eaters in a *S'râddha* repast. (167)

A Brâhmana, who has not studied the *Vedas*, is like unto a rush fire that is soon extinguished, to him oblations must not be offered, as no one casts fire-offerings in the ashes. (168)

The merit which the giver acquires in the other world by giving oblations unto Brâhmaṇas, unfit to be given access to a row of diners, in connection with a *S'râddha* offered to the manes, or to the deities, now hear me describe in detail. (169)

Whatever is eaten by Brâhmaṇas who are non-observant of the *Vaidic* or *S'âstric* vows, or by those who are guilty of the sin of *Parivetta*, or by Brâhmaṇas who are unfit to sit in the row of diners (*apânkteyas*) in a *S'râddha* repast, is eaten by monsters. (170)

A younger brother, who marries or kindles the sacred fire before his elder (brother) has married or kindled such a fire, is called a *Parivettâ*, the latter a *Parivitta*. (171)

A *Parivettâ*, a *Parivitta*, the bride given away in such a marriage, the giver of the bride and the priest who solemnizes the marriage ceremony, all these five, go to hell, (after death). (172)

He, who, otherwise than under an appointment of begetting a son on her, visits the widow of his deceased elder brother, out of passion, is called the husband of a deceased elder brother's widow. (173)

Sons begotten by a man on another's wife are called either *Kundas* or *Golakas*. The son of a woman, born in adultery, during the life time of her lawful husband, is called a *Kunda*, while a son begotten on a widow, after the demise of her husband, is called a *Golaka*. (174)

S'râddha oblations* offered to either of these two kinds of sons, (incestuously) begotten on another man's wife, destroy all the merits of their donors (both in this world and the next. (175)

If a Brâhmana, unfit to be invited to a *S'râddha* repast (*Apánkteya*),† sees a number of competent Brâhmanas eating their meal (in connection therewith.), the unfortunate giver of the repast is deprived of the merit of feeding that number of Brâhmanas, seen eating by the *Apánkteya* one. (176)

[In the event of the dinner being] thus looked at‡ by a completely blind *Apánkteya*, the giver of the repast is deprived of that much merit as is acquired by feeding ninety Brâhmaṇas; looked at by one, blind in the one eye, he is robbed of the merit which is acquired by

---

* Any oblation whether offered to the manes, or to the deities on the occasion of a *S'râddha* ceremony.

† Such as Brahmanas, guilty of gold stealing etc.

‡ How can a blind man see? The meaning is that, if a blind, *Apânkteyâ* intruder can reasonably infer from sounds, etc.., that the repast is going on. KULLUKA explains that a blind, *Apânkteya* onlooker, sitting at a place whence it is possible for one with eyes to writness the repast.

feeding sixty Brâhmanas; looked at by a leper (leucodermic Brâhmana) or by one afflicted with a sinful malady, he is robbed of the merit which is acquired by feeding a hundred or a thousand Brâhmanas. (177)

If a Brâhmana, who is the priest of S'udras, touches with his limbs any number of worthy Brâhmanas, eating a *S'ráddha* repast in the same row with him, the giver of the repast is deprived of the merit of feeding the Brâhmanas so touched (by the priest of S'udras). (178)

Even a *Veda*-knowing Brâhmana, who has accepted, out of greed, any gift from a Brâhmana who serves as the priest of S'udras, shall meet his doom, like an unbaked clay-pot (immersed) in water. (179)

A gift made unto a (Brâhmana) seller of *Soma-plant* is like unto excreta,* a gift made unto a professional physician is like unto pus and blood. Destroyed is the gift which is made to a paid worshipper of a village deity (*Devala*), while that which is given to a usurer (Brâhmana) can not stand† before the deity. (180)

The gift made to a trader (Brâhmana) is of no benefit either here or hereafter. Like libations of clarified butter cast in the ashes is the gift made to a Brâhmana who is the son of a faithless widow, born after her husband's demise. (181)

Oblations offered to the manes and deities, if they are given to the aforesaid impious and condemnable Brâhmanas who are not fit to be invited to a *S'ráddha*

---

* Can never be acceptable to the manes or deities—KULLUKA.

† The text has *Apratishthamtu* which literally means has no *locus standi*. KULLUKA explains it by" *Anàs'rayatayà Nishphalam*, futile as it is not supported (countenanced) by the gods.

repast, are like unto blood, fat, flesh, marrow, bones etc.,* this is what the wise men say. (182)

Hear me speak in detail of those foremost of Brâhmanas whose presence sanctifies a row (of diners) in a *S'ráddha* repast which has been sullied by the presence of an *Apânkteya* Brâhmana, (not fit to sit in the row). (183)

Those (Brâhmanas), who are foremost (*i.e.*, well read) in all the *Vedas* and *Vedangas*,† and whose ten ancestors‡ were well conversant with the *Vedas*, are called sanctifiers of the row *(Panktipávanas)* (184)

He who has taken the vow of reading the *Trinâchiketa*,§ or the three *Suparnas*,‖ or has studied the six allied subjects of *Vedic* study, or sings the *Jyeshtha Sâman*, or keeps the five sacred fires, or is the offspring

---

* KULLUKA says that in the opinion of the wise these oblations are transformed into many an abominable thing, such as raw fat, meat, etc. which their giver to the worthless Brahmanas is obliged to partake of in the next world ; or he is necessitated to take birth in a family in which such impure things are eaten.

† The text has *Pravachaneshucha*. *Pravachanam* means any branch of knowledge which serves to illucidate the meaning of the *Vaidic* text. Yama includes *Nyàya* philosophy and the six allied branches of *Vaidic* study within the *Pravachanam* in as much as he extends the privilege of *Panktipavana* to a student of *Nyàya* philosophy or of any of the *Shadangas* (six sub-divisions) of *Vaidic* study. *Nyàyavichcha Shadangavit.*

‡ The text has *S'rotriyànvayhàjschá* which means descendants of (*S'rotriya*) *Veda*-knowing ancestors. The meaning adopted in the translation is based on an aphorism of *Usana, Chhandasà S'uddha Das'a Purusha*, ten generations of ancestors purified by *Vàidic* study.

§ The fore part of the Yajur Veda.

‖ *Taittiriya Aranyakam* X. 48—50.

of a marriage celebrated in the Brahma form (is a sanctifier of the row. (185)

A knower of the *Vedas*, an expositor of *Vedic* doctrines, a religious student, a maker of many gifts, and a centenarian, should be known as sanctifiers of the row. (186)

On the occasion of a *S'râddha*, at least three Brâhmanas possessing the aforesaid qualifications should be respectfully invited on the day of the ceremony, or on the previous day. (187)

A Brâhmaṇa, on being invited to a repast given in connexion with a *S'râddha* offering to the manes, shall observe perfect continence and refrain from studying the *Vedas;* the celebrant of the *S'râddha* ceremony shall as well observe the same (rules of) conduct. (188)

The manes do invisibly enter the persons of Brâhmaṇas invited (on the occasion of a *S'râddha*), follow them like the air,* and sit by them when they are seated (189)

Even the foremost of Brâhmanas, who, having accepted an invitation (to a *S'râddha* repast), wilfully violates his pledge (to attend it), is sure to incur sin, and will be reborn as a hog in his next birth. (190)

He, who, having been invited to a *S'râddha* repast,

---

* The text has *Vàyuvachchànugachchhati* follows like the air. KULLUKA explains "Vayu" by "*Pràna Vàyu*" vital airs, the whole meaning according to him being that, "Pitris (manes) enter the organisms of the Brahmana guests just as souls of men enter the seeds in their parents' bodies.

sexually knows a S'udra wife,* is associated with all the sin done by the giver of the repast.† (191)

The manes are wrathless, cleanly (in their habits), and magnanimous,‡ are prior to the gods, and have laid aside their arms. (192)

The source of their (manes') origin, those who constitute this region of the manes, and the mode of worshipping their Pitris (progenitors) now hear me describe in detail. (193)

The *Pitris* are the sons of Rishis, Marichi, etc., who are the sons of Manu, the son of Hiranyagarbha. (194)

Of these, Somasadas, the sons of Virat, are the manes of the Sâdhyas; and Agnishattas, the sons of Marichi, who are renowned in the three regions, are the manes of the deities. (195)

Barhishadas, the sons of Atri, are the manes of Daityâs, Dânavas, Gandharvas, serpents, Râkshasas, Kinnaras and birds. (196)

Somapas (Soma-drinkers) are the manes of Bráhmaṇas, *Havirbhujas* (eaters of oblations) are those of Kshatriyas, *Ajyapas* (drinkers of clarified butter) are

---

* The text has *Vrishali* which means a S'udra wife. Both MEDHATITHI and GOVINDARAJA hold that, intercourse even with his Brahmana wife by a man, invited to a *Sràddha* repast, is forbidden. They give the etymology of the term *Vrishali* as *Vrihasyante* chapalâyati Bhartáram, one who covets her husband and makes him restive," in short, an amorous wife." Perfect continence on the part of the guest on the occasion is what is contemplated by the text. For other meanings of "Vrishali" see *Apastambha*.

† The text has *Pratipadyati*, that is, all sin of the giver of the repast is transferred to the incontinent guest.

‡ The text has *Mahabhàgàh i. e.* possessed of the eight moral virtues of clemency, etc. *Kulluka*

the manes of Vais'yas, and *Sukâlinas* are the manes of S'udras. (197)

The sons of the celestial bard (Bhrigu) are called Somapas, the sons of Angira are called Havirbhujas, Ajyapas are the sons of Pulastya; and Sukâlinas are the sons of Vasishtha. (198)

Agnidagdhâs, *Anagniaagdhâs* (lit, not burnt in fire), *Kavyas*, *Barhishadas*, *Agnishattâs*, and *Saumyâs* should be known as the manes of Bráhmaṇas. (199)

Thus the principal ones among the manes have been described, infinite are their sons and grand-sons in this universe.* (200)

From the Rishis† have originated the *Pitris* (manes) and from the manes have sprung the races of demons and divinities, and from the deities have originated all things in the order of immobile, mobile, and so on. (201)

Water, reverentially offered to the manes in a silver vessel, or in a vessel plated with silver, gives them infinite satisfation. (202)

The performance of *Pitri S'ráddhas* (*i.e.*, *S'râddhas* offered to the manes) is more specifically obligatory on the twice-born ones than the performance of *Daiva S'ráddhas* (*i.e.* *S'ráddha*-offerings made to the deities).

---

* The Mârkandeya Purânam describes these sons and grandsons of the *Pitris* as the manes of lower animals such as the cow, the horse, etc.

† Celestial sages such as Marichi, etc. Hence even in *S'ráddha* ceremonies of one's own father, grandfather, or great grandfather, the *Somapa* manes should be as well worshipped, in as much as they are the remote descendants of such soma-drinking *Pitris.*—*Kulluka.*

A *Daiva S'râddha* is held only as a prelude* to a *Pitri S'râddha* (ceremony). (203)

For the protection of a *Pitri S'ràddha* ceremony it should be preceded by a *Daiva S'râddha* offering.† A *S'râddha*, not protected in this manner, is destroyed by monsters. (204)

Hence the *Vis'vedevas* should be invoked at the outset, and formally bid adieu at the close, of a *Pitri S'râddha* ceremony, the manes should not be invoked or dismissed in a *S'râddha* before the invocation and dismissal of the *Vis'vedevas.* He perisheth with his progeny who invites the Bráhmaṇas or dismisses the Bráhmaṇa representatives of his manes in a *S'râddha* ceremony without first worshipping the *Vis'vedevas* (as directed above.)‡ (205)

Let him seek out a solitary and holy§ plot of land for the performance of a *S'râddha* (thereon) and plaster it with cow-dung; the ground must be (artificially) made to slope towards the south, if it is not so by nature. (206)

S'râddhas offered to the manes on river-banks, in solitary places, in recesses of forests,* etc., satisfy them to the greatest degree. (207)

---

* A *Daiva S'râddha* forms only a preliminary and auxiliary function of the *Pitri S'ràddha* ceremony.

† Invocation and offerings to the *Vishvadevas* (*i. e.*, all the deities).

‡ All rites done unto Brahmanas in connection with a *S'râddha* offering to the manes must be preceded by similar rites being done unto the *Vis'vedevas—Devala*.

§ The text has *S'uchi*, sacred, KULLUKA explains it by free from bones and charcoals.

‖ The text has *Avakâs'eshu chokshеshu*, KULLUKA explains it by *Svabhâvenas'uchayo'ranyâdiprades'ânteshu*, Recesses of naturally sacred places such as, forests etc.

There, after they have bathed and duly sipped water, the invited Bráhmanas shall be seated, each on a separate cushion, containing *Kusha* grass.* (208)

Thus having seated these commendable Bráhmanas on comfortable cushinons, they should be worshipped with the offerings of saffron, sandal paste, and garlands of sweet-smelling flowers, those who represent the deities being first worshipped, and after them the representatives of the manes. (209)

Then having offered the water of veneration (*Arghya*), containing sesame and *Kus'a* grass, he shall, with their permission, make fire offerings in the manner following. (210)

At the outset let him satisfy *Agni*, *Soma*, and *Yama* with libations of clarified butter, and, after that, offer oblations unto his manes. (211)

In the absence of the sacred fire,† let him (the celebrant) offer the oblations on the hands of the Bráhmanas. "Fire is the Bráhmana," thus Bráhmanas, well-versed in the *Vedas*, have said. (212)

The foremost of the twice-born ones (Bráhmanas), devoid of all irascible feelings, ever graciously disposed, the oldest born in the economy of the universe, and perpetually engaged to promote the weal of the world, have

* On each of the cushions of Brahmanas who are the representatives of the Vis'vadevas shall be placed two blades of *kus'a grass* with their tips directed towards the east, on each of the cushions of the Brahmanas who represent the manes shall be placed a single blade of *kusa grass* with its top pointed towards the south—*Devala.*

† As is probable in the case of an unmarried religious student, duly initiated with the thread, who has finished his study and returned from the house of his preceptor, or of a widower.—*Kulluka.*

been described by the Rishis as the proper recipient deities of *S'râddha* offerings (oblations). (213)

All acts* in connection with the fire-offering must be done by the offerer, seated in, or looking towards, the south, with his right hand. He shall sprinkle water on the ground on which the oblation will be offered. (214)

Let him make three *Pindas* (oblations) out of the remnants of oblations cast in the fire; and facing the south, with his whole soul bent thereon, let him offer the same on the *Kus'a* blade, with the *Pitri Tirtha*† of his right hand. (215)

Then having offered the *Pindas* on the *Kus'a* blades conformably to the rules (of his own school of *Grihya* Regulation), let him rub his hand over the *Kus'a* roots for the satisfaction of his three generations of ancestors, starting with his great grand-father, in the ascending line, who are fond of such pasty scrapings of oblations.‡ (216)

Then having directed his face towards the north, he must sip water, and gently practise three *Prânâyâmas*, and make obeisance to the six seasons of the year and to the manes.§ (217)

The residue of water, contained in the water-vessels, shall be gently poured out near each of the *Pindas*

---

* Such as *Paryukshanam*, (silently sprinkling water over the fire without muttering any Mantra, etc.—*Kulluka.*

† Part of the hand between the fore-finger and the thumb, considered sacred to the manes.

‡ On the *kus'a* roots let him scrape the sticky paste (of oblation) from his hand—Vishnu.

§ Respectively running as "I make obeisance to spring" (*Vasantâya Namastubhyam*) and "obeisance to you, manes" (*Namo Vah Pitarah*)—*Kulluka.*

16

(oblations), and the *Pindas* shall be smelled in the order in which they have been offered. (218)

After that, let him take a small portion from each of the oblations offered to the fathers, etc., and give them first to the Bráhmaṇas, present, to eat. (219)

In the event of his father living, let him (the celebrant) offer *S'râddhas* to his three ancestors preceding his father,* or feed his own father instead of the Bráhmaṇa, who is usually appointed to represent him in the ceremony. (220)

But he whose father is dead, but whose grand-father is alive, let him offer a *S'râddha* first to his deceased father, and after that, to his departed great grand-father.† (221)

A living grand-father can eat the oblation himself instead of the Bráhmaṇa representing him (in connection with a *S'râddha* offered by his grandson), or the grandson may perform the ceremony in any way he likes with the permission of the grand-father. (222)

Then having given water and *Kus'a* grass in the hands of the Bráhmaṇas, let him offer the first pickings from the oblations thereon, by muttering the *Mantra*, oblation to the manes "(*Pitri Svadhâ*)." (223)

There, carrying the plate of boiled rice with his hands, he, meditating on his departed ancestors, shall place it near the Bráhmaṇas for serving the boiled rice to them. (224)

---

* Grandfather, great grandfather, great great grandfather.

A son is privileged to perform *S'ràddhas*, which are accessory to an expiatory rite (*Pràyas'chittam*) even in the life time of his father.

† Govindaraja, following Vishnu, explains it as, "He whose father and great-grand-father are dead, let him first offer a *Pinda* (*S'râddha*) to his two ancestors, preceding his grand-father.

The boiled rice, contained in a plate which is not carried with the two hands, or is served out only with a single hand, is robbed by the malignant *Asuras* (demons). (225)

[Plates, containing] vegetable curries or soups, milk, curd, honey and clarified butter, must be carefully deposited on the ground before serving them to Bráhmaṇas out of the same. (226)

Articles of confectionary, sweet porridge,* edible roots, fruit, palatable preparations of meat, and aromatic cordials. (227)

These should be gradually brought near the Bráhmaṇas with undivided attention and served to them by commending the actual quantity served out at a time. (228)

One must not shed tears at the time of serving out the dishes (to the Bráhmaṇas), nor give vent to anger, nor speak falsehood, nor scatter the boiled rice, nor touch it with his feet. (229)

Tears shed by one, at the time of serving the boiled rice, augment the satisfaction of ghosts; a fit of anger at the time leads to the pleasure of one's enemies, a falsehood spoken at the time, augments the satisfaction of dogs, boiled rice, trampled under feet, leads to the satisfaction of monsters, and scattering boiled rice, leads to the satisfaction of miscreants. (130)

---

* The text has Bhakshyam, anything that is eaten by chewing, and Bhojyam, anything which is taken in the manner of a sweet porridge or thick barley gruel, etc, KULLUKA explains *Bhakshyam* by *Modakádi* (confection) etc. and *Bhojyam*, *Pàyasadi*, rice cooked with milk and sweetened with sugar, and such like preparations.

Articles of food, to which the Bráhmaṇas show a fondness at the time, must be unstintedly served out to them; a discourse on the supreme Self at the time leads to the satisfaction of the manes. (231)

During the *S'râddha* repast *Vedas*, *Purânas*,* *Itihâsas* and *Khilas*† should be recited to the Bráhmaṇa guests, when they would be eating. (232)

In a cheerful frame of mind, he, (the giver of the repast), shall satisfy the Brâhmanas, feed them gently, and repeatedly ask them to partake more and more of the (proferred) dishes, etc,. by dilating on their excellence. (233)

Let him assiduously feed a religious student, related to the deceased (to whom the *S'ráddha* is offered) as a daughter's son, and honour him with the present of a blanket,‡ and scatter sesame on the ground of the *S'ràddha*. (234)

Three things are sacred in a *S'ràddha*, *viz*., a daughter's son, a blanket and sesame; three things are commended in a *S'râddha* ceremony *viz*., cleanliness (purity of mind and body), non-irascibility and absence of hurry. (235)

Let the Brahmanas silently eat all the cooked food, luke warm, in a *S'ráddha* repast. Repeatedly asked to pronounce on their excellence or otherwise, they must not open their mouths. (206)

As long as the food remains warm, as long as the

---

* In his commentary on *Brihad A'ranyaka*, S'ankara describes *Purânas*, as works dealing with the creation of the universe.

† *Khilas*, KULLUKA explains it by *S'risuktas*, *S'iva Sankal'pas*, etc.

‡ The text has *Kutapam*, KULLUKA explains it by "*Nepâla kamvalam*," a blanket manufactured in the country of Nepala.

Brahmanas eat that in silence, as long as they do not remark on the excellence of the food, so long do the manes eat. (237)

What the Brâhmaṇas eat with their heads, covered, whatever do they eat with their faces towards the south, whatever do they eat with their shoes on, the monsters (and not the manes) eat all that. (238)

Let not a *Chandàla*, a hog, a cock, a dog, a woman in her menses, or a enuch see these Bráhmaṇas eating a (*S'ràddha* repast). (239)

Any thing looked at by (any of these creatures) in the course of a fire-offering, gift-making, repast, or a *S'ràddha* in honour of the manes or deities, produces contrary effect. (240)

A hog by his scent, a cock by flapping his wings, a dog by his sight, and a vile-caste man by his touch, destroys a *S'ràddha*. (241)

A lame or one-eyed man, or one who has a limb in less or excess, even if he chances to be a servant of the giver of the repast, must be removed from the place of the *S'ràddha*. (242)

A householder or a mendicant Brâhmaṇa, if he happens to ask for a meal on the occasion, he shall feed, according to his might, with the permission of the Brâhmaṇas, who are the eaters of the *S'ràddha* repast. (243)

All kinds of cooked curries and boiled rice etc., blended together and mixed with water, shall be deposited on *Kus'a* blades before the repasted Brâhmaṇas. (244)

These leavings deposited on the Kus'â (grass) are unfit to be cast in the fire; they form the portions of spirits of deceased infants, and of faithless wives who had left their husband's familes in life.* (245)

The leavings of food cast on the ground in a *S'ráddha* repast is laid down as belonging to the portion of artless and energetic servants of the house. (246)

S'ràddhas, which should be offered to the spirit of a newly deceased person till the performance of the *Sapindikaranam* rite, should be performed without offering oblations to the *Vishvedevas*; and only a single Bráhmaṇa, a single oblation, and a single blade of *Kus'a* grass are necessary for each of them.† (247)

After the performance of his *Sapindikaranam*, the sons of the deceased, whose funeral rites have been done according to the Regulation, shall offer oblations to his spirit on the day of his death‡ in the manner of a *Párvana S'ràddha*.§ (248)

Having eaten a *S'ráddha* repast, the foolish one, who gives the leavings of his plate to a *S'udra*, falls headlong into the hell of *Kála S'utram* (thread of time). (249)

In the excreta of him, who has sexually known a woman within twenty four hours of eating a *S'ráddha*

---

* The text has *Tyáginám*—KULLUKA explains it by *Gurvádi-Tyáginám* who have abandoned their husbands and superiors. We have adopted *Govindraja's* explanation in our translation.

† With only a single *Arghya* offering, devoid of oblations to the deities, invocation and fire-offerings, and with a single Kus'a blade should be performed such an *Ekoddishta S'ráddha* (*i.e.*) a S'ráddha offered to the spirit of a person who has recently departed this life—*Yájnavalkya*.

‡ On the day marked by the same lunar phase in each month of the year.

§ *Párvana S'ráddha* is a S'ráddha offered to the manes on the day of the full or new moon (*Parva*).

repast, shall his manes lie for a month from that date. (250)

Having asked the Brâhmanas, "have you well eaten?" or "have you been repleted?", he shall ask them to wash their mouths and hands, and after they have so washed, request them to take rest, saying "rest yourselves O, Brâhmanas." (251)

After rest, the Brâhmanas shall say, "*Svadhà Asi*" (let the manes be satisfied);* in all rites of *S'râddha* it is the highest benediction. (252)

After that, he shall ask the Brâhmanas in which way the residue of food (prepared on the occasion) to to be distributed. He shall give it to persons as they will direct him to do. (253)

In all *S'ràddhas* offered to one's father or mother, he shall enquire about the satisfaction of the Brâhmanas, by asking, "have you well eaten?"; in those offered to all the ancestors *(goshthi)* by asking, "have you well heard?" in those offered on auspicious occasion *(A'bhyudaika)* by asking, "is it well done?", and in those offered to the deities, by asking, "does it please?" (254)

An auspicious afternoon,† *Kus'a* grasses, plastering the house with solution of (fresh) cowdung, sesame seeds, unstinted gifts (to the Bráhmanas), purification‡ and cooking of the edibles, and acquisition

---

* The full meaning is that, let the manes be satisfied and let blessing accrue therefrom to the celebrant of the *S'ràddha* ceremony.

† Afternoon in cases of *S'ráddhas* offered on the day of the new moon. According to another *Smriti*, *S'ráddhas* to be offered on auspicious occasions (*Abhyudaiyaka*) should be done in the morning.

‡ The text has *Samskára*, which means either purification of or cooking curries, boiled rice, confection etc.

of row-sanctifying (*Pankti-pâvanas)* Bráhmaṇas, these are the blessed auxiliaries of a *S'ráddha* ceremony. (255)

Kusa' grass, *Mantras*, morning, *Havishyànnam* and things, which have been enumerated as sacred before, are the blessed accessories to a *S'ráddha* offered to the deities. (256)

Food grains used by *Munís* (divine contemplators),* milk, *Soma*-juice, raw meat† and non-alkaline salts‡ are called natural oblations. (257)

Having dismissed the Bráhmanas, let him, pure, silent and self-controlled, longingly cast his look towards the south, and pray the manes as follows : (258)

May the number of gift-makers, O ye manes, increase in our family, may our progeny and wisdom in the Vedas grow from more to more, may veneration towards the Vedas never depart from our family, and may we have many things fit to be gifted away. (259)

Having thus performed the *S'ràddha* and at the close of the prayer, the oblations (*Pindas*) should be caused to be eaten by a cow, or by a Bráhmana, or by a goat, or they should be cast in the water or fire. (260)

Several authorities advise to offer the *Pindas* to the manes after the Bráhmanas have been fed; others advise to give the oblations to the birds to eat, others advise to cast them in the fire or water. (261)

---

* S'ankara in his commentary on the *Brihad Aranyaka Upanishad* defines "*Muni*" as *mananát Muni*, from minding the supreme Self he is called *Muni*. The text has *Munyannáni* that is the kind of food grains which is eaten by hermits in ths forest, such as *Nivára* etc.

† Flesh of an animal which is not forbidden to be eaten, such as venison, hare's flesh, or goat's flesh, which may be offered to the manes as oblations.

‡ Such as Rocksalt, sea salt, etc.

The second oblation* (*Pinda*) should be given to a faithful and lawfully married wife, eager to worship the manes and desirous of conceiving a male child.* (262)

[Thereby] she will give birth to a long-lived, intelligent, well-renowned, opulent, and virtuous son, spiritually disposed, (who, in his turn), will be the father of a large family. (263)

Thus having washed his hands and sipped water, he shall, with the greatest attention, feed his father's cognates, and after that, the relations on his mother's side. (264)

Let not the leavings be removed till the Bráhmaṇas have departed from their seats; and after that, let him make the household offerings, this is the Regulation. (265)

Now I shall describe the kinds of oblations, which, being duly offered to the manes, give them satisfaction which lasts for a long time, or for all eternity. (266)

Sesame, barley grains, Vrihi grains, kidney beans, water, fruits, and edible roots, duly offered to the manes, keep them satisfied for one month. (267)

Páthina fish (keeps them satisfied) for two months; venison, for three months; mutton, for four months; and flesh (of clean) birds, for five months; (268)

Goat's flesh, for six months; flesh of a spotted deer, for seven months; the flesh of an *Ena* deer, for eight months; and the flesh of a *Ruru* deer, for nine months. (269)

Flesh of the buffalo or rhinoceros satisfies the manes

---

* The text has *Madhyamah Pindah* (*i e.*) the oblation offered by her husband to his deceased grandfather, and duly consecrated with the *Grihya mantras*.

for ten months; the flesh of a hare or tortoise, for eleven months; (270)

Preparations of cow-milk, and *Páyasa* for one full year; the flesh of a white, old goat, for twelve years. (271)

The satisfaction, which they derive (from) *Kála-s'áka* (a kind of vegetables), large scaled fishes, flesh of the rhinoceros or of red goat, honey, and food grains lasts for all eternity. (272)

Anything mixed with honey, which is offered to them on the thirteenth day of the fortnight, marked by the asterism *Maghá*,* leads to their satisfaction for eternal time. (273)

"May he be born in our family, who will offer us *Páyasa* offerings, mixed with honey and clarified butter, on the day of the thirteenth phase of the moon, marked by the asterism *Maghá*, or under the auspices of *Kunjara-chchháyá*.† (274)

Anything, which is reverentially offered to the manes, gives them infinite and eternal satisfaction in the next world. (275)

The days of the fortnight, from the tenth day to the day of the new moon, excepting the day of the fourteenth day of the moon's wane, are auspicious for the performance of *S'ráddhas*. (276)

---

* The *Trayodashi* (the thirteenth day of the moon's wane) is specifically mentioned, the thirteenth day of the moon's wane in the month of Bhádra should be considered as meant—as Sankha opines.

† When the sun is in the asterism *Hastá* in the month o *A'shvin*, the thirteenth day of the lunar wane in the month of *Mukhya Bhádra* in connection therewith, marked by the asterism *Maghà*, is called *Kunjara-Chchhàyà*, see Vishnu. Ch. LXXVIII—52, 53.

S'râddhas, offered under the auspices of even numbered asterisms (such as, the second, fourth lunar mansions), or of the even numbered phases of the moon, grant the fruition of all desires ; while those, offered under the auspices of odd numbered asterisms, or lunar phases, grant a family of opulent and erudite sons. (277)

As the dark fortnight is more auspicious than the light one for the purposes of *S'ràddha* offerings to the manes, so evening is better than forenoon for that end. (278)

With the holy thread placed on his right shoulder, and the *Kus'a* grass in his hand, let him assiduously perform all rites in connection with a *S'ràddha* to the manes with the help of the *Pitri-tirtha* of his right hand. (279)

Let him not offer a *S'ràddha* offering in the night ; night is the time for monsters, nor they should be offered at either meeting of the day and night, nor just at sunrise. (280)

In the event of his inability to offer *S'râddhas,* each month, let him in this manner offer three *S'râddhas* in Summer, Rains, and fore-winter (*Hemanta*). (281)

The fire offering to be made in a *S'ràddha* must not be made in any other fire than that in which *Vedic* and *Smirta* rites are performed ; a Brâhmaṇa keeper of the sacred fire must not offer a *S'râddha* on any other day in the dark fortnight except on the day of the new moon. (282)

The foremost of Brâhmaṇas obtains the same merit by offering libations of water to the manes after his bath, as is acquired by instituting the *Pitri-yajnas* (*i.e., S'râddhas, lit.* sacrifices offered to the manes) (283)

The Rishis call the (heirarchy of) fathers as *Vasus*, the (heirarchy of) grand-fathers as *Rudras*, and the (heirarchy of) great grand-fathers as A'dityas (284)

Every day, eat the residue of cooked food left after first feeding the Brâhmaṇas (Vishvasa); eat, every day, ambrosia. The first is called *Vishvasa*, the second is the residue of food left after performing a sacrifice therewith. (285)

Even the eternal S'ruti has aknowledged the divinity of the manes. Thus I have told you all about the mode of performing the five daily sacrifices, and all rites in connection therewith. Now hear me describe the means by which the twice-born ones shall earn their livelihood. (286)

CHAPTER IV.

A TWICE-BORN one shall reside for the first quarter of his life* in the residence of his preceptor, and the second quarter (thereof) in his own house as a married man. (1)

A Brâhmaṇa, other than in the time of distress, shall earn his livelihood and maintain his family by a means, which does not clash, or clash very little, with other men's interests.† (2)

---

* The text has *Chaturthamâyusho Bhagam*, a quarter part of the duration of life, *i. e.* twenty five years, since according to the *S'ruti*, a hundred years is the ordained space of human existence. *S'atâyurvai Purushah*.

† In short by teaching, by celebrating sacrifices on behalf of their celebrants, and by receiving gifts from the pure and the holy, etc., *Yâjanadhyâpana-Vis'uddha-prati grahâdibhiḥ*—*Kulluka*.

He must earn money, enough for his merest existence, by works which do not disgrace the social order he belongs to, and which do not entail much physical labour or hardship. (3)

Let him live by *Ritam* and *Amritam*, or by *Mritam* or *Pramitam*, or by *Satyânritam*, but never by the avocation of a dog.* (4)

Picking up grains of paddy from the stubbly fields (*uncha vritti*), or collecting the ears of paddy constitutes what is called *Ritam*.

Anything obtained without solicitation is called *Amritam* (lit, nectar); to live by begging is called *Mritam* (death), and to live by agriculture is called *Pramritam*. (5)

Trade is called *Satyânritam*, and it is good that a man should live by trade. Service is called the vocation of a dog, hence it should be shunned. (6)

Either be a *Kus'ala-dhânyaka*† or a *Kumbhi-dhànyaka*,‡ or store up enough to support the family for three days, or only enough for the morrow. (7)

Of these four kinds of Brâhmana house-holders (*kus'aladhânyaka* etc), each succeeding one is more meritorious than the one immediately preceding it (in the list), inasmuch as on account of the comparatively greater poverty of their resources they are compelled to practise self-abnegation (lit, self control) by which they are enabled to conquer the whole world. (8)

---

* The text has *S'va-vrittyà* by the avocation of a dog, *i.e.*, by accepting service.

† One who has got food grains stored in his house, enough for three years' consumption of his family.

‡ One who has stored up food grain enough for a year's consumption of the family.

A householder (with a large family) may earn a living by six acts,* one (with a smaller family than the former) by three acts,† one (with a small family) by two acts,‡ and one with a very small family by teaching alone. (9)

A Brâhmana, living by *S'ila* or *Uncha* means of livelihood, should only be devoted to the keeping of the fire, and do the sacrifices which are enjoined to be performed at the end of a *Parva* or *Ayana*. (10)

For a livelihood, let him (Brâhmana) not take to any (vile) means, (usually) adopted by ordinary men,§ let him maintain himself by a profession which is honest, artless, holy and worthy of a Brâhmana. (11)

Resting in contentment, a seeker of happiness must restrain himself from pursuing more and more wealth. Happiness is rooted in contentment, misery is based on discontent. (12)

Following any of the aforesaid professions, a *Snâtaka* Brâhmana should observe the following rules of conduct and vows, which impart fame and longevity in this life and lead to heaven (after death.) (13)

By unremittingly discharging his duties alone, as ordained in the Vedas, to the best of his ability, one comes by the most elevated status. (14)

---

* Such as *Ritam*, obtaining without solicitation, begging, agriculture, trade and money-lending.

† Priesthood, teaching, and gift taking.

‡ Teaching and officiating as priests at sacrifices celebrated by others.

§ The text has *Na Loka Vrittam*, KULLUKA explains it as " not by falsehood, deceit, sycophancy, self advertisement, and imitation of the dress and manners of one's master as is usually done by common men.

He shall not earn money by acts which enthral the senses of man, nor by means forbidden by the Vedas: In the event of his possessing money, or in want, one must not endeavour to earn money from any source, without discrimination.* (15)

Let him not wilfully addict himself to any object of sense-gratification; in case of extreme attachment he must counteract it by means of his will-force. (16)

Acquisition (of wealth, etc), hostile to his *Vediac* studies, must be avoided; if he can study his Vedas, each day, by any how supporting his family, that is his success in life. (17)

His dress, speech and his discernment (feelings) must be in conformity with his birth, wealth, age and *Vediac* knowledge. (18)

He shall peruse, each day, *S'ástras* whose perusal serves to improve the intellect, as well as those which treats on the art of money-making.† Likewise, he shall study the *Nigamas* which illucidate the (true) import of the Vedas.‡ (19)

A man acquires proficiency in the *S'ástras* he reads, each day; and illuminated with their light, his general knowledge increases. (20)

Let him not omit performing the *Rishi-yajna, Deva-Yajna, Bhuta-Yajna* and *Pitri-Yajna*§ according to the best of his might. (21)

---

* "*Prasangena*" is the term that occurs in the text, KULLUKA examplifies it by "dance and music" (*Nrityágitádiná*).

† Dhanyáni, the science of money making, such as the works of *Ushanas* and *Brihaspati*.

‡ The Upanishads, etc.

§ *Rishi-yajna, i. e.* study of the *Vedas, Deva-yajna, i. e.* five offerings to the deities, *Bhuta-yajna* oblations to animals, *Nri-yajna, i. e*, hospitalities to men; and *Pitri-yajna, S'ráddha* offerings to the manes.

Some there are, who, though conversant with the mode of performing both external and internal *yajnas,** perform these five kinds of *yajnas*, by withdrawing the five senses from their respective objects of gratification. (22)

Several wise householders, knowing that immortal is the fruit of performing sacrifices with speech and vital airs, constantly cast offerings of speech in the vital airs, and those of vital airs in the speech.† (23)

Several other Brâhmaṇas, possessed of the knowledge of Brahma, constantly perform these five sacrifices by means of their knowledge of Brahma; with their sight of wisdom (*Upanishad*), they behold that knowledge is the primary end of all (religious) acts. (24)

Let five offerings in connection with the *Agnihotra* sacrifices be offered in the fore-part of the day or night, or in the first or last part of the day, or in the first or last part of the night. At the close of the dark fort-night he shall perform the *Darsha* sacrifice, and at the close of the light fort-night the one known as *Paurnamâsa*. (25)

A Brâhmaṇa must celebrate the *(Agrayana)* sacrifice on the harvesting of the new crops,‡ the

---

* *Vâhya Abhyantara yajnas, Vâhya yajnas* are religious rites or ceremonials, while *Abhyantara yajnas* consist in practising *yoga* with its accessories.

† Mutter the Mantra, "I cast the offering of speech in the fire of vitality, while not speaking; and the one running as, "I cast the offering of life in speech" at the time of speaking.

‡ The text has *S'asyânte,* which literally means after the stock of the previous year's food grains has run out. KULLUKA, grounding his statement on the aphorism of the *Sutra-Kâra, Sâradi Navânnam,* the harvest-sacrifice in *S'rat* (October-November), asserts that the sacrifice must be performed

(*Châturmâsya*) sacrifice at the close of a season,* the animal sacrifice at the beginning of a *Ayana*,† and the *Soma-yajnas* at the close of the year.‡ (26)

A Brâhmana, with the sacred fire, wishing a long life, shall not partake of newly harvested food grain, or cooked meat without first performing the *Navânnam* (new food grain) and animal sacrifices.§ (27)

The fire consumes the vitality of the gluttonous Brâhmana (with the sacred fire), if he partakes of the newly harvested food grains and meat without first offering them as oblations to the fire. (28)

Let not an *Atithi* (guest), unpropitiated with a cushion, bed, food, water, fruit or edible roots to the best of his might, reside in his (Brâhmanas) house. (29)

Let him not welcome with speech even (guests) who go contrary to the *Vedas*, or live by professions other than those peculiar to his order, or are cat-natured|| or dispute the doctrines of the *Vedas* by

---

after the harvest of the new grains has been gleaned, no matter whether the stock of the previous year's food grains has been exhausted or not, as otherwise a rich householder, with several years' provisions in his store, will be discharged from the obligation of of celebrating this sacrifice.

* A *Rituh* (season), according to KULLUKA, consists of four months, a year is divided into three seasons, a fact which shows that, this celebrated commentator of the Manu Samhita was a resident of northern India.

† *Ayana* means the period when the sun is either in the northern, or in the southern solstice.

‡ The text has *Samânte*, (lit, at the close of the year) *i.e.*, in spring, inasmuch as the Vediac year which used to be computed with the first day the lunar month in Chaitra was considered complete with winter.

§ Soma Yajnas such as, Agnishtoma etc.,

|| The text has *Vaidâla Vrittikân* and *Vaka Vratins i.e.* men who are deceitful as cats, or carry cloaks of religion.

false logic, or have no faith in the *Vedas*, or are crane-natured.* (30)

Let him honour the house-holders, who have performed the rites of ceremonial ablutions at the completion of the *Vedic* study, or at the close of a vow, or both, with oblations offered to the gods and manes, and avoid those who are otherwise qualified.† (31)

A householder shall give cooked food to *Brahmachárins* etc.,‡ who do not cook their meals; and after keeping enough food for his relations and dependents, he shall distribute the residue among the birds and beasts. (32)

A *Snátaka* householder, famished with hunger, shall ask money of the king, or of his pupils and disciples, but of no other men. This is the conclusion. (33)

A *Snátaka* Bráhmana must on no account suffer himself to be overwhelmed with hunger;§ and possessing money, he must not wear a torn or dirty cloth. (34)

* Cf Vishnu. Chapter LXXXII. Aphorisms 5 and 7.

† Let him invite them on the occasion of a *S'ràddha*, offered to the gods or manes.

‡ MEDHATITHI and GOVINDARAJA, on the basis of the couplet, *Bhikshàncha Bhikshave dadyàt Vidhibat Brahmachàrine*, etc., say that, *Bhikshus*, *Paribrájakas*, *Brahmachàrins*, etc., have been provided for in the above quoted couplet, and hold that this stanza contemplates the giving of cooked food to mendicants of other pursuasions, or to those who denounce the authority of the *Vedas (Páshandins)*.

‡ Even water should be given to trees and plants, each day, by a Brahmana householder.

§ The text has *Na Sidet Snàtaka Vipra.* KULLUKA explains that a fully educated Snàtaka enjoys the privilege of receiving gifts from proper persons, so he need not beg any thing of the king, as he has many other substantial means of keeping the wolf from the door without depending upon the bounty of the state.

With his hair and beards cleanly clipped and his finger nails decently paired, he, pure in body and spirit, self-controlled and clad in a white garment, shall study the *Vedas*, and be mindful of his own benefit.* (35)

Let him carry a bamboo stick in his hand, an ewer, full of water, his *Veda*, and the holy thread, and wear a pair of beautiful, golden ear-rings. (36)

He must not gaze on the rising or setting sun, nor look at the sun in the mid sky, nor during an eclipse, nor at his reflected image in the water. (37)

He must not leap over the tether of a calf, nor run while it is raining, nor look at his image in the water. This is the injunction (of the Sâstra). (38)

A heap of earth, a cow, a divine edifice, a Brâhmana, clarified butter, honey, a crossing of roads, and large forest trees, these he shall circumambulate (from right to left.) (39)

Even extremely heated, he must not visit his wife during the three forbidden days of her periods, nor share the same bed with her. (40)

Intellect, vigour, strength, eye-sight, and vitality of a man, who goes unto a woman in her menses, are impaired. (41)

Of him, who avoids a woman in her menses, the intellect, vigour, strength, eye-sight and vitality are improved. (42)

Let him not eat in the company of his wife, nor see her eating, nor while she is yawning or sneezing, or sitting (*en dishabille*) at ease. (43)

---

* The text has *A'tmahiteshucha*, KULLUKA explains it by "taking special care of his own health with the help of suitable medicines, if necessary, and by avoiding unwholesome and indigestable food."

Nor while she is applying collyrium along her eye-lids, or anointing her uncovered person with oil; nor while she is giving birth to a child, his wife should be looked at by the foremost of Brâhmaṇas, seeking vigour. (44)

Wearing a single cloth, he must not eat his meal, nor bathe stript of all clothes. He must not pass urine on the road, or in a pasture-ground, or on the ashes. (45)

Nor in a ploughed field or in the water, nor in a cremation ground, nor on the mountain, nor in a dilapidated temple, and never on an ant hill. (46)

Not in a hole dwelt by an animal, neither when walking, nor staying, nor having arrived at a river bank, nor on the summit of a mountain. (47)

Facing the wind, fire, a Brahmana, the sun, the water, or a cow, let him never evacuate urine or excreta. (48)

Covering the earth with wood, clods of earth, leaves, or weeds, with covered head and body, silent, and having washed his mouth, let him evacuate urine and excreta. (49)

In the day he shall evacuate stool and urine with his face turned towards the north, looking towards the south he must do it in the night; at either juncture of the day and night he must do it as in the day. (50)

In the night, in the event of the stars, etc., being enveloped by the cloud, in times of peril to life, let a Brahman evacuate stool and urine, facing any quarter of the heaven he pleases. (51)

Facing the wind, the fire, the sun, or the moon, or looking at a cow, or a Brâhmana, he, who evacuates stool or urine, is robbed of his intellect. (52)

Let him not cast any unholy thing in the fire, nor warm his feet over it. Let him not blow a fire with his mouth, nor look at his naked wife. (53)

Let him not keep a fire underneath his bedstead, nor leap over a fire. He must not place a fire at his foot, nor do any thing that imperils life. (54)

At either meeting of the day and night, let him not eat any thing, or lie down, or walk (*i.e.*, go any where). He must not dig lines in the ground, nor himself remove the garland of flowers he has worn. (55)

In the water he must not evacuate stool or urine, nor cast sputa, poison, blood, or any thing smeared with any excreted organic matter. (56)

He must not sleep alone in a solitary chamber, nor rouse up a superior from his sleep. Let him not speak with a woman in her flow, nor go to a religious ceremony without invitation. (57)

He must keep his right arm free, and uncovered by his upper sheet of apparel, in the chamber of the sacred fire, in a pasture ground, in the company of the Brâhmaṇas, at the time of reading the *Vedas*, and at the time of eating his (meal). (58)

He must not restrain a cow from drinking water or suckling her calf, if he sees her in the act; nor shall he report it to any body. An intelligent person, who has beheld a rainbow in the sky, must not show it to others. (59)

Let him not long reside in an impious village, nor in one infected with any disease. He must not go alone on a long journey, nor stay long on a mountain summit. (60)

Let him not reside in a S'udra kingdom, nor in one teeming with an ungodly population. He must not live in a country abounding in revilers of the *Vedas*, nor in that which is infested by vile-caste men. (61)

He must not eat any thing whose oleaginous essence has been taken out,* nor over-load his stomach† with food; and let him not eat any thing too early in the morning or evening, nor take any thing in the night, if he has been over-repleted in the day. (62)

Let him not make any futile attempt,‡ nor drink water with the united palms of his hands; he must not eat any thing by placing it on his thighs, nor be needlessly inquisitive about any matter. (63)

He must not sing a tune, or dance a measure, or play on a musical instrument, prohibited in the science of music); he must not vauntingly stroke the muscles of his upper arms, nor gnash his teeth, nor bray like an ass out of an exuberance of) emotional feeling. (64)

He shall never wash his feet in a vessel of white brass, he must not eat in a cracked plate, nor in a vessel, repugnant to his sensibility. (65)

A holy thread, an ewer, a coth, a garland of flowers, an ornament, and shoes, previously used by another, he must not wear. (66)

He must not ride on a wild (unbroken), hungry, diseased, beast of conveyance, nor on one with pierced hoofs and mutilated tails, or broken horns. (67)

He shall travel by (horses or elephants) that are

---

* Such as PinyAka, mustard cake, etc.,—*Kulluka*.

† Fill half of the stomach with food, its quarter part with water, and leave a quarter part of its cavity free for the circulation of air.—*Vishunpuranam*.

‡ The text has *Na kurvita Vrithá Cheshtàm*, *i.e.* he must not spend his physical energy to do an act which does not bring him any good either immediate or prospective.

fastgoing, quiet, handsome and good coloured animals, possessed of auspicious features, sparing the mace or the whip as much as possible. (68)

The heat of the autum sun,* the smoke of a cremation ground, a cracked or fissured seat, he must avoid; he must not tear his hair or finger nails, nor cut his finger nails with his teeth. (69)

He must not wantonly grind clay or clods of earth with his hands, nor cut weeds with his finger nails; let him not attempt a futile act, nor do any thing which may create troubles in the future.† (70)

He, who (wantonly) grinds earth (with his fingers), or cuts his finger nails (with his teeth), as well as a malicious calumniator, and one, who neglects his pearsonal cleanliness, soon meet destruction. (71)

He must not lay any wager (as regards matters of *S'ástras* or concerns of life), nor go out wearing a garland of flowers round his neck;‡ in every way it is condemnable to ride on a bullock. (72)

Let him not enter a (walled) village or a house by any other entrance than the front door (or gate); he shall avoid from a distance the roots of trees in the night.§ (73)

---

* The text has *Vâlâtapah*, some commentators explain it by "ray of the morning sun." It really means the heat of the sun when it remains in the sign of *Kanyâ* (Virgo).

† This stanza is not a mere repetition of stanza 63, there *Cheshtà* means physical exertion; the present stanza contemplates all mental acts, such as planning, willing etc, for the performance of an act which does not confer any benefit on its doer.

‡ He must keep it concealed under his upper sheet of garment, when going out. *Kulluko.*

§ He must not think of lying or taking shelter under a tree in the night.

He must not play a game with dice, nor carry in his hand the shoes he wears; let him not gradually eat a morsel of food he has taken in his hand, nor by placing the plate (of food) on a cushion. 74)

He must not eat any preparation of sesame, or any thing, containing sesame, after sunset; let him not lie down entirely naked in the bed, nor go any where without washing his mouth after eating. (75)

He must eat in wet feet, but he must not lie down in wet feet; he, who eats in wet feet, acquires longevity. (76)

Let him not go to a place, which is not easily accessible and which is beyond sight; he must not look at the excreta, nor swim across a river with his arms. (77)

A person, wishing to live a long life, must not stand on the ashes, on skeletal bones, on bits of broken, baked earthen vessels, on heaps of cotton seeds, nor on husks of paddy. (78)

For a moment even, let him not associate with the degraded, with *Chandálas*, with *Pukkas'as*,* with the illiterate, with the purse-proud, and with low caste men (*Antyavasáyins*). (79)

He must not give any worldly advice, or the leaving of his food,† or the residue of the fire-offering to a S'udra; let him not give religious instructions to a S'udra, not grant him (S'udra) sanction to practise a vow. (80)

The Bráhmaṇa, who gives religious instructions to a S'udra, or advises him to practise a religous vow, is

---

* A son of a S'udra woman bya Brahmana is called a *Nishâda*. The son which a *Nishâda* begets on a Sudra woman is called a *Pukkas'a*, and the son begotten by a *Chandâla* on a *Nishâda* wife is called an *Autyavasayin*.

† He can give the leaving of his food to his S'udra servant.

drowned with that S'udra in the hell of *Asamvritam* (unrestrained darkness). (81)

Let him not scratch his head with his united hands, nor touch it without washing his mouth, after eating, nor bathe without immersing his head in the water. (82)

He must not strike any one on the head, nor pull him by his hair; after bathing, head-anointed, let him not touch oil with any other part of his body. (83)

He must not accept the gift of a king, who is not the son of a Kshatriya, nor of him who lives by selling meat,* nor of an oil-presser,† nor of a wine-seller,‡ nor of him who lives upon the income of prostitution. (84)

An oil-presser is ten times as vile as a butcher (meat-seller), a wine seller is ten times as vile as an oil-presser, an enjoyer of the earnings of a prostitute is ten times as vile as a wine-seller, and a non-Kshatriya king is ten times as vile as the enjoyer of a prostitute's earnings. (85)

A non-Kshatriya king is like unto a butcher, who keeps ten thousand slaughter-houses going; and hence, to accept the gift of such a king is a deadly sin. (86)

He, who accepts the gift of a greedy king, who does not rule in conformity with the Regulation, goes to the twenty one hells in succession, known as, (87)

Tâmisram (hell of darkness), *Andha-tâmisram* (hell of sable darkness), *Mahâ-rauravam* (the great howling hell), *Kàla-sutram* (the hell of the thread of time) and *Mahâ-narakam* (the great hell). (88)

---

* The text has *Saunika* which means a butcher, from *Sunâ*, a place of slaughter.

† *Chakram*—an oil-press.

‡ The text has *Dhvajin*, *Dhavja* means a pennon, a wine-seller is called *Dhvajin*, because in ancient India a pennon is used to be hung down on the door-way of each wine-shop.

The *Sanjivanam* (animating hell), *Mahâvichi* (hell of great billows), *Tapanam* (burning hell), *Samprata-panam* (extremely heating hell), *Sanghâtam* (the crushing hell). *Sakâkolam* (hell with crows and owls) *Kudmalam*, *Putimrittikam* (hell of foul-smelling soil). (89)

Loha S'anku (hell of iron tongs), *Rijisham* (frying), *Panthâ*, *Shâlmali*, *Nadi*, *Asipatravanam* (sword-leafed forest) and *Lohadârakam* (iron-breaking). (90)

Erudite, Brâhma-knowing Brâhmaṇas, aware of these things, do not accept gifts from (such) a king, for their good in the next world. (91)

He must leave his bed at the *Brâhma Muhurta** (forty-eight minutes before the sun-rise), meditate on piety and worldly interests, ponder over the form of physical labour by which they can be secured, and ascertain the true import of the *Vedas*.† (92)

Having left his bed and attended to the calls of nature, he, well washed, and pure in spirit, shall, with undivided attention, mutter the morning *Gâyatri* and the *Gâyatris*, which are connected with the other *Sandhyâ* rites as well. (93)

---

* GOVINDARAJA interprets the term *Brâhma Muhurtta* to mean the latter end of the last watch of the night.

† The injunction, ordaining the contemplation of the real import of the Vedas at that time, is for the fact that, intellect becomes fresh and clear in the morning, which leads to a clear conception of the divinity which hedges round our daily duties in life. All our acts are subordinated to the will of the providence, we live in God and live for God only, and all our works are His works. This is the true import of the teachings of the Vedas, and there can be no better moment for thinking of this divine nature of our mission in life than the cool and calm hours of the morning, thus to begin life, each day, with the thought and conviction of divine help and contact.

The Rishis were long-lived because they used to devote greater lengths of time to their rites of daily *Sandhyâ* (prayer), and for this they obtained fame, progeny, celebrity, and the energy of *Brahma*. (94)

Having performed the rite of *Upâkarma** on the day of the full moon in the month of *S'râvana* or *Bhâdra*, he shall devotedly read the *Vedas* for four months and a half. (95)

After that period, under the auspices of the asterism *Pushyâ* (in the month of *Pausha*), he shall, out-side the boundary of his village, do the rite in connection with the completion of his *Vedic* study, or do it on the forenoon of the first day of the light fortnight in the month of *Mâgha*.† (96)

Having duly performed the rite of bidding adieu to the *Vedas*‡ at the out-skirt of his village, he shall refrain from studying the *Vedas* for that day and night, or for that day and night and the next day only *(Pakshini)*. (97)

After that, let him study the *Vedas* during the whole of the light fortnight, and the allied branches of study (*Vedângas* such as Grammar, Prosody, Astronomy, etc.,) during the entire dark fortnight. (98)

He must not indistinctly read the *Vedas*, nor read them near a S'udra; tired with reading the *Vedas* in the last watch of the night, let him not sleep again. (99)

---

* The rite of *Upâkarma* consists in making a fire-offering for the worship and glorification of the *Achâryaya*, preceptor)

† Those who have performed the *Upâkarma* on the full moon day of Bhâdra must do this rite in the first day of the light fortnight in Mâgha.

‡ Fire offerings made after finishing the study of the *Vedas* for four months and a half.

In the aforesaid manner, a BrÂhmaṇa shall devotedly read the metrical *Mantra* portion of the *Vedâs;* and in the absence of distressing circumstances, he shall devotedly read their *Mantra* and Brâhmaṇa portions as well. (100)

Both the reading student and the teaching preceptor must not read the *Vedas* under the following circumstances of non-study (*Anadhyâyam*). (101)

In the rainy season, when the wind is heard roaring in the night, or when the wind is seen raising clouds of dust in the day, (as they are the circumstances, which the learned, acquainted with rule of *Vediac* study, say as occasioning the non-study (of the *Vedas*). (102)

When it rains with thunder and lightning, and when showers of meteors fall from the skies, are the circumstances, said to occasion the accidental non-study of the *Vedas* (from that time to the next day). This is what Manu has ordained. (103)

If these phenomena (thunder, lightning, etc.,) occur at the time of kindling the *Homa* fire in the evening during the rainy season, they should not be regarded as occasions of non-study, but in other seasons of the year the appearance of clouds at the time of kindling the *Homa*-fire will occasion non-study. (104)

Earth-quakes, with rumbling sounds in the earth, and eclipses of the sun and moon, even if they happen in their proper seasons, should be regarded as occasioning periods of non-study. (105)

If lightning and claps of thunder happen to be seen and heard at the time of kindling the *Homa*-fire, the period of non-study will last till the extinction of the luminary,* while it shall extend for the whole day and night, if it happens to rain after the occurrence of either of the aforesaid phenomena. (106)

For extremely pious men, thestudy of the *Vedas* in a crowded village, or in places, always full of foul smell, is prohibited.† (107)

In a village from which a dead body has not been removed, by the side of an extremely impious person,‡ in a crowded place, or in a place where the crying sound is heard, the *Vedas* shall never be studied. (108).

In the water, at mid-night,§ at the time of evacuating stool and urine, in unwashed mouth after eating, and after having eaten a S'râddha repast, let him not contemplate (the *Vedas*) in his mind. (109)

An erudite Brâhmaṇa, on accepting an invitation to an *Ekoddishta* S'râddha repast, must not read the *Vedas* for three days (from the date of such acceptance); (similarly), he must not read them for three days on the birth of a king's son, or on the occasion of a solar or lunar eclipse. (110)

So long as the scent or residue of safforn-pastes etc., with which his body has been smeared on the occasion

---

* Till the sun sets, if it happens in the day, and till the stars disappear in heaven, if it happens in the night.

† The text has *Dharma-naipunya-Kâminah*, KULLUKA explains it by *Dharmâtis'ayârthinah*, those who seek the highest form of virtue.

‡ The text has *Vrishala*, KULLUKA explains it by *Adhârmikah*, impious person, and not a S'udra.

§ The text has *Madhyarâtre*, KULLUKA explains it by *Muhurta-chatushtaya*, 192 minutes in the midnight, and he is supported by *Gâutama*, "*Nis'âyâm Chaturmuhurta*, for 192 minutes in the mid-night. GOVINDARAJA explains it by *Dviprahara*, at the second *Prahara* of the night, a Prahara being equal to three hours.

of an *Ekoddishta* S'râddha, remains on his person, an erudite Brâhmaṇa must not read the *Vedas.* (111)

Lying, or sitting on his haunches, or with his thighs uncovered, after eating cooked flesh, or boiled rice (food) soiled by a birth or death-uncleanness, he must not read the *Vedas.* (112)

In a forest, on hearing the sound of flying arrows,* at either juncture of the day and night, and on the day of the new or full moon, as well as on the eighth and fourteenth days of the fortnight, and on the occasions of *Ashtakâs*, he must not read the *Vedas.* (113)

The day of the new moon destroys the preceptor, the fourteenth day of the fortnight kills the disciple (student), *Ashtaka's* and the day of the full moon lead to the loss of their (*Vedas*) memory; hence, these days should be avoided in reading the *Vedas.* (114)

In dust storms, on the appearance of a meteoric light on the horizon, when the jackals howl, and dogs bark, or the asses bray, and camels scream, as well as in a company, let not a Brâhmaṇa read the *Vedas.* (115)

Let him not read (the *Vedas*) at a cremation ground, at the outskirt of a village, in a pasture ground, wearing the dress he had on when he visited his wife, and on accepting a *S'râddha* gift. (116)

Having accepted a S'râddha gift, whether animate (such as a cow, etc.,) or inanimate, he must not read the

* The text has *Vána S'avde*, several commentators explain *Vána*, which ordinarily means an arrow, by *Viná Visesha*, a kind harp or lyre, the whole meaning according to them being on hearing the notes of a harp.

Vedas, inasmuch as the hands of a Brâhmaṇa are said to be like unto his mouth.* (117)

A terror of thieves and blazes breaking out in the village, as well as all abnormal phenomena of nature must be understood as occasioning periods of nonstudy (of the *Vedas*). (118)

The period of non-study lasts for three nights at the close of the rite of *Upâkarma* or *Utsarga* ;† that in connection with‡ an *Asntakâ* or the completion of a season of the year is one day and night. (119)

Let him not read (the *Vedas* on horse-back, nor while riding on an elephant, or sitting on the bough of a tree, nor while riding an ass or a camel or going in a boat or a vehicle, nor standing on a barren, waterless ground. (120)

Nor while wrangling or fighting, nor near a troop of soldiers, nor in a battle-field, nor immediately after eating,§ nor while suffering from indigestion, nor after vomiting, nor after a sour rising. (121)

Nor without taking permission of a guest (*Atithi*) in the house, nor while the winds are violently blowing, nor after bleeding from any part of the body, nor after a cut from a weapon. (122)

---

* The text has *Pànyàsyah*, lit, hand-mouthed, the meaning is that acceptance of a gift by a Brahmana with his hand is like unto his eating the same.

† For *Utsarga* and *Upàkarma*, see Note. under V. 90 of this chapter.

‡ *Ashtakás.*—The eighth days of the moon's wane during the three months commencing with the day of the full moon in the month of Agrahàyana.

§ *Cf. Vasishthà, Yàvadárdrapàniriti,*" as long as the (washed) hands remain wet after a meal.

He must not read the *Rik*, and *Yajush* (*Vedas*) as long as the chants of the *Sama Veda* will remain audible, nor any other *Veda*, after completing the reading of one *Veda* with its (allied) *A'ranyakam*. (123)

The gods are the presiding deities of the *Rig-Veda*, men are those of the *Yajush*,* and the manes are those of the *Sâma Veda*; hence, unholy are the chants of the *Sâma Veda*.† (124)

Knowing these (tutelary gods), the erudite ones first mutter the *Pranava*, the *Vyahriti* and the *Gâyatri*, the essence of all the *Vedas*, and read the *Vedas* after that. (125)

A cow, etc.,‡ a toad, a cat, a dog, a snake, a mungoose or a mouse, happening to pass between (the preceptor and his disciple) at the time of teaching the *Vedas*, the period of non-study shall be deemed as extending for one day and night. (126)

The impurity of the place of *Vedaic* study,§ and personal uncleanness of the reader, these two are the permanent causes of nons-tudy; let a Bráhmaṇa carefully avoid these two occasions of non-study. (127)

A *Snâtaka* Bráhmaṇa must shun the bed of his wife on the day of the full or new moon, as well as on the

---

* Religious rites and sacrifices to be performed by men and the mode of performing them form the main thesis of the *Yajurveda*.

† The *Bhagavad Gitá*, on the other hand, gives the highest precedence to the *Sâman* among the four *Vedas*.

Cf Vedànàm Sâmavedosmi, I (supreme deity) am the *Sama Veda* among the *Vedas*.

‡ The text has *Pas'u*, which literally means a beast, KULLUKA explains it by *Gavâdi*, hoarned cattle, etc.

§ Such as defilement of the floor of the study with leaving of food, etc., eighth or fourteenth days of the moon's wane or increase, even if his wife be in her menstrual period* at the time. (128)

He must not bathe after eating, nor while ill,† nor at midnight‡ nor with a large number of clothes on,§ nor in an unknown tank or reservoir of water. (129)

Let him not wilfully leap over the shadow of his king or preceptor, nor that of a divine image, nor that of a cow, nor that of a *Snātaka*, nor that of an initiator, nor that of a brown cow, nor that of an initiated person. (130)

He must not long tarry at a cross road at midday or midnight, nor after eating meat in a Srāddha repast, nor at either meeting of the day or night. (131)

Let him not wilfully touch with his feet used cosmatic pastes,|| bathing water, excreted matter, blood, mucous, sputa and vomited matter (lying on the ground). (132)

Let him not associate with (*i.e.*, serve) his enemies, with the friends of his enemies, with impious men, with thieves and other men's wives. (133)

Nothing so shortens the life of a man in this world as the act of (clandestinely) visiting another's wife. (134)

* Twelve days from the fourth day of her period.

† An institutor of a religious ceremony, happening to fall ill and hence incapable of bathing, must bathe without immersing his head in water and by rubbing his body with a wet towel. *Javala.*

‡ Not forbidden in the case of touching a *Chandala*, or a low-caste man.

§ Except those forms of ceremorial ablutions which are made for the fruition of any specific desire, like those performed under the auspices of a lunar eclipse,. etc.

|| The text has *Udvartanam*, KULLUKA explains it as *Abhyanga malāpakarshana pishtakam*, pasted tumeric, Emblic myrobalans etc mixed with oil, with which the body is rubbed for removing its impurities.

A man, however prosperous in life, must not insult a Kshatriya, a profoundly erudite Brâhmaṇa, or a serpent,:(thinking him to be too weak to retaliate); likewise one must not humiliate the weak and the defenceless. (135)

These three, insulted by a man, verily consume him (like fire); hence, the intelligent one must not insult them under any circumstances whatsoever.* (136)

Let him not disparage himself on account of his past failures or misfortunes; let him pursue fortune even to the last day of his life and never think her beyond his reach. (137)

He must speak truth, and truths that are pleasant; he must not speak an unpleasant truth nor a pleasant lie. This is the eternal virtue.† (138)

Even in cases of ungentle dealings he must say "that's good,"‡ "that's good," or he shall say "good" to all; he must not engage in a futile quarrel, nor create a barren enmity, with any person. (139)

In the early dawn or evening, or at midday, he must not go anywhere, nor with a man of unknown character and parentage, nor with a low born miscreant.§ (140)

Persons possessing limbs in less or excess, old men,

* The text has *Buddhimana* KULLUKA explains it by *Kalyána Buddhi* which may mean one graciously disposed, or seeking his own good.

† The text has *Na manyet Durlabham.* He must not think that it is too late or impossible for him to acquire a fortune.

‡ The text has "*Bhadram*" *Bhadram iti Bruyat Bhadram ityeva.* KULLUKA says that the first "Bhadram (good) means instances of ungentle behaviour, or unfair treatment

§ The text has *Vriskala.* KULLUKA explains it by "S'udra," we however find no reason to interpret it in any other sense than that in which it has been used in Stanza 108 of this chapter.

illiterate persons, those devoid of personal beauty and worldly possessions, and men of low birth, he must not taunt for their (unfortunate) deformities or privations (141)

Without washing his mouth, after eating, he must not touch a Bráhmana, a cow or fire with his hand. Impure, when in health, he must not gaze upon the luminaries (*i. e.* stars etc.,) in the heaven. (142)

Happening to touch a cow, etc., while he is in an impure conditon, he must sip water and touch the external orifices of his organs (such as the nose, ears, etc.) and his umbilicus with water. (143)

Not otherwise ill or indisposed, he must not wantonly finger the external ducts of his organs (such as the nostrils, etc.,) nor handle the private hairs of his body. All these should be avoided. (144)

Always he must be of aupicious conduct;* pure in body and spirit and self-controlled, let him unremittingly mutter the sacred *Mantras* and make the fire-offerings. (145)

Calamities† befall not those who constantly be of auspicious conduct, nourish a clean spirit in a clean body, constantly mutter the sacred *Mantras*, and do the fire-offerings. (146)

Let him diligently study the *Vedas*,‡ whenever he finds an opportunity; that is the highest duty of a

* The text has *Mangalàchâra* KULLUKA explains it by *Gorachanádi dhàranam*,. According to him, putting of totems of pasted *Gorochana* (gall stones of oxes) on the forehead, etc. is also included within *Mangalâchâra*.

† *Vinipâta*, KULLUKA explains it by physical disturbances (such as earthquakes, disease, or breavements.

‡ The text has *Vedam* KULLUKA explains it by "the *Vyàhritis Pranava*,. etc.

Brâhmaṇa, all other being his minor or accessory duties. (147)

Constant study of the *Vedas*, cleanliness of the body and mind, contemplation, austerities (*Tapas*) and compassion towards all creatures are what bring to a man the remembrances of his past existences (*Játi-smara*. (148)

Remembrances of his past births make him apathetic to the world and its concerns, and lead him to attain the Supreme *Brahma*; and by existing in this supreme self (*Brahmá*)* he enjoys infinite and eternal happiness (beatitudes). (149)

On the day of the full or new moon, he must make the fire-offerings known as the *Sáavitri* or *S'ánti-Homas*, and worship the manes with *Sráddha*-offerings on the days of *Ashtakás* and *Anvashtakas*. (150)

The stool and urine should be voided at a distance from the fire chamber; at a distance from the fire-chamber should be cast the washings of feet, leavings of food, and the semen. (151)

Voiding stool, performance of toilet, bathing, cleaning the teeth, applying colyrrium along the eye-lids and worshipping the deities must be performed before sun-rise at the close of the night. (152)

On the day of the *Parva* (such as the day of the

---

* *Brahmàbhyàsena* is the term that occurs in the text. KULLUKA explains *Brahma* by "*Veda*". This is however another instance of the attempt to further *Veda* at any costs and even in cases where the terms admit of another kind of interpretation. Even, men like S'ankara, Ràmànuja, Savara Svami, and Kumarila an not free from the fault of advocating their respective cults even at the cost of distorting the true meaning of the text. we, however, find no reason to alter our dicision as regards the true meaning of the stanza.

full or new moon), he must go to pay respect to a divine image, to a protecting king, and to his parents and superiors. (153)

He must welcome the elders (on their arrival to his house), give them cushions to sit upon with his own hands, sit before them with the palms of his hands meekly united together, and follow them when they shall go out. (154)

Unremittingly he must observe the rules of good conduct, commended in the *Vedas* and *Smritis* as proper to the social order he belongs to, as the fountain source of all virtues. (155)

Through (observing) good conduct one acquires a long life, through conduct one acquires a desirable progeny; through good conduct one acquires a decayless wealth, and good conduct kills all the inauspicious (bodily) traits of a person.* (156)

A man of misconduct is condemned in the world, suffers perpetual misery, is afflicted with disease, and dies a premature death. (157)

Even devoid of all auspicious traits, a man of good conduct, believing (in God) and envying no one, is enabled to live for a hundred years. (158)

Works, which make one dependent on others, he must studiously avoid; works, which are entirely under his own control, he must diligently pursue. (159)

Liberty (in all respects) is happiness and dependence, (in all matter) is misery. These know to be the general definions of happiness and misery. (160)

A work, by doing which the inner man is satisfied, do by all means, avoid the contrary. (161)

N.B.—For Sakákolam (crows and owls) read Sakákolam (hell of ravens.)—p. 146.

An *Achâryaya*, an expounder of the *Vedas*, one's own parents or superiors, Brâhmaṇas, cows, and *Tapasvins* (asceties) one must not any wise hurt or injure.*(162)

Let him avoid atheism, reviling the gods and the *Vedas*, arrogance, vanity, anger, and harshness. (163)

Let him not raise a club to any body, nor strike any body with a club, excepting his son and disciple for the purposes of discipline. (164).

With a desire to kill, if a twice born one raises a club to a Brâhmaṇa, he shall live for a century in the hell of extreme darkness (*Andha Támisram)*. (165)

For wilfully striking a Brâhmaṇa, out of anger, even with a weed, the striker shall be reborn for twenty one existences in vile wombs. (166)

He, who draws blood out the body of a non-fighting Brâhmaṇa, suffers extreme misery for that piece of his folly in the next world. (167)

For as many number of years the assaulter is eaten by dogs and jackals in the hell as the number of particles of dust on the ground which are soaked by the (spilt) blood of the Brâhmaṇa. (168)

Hence the erudite one shall not raise his stick to a Brâhmaṇa, nor strike him (even with a weed, nor draw blood from his person (by assulting). (169)

An impious man, he whose wealth is ill-gotten, he who is constantly envious of others, any of these men can not enjoy happiness in this world. (170)

Seeing the reverses of the dishonest and the ungodly, let him not, in moments of scarcity or monetary wants, turn his thoughts to dishonest gain. (171)

Like seeds sown in the earth, iniquities do not take fruit, the same day; but fully evolved out in course of time, they cut the root (*i. e.* completely destroy) their perpetrators. (172)

The iniquities of a sinner will bear fruit in his sons or grand-sons even if they fail to be fruitful in his own self. They can never be fruitless. (173)

By iniquity (dishonesty) a man may thrive, may see many a good in life, may conquer his enemies, but ultimately iniquity is sure to completely overwhelm and destroy him. (174)

Let him, with his tongue, arm, and belly properly controlled, constantly devote himself to truth, piety good conduct and purity, and govern his disciples according to the rules of the *S'âstra.* (175)

Let him avoid money, and desires which are bereft of virtue, let him not practise a virtue by practising which he incurs the enmity of others, or which brings him trouble in the future. (176)

He must avoid all fickleness of hands, feet, eyes, and speech, do what is straight and honest, and never think of doing any hostility to any body. (177)

In virtues of conflicting authority, let him take to the path adopted by his fathers and grand-fathers; by adopting that path, he will not incur enmity of any man. (178)

He must not quarrel with his priests, *Rittvigs* (*i.e.*, celebrants of sacrifices on his behalf), preceptors and maternal uncles, *Atithi* guests, dependants, servants, infants, old men, sick folks, physicians, cognates, marriage-relations and relations. (179)

Nor with his parents, sisters, daughters-in-law, sons' wives, and brothers, and slaves. (180)

By avoiding quarrels with these, a house-holder may

be exonerated of all sin; by conquering these, a householder can conquer all these worlds. (181)

A (propitiated) preceptor leades him to (*lit.* is the master of) the region of *Brahma*, a satisfied father leads him to the region of *Prajápati*; a well-pleased *Atithi* guest leads him to the region of Indra, and a satisfied *Rittvik* leads him to the region of gods. (182)

His well-pleased daughters (and daughters-in-law) lead him to the region of the *Apsarasas*, his friends lead him to the region of the *Vis'vedevas*, his brothers-in-law lead him to the region of *Varuna* and the influences of his mother and maternal uncles are upon the earth. (183)

Satisfied old men, infants, weaklings, and sick folks lead him to the region of the firmament, he shall respect his eldest brother as his own father, and consider his wife and children as parts and parcels of his own self. (184)

He shall look upon his slaves as his own shadow and his daughter as the respectacle of highest affection; worried by them, he must patiently bear with such a worry. (185)

Even capable of accepting a gift, he must give up all attachment to gift-taking; gift-taking speedily extinguishes the energy of the supreme self which is in a Bráhmaṇa. (186)

Ignorant of the regulations of the *Sástra* as regards the taking of gift articles, a (Bráhmaṇa), over whelmed with hunger, must not take a gift. (187)

Gifts of gold, horses, lands, cows, food grains, clothes and sesame seeds, made to an ignorant Bráhmaṇa, are consumed, like a wood cast in the fire. (188)

The life-duration of an ignorant Brâhmaṇa suffers, if he accepts a gift of gold or food grains; by accepting the gift of a land or a cow he suffers in health; for accepting the gift of a horse he is deprived of his sight, for accepting the gift of a cloth his skin suffers, for accepting the gift of clarified butter his energy, and for accepting sesame, his progeny are consumed. (189)

A Brâhmaṇa, who is devoid of all ascetic virtues, is unread in the *Vedas* and very fond of gift-taking, if he takes a gift, is drowned with its donor, like a stone raft with its rider. (190)

Hence, let an erudite (Brâhmaṇa) be afraid of accepting a gift from all and sundry; even by taking a small gift, a Brâhmaṇa is drowned like a cow in the mire. (191)

A virtuous man must not make even an insignificant gift to a Brâhmaṇa, who is cat-natured (selfish), or carries a cloak of religion (*Vakavrata*,) or is not read in the *Vedas*. (192)

By giving a well-gotten wealth to any of these three kinds of Brâhmaṇas, both the donor and the receiver of the gift come to grief in the next world. (193)

Like a man, attempting to cross (a river) with the aid of a stone raft, both the ignorant donor and acceptor of a gift are drowned. (194)

He who, though extremely covetous of wealth, carries a cloak of religion, is deceitful (lit, dissimulating), arrogant, and envious, and can not bear the praise of others, and hence tries to snub down all men, is called cat-natured (*Vidâla-vrataka*). *i. e.*, He is like unto a cat, who assumes meekness only to decoy his prey out of his safe-hold and then pounces upon it with all the native fury of his soul.) (195)

With eyes cast down, to conceal his ferocious purpose, he, who to gain his own ends, roams about in deceit and falsehood, like a crane, is called *Vaka-vrati* (crane-natured.) (196)

Those Brâhmaṇas, who are cat-natured or crane-natured, fall into the hell of extreme darkness through the effects of their (treacherous deeds). (197)

After committing a crime, let him not practise the expiatory penance in the pretext of practising a virtue, for the purpose of duping females and S'udras. (198)

A vow or a penance practised in the way of a pretext goes to the monsters; those Bráhmaṇas, (who are cat-natured or crane-natured), are condemned by the *Brahma-Vâdins*. (199)

A person, who tries to earn a livelihood by falsely wearing the badges or marks of an order he does not belong to, robs all the sin of that order, and is reborn in the womb of beasts. (200)

Let him not bathe in another's tank (not endowed for the public use); by so bathing, he is partly associated with the sin of its owner. (201)

He must not use without its owner's permission a vehicle, a bed, a cushion, a well, or a tank, belonging to another; by so doing, he becomes associated with a quarter part of its owner's sin. (202)

Let him always bathe in rivers, in natural reservoirs of water, such as tanks, ponds, Gartas (lakes less than eight miles in length) and fountains. (203)

Let him constantly practise self-control and not vows only; he, who practises vows only, but no self-control, meets his fall. (204)

Let not a Bráhmaṇa eat anything in a religious sacrifice wherin fire offerings have been performed by a Bráhmaṇa, ignorant of the *Vedas,* or who serves as a village priest, or by a woman or eunuch. (205)

A religious sacrifice in which such persons perform the fire-offerings tends to destroy the prosperity of the Bráhmaṇas, and is not liked by the gods; hence, it should be avoided. (206)

Let him not eat the food offered by an insane, angry, or diseased person, nor that containing hair and flies, nor that which has been wilfully touched by one with his feet. (207)

Nor the food looked at by a fœticide, nor that touched by a woman in her menses or biked at by a bird, nor that touched by a dog. (208)

Nor that smelled by a cow, nor that which has been offered to the hungry and the indigent by proclamation, nor that of a monastery, nor that offered by a courtesan, nor that condemned by the wise. (209)

Nor that of a gold-stealer, nor that of one who lives by singing, nor that of a *Takshanu,* nor that of an usurer, nor of one initiated in a sacrifice (without performing the *Agni Somiya yajna*), nor that of a miser, nor of a chained prisoner. (210)

Nor that of an accursed person, nor that of a eunuch, nor that of a corrupt woman, nor that of an arrogant person, nor the food, containing sweet, that has acquired an acid taste, nor that which is stale or has been prepared over night, nor that which is the leaving of a S'udra's food. (211)

Nor that of a physician, nor that of a hunter, nor that of a cruel person, nor that of one who eats leaving, nor that of one engaged in dreadful acts, nor that of a newly parturient woman, nor of those Bráhmaṇas who continue eating, after a diner in their row has finished eating and washed his mouth (*Parjachánta*). (212)

Nor what has been slightingly offered, nor the flesh which has not been formally offered to the deities, nor the food of an unprotected woman, nor of an enemy, nor that of a city, nor that of the degraded, nor that which has been sneezed over. (213)

Nor that of a scandal-monger, nor that of one who bears false witness, nor that of one who sells the merits of religious sacrifices for money, nor that of a professional actor, nor that of a tailor, nor that of an ungrateful person. (214)

Nor that of a black smith, nor that of a *Nishâda*, nor that of a stage-manager, nor that of a gold smith, nor that of one who manufactures bamboo articles, nor that of one who sells weapons. (215)

Nor that of a keeper of dogs, nor that of a wine-seller, nor that of a dyer of clothes, nor that of a washerman, nor that of a cruel person, nor that of one whose wife's paramour lives disguisedly in his house. (216)

Nor that of one who connives at the misconduct of his wife, nor that of an extremely oxorious person, nor that of one who is affected by a death uncleanness, nor that which fails to give satisfaction. (217)

Food, given by a king, robs its (partaker) of his spirit and energy, that given by a S'udra robs the *Bráhma* energy (of its partaker); food given by a gold smith impairs the vitality, and that offered by a cobbler (leather-seller), destroys the good name (of their partakers). (218)

The food of an artisan kills the progeny, that of a dyer kills strength ; the food of a hotel, or of a courtesan leads to the fall of its partaker from the heaven (he has acquired by his acts). (219)

The food, given by a physician, is like unto pus ; the food given by a corrupt woman is like unto semen, the food given by a usurer is like unto excreta, and the food given by a weapon-seller is like unto mucous. (220)

The food, offered by those whose food is unfit to be taken as mentioned above, should be deemed as respectively like unto their skin, hair and skeletal bones. This is what the learned have said. (221)

Having unwillingly partaken of the food of any of these persons, one must fast for three nights. Having knowingly eaten (food of any of these), he must practise a *Chándràyanam* penance. The same is the penance for eating excreta. (222)

An erudite Bráhmána must not eat the cooked food of a S'udra, devoid of *Sràddhas*; but he may take his uncooked food, enough to last him for a single night. (223)

One is a Veda-knowing miser ; and another, a usurer, though charitable ; deciding about these two persons, the gods came to the conclusion that the food of these two is equally (defiling). (224)

But Brahmá came unto the gods and said, "do not consider the food of these two, virtually possessed of contrary virtues, as of like nature ; the food of the charitable usurer is purified by kindness, but the food, offered by a miserly Veda-knowing Bráhmana, is offered with reluctance, and, hence it is defiled. (225)

Let him with proper feelings unremittingly do

the *Ishta* and *Purta* works.* These works, done with the honest money, bear decayless fruits.† (226)

On obtaining a fit recipient of gift, let him do the *Ishta* and *Purta* works with the greatest self-complacence and to the best of his means. (227)

Let him practise small gift-makings without any feeling of anger or vexation; by them he shall some day obtain a gift-taker who will be able to succour him in every way. (228)

A giver of water enjoys (lit acquires) satisfaction, a food-giver enjoys decayless felicity; a giver of sesame seeds obtains a desirable progeny, and a giver of lamps (lights) obtains a commendable sight.‡ (229)

A gifter of land acquires a landed property, a gold gifter obtains gold; A gifter of houses obtains splended buildings, a giver of silver is blessed with personal beauty. (230)

A giver of clothes attain to the region of the moon-god, a giver of horses ascends to the region of *As'vis*; a giver of bullocks enjoys prosperity, a cow-giver goes to the region of the sun. (231)

A giver of a bed or cushion obtains (a good and handsome) wife; a giver of refuge acquires an unbounded wealth; a giver of paddy enjoys eternal felicity, and a giver of the *Vedas* attains the supreme *Brahma*. (232)

Of all gifts, whether they be of water, cowl, cloth, sesame, gold or clarified butter, a gift of the *Vedas* stands preminently the most meritorious. (233)

---

* Religious sacrifices.

† Endowment of wells, tanks of water, gardens, etc., for the public woal are called *Purta Káryayas*.

‡ The text has *Dipadas'chakshuruttamam*, which may also mean that a gifter of lights is blessed with a supersensous vision in his next existence.

A gift, which one makes out of a certain motive* in this life, shall be returned to him in his next life, honoured with the fulfilment of that motive. (234)

He, who, being duly honoured, makes the gift, as well as he, who, being duly honoured, accepts the gift, both of them go to heaven; if otherwise, they go to hell. (235)

He must not wonder at, nor be proud of the powers (he has acquired by dint of *Yoga* and austerities, nor speak untruth on celebrating a religious sacrifice; even highly oppressed by him, let him not speak ill of a Bráhmaṇa, nor brag of the gifts he has made. (236)

One's sacrifice is decayed by falsehood; (one's merit of) *Yoga* and penitential austerities, by (his) wonder (at the success, achieved). Duration of life is shortend by calumniating a Brâhmaṇa; and one's merit of gift-making, by (his) vaunting of it. (237)

Little by little let him store up virtues, as white ants build up an ant-hill, for his benefit in the next world, without creating hardship on any creature. (238)

In the next world, neither his wife (and children, nor his parents and relations will be of any avail; it is virtue alone that stands by him (in the next world). (229)

Alone a creature comes into being, alone does he meet his death; alone he enjoys the merits of his good deeds, and the consequence of his misdeeds does he suffer alone. (240)

Leaving behind him his dead body, like a log of wood, or a clod of earth, on the ground, his friends and

---

* The text has *Yena Yena tu bhávena (i e.,* out of that, that motive). KULLUKA explains it by the motive out of which a gift is made in this life, either for the enjoyment of celestial bliss, or self-emancipation, etc.

relations go away turning their backs on it; it is virtue alone that follows him (in the darkness of death). (241)

Hence, inorder to have virtue as his ally, let him little by little store up virtue; with the help of virtue a man sails across the shoreless darkness. (242)

The effulgent, ethereal body of a man of dominant virtue, who has extinguished his sin by practising penitential austerities, Virtue herself will swiftly carry up to the other world, after death. (243)

For the elevation of his own family, let him create relationships with nobler families, and avoid those that are mean and humble. (244)

By creating relationships with families that are progressively nobler and nobler and by avoiding connections with low ones, a Bráhmaṇa obtains elevation; by doing the contrary, he becomes (degraded as) a S'udra. (245)

A thorough worker (in the line of good deeds), mild, self-controlled, and bereft of envy, he who does not associate with the miscreants, conquers by his gifts and and self-control. (246)

Fuel, water, edible roots, offered without solicitation, as well as honey and refuge (protection), may be accepted from all.* (247)

Gifts, offered without solicitation, and to which no previous reference has been in any way made, may be received even from the miscreants, this is what Brahmá has acknowledged. (248)

His manes do not eat his oblations, nor the fire convey his oblations to the deities, who insult (refuse) to accept) these gifts. (249)

---

* Excepting corrupt women, eunuchs, etc., as laid down by Yàjnavalkya.—*Kulluka.*

Gifts of beds, houses, *Kus'a* grass, scents, water, flowers, gems, milk-curd, fried rice, fish, milk, flesh, and *s'akas*, these, if offered without solicitation, must not be refused. (250)

For supporting his parents, preceptors, guests, servants, wife, and family, as well as for the purposes of worshipping the deities, he can accept gifts from any person whatsoever, but not for anywise benefiting his own self. (251)

On the death of one's parents, or in the event of his living separate from them, even when they are alive, he must always accept gifts from honest persons for his subsistence. (252)

Among S'udras, a Bráhmaṇa may partake of the cooked rice of one who cultivates his fields, or of one who is an ancient friend of his family,* or of one who keeps his cows, or of his slave or barber, as well as of him who has surrendered himself to his protection. (253)

Let him give out to a proper person his true nature, the kind of work he intends doing, and the extent of service he is capable of rendering him. (254)

He, who gives himself out to honest persons as something different from what he really is, is called the worst of miscreants; truly he is a thief, inasmuch as he dissimulates his real self. (255)

All things are inherent in the meanings of (spoken) words, all things are founded on speech, all things emanate from speech (words); he, who speaks falsehood, is said to be a universal thief (stealer of all things.) (256)

---

* The text has *Kulamitram*, *i.e.*, the descendant of a S'udra-family living in amity with that of his own from a long time.

Having duly discharged the debts to the great sages, to the manes and deities, and entrusted all things to his son, let him live unattached (indifferent) to all things of the world. (257)

Seated in a solitary place, let him always ponder over the good of his Self; by contemplating in a solitary place, he will obtain the supreme bliss. (258)

Thus the eternal duties of a Brâhmaṇa house-holder, as well as the duties of the order of *Snataka*, which augment the quality of *Sattva* in men, have been formulated. (259)

A *Veda*-Knowing Brahmana, who maintains himself by means, laid down in the *S'astra*, is absolved of all sin and is glorified in the region of *Brahma*. (260)

CHAPTER V.

THUS having heard the duties of a *Snâtaka** as duly promulgated before, the Rishis asked the fire-origined Bhrigu as follows, (1)

Bráhmanas who are well read in the *Vedas* and thus duly discharge the duties of their order, how can Death assail them, O lord, (before the appointed time)? (2)

He, the true-sould Bhrigu, the son of Manu, said to the great sages, hear for what fault doth Death destroy the Bráhmaṇas? (3)

* *Snâtaka.*—A Bráhmana, who after the completion of the vow of a religious student, has performed the ceremonial ablution.

† The text has *Anala-prabhavam, i e.,* the fire-origined one. Cf. *S'ruti.*—His first seed, which lay effulgent, was transformed into the primival sun (Aditya), and its residue took embodiment in Bhrigu.

Through non-study of the *Vedas*, through non-observance of the rules of conduct, through idleness, and through partaking of unwholesome food, Death destroys the Bráhmaṇas. (4)

The garlic, turnip, onion, and mush-room are the three (vegetables), unfit to be eaten by Bráhmaṇas, (inas much as) they are originated from impurities (unclean things.* (5)

Hard, red (gummy) exudations of trees, exudations (obtained by making) incisions in trees,† the *Shelu* (fruit) and the milk of a newly parturient cow† should be carefully avoided. (6)

Krisaras,‡ *Samyávas*§ and cakes, not offered to the deities, unconsecrated meat, and offerings not offered to the deities, and clarified butter before being used in a fire-offering. (7)

The milk of a newly parturient cow within ten days of her parturition, the milk of a she-camel, or that of a female animal with unbifurcated hoofs,|| the milk of an

---

* Cf. Inasmuch as they are cultivated with manure prepared from excreta, *Vidjátani* according to Yájnavalkya.

Cf. *Atho Khalu Ya Eva Lohito, yo vá Bras'chanánnir-yasati tasya násya Kámamanyasyeti*—Now, the red exudations of a tree, as well as that which exudes from a cut in the tree should not be taken, exudations of trees other than these should be taken.—*Taittireya S'ruti*.

† The milk of a newly parturient cow, before the tenth day of her parturition, is formed into hard lumps when cooked. —*Kulluka*.

‡ *Krisara* is a kind of preparation of rice and sesame (*Tila Tandula-samparkát Krisara So'bhidiyate*.—*Chhándogya-paris'ish-tam*.

§ *Samya'va*—a cooked compound of clarified butter, treacle, milk, and wheat-flour.

|| The text has *Ekas'apha*, such as a mare, etc.

ewe, or of a cow in her heat,* or that of a cow without her calf. (8)

The milk of all wild female beasts except that of a she-buffalo, the milk of a woman, and all naturally sweet articles (*Suktas*) that have acquired an acid taste (in the course of time). (9)

Of *Suktas*, milk curd and articles prepared from curdled milk,† as well as *Suktas* prepared with the addition of auspicious fruits, flowers, edible roots, etc.. may be eaten. (10)

The flesh of all kinds of carnivorous birds, the flesh of a village fowl, the flesh of an unconsecrated‡ animal with unbifurcated hoofs, and the flesh of a *Tittibha* bird must not be eaten (lit, avoided). (11)

(Similarly,) the flesh of a *Kalavinka*, of a diving swan, of a swan, of a *Chakraváka*, of a domestic fowl, of a crane, of a *Rajjuvalá*, of a *Dyatuha*, of a *S'uka* and of a *S'árika*. (12)

(And) *Pratudas*, web-footed birds, *Koyashtis*, *Vishikiras*, diving fish-catchers, butchers meat and dry meat must be avoided. (13)

---

* The text has *Sandini*, which means a cow that seeks a bull. KULLUKA forbids the use of *Sandini*-milk, on the ground that it is nothing but transformed menstrual blood.

† The text has *Dadhisambhaván*, *i e.*, articles prepared from milk curd such as, whey, butter, etc.

‡ The text has *Anirdishtáms'chaikas'aphàn*, *i.e.*, the flesh of animals with unbifurcated hoops, not slaughtered on the occasion of a religious saçrifice. The Horse-sacrifice of the *Rig* or the *Yajur Veda* is capable of bearing another interpretation than what is usually put upon it. A horse-sacrifice, or the use of horse-flesh as an article of fare ought to have been repugnant to the finer sensibilities of the ancient Aryans, and points to the Scythian origin of the practice or ceremony.

Nor a crane, heron, jackdaw, *Khanjaritaka*, nor, fish-eating animals, swine that eat excreta, and all species of fish. (14)

He, who eats the flesh of an animal, is called the eater of that animal; he who eats fish eats the flesh of all animals, hence let him forswear eating fish. (15)

Páthina, Rohita, Rájiba, and Sakula fish, and all large-scaled fish may be eaten, but all those should be first offered to the gods and manes before being eaten. (16)

He must not eat the flesh of animals that move about alone (like a snake), nor of those beasts and birds whose name and nature are not known, nor of those whose flesh is not forbidden, nor of those which are possessed of five nails. (17)

An attempt to ascertain the true meaning of the term *As'va medha* and the nature of the ceremony which, the *Veduic* Rishis used to celebrate under that denomination, may not be out of the sphere of a commentator of the Manu *Samhitá*, as it will help us to some extent in fixing the date of its recension by Bhrigu, or in other words, of the "Institutes of Manu" as we have it at present.

The term *As'va-medha* according to its usual acceptation means a horse-sacrifice, a sacrifice in which a horse is slaughtered as an offering to the sun-god. By a fiction of *Vediac* ceremony the horse is supposed to absorb in his self the plaints and prayers of the celebrants and is sent to the sun-god as an atonement for their sin. Even before his immolation and at the time he is being brought to the sacrificial ground, heralded by a bleating multi-coloured goat, the priests sing a hymn the first part of which ends with "may this vigorous horse bring us exemption from wickedness," [*Rig-Veda* Ashtaka II. S. VI. (CLXII.)]. According (to the *Yajush* XXIV. 58) and the *Kátyáyana S'utra* (98 etc.), a black goat, a victim sacred to Agni, is tied to the front of the horse at the sacrificial post, and is first immolated.

The Poroupine, Shalyaka, lizard, (*Godha*), rhinoceros tortoise, and hare, may be eaten among the five-nailed animals; of animals possessed of only one pair of teeth, the flesh of a camel may be eaten (on the occasion of a religious sacrifice. (18)

According to the *Kâtyâyana S'utra*, twenty-one posts of various kinds of wood, each twenty-one feet long, are to be set up to which the different animals are to be fastened, amounting to three hundred and forty-nine, besides two hundred and sixty wild animals, making altogether six hundred and nine. The text in the Rigveda does not warrant such a multiplication of posts and seems to say that a single post is intended. We wish to conclude this paragarph with the observation that, the horse, the victim in the sacrifice, must be possessed of thirtyfour ribs, according to the text of the *Rigveda*, which run as *Chatustrins'ah Vájino deva-bandhorvamkriras'vasya svadhitih sameti*, may the axe fully penetrate the thirtyfour ribs which lie on both sides of the swift goer, the beloved of the gods. (Rigveda, II Ashtaka. 162 Suktâ 18 Rk.)

Such is the interpretation of the Sutrakâras, and of Yáska, Sâyana, and Mahidhara. Wilson says that, "although some of the expressions are obscure, and perhaps contradictory, yet it is undeniable that the hymn describes the actual sacrifice of a horse."

Another section of Sanskrit scholars, who hold that the Sarga of the Vediac Rishis is Mongoliâ of our modern geography and the *Brahmarshi Des'a* was a country which was situated to the north of modern Siberia along the Artic Sea, which was then habitable, finds in Rik II of this Sukta, the first domestication of the horse which was first found in Tartary (the Sarga of the *Vedas*) and its employment to the service of man. "*Yamenadattam Trita enamayunagindram enam prathamo adhya-tishthat. Gandharvo asya ras'anâmagribhuat surâdas'vam Vasabo nirtishthat.*

These two sets of opinion practically exhaust all in favour of holding the actual sacrifice of a horse; or interprating the term, *A'sva* in the usually acceptation of the term, (horse).

By wilfully eating a mushroom, a domestic pig, a garlic, a domestic cock, an onion, or a turnip, a twice-born one becomes degraded (*i.e.* loses the privileges of his order. (19)

Agni (the name of a Vediac patriarch) gave it (horse) to Váyu, who yoked it to the chariot, and Indra (the king of Sarga) rode first in this chariot. Gandharva (Soma) took the reins of this horse in his hands, and O ye Vasus, you originated him from the sun (Rik. II. Suskta 162. Ashtaka II).

We, on the other hand, beg to differ from the views of these illustrious glossits and commentators, and make bold to say that, the actual immolation of a horse was never contemplated by the inspired singers of these *Riks*. All shades of religious opinion in India and all forms of creed, whether Paurányik, Tántrika, or pure Vedántik, trace their origin and draw their inspirations from the Mantras of the *Vedas* and *Brahmanas*. Even the *Vámáchárin Tàntriks* find the essential tenets of their cult presaged in the musings of Agastya and Lopamudra (A I. Sukta 172). and in the concluding chapter of the Brihad Aranyakam (*Adhoyajna*. Br. 4 Ch. 6 ; and manifestly the doctrines of the *Vedànta* and *Sànkhya* philosophies are found in embryo in the Sukta 164 of the second Ashtaka of the *Rikveda*. These things show that the *Riks* may admit of different or contrary interpretations in many instances, and it may be that contrary interpretations have been made at different times in order to extort sanctions out of them for some new customs or newer forms of worship or sacrifice, which the increased contact of our forefathers with the neighbouring nations and principalities added to the national code of rituals as new accretions.

Thus we find the *Anukramaniká* enjoys that, the reputable *Purusha Suktam*, the muttering of which, according to the later-day *Dharmas'àstras*, forms the atonement for many a deadly sin, to be read out on the occasion of a human sacrifice. We fail to detect why should it have been so enjoned, when it is capable of bearing a truly grand meaning, a meaning which at once illucidates the loftiest aspirations of the *Upanishads*, and more so, when we consider that the whole spirit of the *Vedaic mantras* is

Having unintentionally eaten these six things, (as are mentioned in the preceding stanza), he shall practise a *Krichcha Sántapanam* penance (which lasts for seven days) or a *Yati-chándráyanam.* For eating any thing other than the six preceding ones (such red gummy exudations of trees, etc), he shall fast for a day and night. (20)

---

absolutely antagonistic to such cruel and barbarous rites. It sounds totally absurd when we consider that the *Veda* was a song of the gladness of life, sung by men with whom life was a joy, a blessing of God to be thankful for, and who would never have denied that gladness to the humblest of creatures that trails on earth. With them it was a high preoragative of man to witness the glorious birth of each song-girdled Day on verdant fields and golden hill-tops, and such atrocities need must have been entirely foreign to their simple understanding when we consider that an act of kindness done to a peafowl has been made use of in the *Vedas* as a mechanism of setting the sympathy of the Universal Heart in favour of its doer. *Vediac* civilisation was singularly conservative of life and its offerings were absolutely blood-less.

Now let us see in which connection does these two Richas occur so that, in accordance with the recognised rules of interpretation (*Tantrayukti*) such as inference (Uhá), concord (etc), we will be able to determine the disguised meaning of a term, if it bears any such disguise. The preceding Suktam (CLXI. A. II) is in honour of the *Ribhus*, the solar rays, the personified leaders of the rays who reside in the unapprehensible sun (Aguhyasya A'dityasya)], for the purpose of fertilising the earth. Indeed, the tenth verse of this Suktam contains a reference, according to Sáyana's interpretation, to the immolation of the victim and the quartering of its body, but this too may be explained in a different way; *S'rondmekam Udakam* may as well mean yellow coloured water as blood (Rudhiram), which is Sayana's explanation. The succeeding Suktam is the 165, the same one which is called the parent of *Vedantism* and which will help us much in our attempt at explaining the so called Horse-Sacrifice *Riks.*

Even a cursory acquaintance with the Vediac literature will disclose the fact that, the explanations of Richas had undergone changes in the hands of different commentators, most probably to suit the spirit of their contemporary times, and to squeeze sanctions out of them for some religious rites or ceremonies that might have been newly added to the code of rituals of the prevailing Brahmanism. Yaska's *Nirukata* deals only with that aspect of their meanings which has its exponents in the physical phenomena of the universe. The causation of rain, the births and deaths of Days, the March of seasons, and such like physical incidents of Nature are, according to him, form the inner meanings of all obscure verses of the *Rigveda*. In his work we completely lose sight of that grand metaphysical spirit of the ancient masters in interpreting the *Vediac Mantras*, which is so markedly prominent in the Upanishads like Brihad A'ranyaka and Chhándogya, etc. Sayana, on the other hand, mainly contents himself with giving the lexicon meanings of the Richas, quoting from the *Niruktam* instances where it differs from his explanations. A Rik of the first Ashtaka of the Rigveda may serve as an illustration of *Sayana's* commentary where *Vrika*, which *Yàska* has explained as *Brinhitasras' mis'chndramá, màsardhamásasamvatsaradikarttà*, (the thick-rayed moon, the creator of months, half months, seasons and full years, etc, he (Sáyana) explains by *Aranyas'va*. (forest dog *i.e.*, wolf). However, the genius of Brahmanic philosophy can not lie asleep for good even in *Sàyana*, the scholarly premier of prince Vakku; and hence, we find him tagging at times philosophical interpretations to those by Yashka and his self, as in the Rik, *striyah sateestán Ume pumsa àhuh*, etc., (Rik. 16, Sukta164, Ashtaka II. Rig). Lastly, let us consider the interpretations put upon the *Vediac mantras* by the immortal S'ankara in his commentaries on the Upanishads, several quotations from which have been given in the preceding pages, and we will find that, they were made at a time when the doctrine of *Vedantism* reigned supreme in India. And all these fully substantiate our theory that, the *Vediac mantras* have been variously interpreted in diverse times to meet the exigencies of the then prevailing forms of faith, and that all of them are capable of bearing metaphysical meanings. In fact, it would be highly interesting to trace the gradual changes in the faith and religious ceremonies of India, if we can hit upon the

23

exact dates of the Ramayanam, Mahabharatam, and Yáshka. We shall presently show that, there might have been no actual immolation of a horse in the *Vediac As'vamedha*, and that the descriptions of the sacrifice, as contained in the Ramayanam and Mahabharatam, strongly intimate the probability that, horse-killing sacrifices were imported from our ancient Scythean neighbours. Most probably when the Scythean or Hungarian settlers in the country came to be assimilated in the Brahmanic faith, the contemporary Brahmanism, by way of a compromise, or concession to the national ceremonies of its new proselytes, had to invent some sort of theological fiction by which they could be shown to have directly carried their sanctions from the *Vediac* text, but which, like all such fictions and stratagems, only serve to disclose the truth by its attempted concealment.

Let us now proceed to examine more closely how far we are justified in holding this view. We all know that, the terms "*Vrisha*" (bull) and "*As'va*" (horse) denote, according to the *Bràhmanas*, the soul of the universe (*vis'vasya atmà*) and also its prototype entombed in the human body. The *Taittiriyam* is sufficiently explicit on the subject when it says, *A'ditya vrishas'va iti* (the sun is the bull or the horse). Thus we see that, the bull, the horse, the self, and the sun are all synonymous in the mystic phraseology of the *Vediac* seers. Moreover, we learn from the Sukta 164, Rik. II of the second Ashtaka of the *Rigveda* that the horses of the Sun (*i.e.*, the *solar rays*), though seven in number, are virtually one; the one horse represents the collective rays of the sun, or the entire manifesting factor (*Saptam yumjanti rathamekachakrameko As'va Vahati saptanàmà*).

Epuipped with these clear cut definitions of "As'va," we must now proceed to discuss the nature of the horse, for whose immolation in the sacrifice our opponents find such an unequivocal and unmistakable sanction in these *Riks* (162—164, *Suktas, II Ashtaka* of the *Rigveda*). The third *Rik* of the 163rd Sukta addresses the alleged horse as, "O thou goer (*Arvan*), thou art *Yama* (fire), thou art *A'ditya* (sun), thou art *Trita* by a mystic act (*Asi yamo Asyàdityo Arvannasi Trita guhyena Vratena*); Thou art *associated* with Soma (*Asi somena samaya viprikta*), thou hast three binding places in heaven, thus say the wise, (*A'huste trini divi bandhanàni*). Sáyana explains this mystic act by "*durdinena*" *i.e*, on a cloudy day, or by dint of *yoga* (*yogadisadhana rupena*) the sun is transformed into *Trita.*

We ask, how Trita, who, according to Sáyana, is a Rishi or sage, can be transformed into a horse or the sun on a cloudy day, or by dint of Yoga? The whole explanation is absurd, but the meaning becomes intelligible enough, if we explain *Tritah* (Tra and Ita) as *Trigunopetah Manushyah*, man or the human soul, enveloped by the three qualities of *Sattva, Rajas* and *Tamas* as its *upadhi* or distinctive attributes, in contradistinction to the *A'ditya* or the universal self (*Vis'vàtmà*). The whole meaning then runs as something like this, O Goer (*i.e.*, human soul,) thou art one in substance with the fire, thou art identical with the universal self (Aditya) in nature, who is transformed in to thy own self through the mysteries of Yoga and psychic transformation. This explanation is further borne out by "*Trini Bandhanàni*" etc., (lit) thy three binding places, three in heaven, three upon earth, and three in the firmament. How can a mere horse have three binding places in heaven, and three in the firmament? Sayana, not to be perplexed by any thing, explains "*Bandhanani*" by "*Utpatti karanani*" (causes of origin), probably in the light of the tenth Rik of the next Sukta (164. c 22. M. I. Ashtaka II.) where *Tisro Matrristrinpitrrinbibhradeka urdhastathau* (Not befriended by any, he, the one (absolute) sun, who, having three mothers and three fathers, is borne up on the high) is explained by Sáyana as three mothers, the three regions of the earth, firmament and heaven (*kshityádi Loka trayam*); and three fathers, by "air, fire and sun, the supporters of the three regions. The sun stands on high, according to Sáyana, as the causal agent of the past, present and future (*Bhutabhavishyadádyátmaná*). We fail to understand why the same acceptation may not be extended to the *trini bandhanàni*. What would be the harm, if we explain it by *Sattva Raja tamánsi, i.e.* (qualities of Sattva Rajas and Tamas, which govern the entombing body of the soul on earth, in heaven and in the astral plain (antariksha)? We know the human body is called *Tristhunam, Tridandi* (three posted exponent of the three preceding principles.) And continuing the metaphor of a horse, (self or goer—*Arvan*), will it not be absolutely legitimate to call the three fundamental principles of its body as its binding stakes or places? It is superfluous to add that, a smattering of Brahmanic philosophy will convince a man that the Sattva, Rajah and Tamas are identical with the future, present and past, or ether (air), fire and water in the parlance of Brahmanic philosophy.

The term *Apsu* (*lit.* in the waters) in the Rik, which Sáyana explains by earth, may be interpreted to mean all created beings (*sarvam Bhuta grâmam*) as he himself has done in the Rik XII. Ch. VII. 3 An. S. (24). As (*Apas'chana praminanti Vratam Vam*) where "Apas" is used by mytonemy "for all beings." And if this view be correct, the three binding places (*Trini Bandhanâni*) can not have any other meaning than the qualities of *Sattva, Rajas* and *Tamas.*

The Vishnupuranam [Ch. I. V.] explicitly enunciates that, the Purusha includes earth, firmament, heaven, etc., and on the basis of its authority we can safely say that, "As'va" of the As'vamedha is the *Purusha* of our subsequent philosophical systems.

We will conclude this portion of our dissertation by enquiring a little more into the nature and origin of the As'va, as set forth in the Richas themselves. In the Rik I, Sukta 162, we find that the coursing *sapta* (which may mean a mover expander or the horse) is originated from the energies of all the gods (*Vájino Deva játasya sapte*). The *As'vo* is identical with various divinites. The various parts of the As'va consists of the energies of various divinities, the Dawn goddess forming its head (*Ushá vá as'vasya medhvasya S'ira iti*—Sruti). A little knowledge of the Upanishads will be enough to disclose that, various divinites, such as Agni, Aditya, Prajápati etc. form (*i. e.*, preside over) the different senses and organs of an individualised self (*Sapta*), which, like its supreme prototype, is ever expanding. Even for once we could have entertained the idea of explaining "*As'va*" by horse, if the Richas had given it thirty-six or thirty eight ribs instead of thirty four. It is our duty now to see if we can explain it in any other way.

Our present contetion is that, how can a horse have thirty four ribs? We cannot deny the *Vediac* Rishis the knowledge of veterinary anatomy, if we once admit that a horse was used to be immolated in the *As'vamedha* sacrifice; since the different parts and members of the quartered body of a sacrificial victim have been enjoined to be carved and quartered in the peculiar fashion. The Aitireya Brahmana fully bears out the point. How can we then account for this anomaly? Sayana explains away the difficulty by saying that, "other animals such as, the goat, etc., have twenty-six ribs, while the horse has thirty-four;" and this is manifestly an error based on the ignorance of veterinay anatomy.

First taking *As'va* to mean the sun (Surya, the motive force or soul of the universe, *Sarvasva preravità*) the thirty four ribs may be explained as the thirteen months, consisting of the twelve solar months and the intercalary one, the fifteen Tithis, and the six seasons. As regards the existence of the thirteenth month, we can refer to the Rik XV of the Suktam 164. Ch. XXII. M. I. Asht II. of the *Rigveda* (*Sàmkajànàm Saptatha màhureka,* some assert that there are seven seasons, born of the sun etc.,) where Sáyana quotes from the *S'ruti*, "there is a thirteenth month" *(Asti trayodas'o màsa iti).* Now let us see if we can reconcile it to *A' sva* in its acceptance of *self* or human soul. The thirty four *panjaras* or essential components of an individualised self are the seven fundamental organic principles of lymph chyle, blood etc., the three *Dhàtus* of Váyu, Pittam and Kaphah recognised by the *Veda* (Cf. *Tridhàtu S'arma Vahantam*), the ten sense organs, the ten senses, the five material elements, the five *tanmàtras* (elementals), and *Manah, Buddhi* and *Ahankàr* (sense of mineness) making thirty-four, together with the self.

The essential components of the individualised Self have been differently computed by different philosophers of India. The holy Agnivesha asserts that, the five elements, together with consciousness, are called the Purusha (Individualised Self), Consciousness alone, according to others, forms the Purusha. On the other hand, the twenty fonr categories such as, the mind, the ten organs, the objects of the senses, etc., are collectively called the Purusha (*Khàdayaschetanà dhàtu Shashthastu Purusha Smritah; Chetanà dhàturapyekah smritah Purusha samjnakah. Punas'cha dhatubhedena Chaturvins'atikah smritah; Mano das'endriyàn-yarthah Prakriti s'chàshtadhatukee* (Charaka. S'àrira, Ch. I. Vs. 14—15). From this it will appear that, the method of computing the constituents of the *Purusha* (individual Self) which we have adapted is not only legitimate and carries the sanction of the ancient masters, but that it would give a total of thirty four, if the common factors are eliminated from these different lists.

It will thus be seen that, the above exaplanation precisely fits in with the number given in the text, and it has this additional advantage that, it does away with the necessity of hypothecating an ignorance of the veterinary anatomy in the Rishis of these Mantras; an ignorance, if they admit, will at once knock off the bottom of the arguments of our opponents, endeavouring to prove the actual immolation of a horse in the *As'vamedha.*

Now let us see who is the immolator of the so called *As'va.* The ninteenth Rik of the Suktam 162. runs as follows: there is one immolator of the radiant As'va, which is Time, there are two that hold him fast, *i. e.*, the day and night, or the earth and heaven *(Ekastashtu ras'vasyá Vis'astá dvá yamtárá bhavatastatha rituh).* Sâyana explains the second line of this *Rik* by "those of thy limbs which I cut up in due season, I offer them made into balls (of meat) upon the fire *(yá te gàtrànàmrituthà krinomi tàtà pindànàm pra juhomyagnau).* We should rather explain it by "the waste which your limbs and organs etc. have suffered in the course of time, them I offer as oblations in the vital fire." This view has been adopted even by Sáyana in his commentary on the Rik 14 of the Suktam, where he explains the five hotris (offerers) of Soma as the five vital airs which Trita, a *yogin,* for the acquisition of super-human powers, suppressed and concentrated with the Chakra or umbilical plexus. The line of the Rik under reference runs as *Trito na yan panchahotrin abhishtaye avavarttad avaran chakriya avase.* He made the vital airs, desirous of issuing from himself. to turn back into his own presence and to concentrate with umbilical plexus, for the entire completion of the rite) those airs such as *Prana, Apana* and the rest constituting the five ministering priests. These Riks clearly demonstrate the fact that, the Rishis had a precise knowledge of the existence of spiritual plexuses in man, and that they used to perform a rite some what analogous to the *Tantrik Shatchakra Bheda* (penetrating through the six occult plexuses) which most probably then went by the denomination of *As'vamedha.* How easily a confusion of the two different meanings of the term (*As'vamedha*) may arise may be illustrated from the last named Rik alone. If we explain *Chakrena* by lance or spear (*Rishtikakhyena A'yudhena*) instead of explaining it by umbilical plexus, the *Pauranik* conception of the rite (Horse sacrifice) will become irresistably patent; and to the mind, blinded by the legendary practice of horse-killing, the true and nobler meaning of these Richas will be utterly incomprehensible. We find no reason which should hinder us from giving the preceding rendering, especially when we know that "Juhomi" in the sense of maintaining the metabolic fire of the orgalnsm either by the ingestion of food, or through the effect of the constructive or destructive metabolism of the body, occurs both in the Charaka and Sushruta, and that Lat (present tense) is used for the past and all the preterites (*Lang, Ling, Lung, Lut,* etc.) in the Vedas. What can be more natural for an institutor of an *As'vamedha* (sacrifice to the soul) to address his soul as, "the wastes of my body, O self, which have been made in the course of time, have been cast in the fire of life, (which is but thy inseparable exponent) as oblations in a fire-offering and have been re-absorbed and re-assimilated in thy essence? The origin and merging of the body with its environments from, and in, the Self is sung in the Riks, XXX and XXXII, of the suktam 164, portions of which have been enjoined by the *Anukramanika* to be used in the middle portion of the *As'vamedha,* which means, according to our view, a sacrifice instituted for the glorification or honorification of the soul (*As'va* self, *medhyate, pujyata,* is worshipped or glorified, *Asmin* herein).

The self, continuing unchanged and undecaying amidst the incessant changes of its organic embodiment, was fitly made the highest object of veneration in the *As'vamedha.* Those who doubt the identity of Self with Aditya we only refer to the R. 5 of the Sukta 164. the seven threads (*dhàtus,* Somayajnas according to Sayana) which the sages have spread to envelop the sun, *Baskaye* *i.e.* the container of reality, the abode of all (*Vatse Baskaye'dhi Sapta Tantun*)

We admit that there are Riks in the Sukta 162. such as the Riks IX, X, XI, XIII, XV. which apparently indicate the actual immolation of a horse and contain references to the cooking of its flesh, to the distribution of the broth, to the caldron, odoriferous with its boiling contents, to its (horse's) grease smeared upon the brush or the axe.

But there is no ground for holding that, even these Richas, if they are not actual interpolations, are not capable of bearing a meaning which may not shake our faith in the bloodless character of the *As'vamedha.* In the Rik 34. Sukta 164 Ashtaka II. of the Rig Veda the Rishi asks what is the seed of this showering sun (*Prichchham Vrishno As'vasya retah*) and the answer to this query is supplied in the Rik XXV of the same Sukta, in the statement that this *Soma* is the seed of the horse (sun) (*Ayam soma Vrishno As'vasya retah*). The Rik 44 of the same suktam says, the three tresses (of the universal self,) fire, air and the sun in proper seasons looks over the earth, one of them shears the tresses, (the cereals, herbs and forest leaves) at the end of the ear (*Trayah keshina rituthà vi chakshati samvatsare vapata eka eshàm*), and in the same Suktam occurs the Rik which says, the priests cook the soma ox as their primary duty (*ukshànam Pris'nimapachanta virah* prathama-nirasyan.) Now, considering that ox is identical with horse which signifies the sun or the self, and that *soma* plant is the body of the ox or horse, and further that the Soma is called the seed of the horse, and the cereals etc. are his tresses, are we not warranted to suppose that the cooking of the different limbs and bodily principles of the *As'va*, described in the Riks of the Suktam 162 of the Rigveda, is only a poetical mode of describing the fermentation of the Soma beverage, whose soul-exhilarating properties had been many times eulogised in the *Vedas*, and which especially in the glorification sacrifice offered to the self (*As'va-medha*) might naturally seem to them to be the only fit and adorable offering to the Real in man? We have seen in the Rik XI. of the Suktam CLXIII. that the hairs of the horse's manes are the flames of the fire which are tossed in manifold directions and spread in the forests (*Tava S'ringani*, *Puratra-ranyeshu*, *charanti* R. 11. S. 163. V22. A II.

Now even if we, like *Yaska*, confine ourselves only to that kind of interpretation of the Riks which reflects only the occurra nce certain physical phenomena, we will be quite justified in holding that, the quartered members of the As'vas body are nothing more than the cereals, foodgrains and Soma plants, which have been figuratively described as the limbs and organic principles of the A'sva, or the sun, or the fire incarcerated in the soil and the womb of the Earth.

We know that in the mystical language of the Bráhmanas the sun (Aswa-goer) or Indra (the burning one) is the soul of the universe; by a poetical analogy and with a little difference of meaning all these terms Indra (the holder of the senses) Asva (the goer the reality that goes out of the body at death, the Surya (the impellor) were extended to denote its human prototype. Prishni the mother of the sun or gods is the Firmament. Prishni, the Soma plant is the seed of the Ashva (Self, and Soma is the name of the most important of the organic vital principles (protoplasmic albumen) which has been described by the Rishis as the quintessence of life, and which is contained in the heart and the visoera (*Hridâveva Kukshaya Somadhânâ.*) According to their view the sun, the Self and the fire, whether called by the epithet of horse or bull, represent the three different aspects of the same substance, if it be right to call force a substance. Similarly, the Soma (protoplasmic albumen), the Soma (plant, the seed of the Self) are the food of both the gross and subtle life. The yellow juice of the red or yellow species of Soma, and twenty four of them are recognised in the Ayurveda (And now this divine Soma may be divded into twenty four species according to the difference of its habitat, virtue, potency, structure, colour, etc.—*Atha Khalu Bhagavan Somah Sthànàkritigunaviryaya vis'eshaischatur-vims'atidha bhavati.*—Sushruta. Chik. C. 29—C3.) have been termed as the blood, its bruesed stem as flesh, and these may account for interpretations which have been put upon theae terms in the As'vamedha Suktam, and which have led many level headed scholars to come to a positive dicision about the actual immolation of a horse in the *As'vamedha*.

The next point that our opponents may urge against our mode of interpretation is that actual cooking etc of horse flesh has been unequivocally described in these Richas. But their contention falls to the ground if we say that these terms, the derivatives of the root *pacha* (to cook) may also unequivocably mean to grow mature to continue in existence. *Kâlah* (Time) *Pachati* (matures) *Bhudtni* (all beings) is a Sanskrit maxim which known even to a veritable Tyro in Sanskrit. The caldron, the ladle etc. which occur in these Richas may also be more consistently explained as the "caldron of time, the ladle of seasons," and scores of instances can be quoted from the Rigveda where *chamasau*, two ladles, have been called the *yoni* of the sacrifice and of all creatures in the shape of Earth and Heaven.

The Singers of the *As'vamedha* Richas were not a race of primitive nomads. They were far advanced in the arts of civilisation and knowledge. Astronomy, prosody, grammar and a rudimentary form of Logic, together with works on ceremonials, and medicine, are found to have been frequently mentioned in the Rig Veda. In fact, the fundamental principles of each abstruse system of philosophy such as, the Sànkhya and Vedànta were presaged in the Suktam 164, the next one to the *As'vamedha Suktam*. There is an unequivocal reference to the Prakriti (Nature) of the Sánkhyas in *Asthnávantam Yadanasthá Bibhartti* (one with bone *i.e.* the primal self, is borne by the boneless (illusive Prakriti).. For the first time we find the oneness of the universal self wtth the individual soul clearly enunciated in the Rik. (18.) of this Suktam which runs as, "he who knows the protector of this universe as the inferior associated with the superior, and the superior associated with the inferior," *Avah parena Pitaram yo asyánuveda para evávarena*; and in the Rik XX of the same Suktam running as, two birds associated together, and two friends (as they are) take refuge in the same tree ; one of them (individual Self) eats the sweet Pippala fruit, the other (Supreme Self,) eating not, merily looks on (*Ová saparnà Sayujà Sakhàyà Samánam Vriksham parishasva Játi; Tayoranyah pippalam Svádvattyanas'nannanyo abhi Chàkasheeti.*) The famous dictum of the *Upanishad* regarding the sexless character of the Self is but the echo of the Rik, *Striyah Sateestmà Ume pumsa áhu etc.* In short, all forms of philosophic ideas had their origin in the Vedas. Under these circumstances, are we not warranted to assert that, the mysticisims of the *Yoga* likewise originated from the metaphysics of the Vedas ? We have shown above that, a rite analogous to the rite of *Tántrika yoga*, commonly known as *Shat chakra Bheda*, was not unknown to the Rishis of the second Ashtaka of the *Rig Veda*, and we must say that, from the metaphysical meaning which the *As'vamedha* Richas are capable of bearing, the Asvamedha (the sacrifice for the glorification of Self), in its original inception, must have been somewhat identical with this *Shatchakra bhedah*. This spiritual or mystic character of the rite was not lost sight of even at the time when Bhrigu made his famous recension of the Manu Samhita. Later on in this chapter we shall come across a couplet, which lays down that, a non-killer of animal life (abstainer of meat diet) is as much meritorious as a performer of a hundred horse sacrifices. This couplet would have been ridiculously absurd, if *As'vamedha* had entailed in fact the immolation of six hundred and nine animals. For in that case the couplet would mean something like this, *viz.*, to forswear meat is as meritorious as killing six hundred and nine animals, a hundred times multiplied. Or in other words, the merit of forswearing false-hood is equal to that of telling a hundred thousand lies.

The greatest obstacle to the acceptance of our view of interpretation is the description of the horse-sacrifice in the As'vamedha Parva of the Mahabharatam (Anugitá Parva Ch. 88 VS 27—35 and Ch. 89. VS 1—5.). Before proceeding further with this dissertation, we must add that, the arguments, which we shall adduce to account for its description in the Mahabharatam, shall apply *mutatis mutandis* to the description of the *As'vamedha* contained in the *Ramayanam*. One thing, which strikes us most in the sufercial view of the matter, is that both in the *Rig Veda* and *Mahabharata* the *As'vamedha* is associated with deep and abstruse metaphysical disquisitions. In the *Rig Veda* the philosophical Suktam follows the *As'vamedha Richas*, in the *Makabharatam* the philosophy precedes the description of the *As'vamedha*. In the Mahabhatam, the A'svamedha was instructed to be instituted primarily for expiating the sin of a disastrous civil war ; but the actual eating of horse-flesh by the priests or the institutor of the sacrifice, as seems to be sanctioned by the Sayana's commentary, was dispensed with in the Mahabharatam. King Yudhishthira then smelled the smoke, capable of purging one of his sin, of the marrow of the horse that was thus cooked (*Asvamedha Parva.* Ch. 89. V. 4). In the Mahabharata the sacrificial horse was made to wander all over the world for the purpose of collecting tributes from the kings of countries through which it had passed. The launching of a campaign of world-wide conquest as a preliminary to the institution of the A'svamedha was never contemplated in the Richas of the Rigveda. A little knowledge of the ancient history of the world will help us to point out the source from which this Horse-sacrifice was imported into Brahmanism, and to trace the steps taken by her priesthood to celebrate this Horse sacrifice with the Mantras, relative to the soul-worship of the Vedas. We know that the ancestors of Huns or Hungarians were proverbially fond of horse-flesh, both literally and metaphorically.

These worshippers of the fierce, tawny coloured god, Rudra, who, in the shape of the bull, begot Maruts on Pris'ni, disguised as a brindled cow (Europa ?), used to celebrate their victories in war with horse-sacrifices. The descendants of these Huns, after their conquest of, and settlement in northern India, came to be assimilated in Brahmanism. And Brahmanism, in its turn, to please the fancy of the conqueror and to prove his lineage from the Vediac gods, sanctioned the sacrifice as a Vedaic sacrifice, adopting and altering the sense of the Mantras to the exigencies of the ceremony, to conceal its character of a foreign and imported innovation.

Several eminent authorities, both Indian and European, hold certain parts of the Mahabharatam such as, the Bhagavad Gitá etc., to be interpolations; and there is nothing to show to the contrary that, the Anugitáparvádhyáya, containing the description of the horse-sacrifice, is not a subsequent addition to that immortal epic, as it gives but the contemporary view of the meanings of the *As'vamedha Richas* as it was understood and celebrated in that age.

We can assert without the least fear of contradiction that, the *Vedas* have been explained in different times according to the genius and intelligence of each age. Yashka's Nirukta, which reads the description of rain, thunder, lightning, or storm in each *Rik*, must have been written at an age when the Brahmanic genius, devoid of its keen-sighted and subtle philosophy, began to look upon the physical phenomena as the highest manifestations of the Divine. The early *Sutrakáras* and Mimánsa (rules of interpretation of Vedaic mantras), were written at a time when the divine authorship of the Vedas came to be first seriously doubted. Sankara's interpretation of the Mantras, contained in the Upanishads, could not help being metaphysical in the face of such a keen and potent Buddhistic opposition of the age (tenth century). Sayana's commentary (14th century A. D.) reflects the spirit of an age in which the reconquest by Brahmanism was once more complete, and all the different forms of interpretation could be equally authoritative and obligatory, and which, discarding none, tended to augment the literary fame of its erudite author. It is impossible within such a narrow compass to fully advance and elucidate all the arguments that favour the mode of interpretation we have adopted. We have given only the main heads of our argument and the line by which we have

To remove the doubt whether he has eaten any unclean article of fare or not, a twice-born one shall practise a *Krichchha* penance, once within a year. Having knowingly eaten any forbidden articles of fare, he must practise penances, especially enjoined to be performed for expiating the sins of eating those articles. (21)

For the purposes of a religious sacrifice, or for the maintenance of his dependants, a Brâhmaṇa can kill the commendable beasts and birds, as did Agastya of yore. (22)

In religious sacrifices instituted by the *Rishis*, Brâhmanas, and Kshatriyas of yore, oblations of meat-cakes used to be made of the flesh of beasts and birds, (therein immolated.) (23)

Commendable articles of food, even after they have become stale, may be eaten with the addition of any oleaginous substance ; residue of oblations (such as sacrificial porridge, etc.,), left after the performance of a fire-offering, may be eaten (even without such addition of clarified butter, etc.) (24)

Articles made of barley or wheat flour, all modifications of milk, even after they have become stale, or if prepared a long time ago, may be eaten by twice-born ones (25)

Thus the commendable and forbidden articles of diet in respect of twice-born ones have been specifi-

---

arrived at that explanation and leave it to our readers, if they approve of our view, to carry on the investigation for themselves.

The discrepancies found in Sayana, Mahidhara, and Mahabharata, etc., regarding the mode of celebrating the actual ceremony, are enough to show that the *Asvamedha* originally meant something other than a mere horse-sacrifice.

cally described, now hear me describe the mode of using or forswearing meat-diet. (26)

Residue of meat-oblations, cast in the fire in a religious sacrifice, as well as that offered in a *S'râddha* repast, may be eaten; flesh may be eaten at the request of Brâhmaṇas, and in diseases, or under circumstances which imperil life. (27)

Whatever exists in the world, all that *Prajâpati* has ordained to be the food of living beings; all, both mobile and immobile, is the food of creatures. (28)

The immobile are the food of the mobile (creatures), the toothless ones are the food of the toothed creatures; the handless, are that of the hand-possessed ones; and the timid, that of the brave. (29)

An eater, eating an animal and thinking it to be his legitimate food, does not commit any sin, inasmuch as the ordainer has created some animals as eaters and the other as their food. (30)

The eating of flesh on the occasion of a religious sacrifice is the divine ordination, to eat flesh for any other purpose is a monstrous practice. (31)

He, who, having brought, or procured, or received the gift of, the flesh (of an animal), eats it after having first offered it to the manes and deities, is not defiled thereby. (32)

[Otherwise than in times of distress,] a Brâhmaṇa, who eats the flesh (of an animal) in a manner condemned by the Regulation, is eaten, defenceless, by that animal in the next world. (33)

A huntsman, who kills animals for money, does not acquire the same demerit in after life, as one who eats flesh in violation of the ordinance. (34)

But the person, who being appointed to do a religious sacrifice, does not eat the (consecrated) flesh, will be re-born as a beast for twenty-one births in succession. (35)

Let a Brâhmaṇa never eat the flesh of an animal, unconsecrated by *Mantras*; conforming to the eternal ordinance, he must always eat the consecrated flesh. (36)

Desiring to eat fiesh. rather let him eat its effigy made of dough and clarified butter than eat the unconsecrated flesh of an animal, not immolated in a religious sacrifice. (37)

For as many number of times does the wanton killer of animal life meets death in his successive re-births hereafter as there are hairs on the body of the immolated animal. (38)

For the purposes of religious sacrifices the beasts were created by the self-origined one, the sacrifice is for the elevation of the whole universe, hence killing is not killing in a religious sacrifice (*yajna*). (39)

Cereals, beasts, trees, animals of the tortoise species and birds, immolated on the occasion of a religious sacrifice, obtain the eternal status. (40)

A *Madhupaika*, a *Sràddha*, offered to the manes and deities, and a religious sacrifice are the occasions on which a beast should be sacrificed, and on no other occasion. This is the dictum of Manu. (41)

By killing beasts on these occasions, a Brahmana, conversant with the inport of the *Vedas*, accords a more elevated status both to his own self and to the self of the (immolated) beast. (42)

Even in times of distress, a self-controlled Brahmana, whether residing in the forest, or in the house of his own, or of his preceptor, must not do an act of killing not sanctioned in the *Vedas*. (43)

Acts of killing which the *Vedas* have sanctioned in the universe should be regard as acts of non-killing, in as much as all virtue has emanated from the *Vedas*. (44)

He, who in quest of his own pleasure kills the harmless animals, does not obtain any happiness, whether dead or alive. (45)

He, who does not wish to inflict on any animal the pain of death or captivity, is said to be the well-wisher of all, such a man obtains perfect felicity. (46)

Whatever he contemplates, whatever he strives for, whatever he puts his heart upon, he gets that without effort, if he does not kill any animal life. (47)

Flesh cannot be obtained without killiug a beast, animal-killing does not lead to heaven; hence, a man must forswear (eating flesh. (48)

Considering the origin of flesh (which is a kind of transformed menstrual blood) and the pangs of death and incarceration the beast suffers, he must forswear eating all kinds of flesh, (whether approved of or prohibited by the ordinance). (49)

He, who does not eat flesh, like a monster, in violation of the ordinance, becomes a favourite with all and is not afflicted with any disease. (50)

He who sanctions the killing of an animal, he who quarters its slaughtered body, the actual immolator, the seller and buyer of its flesh, the man who cooks the flesh, he who serves that cooked flesh to the eaters, and he who eats it are called the killers. (51)

He, who otherwise than for the purposes of *S'raddhas* offered to the manes and deities, tries to augment the flesh of his body with the flesh of a beast, is the greatest of all sinners. (52)

The merit of him, who forswears the use of meat, is equal to that of one who performs the *As'vamedha* sacrifice, each year, for a century. (53)

By living on fruit, bulbs, or food grains used by the holy sages, a man does not acquire the same religious merit as he does by forswearing the use of meat. (54)

He, whose flesh I eat in this life, shall eat my flesh in the next; this is the essential attribute of flesh, as disclosed by its etymological signification, according to the wise. (55)

No sin is attached to wenching, flesh-eating, or wine-drinking; these are the natural propulsions of Man, but abstinence bears greater fruits. (56)

Now I shall discourse on death-uncleanness, as it affects the members of the four social orders in the order of the enumeration, as well as on the mode of purifying the defiled articles. (57)

The *Bandhus* (*i.e.*, *Sapindas* and *Samânodakas*) of a male child, dead before, or after cutting his teeth, or at the age of tonsure or initiation with the thread, become unclean on his death; likewise his *Bandhus* become unclean on the birth of a male child. (58)

Death-uncleanness continues for ten days among *Sapindas*, or until the bones are collected (*i.e.*, for four days as in the case of a fire-keeping Brâhmaṇa), or for three days, or for an entire day and night. (59)

The *Sapinda*-relationship is extinguished in the seventh generation; *Samânodaka*-relationship lasts for all eternity, being extinguished only when the name and *Gotra* are not known. (60)

The term of death-uncleanness, herein laid down, should be also regarded as holding good in respect of birth-uncleanness among *Sapindas*, desirous of obtaining perfect purity. (61)

Personal impurity during the term of a death-uncleannes is equal among all the *Sapindas;* but in respect of a birth-uncleanness, the mother of the (new born) child remains unclean for ten days, while its father regains his purity on bathing. (62)

Having wantonly cast his seed, a man shall regain his purity by bathing; but having cast his seed in a woman other than his married wife, he shall remain unclean for three days. (63)

A Brahmana, who has touched the dead body of a *Sapinda* relation, shall remain unclean for three times three days and one day; a Brahmana, who has touched the dead body of a *Samânodaka* relation, shall remain unclean for three days. (64)

A disciple, happening to perform the funeral rites unto his deceased preceptor, shall remain unclean for ten days like the *Sapinda* relations of the latter. (65)

In a case of abortion or miscarriage (of pregnancy from within three to six months), purification will be effected after the lapse of days, equal in number to that of the months of pregnancy, (the period of uncleanness being three days in respect of an abortion before three months); a chaste woman in her menses will be pure by bathing after the cessation of her flow. (66)

(*Sapinda* relations of a) boy, dead before his rite of tonsure, shall remain unclean for one day and night; while on the death of one, dead after the rite of tonsure (and before his initiation with the thread), they will remain unclean for three nights (days). (67)

His relations shall bury the corpse of a child, dead before completing the second year of his existence, in a pure ground at the out-skirt of the village, fully decorated, without performing the rite of bone-collecting. (68)

His (its) corpse must not be cremated, nor libations of water must be offered to his (its) spirit ; leaving it in the forest, like a log of wood, they (*i.e.*, relations) shall pass three days in uncleanness. (69)

On the death of a boy, less than three years of age, his relations must not do the rite of (offering libations of) water unto him. The departed spirit of an infant, dead after cutting his teeth, or after his rite of nomenclature, becomes happy with such a water-rite, though its performance is not obligatory on his relations. (70)

The period of uncleanness, incidental to the death of one's fellow-student (of the *Vedas*), is one day only, while on the birth of one's *Samânodaka*, one should be regarded pure on the expiry of three days (from the date of the birth) (71)

On the death of a betrothed, (though) unmarried girl, her friends (such as her affianced husband, father, etc.) become purified after the expiry of three days ; her *Sapinda* relations also become purified after the expiry of the same period. (72)

During the term of a (death-uncleanness) they shall eat their meals without any (artificial) salt, must bathe on each of the three days (of uncleanness), forswear meat-diet, and sleep separately on the ground. (73)

The mode of observing a death-uncleanness (by *Bandhus* and relations), residing in the vicinity, has been described; the following should be known as the mode of observing it by *Bandhus* and relations, residing at a distance. (74)

Happening to hear of the death of a relation in a distant country, within ten days of its occurrence, he shall remain unclean for the unexpired portion of (the period of) ten days. (75)

If he hears it after the expiry of ten days, he shall remain impure for three days only. Happening to learn it after one year of its occurrence, he shall regain his purity by bathing. (76)

Happening to hear of the birth of his son, or of the death of his relation, ten days after its occurrence, a man becomes purified by bathing with his clothes on. (77)

On the death of a *Samânodaka* relation, or of a child dead before teething in a distant country, he shall be purified by bathing with all his clothes on. (78)

A birth or death uncleanness, occurring within the term of a pre-existing one, must abate with the expiry of the *latter* (*i.e.*, the previous uncleanness.) (79)

It is said that, one's uncleanness, incidental to the death of his preceptor, lasts for three days; that on the death of a preceptor's son or wife is for one day and night. (80)

On the death of one's fellow student of the Vedas in the same house, the period of uncleanness is three days: On the death of one's brother, disciple or priest, he shall remain impure for two days and the night between them (Pakshini). (81)

On the death of the king of the country wherein he resides, let him observe a death-uncleanness for the day or night in which the death has occurred. The period of uncleanness in respect of the death of of a Veda-ignorant, or Veda-knowing preceptor, is for the entire day or night in which the death has occurred. (82)

A Brahmana shall regain his purity after ten days; a Kshatriya, after twelve days; a Vais'ya, after fifteen days; and a Sudra, after a month. (83)

Let him not extend the period of uncleanness, nor cease to make the Vediac fire-offerings; if he gets them done by a *Sapinda* proxy, he does not become impure. (84)

Happening to touch a *Chandàla*, a woman in her flow, a degraded person, a (newly) parturient woman, a dead body, or a person who has touched a corpse, one shall regain his purity by bathing. (85)

Having seen an unholy sight after the performance of *A'chamanam* (sipping water) in connection with a daily religious rite, one must diligently mutter the Mantras sacred to the sungod, or any other sacred Mantras, to the best of his ability. (86)

Happening to touch a human skeletal bone, smeared with grease or marrow, a Brahmana shall regain his purity by bathing; having touched such a dry bone, he shall purify himself by touching a cow, or by looking at the sun. (87)

A religious student (*Brahmachàrin*), before fulfilling his vow, must not do obsequious rites unto the spirits of his departed relations; after the completion of his vow he shall observe a death-uncleanness for three days, and thereafter regain his purity by offering libations of water unto them. (88)

Unto the (souls of) persons of hybrid castes (begotten by men of inferior castes on women of superior castes) and unto the souls of ascetics and of men who have committed suicide libations of water must not be offered, after death. (89)

(Similarly), not unto the spirits of atheists, defilers of the *Vedas*, moral wantons, and wives who had been drunkards, or faithless to their husbands, or guilty of committing abortions of pregenancy. (90)

For carrying, or cremating the dead body of his own initiator in *Brahmanism*, or of his preceptor, father, mother, or of any other superior relation, a religious student *(Brahmacharin)* must not be considered as dis-associated (*i. e.* to have broken) with his vow. (91)

The corpse of a deceased S'udra must be carried out of his house through the eastern door of its southern portion; that of a Vais'ya, through the western door, that of a Kshatriya through the northern door, and that of a Brahmana through the eastern exit. (92)

Kings (*i. e.* crowned and duly anointed sovereigns of the Kshatriya caste), *Brahmachârins*, and celebrators of Vediac sacrifices are never affected by death or birth-uncleanness, inasmuch as the kings are the representatives of Indra (on earth), and the two last named ones are those of Brahma. (93)

In respect of a king, seated on the glorious cushion of sovereignty, the (period of) uncleanness is laid down as one day only, the reason being that sovereignty exists for the protection and welfare of the subjects.* (94)

No uncleanness exists in respect of the death of persons, killed in a battle not conducted by the king,

---

* Kings are not governed by ordinary Laws of uncleanness as their persons must be kept always pure inorder to leave them morally competent to make gifts and to do other prophylactic rites for the welfare of their subjects in cases of emergency such as famine, etc—*Kulluka*.

or struck dead by lightning, or killed in execution of the sentences of royal tribunals (lit. king's commands), as well as in respect of the death of those who have surrendered their lives for the protection of kine and Brahmanas, or of those whose deaths by the king's command should not give rise to such uncleanness. (95)

The king is the embodiment of the (energies of the) eight lords of regions such as, the Moon, the fire, the air, the sun, Indra, the lord of wealth (Kuvera), the lord of waters (Varuna) and Yama. (96)

Sovereignty is founded on the energies of the lords of the eight regions; hence, a king is not affected by uncleanness. How can he, whose commands make mortals subject to cleanness and uncleanness, be himself affected by uncleanness? (97)

A person, killed with an uplifted weapon (such as a sword, etc) in battle in discharge of the duties of a Kshatriya, instantaneously acquires the merit of (an *Agnishtoma*) sacrifice, and is at that moment purged of uncleanness. (98)

(After the performance of the S'raddha and at the expiry of the period of uncleanness, a Brahmana is purified by sipping water; a Kshatriya, by touching a weapon and a charger; a Vaisya, by touching a goading stick and the reins (of a horse); and a Sudra, by touching a stick. (99)

O you foremost of Brahmanas, thus I have related to you the rules of cleanness among the *Sapinda* relations of the decased, now hear me describe the rules of cleanness to be observed by the *Asapinda* relations of the deceased. (100)

A Brahmana, having carried and cremated the corpse of an *Asapinda* relation, like a relation, becomes pure after a threedays' uncleanness. Similarly, having carried and cremated the corpse of a deceased and intimate relation (uterine brother or sister of his mother), he shall observe a period of three day's uncleanness. (101)

Having partaken of the food in the house of his decased *Asapinda* relation (during the term of uncleanness), a Brahman shall remain unclean for ten days, his mere residence in the house without partaking of the food (of the family) will make him unclean for one day only. (102)

Having followed the corpse of a deceased person, whether related to him as a cognate or not, a man shall effect his purification by bathing with all his clothes on, by touching fire, and by drinking clarified butter (after that). (103)

In the event of his having had relations of his own, the corpse of a deceased Brahmana must not be carried by S'udras; such a corpse (lit, bodily oblation to death), defiled by the touch of the S'udras, leads not its spirit to heaven. (104)

Knowledge (of Brahma), *yoga* and penitential austerities (*Tapas*), the fire, food, the earth, conviction, water, pastes and unguents, the air, deed, the sun and Time are the purificators of embodied creatures. (105)

Of all purifications (or purities the purification or purity of the mind is the greatest purification or purity. He who is pure in intent (thought or idea) is truly pure, purification with the help of clay and water is no (real) purification. (106)

Through forbearance the erudite are purified, through gifts wrong-doers are made pure. Sinners in secret are purified by muttering or mentally repeating (*yapya*, the sacred Mantras, and the foremost of Veda-knowing Brahmanas are purified through the practice of penitential austerities. (107)

Things to be purified are purified with clay and water; a river is purified by its current; a woman, by her flow; and the best of Bráhmanas, by asceticism. (108)

Water purifies the limbs and bodily members (of a person); truthfulness purifies the mind; the individualised Self is purified by knowledge and penitential austerities; and intellect (Discriminative faculty) is purified by knowledge. (109)

Thus the mode of purification in respect of your persons has been descibed; now hear me discourse on the mode of purifying various articles (and substances). (110)

The purification of all gems, metallic articles, and things made of stone should be effected with the help of water, ashes and earth. This is what has been said by the wise. (111)

A golden vessel, bereft of smear (*i. e.*, not smeared with grease or any unclean paste), is purified by washing it with water; the same rule holds good in respect of articles made of stone, of aquatic substances, and of unstriated articles of silver. (112)

Silver and gold have originated from the fire and water, hence the purification of gold and silver should be effected with fire and water, their parent substances. (113)

Articles, made of copper, iron, bell-metal, brass, zinc, or lead, should be respectively purified with alkali (ashes), acid and water, as suited to each of them (See Brihaspati Samhita). (114)

26

All fluid substances (such as oil, clarified butter, etc., defiled by a crow, or by a fly) should be purified by stirring them (with a ladle). Articles, made of the combination of several other things, should be purified by sprinkling water over them, and wooden articles should be purified by scraping them. (115)

During the celebration of a religious sacrifice, sacrificial vessels are purified by rubbing them with the palm of hand, while ladle and spoons are purified by washing them. (116)

Sacrificial porridge, and sacrificial spoons and ladles, known as *Sruk* and *Sruva*, are purified by washing them with hot water; winnows, carts, pestles and mortars are purified by washing them with hot water. (117)

A pile of paddy or clothes, (defiled by any impure contact), is purified by sprinkling water over it; a small quantity of paddy, or a small number of clothes is purified by washing it with water. (118)

The purification of Bamboo articles, as well as of those made of leather should be effected in the manner of clothes; whereas the purification of *Sàkas*, fruit and bulbs should be made in the manner of paddy. (119)

Wearing stuffs, made of the threads of silk-worm-cocoons (*Kausheya*), and stuffs made of sheep's wool must be purified with alkali; blankets, such as are manufactured in the country of Nepal, must be purified with Nimva leaves; cloths made of flax and Jute-twists must be purified with Vilva fruit, while those made of bark-twists (Kshauma) must be purified with white mustard seeds. (120)

Let the knowing one effect the purification of

articles made of horns, conch-shells, bones, or teeth (tusks) in the manner of *Kshauma* cloths, or with water and cow's urine. (121)

Wood, weeds, straws, etc, are purified by sprinking water over them, a room is purified by washing and plastering it (with cowdung, etc, while earthen vessels are purified by baking them again. (122)

Earthen vessels, defiled by the touch of urine, fæces, sputam, pus or blood, are not purified by re-baking them. (123)

A ground, (defiled by stool, by urine, or by the residence of a *Chandála* thereon and such like causes), is purified by brooming, plastering, washing, and scraping it, or by keeping kine thereon. (124)

An article, nibled by a bird (whose flesh may be eaten), or smelled by a cow, or spitted upon, or trampled under foot, or defiled by the touch of an insect or hair, is purified by throwing earth over it. (125)

An article, smeared with any impure substance, must be rubbed with earth and washed with water until the smear and its foul smell are removed. This is the rule in respect of the purification of all articles. (126)

The gods have ordained three things as pure for Brahmanas, *viz.*, those which have not been found to be any wise polluted, those washed with water, and those declared as pure by speech (word. (127)

That quantity of water, which is enough for a cow to quench her thirst with, if it stays on the ground, not bereft of (its proper) smell and colour, and undefiled by the contact of any impure thing, should be regarded as pure. (128)

Always pure is the hand of a maker of flower-garlands, always pure in the shop is an article spread out for sale, and always pure is the article of gift in the possession of a *Brahmachârin*. This is the conclusion of the Sastras. (129)

Always pure are the faces of women, pnre is the bird in the act of felling down a fruit; pure is the mouth of a calf at the time of milching a cow, and pure is the mouth of a dog in catching a game in a hunt. (130)

Pure is the flesh of an animal killed by a dog; as well pure is the flesh of an animal killed by a *Chandâla*, or by a carnivorous beast. This is what Manu has said. (131)

At all times pure are the external ducts of organs situated above one's umbilicus, always impure are the ducts of organs situated below the navel, as well as the refuse matter which are secreted or discharged through them. (132)

Flies, particles of saliva escaped out of the mouth, a shadow, the cow, the horse, the rays of the sun, dusts carried in the air, earth, fire and air have been held as pure in respect of their touch. (133)

Earth and water, enough for the purpose, should be used purifying the parts after defication or urination, or after the discharge of any of the twelve aforesaid bodily excretions. (134)

The fat, semen, blood, marrow, urine, fæces, the waxy deposits in the ears and nostrils, phlegm (mucous) tears, sweat and the mucous deposit in the corners) of the eyes, these are the twelve refuse products of the bodies of men. (135)

A person, wishing purification, must rub his genitals

once, his anus thrice, his left hand ten times, and his both hands seven times, with earth (clay) and water. (136)

This is the (rule of) purification for house-holders; Brahmacharins, forest-dwelling hermits, and anchorites (Yatis) shall respectively double, treble and quadruple the number (of purificatory measures laid down in the preceding couplet). (137)

After defecation or urination, after having eaten his meal, or wishing to study the *Vedas*, he shall sip water and touch the apertures of his organs. (138)

Desiring the purification of his body, he must thrice sip water and thrice wash his mouth with water. Only once must a S'udra and a woman do each of these things. (139)

Following the path of equity, S'udras must shave their heads once, each month, follow the rules of purification laid down in respect of the Vais'yas, and eat the leavings of Brahmanas' food. (140)

Particles of saliva falling on the limbs, hairs of the beard getting into the mouth. and the particles of food retained in the interstices between the teeth must not be regarded as leavings of food (Uchchhishtam). (141)

Drops of water, falling down on the feet of one at the time of helping another to rinse his mouth with water, should be regarded as pure as the water, lying on the ground. (142)

A person, with an article in his hand, happening to be touched by the leaving of food, shall recover his personal purity by sipping water. without placing the same article on the ground. (143)

After purgation or emesis (induced by a medicine) a person shall bathe and drink clarified butter; having belched after taking his meal, he must sip water in the manner of an *Achamanam*. It is said that, after visiting the beds of their wives, men must purify their persons by bathing. (144)

After having slept, sneezed, eaten, spitted, drunk water, or spoken a lie, or before commencing his *Vediac* study, let him assiduously do an *Achamanam*. (145)

Thus the mode of effecting the personal purification, as well as that of purifying (various) defiled articles) has been elaborately and exhaustively described; now hear me discourse on the duties of women of all the (four) social orders. (146)

A girl, or a maid, or an old woman must not do any thing independently (*i.e.*, at her own will) in the house. (147)

In childhood let her remain under the control of her father, under the control of her husband in youth; and under the control of her son after the demise of her lord in old age. A woman must not assume independence under any circumstances whatever. (148)

She must not wish separation from her father, husband or sons: a woman living separate from these (relatives) becomes condemnable in both families. (149)

Skillful in her household duties, let her maintain a happy and cheerful frame of mind, keeping the furniture neat and tidy, and avoiding extravagance. (150)

During the life-time of him unto whom her father, or her brother, with her father's consent, might have given her in marriage, him she must (devotedly) serve, and make no transgression against him, after his demise. (151)

The religious sacrifice, known as the *Prajápati-yajna* and other bliss-giving rites should be instituted on the occasions of their marriage); for auspiciousness; (*i.e.*, for fruition of the object of marriage); the formal giving away (betrothal, or giving of word according to *Kulluka*) creates the right of husbandship. (152)

The lawfully married husband, the doer of the rite of consecration by *Mantra* (*i.e.*, Marriage); is at liberty to visit his wife during her menstrual period, or at any other time, since it is he who gives pleasure to the wife both in this world and the next. (153)

Like a deity, a chaste wife shall always serve her husband, even if he be found devoid of learning, character and conjugal fidelity. (154)

A wife has no other religious rite or vow of her own than an unflinching devotion to her lord, whereby she will be glorified in heaven. (155)

A virtuous wife, desiring to attain the region of the husband, must not do any thing unpleasant to her lord, in life or death. (156)

After the demise of her lord, let her control her passion by living on auspicious flowers, bulbs, and fruit, and never dream of taking the name of another man. (157)

Forbearing, self-controlled, and emulating the excellent virtues of chaste wives, let her pass her whole life in the constant practice of asceticism, (for swearing meat, honey, wine and sexual intercourse, etc.) (158)

Many thousands of celebrated *Brahmachárins* (such as, *Sanaka*, *Bálakhilyas*, etc.,) and thousands of Bráhmaṇas have gone to heaven (even) without (the (merit of) procreating children. (159)

After the demise of her lord, a virtuous wife, by taking to the life of asceticism, may go to heaven, even though not blest with a child, like the *Brahmachárins.* (160)

Out of a greed for progeny, a wife, who makes transgressions against her lord, acquires infamy in this life and is ousted of the region of conjugal felicity (*lit.* region where virtuous wives are re-united with their husbands after death.) (161)

A son, begotten by a man on another's wife, and *vice versa*) can never be called a son, and nowhere a virtuous woman has been advised to take a second husband (*in the Sastra.*) (162)

A woman, who, discarding a former though inferior husband of her own, marries a better and greater husband, (for the second (time), is condemned in society and is called a fore-enjoyed wife *(Parapurvá.)* (163)

For acts of infidelity to her lord, a wife becomes condemnable in society; she will be reborn as a she-jackal, afflicted with many a foul disease (such as leprosy, etc). (164).

Controlled in her speech, body and mind, a wife, who transgreeses not her lord, attains the region of the husband and is glorified as a chaste woman by the world. (165)

Controlled in her speech, body and mind, and by thus faithfully discharging the duties of matrimony, a a woman (wife) acquires glory in this life and attains the region of the husband, after death. (166)

A true-born one (Brahmana), shall cremate the corpse of such a dutiful wife, dead before him, in the *Agni Hotra* fire, together with the wooden utensils used in that sacrifice. (167)

Having thus cremated his deceased wife, the surviving husband shall again marry a second wife, or pass the remainder of his life in doing fire-offerings. (168)

A house-holder must not abandon the performance of the five daily sacrifices, conformably to the rules stated before, and shall reside married in his house for the second division of his life. (169)

CHAPTER VI.

HAVING thus duly discharged the duties of the house-holder, a *Snátaka* Bráhmana, with all the passions of his heart sobered and tranquilised, shall live, self-controlled, in the forest. (1)

A house-holder, when he will find his hairs turned grey and the skin of his body furrowed with lines and wrinkles and see the son of his own son, shall resort to the forest. (2)

Forswearing the use of all kinds of food-grains, as well as that of vehicles and wearing apparels used by (men) in the village, and placing his wife under the protection of his son, or in her company, let him take refuge in the wood. (3)

Taking the *S'rauta* and the *Grihya*-fires, together with the spoons and ladles, etc., used in the *Agni-hotra* offerings, with him, let him come out of the village, and live, peaceful and self-controlled, in the forest. (4)

With food-grains used by Munis (divine contemplators) and holy roots, fruit and *S'akas*, let him duly perform these five great sacrifices. (5)

Let him be clad in skin, rags, or barks of trees, bathe morning and evening, each day, wear beard, mustache and clotted hair, and grow finger-nails. (6)

Out of his own food let him make offerings and gifts to the best of his might to the poor, and worship (serve) the guests in his hermitage with offerings of water, fruit and edible roots. (7)

Always devoted to the study of the *Vedas*, with all his senses under control, beneficient and compassionate to all, let him ceaselessly make gifts without receiving them from any one, and exert for the good of all creatures. (8)

He must do the *Vaitânika Agnihotra** fire offering according to the Regulation, and perform the sacrifices on the days of the full and new moon in turn. (9)

Successively he shall institute the religious sacrifices, known as *Rikshishte*, *Agrayana* (the harvest offering), and *Chaturmasya*, as well as those which are respectively to be instituted under the auspicies of the two solstices (*Uttaráyana* and *Dakshináyana*). (10)

Let him separately offer oblations of sacrificial porridge, etc., cooked with food grains used by *Munis*, in Spring and Autumn, which he himself must glean for the purpose. (11)

Having first offered oblations of holy forest-grains (such as *Nivara*, etc.,) duly cooked, to the deities, let him eat the residue thereof, and use the salt which he himself has manufactured. (12)

---

* The consecrated fire which a house-holder duly inaugurates on the altar in the house is called Gárhapatyágni. The mixing of this fire in the pit with the southern fire is called *Vitânam* and *Vaitánika Agnihotra* consists in casting libations of clarified butter in this fire.

Flowers, fruits and edible roots, whether grown on land or water, and the fruit of holy forest trees, as well as oils pressed out of wild seeds he shall take. (13)

Let him avoid honey, flesh, mushrooms, *Bhustrinam*, *Shigru* and *Shleshmataka* fruits. (14)

In the month of *As'vina*, he must give away his store of food grains, fit to be eaten by *Munis*, and which he might have collected in the previous year, and cast away the old clothes and fruits, bulbs and *Sákas*, collected in the previous year. (15)

Let him not eat any thing grown on a ploughed field even if it be voluntarily offered; even under the most pressing circumstances, he must not eat any bulb or fruit, grown in a village. (16)

He must eat his food by cooking it over fire, or fruits spontaneously ripened in course of time, or by grinding the (edible things) with stone, or by simply grinding, or chewing them with his teeth. (17)

He must store up food grain enough for a day's, month's, half year's, or year's use. (18)

Collecting it to the best of his ability, let him eat his food in the day or night, or on the night of the second day after a fast of the previous day, or on the night of the fourth day after fasting for the three preceding days. (19)

Or he shall live as laid down in respect of the *Chandráyana* penance in the light or dark fortnight, or at the close of the fortnight (*i.e.*, on the day of the full or new moon) he must drink barley gruel only one time. (20)

Or he shall live on fruit, roots and flowers alone, on ro those which have ripened, or witherd in course of time, or live the life of a forest-dwelling hermit. (21)

He shall either stroll on the ground, or stand on the tips of his toes during the day, or gently ramble in the place of his staying, and bathe at morning, noon and evening. (22)

In summer let him practise the five penances,* lie in the open during the rainy season, and wear wet clothes in the fore part of winter. Thus let him gradually increase his penitential austerities. (23)

Thrice bathing, and offering libations of water unto the gods, Rishis and manes, each day, let him purify his body by means of austere penances such as fasting for a month or fortnight at a time). (24)

Having duly installed the sacrificial fire on his own self, as is practised by the forest-dwelling hermits, he must observe the vow of silence; and houseless and unpossessed of fire, he must live on fruit and edible roots (of the forest.) (25)

Apathetic to the objects of pleasure, and continent, he must lie on the bare ground, knowing no other house than the tree-shade, and despising any other place of refuge. (26)

Of *Tapasvins*, forest dwelling or house holder Bráhmaṇas he shall beg his necessaries of life (daily food). (27)

Or having collected it from the village, he shall eat eight morsels thereof in the wood, placing the same in the holow of his palm, or in a chip of bark, or in a cup of tree-leaf. (28)

---

* The text has *Panchatapah* which consists in placing one's self amidst five fires, *i.e.*, the four fires blazing on his four sides and the sun shining over-head.—*Translator.*

Thus living in the wood, a forest hermit shall discharge these duties (of his order); for the realisation and correct knowledge of his own Self he shall ponder over the *Srutis* which apertain to the science of (*Brahma*). (29)

With a view to augment their penance and knowledge, and for the purification of their persons, Rishis, Brâhmaṇas and (even) householder Brahmanas have made use of (lit, served) these *Upanishads.* (30)

On the advent of an incurable disease, let him, living on air and water, and with his Self rapt in Yoga, go straight to the north east until he quits this mortal life. (31)

By quitting his body in any of these modes of the great sages, a Brâhmaṇa, void of fear and grief, is glorified in the region of *Brahma.* (32)

Thus living in the forest, he shall pass the third period of his life; and forswearing company, he shall dedicate the fourth period of his life to the practice of asceticism. (33)

Thus having successively passed from one order of life over to another, he, the conqueror of his senses, and institutor of many a fire-offering, tired with the labour of begging and offering oblations, shall augment or increase his pleasures in the next world by taking to asceticism. (34)

Having discharged his three debts, let him devote his thought to Self-Emancipation; striving to attain emancipation without dicharging these debts, a man obtains a degraded status. (35)

Having studied the *Vedas* according to the Regulation, procreated sons according to the rules of virtue, and performed the religious sacrifices to the best of his ability, let him turn his thought to Self-Emancipation. (36)

For seeking the emancipation of self, without having studied the *Vedas*, and procreated children and performed the sacrifices, a Bráhmaṇa shall obtain a very degraded status in the next world. (37)

Having studied all the *Vedas* and paid honoraria to his preceptor, and performed the *Pràjapatya* sacrifice and installed the sacrificial fire on his own self, a Brahmana must abandon his home and take to the life of asceticism. (38)

Those Bráhmaṇas, who, declaring protection to all creatures, leave their homes and take to asceticism attain the effulgent regions. (39)

The soul of a Bráhmaṇa who gives no cause of terror to any creature, does not obtain a fright from any creature in return, after escaping from his body. (40)

Having abandoned his home, let him, observing the vow of silence and carrying the holy paraphernalia of asceticism (such as, a staff and an ewer*), betake the life of an ascetic, apathetic to all objects of desire (such as, palatable food, etc.) (41)

Alone and unfriended, let him roam about for working out the emancipation of his self. Having thus alone achieved success, he will neither abandon, nor will be abandoned, in his turn, by, any body.† (42)

---

* The text has *Pavitropachitah*. *Medhatithi* explains it by "*Pavitrairmantra Japairathavá pávanai Krichchhrayadibhih* *i.e.*, associated with the sacred Mantras and attached to the practice of austere penances.—Tr.

† Apathetic to feelings of pleasure and pain. He will not miss the absence of his sons and relations, nor will be missed by them.—Tr.

Houseless, bereft of the sacred fire, apathetic and speechless, let him, maintaining the perfect equanimity, enter the village for begging his food. (43)

The carrying of alms bowl, the housing about the roots of trees, companionlessness, the wearing of rags and non-destinction of friends and foes are the characteristics of an emancipated individual. (44)

Life or death he must not court; like a servant waiting for the receipt of his salary, he must bide the time of Death (45)

With his sight he must purify his each foot-step,* drink water which has been strained through a piece of linen, speak the speech which truth has purifie, and do whatever his conscience would approve of (46)

Dispassionately he must bear with his revilers, nor offer affront to any one; let him not, for the sake of this (frail and pathogenic) body, create enmity with any person whomsoever. (47)

Let him not enrage an already angry or infuriated person, speak sweetly and gently to one who is not angry, and refrain from uttering any word about any temporal subject through any of the seven speaking appliances of the mind* (*i.e.*, speak about nothing but Supreme Brahma). (48)

---

* The text has *Saptadvārāvakirnāncha*, lit promulgated through the seven doors of the mind, which, according to the Vedanta comprise the eye, the nose, the ear, the tongue, the skin, the intellect, and discrimination. *Govindaraja*, on the other hand, explains it by speech originating from its seven objects such as, virtue and wealth, desire and virtue, wealth and desire, and virtue and desire. Certain authorities explain it by "seven regions," as correlated to speech. In short, the meaning is that he must not speak of any object of sight, touch, taste, smell etc., which belongs to the earth and is earthly, and does not appertain to Brahma, the only reality in the universe—Tr.

Always brooding upon the thought of Brahma, non-attached to any thing of this world, and desiring nothing both here and hereafter), let him in the company of his self alone roam about in the world for the pleasure of emancipation. (49)

He must not desire to obtain gifts by reading portends and omens, nor by practising (divination or astrology, nor by reading physiognomy, nor by interpreting and preaching *S'astras*. (50)

He must not enter a room, crowded by hermits, Bráhmaṇas, birds, beggars or others. (51)

With his hair, beard and finger-nails clipped, and carrying a staff and an ewer, he shall wander without creating hardship on any creature. (52)

His ewers, etc., shall be made of unbroken non-metallic (vegetable) substances; like that of sacrificial ladles during the celebration of a religious sacrifice, their purification should be made with water. (53)

Vessels made of gourds, wood, earth or bamboo, should be used by the fourth order of ascetics (yatis). This is what Manu has said on the subject. (54)

Once a day, let him stroll out for begging alms and refrain from attempting to secure a large quantity of food-stuff by begging; through attachment to a larger alms-collecting, a *yati* (ascetic) may ultimately become attached to things of the senses. (55)

After (the hearths of house-holders) have ceased to emit smoke, after pestles and mortars have been laid aside for the day, after the hearth-fires have been extinguished, after the house-holders have all eaten their meals, and plates with leavings have been cast away, let an ascetic stroll out for alms, each day (in the evening). (56)

He must not be sorry, if he obtains no alms, nor rejoice at its receipt; collecting alms (food), enough for the purposes of barest existence, he must free himself from the sensibilities of contraries, pleasure, pain, heat, or cold, etc.) (57)

By all means, let him condemn gifts (alms), given with honour; by such glorifying gifts, a *yati*, though emancipated, is enchained again. (58)

By taking small food, and by residing in solitude, he must withdraw his senses from their attracting objects of enjoyment. (59)

By restraining the senses, by annihilating love and aversion, by extending compassion to all creatures, (a *yati*) attains immortality. (60)

He must ponder on the sufferings of human life, brought about through the effect of evil deeds such as, the consignment of (souls) to the tortures of hell, and the dreadful sufferings therein to be endured. (61)

On separation from objects of love and association with those who are loathsome, on the ravages of age and imbelicity, and affliction from desease. (62)

On the exit of the soul from the body, and its re-birth in another womb, after death, and on the transmigration of this inner spirit through tens of millions of wombs. (63)

On the affliction which is endured by all embodied creatures through the predominance of sin, and on the eternal felicity they enjoy through the effect of their virtue and virtuous wealth. (64)

By means of yoga he must comprehend the des-embodied self of supreme Brahma, which, in its gross from, runs through all types of living beings, good or bad, high or low. (65)

Placed in whatsoever station of society, and (howsoever) defiled, let him practise virtue and be equally (compassionate) to all creatures. The mere cloak of virtue (Garb of holy orders) is no virtue. (66)

It is the (actual contact of) a *Kataka* seed which tends to clear water of its impurities, the mere mention of its name can not make (tur bid) water, clear. (67)

In day or night, and even in disease, he must, for the protection of (small) animals such as, the ant, etc.) walk by carefully observing the ground. (68)

For expiating the sin of unconsciously or unknowingly killing animal lives in the night, a *yati* must bathe, and six times suppress his breath in the manner of a Pranayama. (69)

Even three *Prânâyâmas*, coupled with *Pranava* and *Vyâhritis* and duly practised, should be understood as forming the highest penance of a Brahmana. (70)

As burning metals are purged off their dross, so the impurities of the senses are burnt off by practising the *Prânâyâma*. (71)

Let him burn down the defects of his senses (mental propulsions) with Pranayama; sin, by concentrating his mind on Self; attachment to the world, by withdrawing the senses from the external objects; and ungodly attributes of his self, by means of divine contemplation. 72)

The all-pervadingness of this Inner Self, which runs through all creatures, whether high or low, is unintelligible to untrained and uncultured intellects, let him witness this all-pervadingness by means of communionstic contemplation (*Dhyâna* Yoga). (73)

Him, who has fully witnessed this (all-pervadingness of supreme) Self, the acts do not enchain; bereft of this witnessing, a man shall revert to this world. (74)

Universal compassion, annihilation of all killing and injuring (desires,) control of the senses, institution of religious rites enjoined in the *Vedas*, and practice of austere penances are the factors by which one can realise the Supreme Self in life. (75)

Supported by the pillars of bones, bound by ligaments, plastered over with flesh and blood, and covered with skin, this body should he understood as the foul-smelling refuge of urine and excreta. (76)

He shall have to quit this bodily frame, subject to age and imbecility, the abode of diseases, afflicted with pain and suffering, the transitory embodiment of material elements, characterised by the quality of Rajas. (77)

As a tree tumbles down from the bank of a river as a bird quits a tree (at day break), so the self, like an aquatic animal freed from the jaws of an aquatic monster (crocodile,) with the greatest difficulty, becomes liberated from this body. (78)

Leaving his good to his dear ones and his evil to his enemies,* let him, by dint of contemplation, attain the eternal Brahma. (79)

When through the effect of contemplation he will be entirely desireless about things of the world, then

---

* Let him leave the good he has done to his friends and the evil which he has suffered at the hands of his enemies work out their respective effects in them, and let him not any wise associate his Self with them and banish their thoughts from his mind.—*Tr.*

he shall acquire eternal felicity both here and hereafter. (80)

Thus by gradually abandoning all associations, and becoming free from pairs of contraries, his self will merge in *Brahma*. (81)

All these aforementioned, (latent possibilities of his nature such as, the knowledge of identity of his self with Supreme Brahma, extinction of all feelings of mineness, etc.,) become patent only through the practice of meditation; he who has not acquired the knowledge of this identity will not obtain the highest good (emancipation of self) through meditation. (82)

He must constantly mutter the sacred *mantras* which are related to the performance of *Vediac* sacrifices, or to the adoration of *Vediac* deities, or to the knowledge of self, as well as those of the Vedanta which treats of eternal realities.* (83)

This Brahma is the refuge of all knowing as well as ignorant beings. It is the final goal of the aspirations of all heaven-desiring individuals. (84)

A Brâhmaṇa, who, following these graduated steps, takes to asceticism, shakes off all sin and attains the supreme Brahma. (85)

Thus have I disclosed to you the duties of the self-controlled *yatis* (fourth order of ascetics), now hear me promulgate the duties *Vediac Sannyâsikas*.† (86)

---

* The text has *Adhiyajnam* which means the spirit of *Vishnu* (all-pervading self) residing as the tutilary divinity of religious sacrifice in his eternal and infinite embodiment. Compare *Adhiyajnohamevatradehe* (I am *Adhiyajna* in this body).

Bhagavadgita.—*Tr.*

† *Veda Samnyâsikas*, cottage-dwilling anchorites who have abandoned the performance of *Agni-hotras* and other religious sacrifices enjoined to be performed in the *Vedas*.—*Tr.*

Brahmachàrins, *house holders*, forest dwellers and *yatis* (fourth order of ascetics, all these four several orders have sprung from the order of house holder. (87)

All these orders, adapted and gone through according to the Regulation, lead a Bràhman, who has duly discharged the duties they respectively entail, to the supreme status. (88)

Of all these orders, the order of householder is said to be the highest according to the ordinance of the Vediac Law code, since it is the order of householder that supports all the other three orders. (89)

As all rivers, whether bearing masculine or feminine names, finally draw their support from the ocean, so all the orders (of ascetic, *Brahmacharins*, etc.,) draw their maintenance from the order of householder. (90)

By Bràhmanas, belonging to all these four orders, should be assiduously pursued the ten-attributed virtue. (91)

Contentment, forbearance, non-attachment to worldly concerns, non-avarice, purity, subjugation of the senses, knowledge of the immutable principles, erudition, truthfulness, and non-irascibility, are the ten specific attributes of virtue. (92)

Bràhmanas, who having throughly learnt of these ten attributes of virtues, practise them in life, attain the most exalted status. (93)

A Bràhmana, having discharged the three-fold debt of life and practised the ten-attributed virtue and heard the discourse on Vedanta according to the Rugulation, must be take to asceticesm. (94)

Having abandoned all acts and annihilated the demerit arising from work, let him constantly study the *Vedas*, living in the maintenance of his son. (95)

Bereft of all work, apathetic to the pleasures of heaven as factors of enchainment, on account of the privilege of witnessing his Self, and by constantly brooding over Brahma, a Brâhman attains the highest bliss. (96)

Thus the fourfold Virtue of Brahmanas, auspicious and bearing eternal fruits, has been narrated to you, now hear me discourse on the duties of kings. (97)

CHAPTER VII.

Now I shall relate the rules of conduct which should be followed by the king, and the mode by which he shall achieve the highest success. (1)

The protection of all should be justly and lawfully made by a Kshatriya (king), intiated with all the initiatory rites inculcated in the *Vedas*, according to the laws of his own realm and in the exercise of the functions peculiar to his own order). (2)

Out of terror all creatures run about when the world suffers anarchy; hence, the lord created the king for the protection of all. (3)

Out of the eternal essence of the deities, Indra, wind god, Yama (Death), Sun, Fire, Varuna (water god), Moon, and Vittesha (the lord of riches.) (4)

Since the king has been made out of the essence of Indra, and such like deities, his energy overwhelms all creatures in the world. (5)

Like the sun, he dazzles the sight and mind; no one can look at his face in this world. (6)

In his energy he is like unto *Agni* (fire,) *Vayu* (wind god) *Arka* (sun) *Soma* moon, the lord of virtue Yama, *Kuvera*, Varuna and the great Indra. (7)

The king, if he be an infant, must not be belittled in the knowledge of his human birth, he is the great divinity manifest in the shape of a man. (8)

Fire doth consume a man who may unconsciously come in its contact, the fire of king's wrath burns down one's whole family with all its animals and possessions. (9)

He (the king), in due consideration of the exigencies of the work, force, country and time, assumes diverse attributes under diverse circumstances for the realisation of the inceptive principle of his existence.* (10)

He, in whose grace dwelleth the goddess of opulence, in whose prowess resides victory and in whose wrath abideth death, needs must be full of all energy (*i. e.* all effulgent.) (11)

He, who, out of folly, incurs the enemity of the king, certainly meets his doom; speedily doth the king resolves his destruction. (12)

Hence, let not a man violate the gracious or ungracious command of the king which he might be pleased to make in respect of his friends or foes. (13)

For the achievement of his (king's) end, the lord (Brahma) created, out of his own essence, his son, the punishing rod of sovereignty for the protection of all creatures. (14)

Out of fear of that (rod), all created things, whether mobile or unmobile, are enabled to enjoy their respective enjoyments and do not diviate from their specific duties in life. (15)

In due consideration of the time, place, knowledge and specific nature of his offence he must inflict proper punishment on an offender. (16)

That rod of sovereignty is in fact the sovereign; he is said to be the leader and regulator (of society,) the surety for the due discharge of their duties by (the members of) the four social orders. (17)

The rod of soverignty governs the subjects, the rod of punishment protects all the subject people; it is the rod of punishment that wakes up by the side of those who are asleep, the erudite ones call punishment the embodiment of virtue. (18)

Punishment, justly inflicted after due deliberation, endears all subjects; unjustly inflicted, it destroys them all. (19)

When the king fails to unremittingly inflict punishments on offenders, the powerful will torture the weak, like fishes fried on gird irons. (20)

(Had there been no terror of punishment), crows would have drunk the sacrificial porridge, the dogs would have licked off sacrificial clarified butter, no one would have had the right of ownership in any thing and the miscreants would have been paramount in society. (21)

Men are dominated by the fear of punishment, rare is the man who is moral for the sake of morality; it is the terror of punishment that enables all men to enjoy their earnings or possessions. (22)

Even gods, and demons, Gandharvas, Rakshas, and celestial serpents and birds, dominated by the fear of divine retribution, tend to discharge their respective duties (for the advancement of the universe). (23)

Extinction, or anomaly of, punishment will vitiate all the social orders, cause all bridges to be broken down, and create a panic among all ranks of the society. (24)

Subjects are not agitated (in the country where stalks the blue-coloured, red-eyed rod of punishment, if its wielder (king) fails not to see things in their true light. (25)

Such a truthful, intelligent, inflictor of punishments, who is possessed of good deliberations and understands the principles of virtue, desire and wealth, men call the king. (26)

The three categories (of virtue, desire and wealth) of the sovereign, who justly and properly inflicts punishment, become augmented; while punishment destroyeth a self-seeking, sensuous, deceitful, and arrogant king. (27)

This mighty rod of punishment, which is too heavy to be borne by an uncultured king, will destroy, with his friends and relations, a sovereign, who has deviated from the path of virtue. (28)

After that (*i.e.*, after the complete ruin of an iniquitous king with his progeny, etc.,), an unjustly inflicted punishment (will) lead to the destruction of his kingdom, forts and subjects, both mobile and immobile, and then proceed to oppress the gods and holy sages, who reside in heaven, (by making the offering of oblations to them impossible). (29)

Devoid of the co-operation of his allies (ministers, generals, priests etc.,), foolish, greedy, uncultured, and attached to the pleasures of the senses, such a king becomes incapable of inflicting punishments in proper cases. (30)

A pure, truth-seeking, intelligent king, possessed of good allies (cohorts) and acting conformably to the teachings of the Sastra, is alone capable of exercising the rod of punishment. (31)

Let him be just and equitable in his own dominion, hard-hitting in respect of his enemies, straight in his dealings with his friends, and forbearing to the peaceful Bráhmanas. (32)

The fame of a king of such conduct, even if he lives on fares of poverty, shall expand in this world, like oil-drops on water. (33)

The fame of a king of (contrary conduct, who has not controlled his senses, shall contract in this world, like drops of clarified butter on water. (34)

Of the members of all the (four) several castes in their order of enumeration, true to the duties of their respective orders, the king has been created the protector. (35)

Now I shall enumerate to you in due order the duties of the king and his servants in protecting the subjects. (36)

A king, leaving his bed at early dawn, shall worship old Brâhmaṇas, well-versed in the three Vedas, and abide by their instructions. (37)

Daily he shall abide by the instructions of pure, old, and Veda-knowing Brâhmaṇas; a king, who acts according to the instructions of the old, is certainly and always worshipped even by Rakshas (38)

Even though humble in spirit, he must learn humility from them (Brâhmaṇas), each day; a king, who is humble in spirit, can never be destroyed. (39)

Many kings, with their progenies, have been destroyed through arrogance (hauteur); and kings, who had been exiles in forests, have regained their kingdoms, through humility. (40)

Vena, king Nahusha, Sudâsa, Yâvani, Sumukha and Nimi were destroyed through hauteur. (41)

Through humility, Prithu and Manu regained their kingdoms; through humility Kuvera obtained wealth and opulence; and the son of Gádhi (Vis'vâmitra), the status of a Brâhmana. (42)

From Brâhmanas, well-versed in the three Vedas, he must learn the three Vedas, the eternal principle of punishment, the science of reasoning, the science of Self-knowledge, the principles of trade, agriculture, and cattle rearing, and the science of wealth. (43)

Day and night, he must be engaged in conquering his senses; a king, who has conquered his senses, is enabled to keep his subjects under control. (44)

Let him assiduously avoid the ten evil habits, which originate from desire (lust), as well as those eight, which result from anger, and which are sure to end in grief. (45)

A king, addicted to vices resulting from desire (lust), becomes dis-associated with virtue and wealth; addicted, to those which result from anger, he meets his doom. (46)

A hunting excursion, a game with dice, day-sleep, calumny, promiscuous intercourse (lit, a large concourse of wives), intoxication, singing, dancing, music, and idle rambling, these are the ten vices which originate from desire. (47)

Deceit, or crookedness of temper, rashness, the seeking of other men's discomfiture, envy, the spirit of fault-finding, the robbing of other men's money or non-payment of just debts, use of abusive language, an battery, these are the eight vices which originate from anger. (48)

Assiduously he must conquer that greed which all erudite men have described to be the parent of these two sets of vices. (49)

Abuse of wine, gambling with dice, promiscuous sexual intercourse, and a hunting excursion, these four should be successively regarded as the most inveterate of vices originating from desire. (50)

Battery with a club, use of abusive language, and encroachment on other men's wealth, these three should be always regarded as the most inveterate of vices resulting from irascibility (anger,) (51)

A self-controlled king must know these seven concomitant evils (such as, the abuse of wine, gambling with dice, promiscuous intercourse, hunting excursion, assault, use of abusive language, and encroachment on other men's wealth) of the two (preceding) sets of vices as most heinous, each preceding one being more heinous than the one immediately following it in the list. (52)

Of vice and death, vice is more painful, in as much as a vicious man, after death, will sink down to a lower and lower status, whereas a non-vicious man will ascend to heaven. (53)

He shall select seven or eight ministers of tested virtue and ability who would be conversant with the prices of lands, well-versed in the Sastras, valorous, and born of noble families, with unmissing aims in archery or in the use of arms. (54)

Even a work, which may be easily accomplished, may appear difficult to an unaided man to accomplish; how can a kingdom, which involves so many mighty issues, be governed by a single, unaided person? (55)

With them he must deliberate on all general topics of treaty and war, on the maintenance of forces, on the state of the exchequer, on the capacity of the capital and the kingdom as regards the location and food-supply of their inmates, on ways and means, on the protection of his person and kingdom, and the distribution of revenue among its worthy recipients (public officers) (56)

Having heard the several and independent' opinions of these counsellors, let him carry that much of those opinions into practice which conduces to his welfare. (57)

The King shall deliberate with the most erudite Brâhmaṇa among these concillors on the most important topic regarding the six predicatives of the kingdom (*viz.* treaty, war, expedition, etc.). (58)

Having been confident of his integrity, let him entrust all works to him (*i.e.*, ot the Brâhmaṇa premier) and undertake all works, after first having deliberated with him. (59)

Other councillors, pure, intelligent, affluent in wealth, and of tested virtue and comprehension, he shall also appoint. (60)

Kings shall appoint so many skillful, intelligent and hard-working officials, as may be considered necessary for the due discharge of their kingly duties. (61)

Out of these he must appoint skillful, valorous men of noble parentage in protecting the wealth of the kingdom, and in supervising the mines (sources of revenue); and conscientious men he shall appoint in matters of domestic economy. (62)

An intelligent, pure-hearted man of noble family, efficient, well-versed in all the Sâstras, and capable of interpreting other men's feelings from their meins and demcanours he shall appoint as an ambassador. (63)

A person, handsome-looking, intelligent, skillful, pure-hearted, devoted to his person, capable of judging the spirit of the place and time, fearless and eloquent, is recommended to be the ambassador of the king. (64)

The forces of the realm, as well as the maintenance of its internal peace should be in the hands of the General (Amátya) ; the government and treasury in the hands of the king, and the (declaration of) war and treaty in the hands of the ambassador. (65)

The ambassador is fit to create or break an alliance ; he does that, by which those who are not united are united in alliance, and those who are allies are severed from one another. (66)

He (the ambassador) shall ascertain from the gestures and demeanours of the intimate friends (associates) and relations of a (foreign king), as well as from those of his servants, the scope and nature of his works and undertakings. (67)

Having ascertained the nature and scope of the works (of a foreign king), he shall so deport himself (in his realm) so as not to any wise imperil his personal safety. (68)

He, (the king) must live in a dry, fertile country, (enjoying much of sun light and bereft of swamps and jungles), containing large stores of food-grain and a large population of Aryan settlers, clear (free from disease and disturbing physical phenomena), beautiful with shady trees and creepers, bordered by (adjacent to) the territories of his submissive vassals, and which offers means of livelihood (by trade or agriculture. (69)

He shall live by taking refuge either in a fort (girdled by deserts), or in a land-fort, or in a water-fort, or in a wood-fort, or in a fort composed of men (*i. e.*, guarded by troops of soldiers). (70)

By all endeavours let him take refuge in a hill-fortress; a hill-fort is the best of all forts for its many excellent features and advantages. (71)

Of these, the first three forms of forts are respectively inmated by quadrupeds, hole dwelling animals, and aquatic creatures, and the remaninig three are respectively inmated by monkeys (quadrumanas), men and deities. (72)

As huntsmen can not hurt these animals, while residing in these fortresses, so his enemies cannot assail a king who has taken refuge in any of them. (73)

Since from behind the battlement of a castle an archer can fight a hundred archers, and a hundred archers can fight a ten thousand archers, so the building of a castle is imparatively obligatory (on a king.) (74)

The fort should be equipped with weapons, money, food grains, transport-animals, Brâhmaṇas, artisans, engines, forage and water. (75)

Within this fort the king shall cause his palace to be built, commodious, secret, white, fit for all seasons of the year, and provided with trees and water. (76)

Residing therein, he must marry a wife, beautiful, accomplished, possessed of commendable bodily features, born of noble parentage, and belonging to his own caste. (77)

He shall appoint a priest and a *Ritvik*, who will respectively perform his domestic sacrifices and the *Vaitánika* fire-offerings. (78)

The king shall institute various sacrifices, and pay honoraria to priests officiating at them; for the acquisition of virtue likewise he shall make gifts of money and articles of enjoyment to Brâhmaṇas (79)

At the end of the year, he shall collect revenue from men appointed to collect it (from his subjects); and he shall be like a father unto persons, true to the Sastra, and residing in his dominion. (80)

And in those matters he will appoint efficient supervisers (agents?), who will superintend the works of men (appointed by the king. (81)

The king must be the worshipper (pecuniary helper) of Bráhmaṇas, returned from the houses of their preceptors. This (worship) is said to be the eternal treasure of a king in *Brahma*. (82)

That treasure) the thieves steal not, nor enemies destroy; hence a king should deposit that eternal treasure in Bráhmaṇas. (83)

Oblations (food) cast in the mouths of Brâhmaṇas are superior (in respect of merit) to those offered in *Agnihotrâ* fire-offerings, inasmuch as they do not deteriorate, nor wither, nor decay. (84)

A gift, made to a non-Brâhmaṇa, bears ordinary merit; those made to a degraded Bráhmaṇa, to a well-read one, and to a *Veda*-knowing Brâhmaṇa respectively bear double, hundred thousand and eternal merit. (85)

Through the difference of characters of its recipients, and the variation in the sincerity of feeling with which it is offered, a gift acquires a greater or lesser merit in the next world. (86)

A king, protecting his subjects, if called by an equally powerful or more or less powerful adversary to battle, must not be reluctant to fight in consideration of his martial duties (87)

A non-reluctance to fight, the protection of subjects and serving the Bráhmanas are the most auspicious duties of kings. (88)

Of two kings, trying to kill each other with superior forces, the one, who does not turn his back on the battle-field, goes to heaven, after death. (89)

Fighting, he must not kill his enemies in battle with hidden weapons, nor with barbed, poisoned, burning or fire-mouthed arrows. (90)

Himself riding in a chariot, he must not kill an adversary, standing on the ground, nor one who is a eunuch, or prays for life, or surrenders himself. (91)

Nor one who is asleep or unarmoured, nor one who is unarmed or stript of clothes, nor one who is a mere non-fighting on-looker, or is engaged with another. (92)

Nor one whose weapon is broken, or who is bemoaning the loss of a killed relation, or is seriously wounded; nor one who is afraid of life, or flying from the battle-field in consideration of his martial duties. (93)

Afraid of life, if one, while flying from the field of battle, is killed by the enemy, he acquires all the demerit of his master (employer) (94)

All the merit, which such a run-away (from battle) might have acquired for heaven, his master will acquire in the event of his being killed during flight. (95)

A car, a horse, or an elephant, as well as paddy, wealth (money), women and all other articles, or any me tal other than gold or silver, whatever one might have conquered (captured in war), would be his own. (96)

"The residue shall go to the king" is the dictum of the *Vediac* law on the subject; a thing, which has not been captured by any particular man (*i.e.*, all such articles), he (king) shall divide among all the soldiers. (97)

The eternal and commendable duty of a warrior is (thus) described; a Kshatriya, while engaged in killing his adversaries in battle, must not deviate from this duty. (98)

(A king) must covet what has not been acquired, assiduously protect what has been acquired, augment what has been kept and protected, and distribute this augmented wealth among worthy recipients (*i. e.*, spend it on worthy projects.) (99)

The preceding four acts he must regard as the highest good in his life; and hence, assiduously he must do them from day to day. (100)

A king shall covet a thing, ungained, by means of force; keep the acquired wealth by giving due attention to its increase (*i.e.*, the acquired wealth with interest accrued thereon), and pay over the increase to worthy recipients, (101)

Each day, he must maneuver his forces; each day, he must manifest his prowess; each day, he must conceal the performances of incantationary rites; and each day, seek the weak points (watch the discomfitures) of his enemies. (102)

The world is overwhelmed with the terror of a king, who daily maneuvers his forces: hence, he must bring to submission all the world with the (show of his) might. (103)

Secret in his design, he must be straight-forward in his dealings, and never live by deceit; but he must be wise enough to understand the stratagem of his adversary. (104)

He must not let his enemies know of his weak-points, but he must learn them of his adversaries; like a tortoise hiding his limbs (within the cavity of its shell), he must conceal his own weaknesses (lit, holes.) (105)

(Patiently, and concealed,) like a heron, he must watch his own interests (*i.e.*, the discomfiture of a fish-like fickle adversary), attack his enemy (even if big like an elephant) with the courage and prowess of a lion, dart upon (his prey) like a leopard, and beat out a retreat (with the fleetness and subtility of) a hare. (806)

Those, who will (dare) being the enemies of such a conquering king, he must bring under his control with the appliances of conciliation, etc. (107)

If thy do not stand (*i.e.*, can not be conquered with) the application of the first three appliances (conciliation, buying off, and division,) he must conquer them at once or gradually with his forces. (108)

Of the four expedients (of Government such as, conciliation, buying off, division and war), wise men recommend the adoption of conciliation and war for the advancement of the kingdom. (109)

As a weeder weeds out the weeds and preserves the paddy plants in the field, so a king must protect the kingdom (loyal subjects) and destroy its enemies. (110)

A king, who has indiscriminately ploughed (the field of) his kingdom, shall be ousted thereof; he shall meet destruction with his relations (progeny, etc). (111)

As the vitality of a man ebbs away (on account of the aggravation of his bodily humours) through fasting (and such like depletory causes), so the life of a king ebbs away through the enragement of his subjects. (112)

This measure should be always adopted for the management of the state; a king whose kingdom is well-managed (well-ordered) attains happiness. (113)

For the orderly management of the state, he shall appoint governing officers over each circle *(gulma)* of one hundred, two hundred, three hundred, or five hundred villages. (114)

He shall appoint a head man of each village, a headman over ten villages, a headman over twenty villages, a headman over hundred villages, and a head man over a thousand villages. (115)

The governor of the village shall try all cases of offence occurring therein; cases which he is not competent to decide, he shall refer to the governor of ten villages. In cases of doubt or incompetency, the lord of ten villages shall refer to the lord of twenty villages; and the latter, to the lord of a hundred villages; and he too, under similar circumstances, to the lord of a thousand villages. 116—117)

The king's daily dues from the inmates of a village, (such as articles of food or drink, and fuel etc.,) the governor of the village shall receive (enjoy), each day. (118)

A governor of ten villages shall enjoy a *Kula* measure* of land; a governor of twenty villages, five *Kulas*; a governor of a hundred villages shall enjoy a village; a governor of a thousand villages, a town. (119)

* The measure of land which a cultivator can plough with a plough yoked with six bullocks, in a day (morning and evening) of six hours.

Other confidential ministers of the king shall assiduously supervise the works of these village-governors and other works as well. (120)

In each city the king shall appoint officers, mighty like the mighty planets, seen among the stars in the higher spaces of heaven, who will think of all matters relating to its government. (121)

He (city governor) shall go out on tours, inspecting the works of headmen of villages, and of the works of these city-governors the king shall be cognisant through spies. (122)

The king's servants, connected with the government of the realm, are often found to be exacting and deceitful; the king shall protect his subjects from (the exactions of) these officials. (123)

The king shall excommunicate from the country corrupt officials, who would receive undue gratifications from suitors (at their courts), and confiscate their goods as well. (124)

Maids, messengers, and minials, engaged in the king's service, shall be daily paid their wages at rates varying according to the nature of their posts and services. (125)

One *Pana* (Anna) should be the daily wages of menial servants, and six *Panas* those of higher ones. Each menial should get one *Drona* of paddy, every month; and a higher servant, six *Dronas*; each menial should obtain a cloth, every six month, while a higher servant should get six pieces (three pairs). (126)

Taking into consideration the baught-price as well as the sale-price of his goods, the cost of conveyance, the costs of his daily living, and other contingent expenses, as well as the cost of ensuring safety to his goods (*yoga-kshema*), the cost of policing the forests, rivers, hill-passes, etc.) he shall levy taxes on merchants. (127)

The king, after due deliberation, shall always impose taxes on profits of traders and cultivators, as well as on those of the state. (128)

As leeches, calves and bees, little by little, draw their respective sustenances, so the king shall draw his revenue from his realm, little by little, each year. (129)

A fiftieth part of its value should be the tax on gold or animal; and a sixth, eighth or twelfth part of its value on food-grain, according to circumstances, should be collected by the king, each year, from his subjects. (130)

He shall take a sixth part of profits derived from trees, honey, clarified butter, scents, cereals, saps, flowers, roots and fruits. (131)

As well as of that derived from leaves, *s'âkas*, weeds, leather, bamboo-made articles, earthen vessels, and all kinds of stone-ware. (132)

A king, even at the point of death, must not receive any revenue from a *S'rotriya* Brâhmana; nor must he suffer a *S'rotriya*, living in his territory, to be oppressed with hunger. (133)

The kingdom of a king, wherein a *S'rotriya* is overwhelmed with hunger, is soon consumed by that hunger. (134)

Informed of his *Vediac* knowledge and holy rituals, the king shall provide for his proper means of subsistence; and like a son of his own loins, he shall protect him (*S'rotriya*) from thieves, etc. (135)

The religious rites which a *S'rotriya*, protected

by the king, performs every day, tend to increase the longevity, riches, and territories of the king. (136)

The king shall levy a nominal tax on poor men, living by plying small trades in his kingdom. (137)

The king shall cause each artisan, manufacturer, S'udra and labourer, to work for him for a day, each month. (138)

Out of affection for his subjects, he must not bring about his own ruin by forswearing to collect his revenue from them, nor cause their ruin by his greed; by so bringing about his own ruin, he will become an oppressor of his own self, as well as of his subjects. (139)

The king must be mild or sharp (hard) according to the exigency of each case. Endeared to all is the king who can be thus mild and hard, (140)

Tired or incapable of personally attending to the affairs of the state, the king shall place in his own stead (*i. e.*, delegate his authority to) his wise, nobly-born premier, who has controlled his senses. (141)

An energetic sovereign, free from folly, thus formulating and ascertaining his duties, shall protect his subjects. (142)

The king, who with his ministers and officials, sees and suffers his subjects to be harassed by thieves and robbers, is a dead, and not living, king. (143)

The highest duty of a Kshatriya (king) is the protection of his subjects; a king, who enjoys the just and properly levied revenue (of his realm), becomes associated with (*i. e.*, acquires) virtue. (144)

Having left his bed in the last watch of the night, and attended to the calls of nature, and carefully washed himself, he, after having cast oblations in the fire and worshipped the Brahmanas, shall enter the auspicious hall of assembly. (145)

Seated in that (assembly-hall), he shall graciously speak to and (courteously) dismiss his subjects; and having dismissed them all, he shall deliberate with his ministers. (146)

On the hill-top, in the solitary chamber of his palace, or in the dense solitude of a lonely forest where even birds cannot penetrate, he must deliberate (with his ministers without letting his resolution being in any way detected (by them). (147)

A king, whose counsels the vulgar can not detect, is enabled to enjoy the whole world, even if he be bereft of treasure. (148)

He must avoid the (presence of) idiots, of dumb or deaf ones, of birds (such as parrots, etc.), of extremely old men, of women, of *Mlechchhas* (barbarous people), of sick folks, and of those who have got limbs in less. (149)

It is fickleness, and parrots and women in special, who disclose the counsels of kings; hence, they should be studiously avoided (at the time of deliberation). (150)

Reposed and refreshed, either alone, or in their (*i. e.*, ministers') company, he must ponder on (themes) of virtue, desire and wealth at midday, or at midnight. (151)

Acquisitions of virtue, desire and wealth, which do not conflict with one another, should be made; the daughters should be married; and sons, protected. (152)

The sending of spies (into the realm of his adversary), the execution of acts already undertaken, the contemplation of departments of the female inmates of the palace,* as well as of the endeavours of his spies in foreign countries, should be made (by the king). (153).

His entire eight-fold duty,† his five-fold espionage (*Varga*),‡ love and aversion of (his subjects, and the usages of his country he must ponder on. (154)

He must assiduously watch the expansion of a

---

* His queen killed king Viduratha with a weapon, which she previously kept concealed within the braid of her hair, and the queen of the knig of Kasi killed her lord with the contact of her poisoned anklets (*Nupur*).

‡ *A'dánecha Visargecha tathápraisha-nishedhayoh ; Pancha-mechártha-vachane Vyavahárasya chekshane. Danda s'uddhyoh sadá Yuktastenáshtagatikonripah.—Ushaná.*

Collection of revenue, disbursement of the revenue in the shape of salaries to state-officials, restraint on ministers and officials in affairs of the state, declaration of injunctions in respect of hostile acts done by the king's servants, supervision of the administration of justice, infliction of punishment, and the institution of purificatory rites for expiating the sin of an iniquitous act, these are the eight duties of the king. *Kulluka* gives the above extract from *Ushaná* in support of the explanation he has offered. *Medhátithi*, on the other hand, describes the duties of sovereignty as undertaking of acts not already undertaken *(Akritárambha)*, completion or execution of those, already undertaken *(Kritánushthánam)*, specification of an act already executed *(Anuskthita-visheshanam)*.

Construction of roads, caravans and bridges, the building of forts, repairing forts and other public buildings already constructed, capture of elephants, working of mines, construction of barracks for soldiers, and clearing of forests, according to others.

† Appointment of spies such as, those who disguise themselves as (1) students (*Kapatikas*), or (2) *Sannyásins*, or (3) peaceful householders, (4) or Merchants (*Vaidehikas*) or as (5) shaven-headed ascetics *(Tapasvins)*

Madhyama,* or *Udâsina*† sovereign, and the movements of a *Vijigishu* king (*lit.*, of a king bent on conquest *i. e.*, the central monarch). (155)

These four sovereigns (*Prakritis*) collectivly form the basis of the circle of sovereignty (*Mandalam*, balance of power). Together ;with the eight other *Prakritis*,* they are twelve in number, and constitute the *Prakritis* (constituent elements of the state and allies, etc.) (156)

Each of these twelve *Prakritis* (sovereigns, allies) has five *Prakritis* (essential constituents of the state) of their own such as, ministers, government, forts, treasury, and punishment (administration of justice), thus forming seventytwo in all. (157)

The king, whose realm adjoins that of his own, (2) he mast reckon as his adversary (*Ari*), as well as him who is the ally of that adversary; him whose realm is contiguous to that of his foe as his ally (*Mitram*); and him who is other than these two (foe and ally) as indifferent (*Udasina.*) (158)

With the expedient meaures of state-craft such as, concilliation, division (breach-making among allies), etc., either jointly or severally applied, or with prowess or diplomacy, he must bring these (sovereigns) under his control. (159)

---

* A king whose territory lies between the realm of a conquest-intending sovereign (*i. e.*, central monarch and that of his adversary (*Ari*) and who is capable of doing good to them when combined, but is powerful enough to subdue them severally when not allied with each other, is called a (*Madhyama*, intermediate) sovereign —*Kulluka*.

† *Udâsina* (*lit.* indifferent) means a sovereign who is capable of benefiting or suppressing the *Madhyama*, *Ari* and *Vijigishu* kings at will, whether they are combined or uncombined—*Kulluka*.

He must constantly ponder on the six political expedients of treaty, war, military expedition, toleration (*i. e.*, waiting for opportunity), dividing the army and attacking the enemy in detachments,* and making alliance with a more powerful king (when attacked by an enemy). (160)

According to circumstances, he (the king) mast take recourse to the expedients of toleration, expedition, treaty, war, guerilla skirmishes (*Dvaidhi*), or alliance with a more powerful sovereign. (161)

Of twofold nature is Treaty, of twofold nature is War, of twofold nature is expedition, of twofold nature is toleration (waiting for opportunity), and of twofold nature is an alliance with a more powerful ally. (162)

A treaty entered into by two sovereigns, for offensive (and defensive) purposes for the time being, is called *Samána-yâna-karmá*; while the one, which is entered into for a prospective benefit and which takes effect in some future time, is called *Viparita*. These are the two forms of treaty. (163)

A war, whether declared in the proper or improper season,† by a king for his own good, and a war so declared by him for the protection of his ally (illustrate) the two kinds of war. (164)

Twofold is the nature of a military expedition (campaigning) according as it is undertaken at will by a

---

* The text has *Dvaidhibhávam*, which, according to several authorities, implies double-dealing, *i. e.*, keeping an apparently frienely relation with the enemy. We, however, have adopted *Kulluka's* explanation.

† *Akàle* (lit, at an improper time) *i.e.* in any month of the year other than that of *Márgas'irsa—Kulluka.*

Kàle (at the proper time), *i.e.* when the enemy is in distress.

king alone (on the sudden discomfiture of his enemy), or in combination with an ally. (165)

Twofold is the nature of *A'sanam* (toleration of, or bearing with, the rising supremacy of his enemy, according as it is either made by a king on account of the loss of his forces through his past follies or as the effect of sin of his former birth; or as it is resorted to by a capable or powerful sovereign at the request (and for the welfare) of his ally). (166)

Twofold is the nature of the division of the army, accordingly as it is made for the achievement of the object (of the war), or for the protection of the sovereign. This is what has been said by experts on the six expedients of state-craft. (167)

Twofold is said to be the nature of alliance with a more powerful ally, according as it is made by (a sovereign) hardly pressed by his enemy at the time, or only as a pretext to intimidate his future and intending invaders. (168)

A sovereign, when he shall find that, at the cost of an inconsiderable pain or loss for the present, he can purchase his permanent superiority in future, must then enter into a treaty even at the cost of that little pain or loss (payment of money). (169)

A king, when he shall find his subjects and allies fully contented (with his gifts and honours, etc.), and himself in a very exalted position in respect of his forces (*i e.*, at the head of a spirited and well-equipped army), shall then declare war (with his adversary). (170)

When he shall find his forces exhilarated and largely augmented and those of his adversary in a contrary condition, then the king must go out campaigning against him. (171)

Having lost his forces and transport animals, he shall gradually concilliate his enemy, and enter into a defensive alliance with a more powerful ally. (172)

The king, when he shall consider his adversary more powerful than his own self in every respect, then having divided his army into divisons, shall proceed to achieve his own purpose. (173)

The king, when he shall apprehend to be made a captive by the forces of his adversary, shall then enter into an alliance with (*lit.* place himself under the protection of) a virtuous, powerful sovereign (ally). (174)

Him (*i.e.*, the ally), who is capable of punishing both the subjects (generals ministers, etc., through whose infidelity his capture was made possible) and the adversary, the king must daily and assiduously worship as his preceptor. (175)

If he detects any treachery in that ally, let him fearlessly wage an honourable war* against him. (176)

By means of all political expedients, a king, well versed in the laws of state-craft, shall so exert that, his allies, foes, and indifferent sovereigns may not acquire a higher supremacy than his own Self. (177)

He must righly ponder on all works (of the state) in their relations to the past, present and future, as well as on the good or evil accruing therefrom (178)

---

* The text has *Suyuddham, Kulluka* explains it by *Sobhanam yuddham*, honourable war. Though there is little chance of his coming victorious out of the contest with such a powerful, though treacherous ally, and although there is every probability of his being killed in the conflict, yet it is infinitely more honourable to die like hero, than to put up with affronts offered by a cowardly though powerful potentate, who can violate the laws of hospitality and take advantage of an ally in distress.

A king, who can rightly and speedily ascertain the good or evil of all past, present, or future issues, suffers no discomfiture at the hands of his adversary. (179)

The king shall so arrange all matters that, neither his enemies and allies, nor indifferent kings (*Udasinas*) may deceive him (surprise him unprepared). This is the synopsis of the Law of state-craft. (180)

When the lord (king) shall march on the capital of his adversary in a campaign, he shall slowly approach it by arranging all matters in the aforesaid manner. (181)

In the auspicious month of *Màrgas'irsha* (November December), or in the month of *Phàlguna* (February March), or in *Chaitra* (March-April), the king, at the head of (the four divisions of) his army, shall march out (aginst his adversary). (182)

In seasons (months) other than the aforesaid ones, he (the king) shall break all treaties, march out with his forces against his adversary, if he will find the prospect of a sure victory, or the (internal) distress of his enemie's (realm) due to the infidelity of his ministers, etc). (183)

Conformably to all rules which should be followed in respect of the protection of his own realm at the time of marching,* and having won over the servants and officials of that part his enemie's territory wherein he intends to mobilise; and having stationed spies in due order, (184).

And having cleared the three kinds of ways, and

---

* Strengthening the fortifications of his own kingdom, protection of the rear of his realm with trustworthy rear-guard allies (*Pàrshingrahas*), distribution of proper forces for the preservation of its internal peace, collection of food, forage, water, transport animals, armours, and arsenals, etc.

purified the six kinds of his own forces, he (the king), fully equipped with all the munitions of war, shall slowly march into the kingdom of his adversary. (185)

An ally, who secretly serves the adversary, and who had once been openly in alliance with the enemy but has again been won over to his side, thus serving as a link between the two beligerents, should be regarded by a king as the more dreadful (treacherous) of the two enemies. (186)

With his forces drawn up in the array, known as *Danda*,* *S'akata*,† *Varàha*,‡ *Makara*,§ *S'uchi*‖ or *Garuda-vyuha*,¶ he shall march that way (*i. e.* on the road to his objective) (187)

He shall extend the (front of his forces in the quarter from whence he will apprehend any danger, and shall himself remain in the midst of the corps

---

* The array, in which the general (*Balâdhyaksha*) leads the van; the king, the centre; and the lieutenant general, the rear of the army, and each of its wings is composed of elephant-men, cavalry soldiers and infantry in the order of their enumeration *viz.*, first the elephant-men, flanked by the cavalry, and the cavalry, flanked by the infantry, is called the *Dandaka Vyuha.*

† The array, in which the van of an army is drawn up in a narrow and compact order, its rear expanding in extended columns like the back of an Indian cart (S'akata), is called the *Sakata Vyuha* (cart array.)

‡ The array, in which the army is drawn up in the order, narrow at the van and rear, and thick and extended at its centre, is called the *Varâha Vyuha* (boar-array).

§ The reverse of *Varâha Vyuha* is called the *Makara Vyuha.*

‖ The array of soldiers in extended columns, one man, following one another like a swarm of ants, is called the *S'uchi Vyuha.*

¶ The array, in which the centre of the army is thick, and bulges out both ways, is called the *Garuda Vyuha.*

guarded by soldiers, drawn up in the array, known as Padma *Vyuha** (188)

Let him place *Senàpati* and *Balàdhyakshas*† in all quarters, first placing them in that quarter from whence the danger is apprehended. (189)

He shall place piquets or patrols of trusted (*Gulma*)‡ troops, to fall in at the sound of any particular instrument, expert in fighting as well as in covering the retreat, valorous and incorruptible, (for the purpose of guarding the entrance of hostile soldiers into the line). (190)

He shall fight, placing the soldiers of lesser fighting capacities in compact squads, and placing the veterans in extended lines; drawing up his troops in the *Suchi* (needle) or *Vàjra* (thunder-bolt) array,* he shall fight (the hostile army). (191)

On the even ground he shall engage his charioteers and cavalry, in swamps he shall engage his elephant riders, on the water he shall engage his flotilla, on grounds covered with trees and shrubs he shall engage his archers, and on the level ground he shall engage his bucklers and swordsmen. (192)

---

* The array, in which the king is protected by troops drawn up in circles, within a compact square of soldiers, is called *Padma* (lotus) array..

† The leader of one elephantman, one horseman, and ten foot-soldiers is called a *Pattika*. An officer who commands ten such *Pattikas* is called a *Senâpati*, the leader of ten *Sendpatis* is called a *Balâdhyaksha* (general).

‡ 9 Elephant-soldiers, 9 charioteers, 27 horsemen, and 45 foot-soldiers from a *Gulma* (group).

For a better knowledge of the formations of brigades, army-corpses, battle-arrays, and orders of attack and retreat, the reader is referred to the English translation of the *Agnipurànam* (Wealth of India series). Vol. II. CH. CCXLII. pp. 871—880.

He shall fight placing in the front line of fighting such tall and light-limbed soldiers as men of Kurukshetra, Matsya, Pánchála and Surasena countries. (193)

Drawn up in the battle array, let him supervise and encourage his troops and ascertain their feelings towards the enemy. (194)

Let him closely besiege the enemy and harass his territories; likewise he must constantly vitiate (envenom) its food stuffs, forage and water. (195)

Let him demolish fortwalls and cut down the banks of dykes and water-tanks (of the enemie's country); safely encamped for the night, he must constantly harrow his enemy with terror. (196)

Having severed those (such as, ministers of the enemy) who would be capable of being severed (from the cause of their master) and ascertained the intention of the enemy, he (the king), fearless and intending to win the victory shall fight his enemy on the auspicious moment (*i. e.*, watched by auspicious stars). (197)

With concilliation, payment, and breach-making, severally or combinedly applied, he must endeavour to conquer his enemy; and never by fighting. (198)

Since, dubious is victory in a battle between two belligerents; and since, defeat in battle is sometimes seen, let him accordingly avoid war. (199)

In cases when the three aforesaid expedients (of concilliation, etc.,) would be unavailing, let him, fully equipped, so fight his enemies that, Victory might certainly wait on his banner. (200)

Having won the victory, he must worship the deities and virtuous Brâhmaṇas, give gratuities to the inhabitants of the conquered country (for the advancement of the public weal), and declare a general pardon (amnesty). (201)

Thus having ascertained the intention (of the ministers, etc., of the conquered king), he shall re-instate a scion of that family on the throne of the country, and determine (formulate) his duties and obligations. (202)

He shall verify their laws and usages, and glorify the (newly-appointed) king and his ministers with presents of gems. (203)

Unpleasant is the non-giving (confiscation or withholding) of the desired objects (of individuals) and pleasant is their giving; but such withholding is recommended under certain circumstances. (204)

All these works are contingent on the laws of men and gods; unthinkable (unscrutable) is the divine dispensation, while measures are possible in respect of human affairs. (205)

Having found the three kinds of benefit such as, land or territory (ceded to him), gold, and an ally (in the person of the conquered sovereign), let the king depart with his (forces and allies) after assiduously making the treaty. (206)

Having judged the attitude of the hostile king in the rear of his realm (*Pârshnigrâha*), as well as that of one *(A'kranda)*, whose conduct controls the action of the former, and from their amity or enmity, let him infer the success of the expedition. (207)

With the acquisition of gold or territory a king does not prosper so much as with the acquisition of a true and steady ally, who can be powerful in future. (208)

An ally, virtuous, grateful, contented, devoted, and

resolute in his undertakings, even if he be weak, is recommended (as worth-having). (209)

An enemy, who is intelligent, well-born, valorous, efficient, grateful, munificent and possessed of a good comprehension, the wise call the most inveterate of foes. (210)

Urbanity, with a knowledge of men, valour, generosity, and munificence in gifts, are the excellent traits in an *Udâsina* (indifferent) sovereign ally; (and hence, the alliance of such a one should be always courted.) (211)

A king, in consideration of his own safety (*i.e.*, in the absence of any other means of self-protection), shall unhesitatingly give up a land (country), possessed of auspicious traits, fertile (*i.e.*, well-watered by rivers), and always affording excellent facilities for the rearing and increase of cattle. (212)

Let him preserve money for (times of) distress, protect (his) wives at the sacrifice of wealth, and always protect himself at the cost of wealth and wives. (213)

Finding all dire distresses to be simultaneously present, let a wise man apply these expedients either severally or combinedly. (214)

Considering his own self (his own capacity), the nature of the object to be obtained, and the expedients (to be applied for its realisation), he must proceed to achieve his own end. (215)

The king, having thus deliberated on all these subjects with his ministers and taken physical exercise, shall enter the seraglio to eat his meal at midday. (216)

There he shall eat his meal, well-tested (as to its being free from poison) by trusted, incorruptible (*lit.* inseparable) cooks, who are acquainted with the hours of his meals, by consecrating it with *Mantras* of anti-toxic virtues. (217)

All articles of his (royal) use should be protected with (the admixture of anti-toxic drug-compounds (*Agadas*), and he must always bear on his person gems of venom-destroying properties. (218)

Respectful and well-dressed ladies, well-examined (that they do not secrete any weapon or poison in the folds of their garments), shall fan him, and carry his water goblets, and burn (fragrant) incense before him. (219)

Thus he must exercise caution in respect of his vehicles, beds, seats, baths, toilet, and all personal decorations. (220)

Having eaten his meal, he must sport in the company of the ladies of the seraglio; and having reposed a little, he must again ponder on the affairs (of the state). (221)

Decorated, he must inspect his troops, arsenals, animals of transport and conveyance, and all weapons and ornaments (*i.e.*, state jewels, etc) (222)

Having performed his *Sandhyá* (prayer), he, armed with weapons, shall hear tales of wonder and the reports of his spies in an inner chamber of the palace. (223)

Then having entered another chamber and directed them (spies) as to their fresh undertakings, he, surrounded by the ladies (of the palace), shall enter it again to take his (night) meal. (224)

Then having eaten, and been exhilarated for a while with the sounds of music, he shall go to bed and leave it, fully refreshed, at the proper time (*i. e.*, at early dawn.) (225)

The king (*lit.* lord of the world) shall observe these rules of conduct in health; and in disease he shall delegate these duties to his servants. (226)

CHAPTER VIII.

WISHING to see (*i.e.*, attend to adjudications of) law suits, the king, in the company of Bráhmaṇas and ministers, versed in law (*lit.* judgment or deliberation), and in a gentle mein, shall enter the assembly (court). (1)

Seated in, or staying at, that (assembly) in plain (*i. e.*, as opposed to gaudy or majestic) garments and ornaments, he shall supervise the cases of suitors. (2)

Each day, conformably to the rules of the *S'ástra* and usages of the country, he shall severally adjudicate (cases arising from) the eighteen sources of law-suits (subjects of legal contest such as, the non-payment of a money debt, etc.) (3)

Of these (subjects of contention), the non-discharge of a debt, creation of a trust, sale of a property by one other than its lawful owner, co-partnership transactions (mercantile causes), resumption of a gift, non-payment of his salary to a servant, non-performance of a promise or contract, non-delivery or non-claiming of a good bought or sold, dispute between a cowherd and an owner of cattle, dispute in respect of a boundary, assault and use of abusive language, theft, rash act (robbery), adultery, duties of husbands and wives, the division of an ancestral estate, gambling with dice, and wagers in respect of animal-fights, form the eighteen legs (subjects of law suits). (4—7)

In these matters of men, variously contesting with one another, he, conformably to the eternal Law, shall adjudicate. (8)

When the king can not himself attend to the adjudication of a law suit, he must delegate his authority to an erudite Bráhmaṇa for its decision. (9)

He the appointed Bráhmaṇa), accompanied by three other jurors, shall enter the assembly-room (court room); and there, either seated or standing, they shall witness these transactions. (10)

(The assembly), wherein are present (seated) three *Veda*-knowing Bráhmaṇas and an official of the state (judge) is called a Brahma assembly. (11)

All the members of the tribunal, in which truth (or justice) is conquered by falsehood (or injustice) and falsehood is not pierced by the needle of justice, should be regarded as smitten with impiety. (12)

Rather one should not attend a tribunal, but once there, he must speak nothing but truth; by keeping silent or speaking falsehood in a tribunal, a man becomes guilty of vice. (13)

The members of a tribunal, wherein truth is killed by untruth, and virtue by vice, are killed by that (partial or prejudiced) sight. (14)

Virtue (justice), killed, kills (in its turn); virtue, (justice), preserved, protects (in its turn); hence, virtue should not be destroyed; may not killed virtue (*i.e.*, failure of justice) destroy us all. (15)

Virtue (justice) is the showerer;* he, who impedes the (full working of) virtue, is called *Vrishala*; hence, virtue should not be obliterated. (16)

Virtue is the one true friend of man who follows him even after death; with the death of (his) body all other (friends) fall off. (17)

A quarter part of the (sin of) injustice is attached to the person making the false complaint, a quarter part is attached to his false witnesses, a quarter part is attached to the members of the tribunal, and another quarter part is attached to the king. (18)

The king becomes sinless, the members of the tribunal are absolved of the sin, and sin goes to its perpetrator, when the offender is righly condemned (punished). (19)

The Judicial officer of a king must be a Brâhmana, even if he be a mere Brâhmana by birth (and bereft of the virtues of his order), or a mere professional adjudicator of issues, and not a S'udra under any circumstaces whatsoever. (20)

The realm of a king, wherein a S'udra official administers justice, is destroyed under his very eyes, like a cow merged in the mire. (21)

The kingdom, wherein S'udras abound and which is infested with an atheistic, non-Brâhmana population, is soon destroyed in its entirety, stricken with famine and pestilence. (22)

---

* *Vrisha* (which usually means a bull) is the term that occurs in the text. *Vrisha* here means a showerer of desired benefits, *Kamânàm Varshità*. The whole meaning of the couplet is that, by birth alone a man does not become a S'udra; a man of easy virtue is as much a S'udra as one born of S'udra parents.

Seated on the judicial seat, the king, with his body well-covered, and having made obeisance to the lords of the quarters of heaven, shall commence to witness the affairs of the court (adjudications of law-suits). (23)

Bearing in mind the good (of the protection of subjects) and the evil (of their destruction), and piety (justice) and impiety (injustice) alone, (so that they may not clash with each other), the king shall attend to the (judicial) matters in court, and take up cases in preference to the castes of the suitors. (24)

From external features such as, their meins, demeanours, tones of voice, gestures, and looks, he shall ascertain the inner feelings of men. (25)

From meins, gestures, movements, deportments, tones of voice, and expressions of faces and eyes should be comprehend the inner mind. (26)

The estates of friendless orphans the king shall keep in his custody for so long as they do not come up to age and marry. (27)

So shall he protect the estates belonging to sterile or sonless women, to women who have not got any *Sapinda* relation (and whose husbands are absent in distant countries), to widows, and to chaste but sickly wives. (28)

A virtuous king shall punish, like thieves, those of their male (relations) who might have attempted to rob them (of their estates) during their life-times. (29)

For three years, the king shall hold in trust a property whose rightful owner cannot be ascertained; after three years, he shall confiscate it (by law of escheat.) (30)

"Saying it mine," he, who shall claim such a treasure, must give its exact (measure and description, and if they be found correct, the king shall make it over to him. (31)

Failing to give the correct colour, size, and description of the lost article which he has claimed, as well as the time and place of its loss, the king shall fine him its equal value in money. (32)

The king shall receive from the owner of a lost article in case of its recovery, a sixteenth or twelfth part of its value according to the superior, middling, or inferior status of its owner. (33)

The king's official shall make over to the king all lost articles which might have come into their possessions, and the king shall cause all thieves caught (in his realm) to be (trampled down) killed by elephants. (34)

From the man, who shall truly claim a lost treasure as his own, the king shall realise a sixth or twelfth part of its value. (35)

In the event of one's falsely claiming such a lost article, the king shall fine him an eighth part of its value, or a lesser fine in the case of doubt. (36)

An erudite Brâhmaṇa, having received a treasure previously given by another, shall take the whole of it, inasmuch as he is the lord of all (wealth). (37)

The king having found an old treasure, buried underneath the ground, shall give a half thereof to Brâhmaṇas, and half he shall deposit in his treasury. (38)

Of old treasures, and metals (and minerals, etc., found underneath the soil, the king shall retain a moiety thereof, inasmuch as he is the owner and protector (of mines). 39)

The king shall recover from thieves all articles they have stolen, and make them over to their respective owners without any distinction of castes; a king, by enjoying such stolen articles, acquires the sin of a thief. (40)

The king, cognisant of laws, and in consideration of the duties of the (four) several orders of society, as well as of usages and customs of different localities, guilds, communities and families, (not incompatible with the doctrines of the *Vedas*) shall discharge his own duties (*i.e.*, enact and enforce laws, recognizing the valid authority of those customs and usages). (41)

Men, discharging their own specific duties, even if they happen to be remote, become endeared to the world for the fact of their being true to their respective works (duties). (42)

The king, or king's officials (judges, etc.) shall never fabricate a false case, (or institute a false law-suit) out of greed,* nor put off (*lit.* be indifferent to the hearing of a case for (illegal) gratifications. (43)

As a huntsman traces the wounded quarry to its lair by means of its blood-streaked foot-prints on the ground, so the king shall administer justice (*i.e.*, adjudicate cases) by means of inference (and positive proof. (44)

The king, presiding over a tribunal, shall ascertain the truth and determine the correctness of the (allegation regarding) the subject of the suit, the correctness of the testimonies of witnesses, the description, time, and place (country) of the transaction (or incident) giving rise to the case, as well as its usages, and prononnce the true judgment in consideration of the merit he will acquire (in heaven by so doing). (45)

---

* The king, out of partiality or greed, must not drag non-litigant men into a law suit; he must not fabricate false cases, nor falsely start law suits against his subjects for money. *Kātyana.*

Whatever has been done by good men, or what ever has been done by the virtuous Brâhmaṇas, should be regarded as valid, if they be not contrary to the law and usages of (their country), and the king shall shall give judgment in conformity therewith. (46)

If a creditor makes an allegation (institutes a suit) against a debtor for the recovery of his money, the king, after the debt has been proved, shall cause such money to be realised from the debtor, and make it over to the creditor. (47)

By those means, by which the creditor can realise the amount of claim from the debtor, the king shall cause it to be realised from the debtor and make it over to the creditor. (48)

By means of friendly pursuasion,* by getting its payment assured by a bond or oath,† by means of fraud,‡ by arresting the person of his son, etc, or by employing force,¶ which forms the fifth means, a creditor can realise the money from his debtor. (49)

He, who will thus realise his money from his creditor, must not be indicted by the king for his having realised the same. (50)

---

* The text has *Dharma, Suhrit Sambandhi-sandishtaih Sámena Chánugamenacha ; Práyena Vá rini dâpyo dharma esha Udâhritah.*

Realisation of a debt by a creditor from a debtor by means of gentle pursuasion, or by following him, or through the pursusion of his friends is called *Dharmah.*

† The hypothecation of his property to, or execution of a bond by him in favour of, his creditor by a debtor is called *Vyavahâra.*

‡ As by seizng another man's money kept with or in the possession of the debtor *(Anyahritâdi Váhritya dapyate tatra sopadhih).*

¶ By dragging him bound to his (creditors) own house and intimidating him with sticks and cudgels *(Baddhâ Svagrikamániya tâdanâdyairupa Kramaih).*

If a debt or does not admit the debt, and if that debt be subsequently proved in court (by means of documents, etc.), the king shall recover and make over the debtal amount to the creditor, and impose a small fine upon the debtor according to his pecuniary circumstances. (51)

In the event of the debtor not admitting the debt even after the tribunal has ordered him to pay it off, the complainant shall substantiate his claim with documents (and witnesses), and the king, after the proving of the debt, shall impose a fine upon the debtor for this fraudulent denial. (52)

[The king shall dismiss the suit, instituted by] a plaintiff who has cited witnessess who can not be possibly present at the time of the transaction (*i.e.* payment of the money), or has purposely failed to produce witnesses, he has already cited, or does not understand that his later allegations contradict his former ones.

Or tries to amend a former statement by alleging a new and different fact,* or who, relevently interrogated by the court, refuses to give any answer. (54)

Or consults with his witnesses in a solitary place where he should not so consult, or does not answer

---

* As for example, having said that, the debtor took a *Palam* weight (four tollas) of gold from my hand" the creditor or the plaintiff corrects himself afterwards, "yes, the debtor took a *Palam* weight of gold from my son."—*Kulluka.*

† The text has *Samyak Pranihilanchartham* *i.e.* interrogated as to why did he lend that money in the darkness of the night and in the absence of any witness, the plaintiff does not give any reply *(Kasmat tvayâ râtrâvasâkshikam dattamityevamâdi prâdvivekena prishtah Sanna Samadhatte)*—*Kulluka.*

questions by the court, or hurriedly leaves the premises of the court. (55)

Or refuses, when asked (by the court to speak out, or fails to prove his allegation, or understands not what is required to be proved and the means by which that proof can be established. In such cases creditors shall not be entilled to recover from debtors their claims. (56)

And for these reasons the judge shall dismiss the suit of a plaintiff, who, having alleged to have witnesses, shall fail to produce them in court, after being so directed by it to do. (57)

A complainant who refuses to depose any thing in court after filing his written statement (plaint or complaint) shall be punished with death (in a complaint of grave and serious nature), or with a lighter penalty (in a light case); and his case shall he dismissed if he refuses to answer for three weeks. (58)

If a (defendant fraudulently disowns a true debt, or if a plaintiff sets up a false claim, in court, the king shall fine them double the amount, so fraudently disowned or claimed. (59)

If a debtor (defendant), interrogated by the judge) denies the debt, then he shall have to prove his non-indebtedness before the king and Brâhmaṇas with (the testimony of at least) three witnesses. (60)

Now I shall discourse on witnesses by whom creditors shall get their transactions attested, and the mode in which they shall bear the true testimony. (61)

Kshatriya, Vais'ya and Sudra house-holders who are residents of the same village or town) with the creditor, are fit to be witnesses. In times of distress any person may be a witness. (62)

In all matters, trustworthy, non-avaricious men, who are conversant with all forms of virtue, should be made witnesses; and men of contrary characters should be avoided. (63)

Persons having pecuniary relations with the parties (or having any interest in the transaction), or their relations, dependants (cohorts), or enemies, as well as sick folks or persons degraded for any heinous crime, or those who have known to bear false witnesses, should not be made (*i.e.*, cited as) witnesses. (64)

The king, an artisan, a professional actor, a musician, a *S'rotriya Brahmana*, an ascetic, and a religious mendicant can not be called as witnesses. (65)

A born dependant, a man of condemnable character, a highway robber, a miscreant, an infant, an old man or one deprived of any bodily organ (must not be cited as a witness). (66)

A man in bereavement, an intoxicated person, one afflicted with thirst or hunger, a fatigued, angry, or sexually excited person, and a thief, (must not be made witnesses) (67)

Women shall be the witnesses of women (in money transactions etc.,) and members of twice born orders shall be the witnesses of men of their respective orders; virtuous S'udras shall be witnesses on behalf of S'udras and members of vile orders, on behalf of men of their own castes. (68)

Any one, who is aware of the acts of the litigants, done in a room or forest, or at the time of death, is competent to bear witness. (69)

In the absence of any other available evidence, a woman, an infant, an old man, a disciple, a friend, a slave, or a servant may bear testimony. (70)

The faltering speech is the indicator of an old man, infant, or a sick folk deposing any thing false; under these circumstances their real mind should be inferred from gestures and demeanours. (71)

In all cases of violence,* theft, kidnapping, (or elopement of females), abuse, assault, or battery, witnesses (of aforesaid qualifications) should not be (regarded) and examined as the only competent witness.† (72)

In cases of conflicting testimonies (lit, wherein witnesses contradict one another) the king shall cause the evidences of many witnesses to be taken down; in cases of equal number of testimonies (on each side), testimonies of witnesses of commendable qualifications will prevail, and in cases where their (qualified witnesses') number is equal, the testimonies of excellent Bráhmaṇas shall prevail. (73)

The testimony of an eye-witness in respect of a fact which can be seen, or the hearing by a witness of a matter which can be heard, should be regarded as valid; a witness by spea king truth, in respect thereof is not disassociated with virtue and wealth (and does not become liable to a fine or money penalty). (74)

A witness, who has spoken in the assumbly of venerables (in court) any thing other than what he has actually seen or heard, shall be ousted of heaven, and fall headlong into hell, after death. (75)

---

* Such as acts of incendiarism, poisoning (administration of poison, etc)—*Rulluka.*

† In these cases the court must not refuse to record the testimony of men who are not possessed of the qualifications mentioned in verse 62 of this chapter, but is at liberty to taken down evidences given by infants, old men, in short by all persons considered able to give material informations.—Tr.

A person, (present in court) must depose truly as to what he has seen or heard, when asked, even though he may not have been cited as a witness (by any party to the suit). (76)

A single non-avaricious male witness should be regarded as enough and competent for testifying to a fact, while a host of virtuous women should not be regarded as competent witnesses owing to the fickleness of the female temperament. Likewise, those, who bear stigmas on their characters, (whether male or female), are not competent to be witnesses. (77)

Whatever a witness has spontaneously (*i. e.*, voluntarily) alleged shall be taken cognisance of for the adjudication of a case by the court); his allegations of a contrary character (*i.e.*, those made out of fear, or through inducement or pursuasion etc.,) should be rejected as worthless. (78)

The presiding officer of the court (*Pràdviveka*), shall interrogate the witnesses, present, in the presence of the complainant and defendant, courteously addressing (lit, consoling) them in the manner following. (79)

Speak truly what you know regarding the dealings between the plaintiff and the defendant which form the subject of the present suit you have been cited as a witness in this matter. (80)

A witness, who alleges truth in his deposition, attains the exalted regions after death and acquires an excellent fame in this life; this is a statement which Brâhma has approved of (*lit.*, worshipped). (81)

A witness, for giving false testimony, shall be oppressed, a captive, for a hundred existences, under water, tied with the serpent nooses of *Varuna* (water god); hence, a witness must speak truth. (82)

Truth purifies a witness, and it is Truth that augments virtue (justice); hence, witnesses of all castes must speak truth. (83)

His Self (soul) is the witness to his own self (*i.e.*, to all his acts); Self is the refuge of self; hence, by bearing false witness, one must not insult his own self, (the omniscient and eternal witness to all incidents). (84)

Miscreants think that, there is none to witness their secret vices; the gods and their inner Selves are the witnesses to their misdeeds. (85)

The two worlds (Heaven and Earth), the water, the heart, the sun, the moon, the lord of Death, the wind-god, the night, the two junctures of the day and night, and virtue are cognisant of the thoughts of all creatures. (86)

In the presence of the gods (divine images) and Brâhmaṇas, let him, pure (in body and mind), question the pure Brâhmaṇa witnesses, with their faces turned towards the north or the east, about the truth, in the forepart of the day. (87)

He (*i. e.* the judge) shall say unto a Brâhmaṇa (witness "speak," "speak truth" unto a Kshatriya; by the sin of stealing a cow, gold or seeds he shall charge a Vais'yu witness to speak truth; and a Sudra (witness), by all sins. 88)

To regions, which are said to be reserved for killers of Brâhmaṇas and women, for infanticides, for the violators of friendship, and for the ungrateful, go (the souls of) those who speak falsehood, (after death). (89)

O thou gentle one, may the (merits of) virtues, which thou hast practised since thy birth, all go to the dogs, if thou speakest falsehood. 90)

Think not, O thou gentle one, that, "I am the soul, and nothing exists but my own self;" for, the eternal witness to virtue and vice always dwelleth in the heart. (91)

If you quarrel not (by telling lies) with the Supreme Self, the representative of the sun and Death, which is ensconced in the heart (*i.e.* conscience), you need not go to the (sacred) Ganges or Kurukshetra (for the expiation of sin). (92)

Bare-bodied, shaven-headed, blind, and oppressed with thirst and hunger, shall he go (to the doors of) his enemies for begging his food, who shall bear false witness. (93)

In respect of ascertaining the truth (*lit*, virtue), the sinful one, who, being duty interrogated, shall speak falsehood, shall fall headlong into the hell of extreme-darkness (*Andhá-támisram*). (94)

He, who being summoned to court (*lit.* present in the tribunal) alleges distorted facts, or facts which he has not personally witnessed, (in consideration of bribes offered to him), does not know that his conduct is like that of a blind man attempting to eat a fish with its bones. (95)

A greater being than the Self of a man, which at the time of his deposing (in court) never apprehends that, he will speak falsehood, the gods know not in this world. (96)

O thou beloved one, hear me describe the specific kinds of falsehood and the numbers of his ancestors which one kills by telling lies. (97)

By telling a lie in respect of an animal, one kills five (generations of) his ancestors; ten (generations of his ancestors, by telling a lie) in respect of a cow; a hundred (generations of his ancestors, by telling a lie) in respect of a horse; and a thousand generations of his ancestors by telling a lie) in respect of a person. (98)

By telling a lie in respect of gold, one kills all his ancestors and unborn (descendants); by telling a lie in respect of a land one commits the sin of killing all creatures. Hence, one should not tell a lie lor a land. (99)

False evidence given in respect of waters (*i.e.*, tanks ponds, etc.), carnal knowledge of a woman, gems, or any kind of stone-ware is as sinful as a lie spoken in respect of land. (100)

Considering these evils of giving false evidence (*lit.* speaking falsehood), you must speak what you have actually seen or heard. (101)

Brâhmaṇas, who live by tending cattle, as well as those (Brâhmaṇas) who are traders, artisans, professional actors or musicians, money-lenders, or are in the service (of any body), should be treated as S'udras, (if summoned to a court as witnesses). (102)

A witness, who, out of compassion, has knowingly stated a fact otherwise than it is in reality, shall not be ousted of heaven therefor, since such a speech (statement) is called a divine allegation. (103)

In cases where the allegation of truth would lead to the (lawful execution (*lit.* death) of a S'udra, Vais'ya, Kshatriya or Brâhmaṇa, a witness is warranted to speak falsehood. In such a case a lie is greater than truth. (104)

Such (false) witnesses shall worship the deity of Speech with offerings of sacrificial porridge, that being a good expiation for the sin of speaking such lies. (105)

Or muttering the *Kushmándi Mantra*, or the three *Richas* running as *Uditi*, or the three *Richas* sacred to *Varuna*, he shall duly cast libations, of clarified butter in the sacrificial fire. (106)

A witness in health (*i.e.*, not incapacitated by disease or sickness), having refused to depose in respect of a money-debt in court, shall pay the equal amount of the debt to the creditor and a tenth part thereof to the king. (107)

The witness, who, within a week of his deposition in court, is found to be punished with a disease, or with the death of a relation, or with the burning of his house by fire, shall be liable to pay the debt (*i. e.*, the amount in claim) and a fine to the king.* (108)

In a suit without witnesses, the truth should be ascertained by causing the contending parties (litigants) to swear or affirm on oath. (109)

The gods and great sages have sworn for determining the truth (in suspicious cases); Vas'ishtha swore in the court of king Paiyavana† (of yore). (110)

A wise man shall never wantonly swear for a small thing; by unnecessarily swearing a man is destroyed both in this world and the next. (111)

A swear (falsely made by a husband of many wives as to his preference to one of them, present at the time), as well as that made in respect of a matrimonial

* Such calamities are considered to be the effects of divine retribution for the false evidence of the witness, he must make good the amount of money which the defeated creditor might have lost in conrt, and also pay a fine to the king for perjury.

† Once on a time, Vis'vamitra accused Vas'ishtha of having eaten a hundred sons of his own. Vas'ishtha to exculpiate himself swore to his own innocence in the court of king Sudámá, the son of Piyavana.

(negotiation) in respect of forage for cattle, in respect of fuel, or the one made for the advancement of a Brâhmaṇa, does not entail any sin. (112)

A Brâhmaṇa shall be caused to swear by truth; a Kshatriya, by his weapons and riding animals; a Vais'ya, by his cattle and seed-grains; and a S'udra, by the sin of all the crimes. (113)

Or he (s'udra) shall be caused to carry fire* in his hands, or to be drowned in water,† or to swear by touching the head of his son or wife. (114)

Him, whom a well-kindled fire burns not, nor water can drown, nor disease does strike, should be speedily pronounced innocent in an ordeal. (115)

Of Vatsa, who was accused (of his S'udra origin) by his younger (step) brother of yore, the fire, in congnisance of the good of the world, did not burn the hair, on account of the truth of his assertion. (116)

In all litigations (*i.e.* partly heard or adjudicated suits) in which false evidence would be subsequently detected, all orders and proceedings must stay, and whatever has been done (in connection therewith) must be regarded as undone. (117)

False evidence is said (to emanate) from greed, ignorance, fright, friendship, desire, anger, foolishness, and juvenile (fickleness.) (118)

I shall enumerate in due order the punishments to be inflicted on a witness who gives false evidence under circumstances (*i. e.*, out of reasons) other than these. (119)

---

* A red hot iron ball, weighing fifty *Palas* and to the girth of eight fingers, should be carried on the palm, strewn over with *Asvatha* leaves.

† As regards other forms of ordeals see *Vishnu Samhita*.

For giving false evidence out of greed, out of mental agitation, out of terror, or out of affection, one shall be respectively punished with a fine of a thousand, two hundred and fifty, one thousand, and a thousand *Panas*. (120)

For giving false evidence out of lust (*i. e.*, sexual obligation) one shall be punished with a fine of two thousand and five hundred *Panas*; for giving false evidence out of anger or spite the penalty shall be a fine of three thousand *Panas*, for giving false evidence out of ignorance one shall be punished with a fine of two hundred *Panas*, while the penalty for giving false evidence through inadvertance shall be a fine of a hundred *Panas*. (121)

For guarding against the failure of justice, and for repressing crime, wise men have laid down these penalties for giving false evidence. (122)

A virtuous sovereign shall punish false witnesses of the three social orders in the aforesaid manner and banish them from the country; while he shall simply exile a false witness of the Brâhmaṇa caste from the realm (without punishing him with a money-penalty). (123)

Unhurt even in those ten places (limbs), on which the self-origined Manu has directed that punishment should to be inflicted, a Brâhmaṇa offender shall be banished from the country. (124)

The reproductive organ, the tongue, hands, legs which (stand) fifth (in the list), the eye, the nose, the ears, property and body (are the ten places of punishment. (125)

Considering the wilful repetition (*i. e.*, wilful and repeated perpetration) of a crime by (an offender), as well as the time, place, and circumstances of its perpetration, the light or serious nature of the offence committed, and the bodily strength (and pecuniary circumstances of the offender to bear the penalty), punishment should be inflicted on an offender. (126)

An unlawful punishment destroys fame and renown and shuts out the heaven in the next world; hence, (the king) shall withold an illegal punishment. (127)

By punishing those who should not be punished, and by not punishing those who ought to be punished, the king acquires a great infamy and goes to hell, after death. (128)

A first offender should be let off with a (warning, a second offender (*i.e.* one who has committed the same offence for the second time) should be let off with a strong censure; one, who has committed the same offence for the third time, should be punished with a fine; while death (corporeal punishment, or mutilation of a limb) should be the penalty for one who has committed the same crime for the fourth time. (129)

In cases where corporeal punishment would not prove sufficiently deterrent, all these four forms of penalty should be simultaneously inflicted on the offender. (130)

Now I shall enumerate the measures of copper, silver, and gold as they are known in daily use (*i.e.*, barter or exchange by men), and by which names they are current in the world. (131)

The smallest particle of dust, which is seen to float in a ray of sun-beam, admitted through a hole in the window, is called a *Tasra-renu.* (132)

Ei htsuch *Tasra renus* make a *Liksha*; three

Likshas make a *Râja-Sarshapah*; and three *Raja Sarshapas* make one *Gaura Sarshapah.* (133)

Six *(Gaura) Sarshapas* make one *Yavamadhya*, and three *Yava-(madhyas)* make one *Krishnalam* (*Ratti*); five *Krishnalakas* make one *Másha*, and sixteen *Máshas* make one *Suvarna* weight of a (Gold mohur). (134)

Four *Suvarnas* make one *Palam*, ten *Palas* make one *Dharanam*; two *Krishnalas* of equal weight make one *Raupya-máshaka.* (135)

Sixteen such *Raupa* (silver) *màshakas* make one *Dharanam* or *Raupa* (silver) *purànam*; one *Kàrshika* (eighty *Rattis* or a quarter *Palam*) of copper is called a *Panah* or *Kárshàpanah.* (136)

Ten *Dharanams* make one *Raupya* (silver) *Sátamaua* and four *Suvarnas* make one *Nishka.* (137)

Two hundred and fifty *Panas* constitute what is called *Prathama Sáhasa*; five hundred *Panas*, *Madhyama Sahasa*; and a thousand *Panas, Uttamasáhasa.* (138)

In the event of the debtor acknowledging his debt to the creditor, the king shall fine him (at the rate of) five *Panas* for each hundred *Panas* of the debtal amount; while in the case of his falsely denying the debt (the king shall fine him) double the amount (*i.e.* ten *Panas* for each hundred *Panas* of the amount in claim.) This is the injunctiou of Manu. (139)

A money-lending creditor shall charge interest (on the money lent and advanced on a mortgage) at the rate fixed by Vasishtha, *i.e.*, an eightieth part of each hundred per *mensum.* (140)

Conformably to the practice of virtuous men, let him take interest at the rate of two *Panas* for each hundred *Panas* per *mensum*; by charging interest at the rate of two *Panas* for a hundred *Panas* per mensum, a man does not commit any sin. (141)

Interests shall be respectively charged from (the members of the (four) social orders in the order of their enumeration at the rates of two, three, four and five *Panas* for a hundred *Panas*, per *mensun*. (142)

No interest shall accrue when the debtor will borrow money by assigning the use of the mortgaged property to the creditor; and the mortgaged premises, for being long held in mortgage, shall not be considered as any thing other than a mortgage, and as such, incapable of being sold. (143)

A creditor, forcibly enjoying a mortgaged property which ought not to be so enjoyed, shall remit the interest on the money (lent and advanced) and satisfy the debtor with the price thereof; in default whereof he shall be punished as a stealer of the mortgaged property (article). (144)

An article, held in trust or under a mortgage, should be returned to its owner on demand without the least delay; even after the long continuance of such an article in trust or mortgage, its return or reconveyance to its owner must not be withheld. (145)

It may be necessary to make use, out of amity, by a person of a cow, horse or camel, made over to him to be tamed or broken to harness, but such an use will not extinguish the right of its owner in the animal. (146)

If the owner of a small property (money), knowingly connives at its possession and enjoyment by another for ten years, he shall not be competent to recover or claim it back as his own after the lapse of that period. (147)

If the owner of such a property be not an idiot or a minor, an uninterrupted possession thereof by a person (holding it in adverse possession) will create his right of ownership therein. (148)

Enjoyment of a mortgaged article, of a boundary land, of a minor's property, of a trust property, of a (sealed) deposit, or of a woman, does not extinguish the right of ownership. (149)

A foolish mortgagee, who without the consent of its owner (the mortgager) has enjoyed (the mesne profits of?) a mortgaged property, shall have to remit a moity of interest to him by way of compensation. (150)

Principal and interest, simultaneously recovered at one time, must not double the amount (originally lent and advanced); in respect of paddy, fruit, wool and animals of conveyance five times the quantity or number (originally lent) may be recovered, and not more. (151)

A rate of interest other than what has been laid down in the S'astra (in respect of the members of a certain caste), if agreed upon (by them), must not be held as valid, in other instances interest may be charged at the rate of five percent (as sanctioned by Manu.) (152)

A creditor shall not recover from a debtor interest (accrued due on money advanced by him) not later than a year,* nor at rates disallowed by the Sastra

---

* The text has *Nátisamvatsarim Vriddhim*, *i.e.* a creditor, who has agreed to receive interests after three, four or six months, must not let it accrue due for more than one year. He shall demand and receive it within that period.

such as, *Chakravriddhi* (compound interest), *Kála-vridhi*,* *Karita*† and *Kayika*.‡ (153)

A debtor, incapable of discharging his debt and willing to renew the bond, must pay off the whole amount of interest accrued due thereon and execute a fresh one in the favour of the creditor. (154)

Failing to pay off the whole amount of interest, he shall add up the principal and the balance of interest, and execute a bond (in favour of the creditor) entering therein the consolidated amount as the principal). (155)

A (carrier) who has stipulated to carry (a thing) for a certain time, or for a certain distance (*lit.* place) in consideration of fares, charged at the rate of compound interest, shall not be entitled to it (compound interest), if he fails to carry it for that much time or distance.* (156)

In such cases, the rates of interest on fares, which traders by land or sea (*lit.*, seafaring merchants), conversant with the laws of time, place and fares, might have thought fit to lay down and fix, shall prevail. (157)

He, who stands surety for the appearance of a debtor (in court), is bound to discharge the debt with his own money, if he fails to make the debtor enter appearance. (168)

A son is not bound to discharge the gambling debt of his father, or the unrecovered balance of a fine

---

* *Kálavriddhi, i.e.*, the interest must not double the amount originally lent and advanced, no matter how long the debt might have been standing unrealised.

† *Karita*, the heavy rate of interest which a debtor in distress may be agreed to pay.

‡ *Káyika*, the exorbitant rate of interest which is exacted from a debtor by means of threat or violence.

imposed upon him, nor to pay off the money, due from him for standing surety for another (money recognisance) or a gift made by him to a unworthly person. (169)*.

The rule in respect of one's standing a surety for the appearance of another has been stated above; in the event of the death of one who has stood a surety for goods, his heirs shall pay off the recognisance-money.)160)

(If it be asked) why should the heir of a person who has entered into a recognisance for the appearance of another or for (the delivery of) goods, pay the recognisance money, (the answer is) that, on the death of one who has stood such a surety on having received a proper sum of money from the debtor (or the defendant) his heirs are bound to refund it to him (*i.e.* debtor.) (161)

In the event of the surety having received enough money from the debtor to pay off his recognizance, his heirs shall pay it back to the debtor out of their own funds. (162)

An act (money-transaction), done by an insane, intoxicated, or diseased person, or by an infant or old man, or by one, not duly authorized in that behalf, can never be valid. (163)

A deed of agreement or contract, (containing provisions) contrary to law (Dharma) and confirmed usages, if it be executed by one, must not be held as valid. (164)

A mortgage, sale, gift, acceptance, or trust, if found

---

* The text has *Vrithâddânam*, KULLUKA explains it by *parihâsa-nimittam Bhandâdibhyo deyatvena pitrângikritam*, money gifts promised by the father to fools and jesters, etc., for jokes or oolings.

to be fraudently done, shall abate, and all proceedings made under it should be regarded as unmade. (165)

If one dies after having made a debt for (the maintenance of the) family, then all the members of that family, whether joint or divided, shall discharge that debt out of their own funds. (166)

A debt, contracted by a slave for the maintenance of his master's family, the master, whether residing in that or in a distant land, is bound to acknowledge and approve as one contracted by himself. (167)

Anything given, or written (executed) through the application of force, or forcibly enjoyed, (as well as) all acts done under force, should be considered as undone; this is what Manu has said. (168)

A witness, a surety, and an umpire are the three (persons) who suffer pain for the sake of others; and a king, a capitalist (*lit.* rich man), a Brâhmaṇa, and a merchant are the four (persons) to whose thriving do the others contribute. (169)

A king, even in direst need, must not take what ought not to taken; even when most affluent in wealth he must not give the veriest trifle of what ought not to be given. (170)

By taking what ought not to be taken, and by giving what ought not to be given, the weakness of a king is proclaimed; he perisheth both here and hereafter (171)

By receiving his just dues, by preventing the intermixture of castes, and by protecting the weak, the strength of a king is augmented; he thrives both in this world and the next. (170)

Hence, the king shall conquer his anger and senses; and forswearing personal love and derison, he shall be, like unto death, impartial to all. (173)

The bad-souled king, who fails to administer even handed justice out of greed or folly, his enemies soon do subjugate. (174)

Him, who, with his anger and desire fully controlled, administers justice (*lit.*, adjudicates cases), do the subjects fondly follow, like the rivers, following the sea. (175)

If a debtor lodges a complaint against a creditor, endeavouring to realise his just money from the former, the king shall punish the debtor with a fine, equivalent to a [quarter part of the debtal amount, and realise, and make over to the creditor, his just dues. (176)

If the debtor be of the same caste with the creditor or belongs to a caste inferior to that of the creditor, he shall pay off the debt by bodily work (compatible with his social order); while a debtor, belonging to a caste superior to that of the creditor, shall repay his debt by easy instalments. (177)

Conformably to the aforesaid rules, the king shall decide law-suits between the parties thereto with the help of witnesses, and testimonies, etc. (178)

A wise man shall deposit money in trust with a high-born, good charactered, virtuous, truthful and opulent person with a large family (of sons and relations. (179)

In the same manner, in which a man will deposit any money in the hand of another, will it be returned to him on demand. As the deposit is, the refund is. (180)

On the deposit-holder failing to refund the trust (*lit.* deposit) money to the depositor on demand, the latter shall apply to the judge, and the judge, at the back of the depositor, shall demand the money of the trustee. (181)

In the absence of any witness in such a transaction, the judge, for the determination of truth, shall cause a handsome looking attendant (officer of the court) disguised so as to conceal his identity, to deposit gold with the alleged (deposit-holder) and to demand the same of him. (182)

If the holder of such a deposit can return the gold in the same form and in the same condition (*i e.*, sealed or unsealed) in which it was originally deposited, it shall be presumed that he does not hold the deposit as alleged by the complainant (plaintiff). (183)

But if he fails to return the deposit (gold) made by his attendant in its original form and condition, the judge shall recover from him both the deposits (*i.e.*, gold and the article or money alleged to be deposited by the plaintiff) This is the decision of law. (184)

One shall not give an article, mortgaged to or deposited with him, to his heir, inasmuch as either in his life-time or after his demise (such a giving may lead to the probable destructiou of such a pledge or deposit article. (185)

If after the demise of the depositor, the holder of the deposit, out of his own motion, returns the deposit article to his (depositor's lawful) heir, the relations of the depositor shall not be competent to bring an action against him (*i.e*, the holder of the deposit) in the king's court (on the allegation of the existence of more such deposits with him.) (186)

On the institution of such a suit (*lit.* after the filing of such a complaint), the king, forswearing all duplicity, shall endeavour to recover the deposit article with amicable means; and in consideration of the character of the deposit-holder he shall achieve his end with concilliatory appliances. (187)

This rule holds good in respect of realising all kinds of deposit articles; if the deposit-holder returns a sealed deposit article with the seal intact, or does not take anything out of it, he shall not be indictable. (188)

A deposit-holder is not liable to make good the deposit article in the case of its being stolen by a thief or in the event of its destruction by water or fire. (189)

(The king shall) examine the stealer of a deposit-article, as well as the one who fraudently demands an article that has never been deposited as a trust, by means of all the aforesaid expedients (of concilliatory measures, etc.,) as well as by means of ordeals mentioned in the *Vedas*. (190)

He who refuses to give back a deposit article, and he who demands an article without having kept it as a deposit, both of them should be punished as thieves, and the value of such an article should be recovered (from either of them.) (191)

The stealer of a deposit article shall be punished with a fine equal in value to that of the article deposited with him* and the king shall punish a stealer of a pledged article with a fine, equal to its value, without any distinction of caste or person.* (192)

He, who on a false† pretext robs another of his

* This couplet is not a mere repetion of what has been stated in the preceding verse, but contemplates cases where Brahmanas, who were above all corporeal punishments, would be guilty of offences enumerated here in.—*Kulluka*.

† The text has *Upadhabhisha* on a false pretence. Kulluka exemplifies it by illustrations such as, when a man goes to his neighbour and says "the king is angry upon you, pay me so much money and I shall shield you from the king's wrath.

money, shall be punished, together with his abettor, with any of the various corporeal punishments* (mentioned before). (193)

An article (such as gold, etc.,) deposited with a man in the presence of a witness, should be returned to the depositor (on demand) in the same quantity or measure in which it was deposited; and such a witness, deposing falsely to its (original measure or quantity), shall be liable to punishment. (194)

An article, which has been deposited and received in secret, should be secretly returned (to its depositor on demand); like the deposit is the taking back. (195)

The king, without anywise oppressing the deposit-holder, shall ascertain the fact whether the article is actually a deposit, or a pledge, or a deposit out of love or affection.† (196)

The king shall never accept the testimony of him, who, without having any right of ownership in it, sells an article without the consent of its rightful owner, and who, although a thief in reality, does not consider himself as such. (197)

Such a person, who is equally culpable as a thief, if he happens to belong to the family of the rightful owner, should be punished with a fine of six hundred *Panas*; otherwise he shall held guilty as a thief and punished with the penalty for theft. (198)

A sale or mortgage of a thing by a person other than its right and lawful owner, as well as all acts

* Imprisonment, or mutilation of any limb or organ such as, the hand, leg, etc.—*Kulluka.*

† The text has *Prityopanihitasya.* That is, an article deposited with a person, out of love by the depositior, for its temporary use by the former. *Kulluka.*

done by him (in connection therewith) must be regarded as invalid (lit, not done). This is the decision of Law. (199)

In the case where possession (of a property by one) is evidenced, but not the means (right or little) under which he has come by it, the title will determine the right of ownership therein and not the possession. This is the decision of law. (100)

At a public auction, the man, who purchases a property (lit, wealth) for a (good) value in the presence of legally competent witnesses, is said to lawfully come by it, since (a good) value or consideration purifies the property, *i.e.*, removes any defect in its little after the sale. (201)

If the auction-purchaser (vender of an article or property), on his failure to produce (lit, show) the vendor,* can prove (the fact of his purchasing the same at a public [lit, open auction and] its consequent purity for its being so purchased, he shall not be punishable for purchasing it from one who is not its rightful owner; but the rightful owner of the article in such a case shall have it back on payment of half the consideration to the purchaser. (202)

An article (of one species) mixed with another of a different (species), a pithless substance, an article weighing less than its surface or manifest weight, and an article that is under a cover or lies at a distance, must not be sold. (203)

If by showing a (more handsome) bride (at the time of fixing the dowry) another (of more homely

---

* As in the event of his death, of departure to a distant country.—*Kulluka.*

features) is given in marriage, than the [bridegroom shall be entitled to marry both of them on payment of that (single) dowry; this is what Manu has said. (204)

He who gives away in marriage an insane girl, or one who is not virgin, or is afflicted with any form of cutaneous affections, without informing (the bridegroom) of her such disqualification shall be liable to punishment. (205)

If a *rittvik* (priest) duly appointed to officiate at a religious sacrifice, abandons his office, the institutors of the rite shall be bound to pay him his honorarium (*Dakshiná*) proportionate to the work he has performed. (206)

Having officiated as a priest at a sacrifice till the payment of the honorarium (*i.e.*, nearly up to the completion of the rite), if he is compelled to abandon his office, he shall be entitled to the entire amount of *Dakshiná*, and to get the remaining rites done by another. (207)

The query is whether in respect of a religious rite, for the performance of each part whereof a separate *Dakkiná* (Honorarium) has been sanctioned by the *S'ástra*, persons who have respectively performed those parts shall each obtain a *Dakshiná*, or shall they aportion among themselves the entire *Dakshiná* (paid in one lump sum at the close of the sacrifice. (208)

(Among the followers of certain branches of the *Vedas* the practice is that) the *Adhvarju* shall obtain a chariot, the Brahma shall receive a swift-going horse, the *Hota* shall obtain a horse, and the *Udgátá* (chanter of the *Samveda*) shall obtain the cart in which the *Soma* plants have been carried.* (209)

In a Jyotishtoma sacrifice the *Dakshinâ* (which consists of a hundred kine should be distributed among the sixteen priests as follows, *viz.*,) the (four) principal priests (*Hotâ*, *Adhvaryu*, *Brahma* and *Udgâtâ*) shall each receive a *Dakshinâ* of a dozen kine, those known as *Maitravaruna Pratistotá Brahmananch-chchhansi* and *Prastotá* shall each receive a half of the *Dakshinâ* of the former (*i.e.*, six kine each); the priests of the third set *Achchhâvak*, *Nashtri*, *Agnidhra*, and (*Pratihartâ*) shall each have a third part of the *Dakshinâ* (of a principal priest, *i. e.*, four kine each), and the priests of the fourth set *Grâvastut*, *Unnita*, *Potâ* and *Subrahmanya*) shall each have a quarter part of the *Dakshinâ* of a principal priest (*i. e.*, they shall have three kine each).† (210)

---

* The text *Chàpyanahkraye*, which Kulluka explain by *Soma-vahana-Sakatam*, a cart or barrow employed to bring the soma plant to the hall of sacrifice. In the Rick 19 of the Sukta IX (XLI) of the second Ashtaka (Eighth Adhyaya of the Rigveda, we find a reference to these carts or barrows which are placed in front of the hall of sacrifice; north and south of an altar erected outside. The *Sakatas* are requested, according to Sayana, to proceed to the west part of the northern *Vedi*, or altar; according to Kâtyayana, they are also termed *Havirdhànas*, oblation-containers, and part of the ceremony consists in dragging them into different positions at different periods accompanied by appropriate Mantras which are given in Yajur Veda. V. 14-31.

† The sixteen are thus enumerated by KULLUKA BHATTA, in the order and proportion in which they are entitled to share in a *Dakshina* of a hundred cows, being arranged in four classes, of which the first four are severally the heads, and the others subordinate to them, in the same course of succession:— I. *Hotri*, *Adhwaryu*, *Udgâtri* and *Brahman*, are to have

The shares of several men, jointly doing a work in this world, should be respectively determined by applying the above-said principle (of division of *Dakshiná*). (211)

---

twelve each, or forty-eight in all. 2. *Maitrávaruna*, *Pratistotri*, *Brahmanachchhansi*, and *Pratiharttri*, six each, or twenty-four. 3. *Achchavaka*, *Neshtri*, *Agnidhra* and *Pratiharttir*, four each, or sixteen; and 4. *Grávadut*, *Netri*, and *Subrahmanya*, three each, or in all twelve; making up the total of one hundred. *Ramánátha*, in his commentary on the *Amara Kesha*, VII. 17, also gives the names of the sixteen priests, with a few variations from KULLUKA. *Grávastut* is his reading, instead of *Grávvadut*, and it is the more usual one; and in place of the *Prastotri*, *Netri*, and *Potri*, he gives, *Prasthatri*, *Prasastri* and *Balachchha*: We have the *Potri* repeatedly named in the text of the *Rich*, as well as the *Prasastri*. In the *Aitareya Brahmana* b. VII. I, the sixteen priests to whom portions of the offering are assigned are also enumerated with some modifications, having, instead of the *Pratistotri*, *Grávadut*, *Netri*, and *Subrahmanya*, of the first list, *Pratiprasthatri*, *Upagatri*, *A'treya*, and *Sadasya*. The same authority, however, adds as priest not included in the sixteen, *Gravastut*, *Unnetri*, *Subrahmanya* and the *Samitri*, immolator, when a Brahman. In *Madhava's* commentary on the *Nyáya málá vistára* of *Jaimini*, for an extract from which I am indebted to Dr. Goldstucker, he enumerates the sixteen priests as classed in four orders, following the authority of *Kumaril Bhatta*, much to the same effect as KULLUKA; they are: I. The *Adhwaryu*, *Pratiprasthatri* and *Unnetri*; 2. the *Brahma*, *Brahmanachchhansi*, *Agmdhra* and *Potri*; 3. the *Udgatri*, *Prastotri*, *Pratiharttri*, and *Subrahmanya*; and 4. the *Hotri*, *Maitrávaruna*, *Achchhavaka*, and *Gravastut*. The four first are especially charged with the ceremonial of the *Yajur-Veda*; the next four superintend the whole according to the ritual of the three *Vedas*; the thir class chant the hymns, especially of the *Sama Veda*, and the fourth repeat the hymns of the *Rich*; the head of each class receives the entire *Dakshina*, or gratuity; the second, one-half; the third, one-third; and the fourth, a quarter: the several functions are not very explicitly described.

One, who has given, or has promised to give a small sum of money to a person for a religious rite, shall get back the money or withhold the gift in the event of the latter's failure to perform the same. (212)

If the supplicant, out of greed or foolishness, fails to refund the money to the giver, the king shall fine him a *Suvarna* (gold mohur) for the theft. (213)

Thus is described the law relating to malefeasance in respect of trusts or deposits ; now I shall discourse on (the law relating to) non-payment of wages (to servants, etc.) (214).

A servant, working for a stipulated pay, if he refuses to do, without being sick or indisposed, the work agreed upon out of insolence or impertinence, shall be punished with a fine of eight *krishnalas* of gold ; and the wages shall not be paid to him. (215)

(But) if he had been really ill, and if after recovery he resumes his work as originally agreed upon, he shall be eutitled to his pay, due to him for howsoever long a period. (216)

He, who fails (to get the stipulated work done by others), when ill, or refuses to do it himself, when well, shall get no wages, even if a very small part of the work is left undone. (217)

Thus the law relating to the payment of wages has been fully set forth, now I shall discourse on the law relating to breach of promise or contract. (218)

Him, who, having promised on oath to abide by the rules of the guild or assembly of his village or country, breaks that promise (*i.e.*, transgresses the rules) out of greed, (the king) should banish from the country. (219)

Having thus punished the breaker of promise, (the

king shall impose upon him) a fine of four *suvârnas* or six *Nishkas*, or one hundred silver coins. (220)

A virtuous king shall adopt this law of penalty (*i. e.*, inflict these penalties on) in respect of persons who have violated their compacts with their caste-guilds or village-assemblies. (221).

He, who, having purchased or sold an article repents his sale or purchase, must return it (to the seller or purchaser) within ten days of the sale or bargain. (222)

After the expiry of ten days such an article must not be given or taken; for giving or taking it (after the lapse of ten days) the king shall punish the giver or the taker with a fine of six hundred *Panas*. (223)

Him, who gives a faulty girl in marriage without mentioning the defect, let the king punish with a fine of ninety-six *Panas*. (224)

He, who, out of spite, calls a virgin, unvirgin, shall be fined a hundred *Panas*, on his failure, to substantiate his statement. (225)

Nuptial *Mantras* are related to (*lit.*, established on) virgins,* and they are never applicable in respect of unvirgined brides, inasmuch as they stand outside the pale of (*lit.*, are bereft of) all religious rites. (226)

* The text has *Kanyâ* which KULLUKA has explained by *Akshatayoni*, which is ordinarily interpreted to mean a girl who has not menstruated. It would have been far more desirable, if the celebrated commentator could have used any other term less equivocal and less confounding. The intention of the author is plain enough, and we would prefer to explain *Kanyâ* by *Akshunna-Sati-Chchhadâ* (a girl with unruptured hymen, which is the recognised evidence of virginity in a girl). The marriage of a girl, after menstruation, is not condemned by Manu, nor does his Samhita depict her status as a wife in any way inferior to that of one married before the age

The nuptial *Mantras* impart the status of a wife, and the rite of *Saptapadi* (walking seven steps), gone through by the bride completes the creation of wife-hood. (227)

In whatsoever transaction (*i. e.*,) not only in a sale, or purchase, or payment of wages), him, who shall have any cause of complaint, the king shall give this equitable relief in accordance with the abovesaid rules. (228)

---

of puberty. In the verse XC of the IX. Chapter we find that, an unmarried girl, after menstruation, is enjoined to live for three years in her father's house, and to seek out a husband thereafter; and the verse XCIII. of the same Chapter exempts a man, marrying such a girl, from the obligation of paying a dowry to her father. The right of using *Vediac Mantras* in marriages of pregnant brides, and the privilege of recognising such marriages as sacrements were not denied to the parties thereto by Manu, as would from *Yá Garbhini Samskriyati* or *Vadhu Kanyá Samudbhabam etc.* In respect of the *Gandharva* form of marriage, which may be solemnised even after its actual consummation by the couple, *Devala* enjoins that *Vediac* Mantras and rites should be respectively recited and gone through on the occasion of its solemnization before the nuptial fire. (*Gandharveshu Viváheshu punar Vaiváhika Vidhih; Kartavyas'cha tribhirvarnaih Samayanágni Sákshikah*). The couplet in the ninth chapter of this Samhita which lays down that a man of thirty should marry a handsome girl of twelve (*Trinsadvarsho-dvahet Kanyám hridyám Dvádas'avárshikim*) does not necessarily suggest that girls should be married before puberty, since menstruation has been known to occur in many cases earlier than that age. What the couplet does at best is to fix the highest desparity of age allowable between the married couple. The intention of the Samhita is to ensure the highest sanctity of marriage and this verse evidently contemplates that a bride must be a chaste virgin in order to be consecrated with the sacrament of marriage. (*Dharmay Viváha*), which the loss of her virginity before the wedlock does not entitle her to claim.

Now I shall duly discourse (on the law relating to) disputes between owners and keepers of cattle, arising out of their (respective) short-comings (*i.e.*, negligence, or omissions). (229)

The keeper of an animal, made over to him for tending, shall be answerable for any injury done to it during the day, while its owner shall be answerable for an injury done to it in his house during the night; but if the terms of tending be otherwise (*i. e.*, for the day and night) the keeper shall be answerable for injuries done to it both in the day and night. (230)

A cowherd, who has agreed to take milk in lieu of his wages, shall milch with the consent of the owner, the best one among (each group of) ten cows. In the absence of a stipulation for any other form of wages, this should be held as the (standard) wages of cow-keepers. (231)

If an animal strays out of sight, or is killed by a reptile or, by falling into a pit (*lit* uneven ground) through the wilful negligence of the keeper of his duties, the keeper shall be bound to make good its loss (to the owner of the beast. (232)

If a beast be stolen by a gang of thieves, who have perpetrated the crime with the beat of drum, the keeper of the flock shall not be liable to make good its loss if he informs its owner of the fact at the proper time and place. (233)

If a beast dies a natural death, its keeper shall cut off its ears, skin, hairs, bladder, sinews, gall-stones, or other bodily appendages which may testify to its natural death, and show them to its owner (for his better conviction). (234)

In the absence of the flock-keeper, if a wolf attacks

the flock and carries away a beast, the flock-keeper shall be answerable for, and liable to make good the loss of, that animal to its owner. (235)

But if a wolf darts upon and kills one of the animals, grazing in flocks in a wood in his presence, the flock-keeper shall not be answerable (for the death of that animal to its owner.) (236)

A strip of land to the extent of four hundred cubits or to the width of three large sticks at the outskirt of a village should be set apart for pasturage; a ground of thrice as much measure should be kept reserved for the purpose at the outskirt of a town or city. (237)

If the cattle graze on and destroy the crops standing on an unfenced ground, adjoining the pasture-land, the king shall inflict no penalty on the cattle-keepers (for such destructions of crops.) (238)

Such a land (*i.e*, the one adjoining or close to the pasture ground) should be enclosed with a fence or enclosure over which a camel would not be able to see, and too dense to allow a dog or a hog to thurst its nose or snout into it. (239)

If a flock of cattle, attended by its keeper, trespasses on an enclosed field near the road side, or at the outskirt of a village, or close to a pasture ground (and grazes upou the growing crop), the king shall fine him a hundred *panas*; the owner of the field is bound to keep them off, if the cattle, unattended by the keeper, attempt to enter upon it. (240)

If the cattle trespass and graze on fields other than those described above, the keeper shall be punished with a fine of one *Pana* and a quarter; but under all circumstances he shall be liable to make good the loss to the owner of the field. (241)

No penalty exists in respect of the destruction of a crop by a cow within ten days of her parturition, or by a bull branded with the sign of a discus or trident, or by a bull, dedicated to a deity, whether attended by the the cowherd or otherwise. This is the decision of Manu. (242)

In the event of the destruction of the crop through the negligence or omission of the owner of the field, he shall be punished with a fine of ten times the measure of grain payable (as revenue) to the king (in respect of that field); and half of the above fine shall be the penalty when the loss will occur through acts of the owner's servants and without his knowledge. (243)

Conformably to these rules the virtuous king shall settle disputes between keepers and owners of animals, arising out of their respective omissions or short-comings. (244)

In a dispute as to boundaries between two villages, the boundary should be determined in the month of *Jaishtha* (May June) after the border embakments have become fully apparent (on the recedence of water. (245)

Trees such as the *Nyagrodha*, *Ashvattha*, *Kins'uka*, *S'almali*, *Sâla*, *Tala*, and *Ksheri* should be made (*i.e.*, planted to demarcate) boundaries. (246)

Boundaries, demarcated by shrubs, bamboos, various kinds of Shamis, ( ), creepers, mud-pillars, or *Kuvjaka* plants are never obliterated. (247)

At the meeting of boundaries, tanks, ponds, fountains or reservoirs of water should be made, or divine temples should be erected. (248)

Considering the blunders committed by men in determining or ascertaining boundaries, other hidden signs of boundary-demarcation should be made. (249)

Stones, bones, cow's hairs, husks of paddy, ashes, bits of broken pottery, dried cow-dung cakes, bricks, charcoals, broken bits of baked clay and sands. (250)

(Or in other words all things which the earth may not consume in course of time should be buried underneath the soil for the purpose of fixing the boundaries. (251)

The king shall lay down the boundary between the two contending (villages) by the abovesaid demarcating substances, having determined it by previous possession and (the existence of) water-courses. (252)

In the case where the existence of boundary-marks would give rise to a suspicion the testimony of witnesses would settle the dispute as to the boundary. (253)

He (*i.e.*, the king) shall interrogate the witnesses as to the bonndary marks in the presence of the disputants and the inmates of the same village. (254)

Statements made by the witnesses regarding the determination of boundaries, together with their names, the [illegible]ing shall cause to be entered into the boundary-paper (record). (255)

The witnesses, clad in red garments, decked with garlands of red flowers round their necks, and carrying loose earth on their heads, shall swear as to the correctness of the boundary by their respective good deeds. (256)

Their true testimony shall purify these truthful witnesses, but the king shall punish each of them with a fine of two hundred *panas*, if they give false evidence. (257)

In the absence of witnesses, four persons, living at the four angles of the village (*S'amantas*), shall assiduously determine the boundary in the presence of the king (258)

In the absence of *Samantas*, persons who are the members of old-established families in the village shall be cited as witnesses, and in cases where even they would be unavailable the foresters, [such as trappers, fowlers, cowherds, '*Kaivartas*' (fishermen), herb-collectors, snake-catchers, and grain-pickers] shall be interrogated. (259—260)

Interrogated by him, whatever they will say as to the mode of demarcating the boundary between the two villages the king shall lay down the boundary in accordance therewith. (261)

In demarcating the boundaries of a field, well, pond, orchard, or a house, the testimony of a man, living in the neighbourhood and cognisant thereof, shall be taken. (262)

The king shall punish each of these witnesses with a fine of *Madhyama Sâhasa* (five hundred *Panas*), if they give false evidence in respect of the boundary. (263)

For having wrongfully taken possession of a house, or orchard by intimidation, one shall be punished with a fine of five hundred *Panas*, for having unknowingly taken possession thereof one shall be punished with a fine of two hundred *Panas*. (264)

In the case where it will be impossible to (rightly) demarcate the boundary, the king shall go to the spot in person and allot the lands (in dispute) to such (of the disputants) to whom they may be most useful. (265)

Thus the law (*i.e.*, procedure) relating to boundary disputes has been laid down in its entirety; henceforth

I shall discourse on the law relating to the use of abusive language. (266)

For having used any abusive language to á Bráhmaṇa, a Kshatriya shall be punished with a fine of one hundred *Panas*; whereas for the same offence a Vais'ya shall be punished with a fine of one hundred and fifty or two hundred *Panas*; and a S'udra, with a corporal punishment (flogging, etc.) (267)

For having used abusive language to a Kshatriya a Bráhmaṇa shall be punished with a fine of fifty *Panas*; while for having used abusive language to a Vais'ya or S'udra he shall be punished with a fine of twenty-five or twelve *Panas*. (268)

In the case of abusive language among members of the twice-born castes, the offender shall be punished with a fine of twelve *Panas*, while in the event of filthy language being used the offender shall be punished with a fine of double value (twenty four *Panas*.) (269)

If a S'udra uses any offensive language to a member of the twice-born caste (Brahmana), his tongue shall be slipped off, inasmuch as he (S'udra) has originated from a vile place (of the body of Supreme *Brahma*). (270)

If a S'udra abuses a member of the twice-born order by mentioning his name and caste, a burning tong to the length of ten fingers shall be inserted into his mouth. (271).

If a S'udra insolently gives any religious or moral advice to a Bráhmaṇa, the king shall cause hot oil to be poured into his mouth and ears. (272)

For having cast unjust aspersions on one's learning, country, caste, deeds, or bodily features, the king shall punish the offender with a fine of two hundred *Panas*. (273)

For having taunted a man for his physical deformity (*lit.* for having called a lame man, lame, and a blind man blind) or for having committed a similar offence out of insolence, the king shall punish the offender with a fine of one *Karshá Panam* (sixteen *Panas*. (274)

For having used abusive language to his mother, father, wife, brother, or son, and for not having given way to his preceptor, the king shall punish the offender with a fine of one hundred *Panas*. (275)

In the case where a Bráhmaṇa has used abusive language to a Kshatriya, and *vice versa*, the king shall punish the Bráhmana with a fine of the *Prathama Sahasa* class (one hundred *Panas*) and the Kshatriya with a fine of the *Madhyama Sahasa* class (two hundred and fifty *Panas*. (276)

For such a (quarrel) having occurred between a Vais'ya and a S'udra, the Vais'ya shall be punished with a fine of the *Prathama Sáhasa* class, and the S'udra, without having had his tongue clipped off, shall be punished with a fine of the *Madhyama Sáhasa* class. This is the decision of law in respect of punishment (for these offences). (277)

Verily thus the punishment for the use of abusive language has been described. Now I shall discourse on the law relating to assault or battery. (278)

The limb with which a member of a vile caste shall assault a member of a superior caste shall be cut off. This is the injunction of Manu. (279)

If a member of a vile caste raises his hand against, or assaults, a member of a superior caste with his hand, his hand shall be cut off by way of punishment; if he commits the same offence with his leg out of anger, his leg shall be cut off. (280)

If a vile person attempts to sit on the same seat or cushion with a man of superior caste, the king shall punish him by branding his waist and exiling him from the country, or by lopping off his hips. (281)

If any one insolently spits on the person (of a Brâhmaṇa) the king shall cause his lips to be cut off; if any one urinates or passes flatus (out of insolence) on the person of a Brâhmaṇa the king shall cause his penis or rectum to be cut off. (282)

If any body pulls him (Bráhmaṇa) by the hair or beard, the king shall cause his (offender's) hand or leg to be cut off, if any body pushes him (Brâhmaṇa) by the neck the king shall causes his testes to be severed. (283)

A Breaker of skin or drawer of blood (on the body of one of his own caste) shall be punished with a fine of one hundred *Panas*, a piercer of flesh, with a fine of six *Nishkas*; and breaker of bone with exile. (284)

Any one injuring the factors by which the trees and vegetables may be used and enjoyed (such as fruits, flowers, etc.) shall be punished with penalties determined according to the gravity or lightness of his offence. (285)

If men or beasts are grieviously hurt, let (the offender) be punished with a punishment proportionate to the greviousness of the hurt. (286)

In (a case of assault attended with) the injury of a limb or organ, or with a wound or bleeding, the king shall cause the assaulter to pay to the assaulted person the costs of the medical treatment necessary for his cure; in default whereof he shall be punished with a fine, double of such costs in value. (287)

For having knowingly or unknowingly done any mischief to another's property (or goods), the offender shall satisfy the injured party by paying off its price or by replacing the same, and also he shall pay a fine of equal value to the king. (288)

For having knowingly or unknowingly destroyed a leather, or a leathern article, a wooden or earthen vessel, or a flower, bulb or fruit, (belonging to another) one shall pay a penalty of five times its value. (289)

Except under the ten circumstances (hereunder mentioned) the carman, passenger and the owner of a car shall be liable to punishment. (290)

If a mischief happens to any beast or person (on the road) on the breaking of the nose-rope (of a bullock yoked to a bullock cart), on the breaking of the shaft (of a horse car), on account of the uneven nature of the ground, on the breaking of a wheel or its spoke, on the breaking of the straps, reins, or headrope, or even after being loudly warned of the danger, (the carman, or carowner etc,) shall not be liable to punishment. This is what Manu has said (on the subject.) (291—292)

If for the inefficiency of the driver any mischief (or accident) happens (to a person or beast), the owner of the car shall be punished with a fine of two hundred *Panas* (for having employed an unskillful carman. (293)

If the driver (car-man) be an efficient one, he alone shall be liable to a fine of two hundred *Panas*; otherwise the riders, car owner etc., shall be each liable to a fine of one hundred *Panas*. (294)

If for being obstructed in his way by beasts or carts, a charioteer, while driving his chariot, happens to kill any creature, he shall be summarily punished (for that rash act.) (295)

For thus having killed a man, he shall be summarily punished with the penalty for theft (*i. e.,* with a fine of one thousand *Panas* and not with the punishment for man-slaughter), while the penalty shall be half as much (*i.e.,* five hundred *Panas*) if he chances to kill a large quadruped such as, a cow, elephant, horse or camel) (296)

Two hundred *Panas* shall be the penalty for killing small beasts under the circumstances, while that in respect of kiliing an auspicious beast (such as, deer) or bird (such as a parrot, etc., is fifty *Panas.* (297)

Five *Máshas* (of silver) is the penalty for (thus) killing as ass, goat or lamb, while a *Másha* of silver is the penalty for killing a dog or a hog (under the circumstances) (298)

A wife, son, servant, disciple, or uterine brother, found guilty of an offence, should be punished with a chord or with (a foliated) bamboo stick. (299)

They shall be chastised on the lower parts of their bodies, and never upon the upper limbs. For having flogged them in any other fashion one shall be liable to punishment for theft. (300)

Thus the law relating to assault and battery has been fully set forth ; now I shall discourse on the law relating to theft. (301)

The king shall assiduously endeavour to repress the thieves in his kingdom ; by repressing theft the fame and kingdom of a king are augmented. (302)

Always worshipped is the king who grants protection from thieves (to his honest subjects) ; verily augmenteth his sacrifice (of sovereignty) which grants perpetual protection (to his subjects) as its *Dakshinâs* (honorarium) (303)

The king receives a sixth part of the religious merit of his subjects whom he in every way protecteth, and a sixth part of their sins if he fails to properly protect them. (304)

Whatever *Vediac* studies do his subjects do, whatever sacrifices do they perform, whatever gifts they make, and whatever prayers they offer to the deity, through his properly protecting them he enjoyeth a sixth part of the merit thereof. (305)

By lawfully protecting his subjects, and by punishing those who deserve punishment, the king acquires the merit of a sacrifice which is performed daily with a *Dakshinâ* of a hundred thousand cows. (306)

The king, who without protecting his subjects realises from them a sixth part of the produce of their fields, revenue, duties, royalties* and fines, goes to hell after death. (307)

The wise have called such a king, who realises a sixth part (of the agricultural products of his subjects without giving them the safety of life and property, as the filth-taker of all. (308)

A law-breaking, avaricious, non-protecting, oppressive, king who sucks up the life-blood of his subjects (*i. e.* squeezes out their substance by means of unjust and oppressive taxes) should be regarded as one (already) doomed to a vile existence (after death.) (309)

By the three lawful expedients of imprisonment,

---

* The text has *Pratibhâgam*, KULLUKA explains it by *Phala-kusuma, S'âka-trinâdyupâyanam Pratidinagrâhyam* Tolls or royalties of fruits, flowers, edible bulbs, hays, etc., daily pàid to the king.

enchainment and various forms of corporeal punishment (such as the mutilation of a limb, etc.,) let him assiduously repress the miscreants. (310

By repressing the wrong doers and encouraging the virtuous, kings are constantly purified as Bráhmanas are purified by the performance of religious sacrifices. (311)

A king, seeking his own welfare shall always tolerate the calumnious remarks made by suitors, defendants, infants, old men and sick folks regarding himself. (312)

He who bears with ill-reports (adverse criticisms) made by the aggrieved is glorified in heaven ; he who out of pride of wealth can not tolerate such criticisms goes to hell for that. (313)

A thief, with his hairs dishevelled, must run to the king, confessing his own guilt and asking him to punish his self. (314)

Carrying a cudgel, or a club of catechu wood, or a sharp spear, or an iron rod on his shoulder. (315)

Killed, or alive after being punished by the king, a thief is exonerated from his crime ; but the king who lets off a thief without punishment himseif acquires the guilt of theft. (316)

The sin of a fæticide is transferred to the person who partakes of his food, the husband of a faithless wife obtains the sin of her adultery, the sin of the disciple is contaminated to his preceptor, and the sin of a *yajámana* (institutor of a religious rite) is transmitted to the priest officiating at the ceremony. (317)

After having committed crimes, men, punished by the king, become free from impurity and go to heaven after death as honest and virtuous men do. (318)

He who has stolen a pitcher from a well, or broken down a water house,* shall be punished with a fine of one *Mâsha* and liable to return the stolen good to its owner. (319)

For having stolen paddy of more than ten *kumbha*† measures a person shall be punished with death (corporeal punishment or mutilation of a limb); for having stolen paddy of a lesser measure he shall be punished with a fine of eleven times the quantity of the stolen paddy, which should be restored to the owner. (320)

Capital punishment should be inflicted on a thief for having stolen a *tula* weight of gold or silver or precious silk) cloths, weighing more than a hundred *palas*. (221)

Mutilation of a hand should be the punishment for stealing the abovesaid articles, numbering more than fifty and less than one hundred. For stealing less than fifty (pieces of cloth) the penalty should be eleven times their value. (322)

Death should be the punishment for stealing jewels and precious gems belonging to high born ladies and men. (323)

For stealing large quadrupeds, weapons, and medicines, the king shall inflict proper punishments in consideration of the hardness of the time and the gravity of the offence or otherwise. (324)

Half of the leg of a thief should be cut away for

---

* The text has *Prapà* [which means a house where water is given to the passers.

† Two hundred *Palas* make one *Drona*, and twenty *Dronas* make one *Kumbha*.

having stolen and threaded the nose of a Bráhmana's cow, or for robbing an animal intended to be immolated in a sacrifice. (325)

For the theft of cotton-threads, cotton, enzyme, cow-dung, treacle, milk-curd, thickened milk, whey, cordials or hays. (326)

(Or of) bamboo made vessels,:salts, earthen vessels, earth and ashes as well. (327)

(Or of all kinds) of fish, birds, oil clarified butter, meat, honey, or any other animal produce. (328)

Or of other articles, wines, intoxicating drugs, articles of food, or confection, the penalty shall be a fine double the value of the article, stolen. (329)

For the theft of green paddy, of a shrub or creeper, or of any other kind of unthreshed grains the penalty shall be a fine of five *krishnalas.* (330)

For the theft of threshed paddy, *Sákas*, edible roots or bulbs, or fruits by one who is not related to their owner the punishment shall be a fine of one hundred *Panas*, whereas the fine shall be fifty *Panas*, if the offender is found to be a relation of the owner. (331)

The forcible taking or carrying away of a thing (with the knowledge and in the presence of the owner) constitutes what is called *Sáhasa* (robbery), taking away of a thing in the absence of its owner constitutes *Steyam*, and the hiding of a thing after having stolen it is called *Chauryam.* (332)

Him, who has stolen any of the abovesaid articles made suitable for human use or has robbed the sacred fire from the fire-chamber, the king shall punish with a fine of the *Prathama Sáhasa class* (*i.e.*, one hundred *Panas.*) (333)

With whatsoever limb of his body one shall attempt to commit theft, the king, for checking the recrudescence of that crime, shall cause that limb to be cut off. (334)

A father, preceptor, relation, mother, wife, son or priest, who fails to discharge his specific duties, should be punished by the king. (335)

For the offence for which an ordinary person would be punished with a fine of one *Kárshápanam*, a penalty of one thousand *Káshápanam* should be inflicted on the king, if he is found guilty thereof. This is the conclusion. (336)

For having committed theft, a S'udra, cognisant of the law, shall be punished with a fine eight times the usual one in value; a Vais'ya, with a fine sixteen times; a Kshatriya, with a fine thirty-two times; and a Bráhmaṇa, with a fine sixty-four, hundred, or hundred and twenty-eight times the usual one in value. (337—338)

The taking of fruits and roots of trees, fuel wood for fire, and hays for cattle, if they belong to others, does not constitute theft. (339

A Brâhmaṇa, if he wishes to take even his just fees for teaching (a pupil) or performing a religious sacrifice) from the hand of one whom he knows to be a thief (and which money he knows to have been obtained by theft) shall be liable to punishment as a thief. (340)

For having taken two pieces of sugar cane and two edible roots from another's field, an indigent, way-faring Brâhmaṇa, shall not be liable to punishment. (341)

Wrongful detainers of stray cattle, as well as those who let loose the horses tied to their posts in a stable and those who rob slaves, horses and chariots should be punished as thieves (*lit.* are guilty of theft.) (342)

A king, by thus repressing the thieves (in his realm) acquires renown in this world and enjoys perfect felicity in the next. (343)

Wishing to attain the status of Indra (king of the deities) and an etrnal fame, let the king show not the least indulgence for a moment to a robber. (344)

A robber should be regarded as a worse miscreant than a thief, assaulter or foul-mouthed person (345)

The king who tolerates (the depredations of a robber soon incurs the ill will (of his subjects) and meets his doom. (346)

Let not a king, out of feelings of friendship, or in consideration of a large pecuniary gain, let off unpunished robbets, who are the dread of all creatures. (347)

When (the practice of) virtue is obstructed (by tyranny), when the eternal division of castes is any wise jeopardised, Bráhmanas may wield arms (for the preservation of law). (348)

He, who destroys life (commits man-slaughter) for the defence of his life and property, in a just and fair fight, or for the protection of women and Bráhmanas, does not become thereby morally condemnable. (349)

A preceptor, old man, infant, Bráahmana, or vastly erudite person, coming as an *A'tatáyin,** must be killed without the least hesitation, (350)

---

* *Agnido Garadas'chaiva S'astrapáni Dhanárpahak kshetra dárápahárícha S'adeti átatáyinah.* He who administers poison, sets fire to his house, comes to assault him with a weapon, or robs him of his treasure, or defiles his mother or wife are said to be the siz Atatyanis (mortal enemies) of a man.

By killing an *A'tatayin* the killer acquires no demerit, inasmuch as it is anger that kills anger in fact in such a case. (351)

The king, having clumsily mutilated their persons, shall cause the defilers of other men's wives to be banished from the country. (352)

Since it is through such men that hybridisation of castes is effected; and intermixture of castes is the primal cause of vice which leads to universal destruction. (353)

A man, who is known to have held incests with other men's wives before, if found conversing in solitude with another's wife, should be punished with a fine of the *Prathama Sâhasa* class (*i. e.*, one hundred *Panas*). (354)

But a man, who is not impeached with an act of previous incest, if found conversing in solitude with another's wife for any just reason, shall not be liable to punishment, inasmuch as there is no delinquency on his part. (355)

If one accosts, and converses with another's wife in a lonely wood or forest, or at a holy pool or confiuence of rivers, he shall be guilty of the offence of adultery punishable with a fine of one thousand *Panas*. (356)

Sending presents of scents and flower-garlands to another's wife, cutting jokes with, or embracing her, touching her ornaments and catching hold of her wearing apparel, and eating, or sharing the same bed-stead, with her are acts which are said to constitute *Stri-samgraha* (adultery with another's wife) (357)

A woman who tolerates being touched at het private (*lit.*, untouchable) parts by a man, and a man who tolerates being similarly touched by her are said to be guity of adultery by mutual consent. (358)

A non-Bráhmana (S'udra), found guilty of adultery, shall be punished with death, inasmuch as it is incumbent on men of all the four castes to protect their wives above (all other possessions). (359)

Beggars, professional panegyrists, men initiated in a sacrifice, and artisans (such as cooks, etc.,) may, if not otherwise forbidden, speak with other men's wives (while alone) (360)

Forbidden to speak with another's wife, one must not converse with her. For thus conversing inspite of the warning the offender shall be liable to a fine of one *suvarna* (gold Mohar.) (361)

This rule does not hold good in respect of wives of *Chåranas* (professional actors or musicians), *A'tmopojivins*,* and of those who sell their wive's embraces for money, inasmuch as they deck out their wives for the embrace of others, or lie concealed to help them (to carry on their obnoxious trade.) (362)

For having conversed with the above said females, maid-servants, and false female ascetics (nuns) in solitude, the offender shall be liable to pay a very small fine. (363)

He, who defiles a maid, not amatively disposed, should be punished (with the mutilation of his reproductive organ), but for having visited an amorous maid of his own caste one shall not be liable to corporeal punishment. (364)

For sharing the bed of a man of superior caste, a maid must not pay any fine, for having carnally

* Those who connive at the adultery of their wives for money and live upon the earnings of their infidelity.

known a man of inferior caste she should be kept incarcerated in the house. (365)

For having visited a woman of superior caste a man of inferior caste must be punished with death; but if for having visited a girl of his own caste, the father of the girl asks for a money compensation (lit, duty) he shall have to pay it to the father. (366)

The fingers of him who forcibly ruptures the hymen of a virgin therewith shall be clipped off, and he shall be further liable to pay a fine of six hundred *Panas*. (367)

A man, found guilty of destroying the virginity an amorous girl of his own caste with his fingers, shall have his fingers clipped off; and for checking the recrudescence of the crime, the offender shall be punished with a fine of two hundred *Panas*. (368)

A girl committing the same offence upon another girl shall be punished with stripes and a fine of two hundred *Panas*; she shall be (further liable to pay a compensation of double value (four hundred *Panas*) to the father of (the deflowered girl). (369)

A woman found guilty of committing the same offence on the person of a girl shall have her head shaved and fingers clipped off; and thus mutilated) she shall be perambulated on an ass (round the town). (370)

A wife, who out of pride of personal beauty and opulent relationship, has made transgressions against her husband, the king shall cause to be devoured by ferocious dogs in a well-crowded locality. (371)

The king shall cause the male miscreant (adulterer) to be laid down on a hot bed of iron and the public executioners shall cast logs of wood in the fire-bed till his body is consumed to ashes. (372)

A person, found guilty of adultery within one year of his having been punished for the same offence, shall be liable to double the penalty; for sexually visiting a girl of unconsecrated caste (*Vrâtya*) the penalty is the same as that for carnally knowing a *Chandala* woman. (373)

For having sexually visited a woman, of any twice-born caste, whether protected, or unprotected by her husband, a S'udra shall be punished with the mutilation of his reproductive organ and a confiscation of all his goods and estates in the first named instance (*i.e.*, for knowing an unprotected twice-born woman), and in the last named case he shall pay the penalty with his life and all his (goods and estates) will be escheated to the sovereign. (374)

A Vais'ya, found guilty of carnally knowing a protected Brâhmana woman, shall be punished with imprisonment for one year, after which all his estates will be escheated to the king. A Kshatriya, found guilty of the same offence, shall be punished with a fine of one thousand *Panas* and his head shall be shaved with urine. (375)

A Vais'ya and a Kshatrity found guilty of carnally knowing an unprotected Brâhmana woman shall be respectively liable to pay fived hundred and one thousand *Panas* (to the king.) (376)

Either of them, found guilty of carnal knowledge of a protected Brâhmana woman, shall be punished as a S'udra guilty of the same offence and burnt in a hay fire. (377)

For having forcibly ravished a protected Brâhmana

woman, a Brâhmana shall be punished with a fine of one thousand *Panas*, for having known such a Brâhmana woman with her knowledge and consent he shall be punished with a fine of five hundred *Panas*. (378)

In respect of a Brâhmana a death sentence must be commuted to one of shaving the hair of his head; death-sentences may be passed on members of all other castes. (379)

Let him (king) not kill a Brâhmana even if he be found guilty of all the crimes; he must banish him (Brâhmana) from the realm unhurt and with all his possessions. (380)

A more heinous sin exists not in this world than murdering (killing) a Brâhmana; let not a king even think of such a project in his mind. (381)

If a Vais'ya is found guilty of the carnal knowledge of a protected Kshatriya woman, or if a Kshatriya is found guilty of visiting the bed of a protected Vais'ya woman, either of them must be punished with the penalty laid down for the carnal knowledge of an unprotected Brâhmana woman. (382)

For having visited the bed of a protected Vais'ya or Kshatriya woman a Brâhmana shall be punished with a fine of one thousand *Panas*; a Vais'ya or a Kshatriya, guilty of the carnal knowledge of a protected S'udra woman, shall be fined one thousand *Panas*. (383)

For having carnally known an unprotected Kshatriya woman, a Vais'ya shall be punished with a fine of five hundred *Panas*; a Kshatriya, guilty of the same offence, shall have the hair of his head shaved with (ass's) urine, or he shall pay a fine of five hundred *Panas*. (384)

For having visited the bed of an unprotected Kshatriya, Vais'ya, or S'udra woman, a Brahmana shall be punished with a fine of five hundred *Panas*; for having gone unto a vile caste woman, he shall be liable to a fine of one thousand *Panas*. (385)

The king in whose realm there exists not a thief, a defiler of another's wife, a foul-mouthed person, a robber, or an assaulter attains the region of Indra (the king of the celestials). (386)

The repression of these five kinds (of miscreants) by a king in his own realm grants him suzerainty over his compeers (contemporary sovereigns) and a high fame in this world. (387)

Either of the *Yajamâna* (institutor of a religious ceremony) who unjustly renounces a priest, capable of performing (that sacrifice), or the priest who renounces a *Yajamâna*, not in any way defiled or degraded, should be liable to pay a fine of one hundred *Panas*. (388)

It is not proper (for a man) to desert his mother, father, wife, or son; for having deserted any of them, not in any way degraded, the king shall punish him with a fine of six hundred *Panas*. (389)

In a dispute among Brahmanas regarding the proper interpretation of a procedure of ritual (lit, domestic sacrifice) the king, for the reason of his own wellfare, shall refrain from passing any decisive opinion on the subject. (390)

In such a case the king having properly honoured the Brahmana (disputants), and appeased their anger by conciliatory words must proceed to give the proper interpretation of their duties with the help of (other) Brahmanas (of his court). (391)

In connection with an auspicious rite in which it is necessary to feed twenty Bráhmaṇas, if a Brâhmaṇa feeds others in exclusion of his neighbours and the inmates of his house, he shall be liable to pay a fine of one *Másha* (of silver to the king.) (392)

A *S'rotriya* (*i. e*, *Veda*-knowing) Brâhmaṇa, failing to feed a virtuous *S'rotriya* (neighbour or inmate of his house) on the occasion of a rite of prosperity (*lit.* that which confers progeny and prosperity such as, marriage, etc.) shall give him twice as much food, and a fine of one *Másha* (of gold to the king.) (393)

A blind or lame man, an idiot, one above seventy years of age, and one who does any benefit to a *Veda*-knowing Bráhmaṇa must be exempted from paying any tax (or revenue to the king). (394)

Let the king always do honour to (*i.e.*, provide for) a *S'rotriya*, sick man, invalid, or infant, as well as to the indigent, high-born and the revered. (395)

A washerman must gently wash the clothes on a smooth-board of S'âlmali (Bombax Malabaricum) plank, he must not mix one's clothes with another's, nor give one's clothes to another for use or wearing. (396)

For each ten *Palam* weight of cotton thread given to a weaver, he must return eleven *Palam* weight of manufactured cloth; otherwise he shall be liable to pay a fine of twelve *Panas*. (397)

At toll stations or customs houses, the king shall receive a twentieth part of the profit on the price of an article, determined by men, expert in fixing the prices of commodities. (398)

The king shall confiscate all the goods (estates etc.,) of him, who, out of greed, shall attempt to sell a commodity which is the king's monopoly, or to export commodities which are forbidden to be exported (contra-bands) to foreign countries. (399)

For having avoided the public highway or sold his goods in the night, or given out a lesser number (*i. e.*, a false manifest of) of his goods with a view to defraud the toll duties or customs, one shall be liable to pay a fine eight times the value of the defrauded duties. (400)

In consideration of the distance from which an article has come or to which it shall be despatched, and for which periods must it be kept in stock and what prices it will obtain thereby, and the expenditures to be incurred under these heads the king shall fix the prices of articles of merchandise (401)

At the end of each fifth day, or at the close of each fortnight, the king in the presence of the appraisers of prices and in consideration of their stock in the market shall lay down the prices of commodities. (402)

Weights and measures of trade let the king personally determine and lay down, and let him examine those weights and measures at the end of each six months. (403)

The freight for taking a vehicle across a ferry is one *Pana*, that for taking a load, which can be carried by a man, across a ferry is half a *Pana*, the freight for taking a beast or a woman across a ferry is a quarter *Pana*, and that for taking a man without luggage is one-eighth *Pana* (*lit.* half of the latter amount) (404)

Ferry rates in respect of vehicles, full of goods of merchandise, should be determined according to the preciousness or otherwise of those commodities, those in respect of indigent persons and empty sacks and guny-bags must be very small. (405)

The hire of a boat should be proportionate to the distance of the journey and must be determined in consideration of the nature of the season and the current of the river. No rule exists in determining freights of sea-going vessels. (406)

Pregnant women till during the second month of gestation, sages who have taken the vow of asceticism, Brâhmaṇas, and *Brahmachárins* (religious students) are exempted from paying ferry-tolls. (407)

Whatever loss the passengers of a boat might sustain through the fault of the crew, the crew must make that good out of their respective shares (in freights). (408)

Thus the law relating to boatmen has been set forth; any thing lost in water through the fault of the crew must be made good by them, who are not liable for any thing destroyed by an act of providence. (409)

The king shall cause a Vais'ya (*i.e.* members of the Vais'ya ccste) to carry on trade, money-lending, agriculture and cattle rearing; and a S'udra, to serve the Brâhmanas. (410)

A Bráhmana shall lovingly support a Vais'ya and a Kshatriya, incapable of maintaining themselves, by engaging them in their proper works or professions. (411)

For having compelled an initiated Brâhmana to serve as a servant inspite of his disinclination for such service, a Brâhmana shall be punished by the king with a fine of six hundred *Pánas.* (412)

A S'udra, whether a slave purchased or otherwise, must be employed in service, inasmuch as it is for seving the Brâhmana that he has been created by the self-begott en one. (413)

Even set at liberty by his master, a S'udra can not be liberated from service: service is his vocation by nature; who shall emancipate him from that? (414)

A captive of war, a slave for maintenance, the son of a female slave, one purchased for money, a slave obtained as a present, a hereditary one, and one condemned to slavery for any offence, these are the seven kinds of slave (*lit.*, sources of slavery). (415)

A wife, a son, and a slave can never acquire any property for themselves; whatever they earn go to him to whom they belong. (416)

Let a Brâhmana unhesitatingly appropriate to himself whatever (his) S'udra (slave) has earned, inasmuch as nothing can belong to the latter, he being himself an enjoyable good of the Bráhmana. (417)

Let (the king) assiduously cause the Vais'yas and S'udras faithfully discharge their proper and specific duties, since their non-performance tends to oppress (disturb) the whole world (*i.e.* social economy.) (418)

At the close of his duties, let the king regularly supervise his income, expenditure, treasures and mines, each day. (419)

A king by observing these rules (*lit.* fulfilling these duties) becomes exonerated from all sin and acquires an exalted status (after death). (420)

CHAPTER IX.

I SHALL discourse on the eternal duties of the husband* and wife, leading a virtuous life, as well as on those which are obligatory on them when they live together or apart.* (1)

Men should never give any license to their wives in day and night; by keeping them engaged in commendable pursuits,† they should keep them under their own control. (2)

The father protects her in infancy; the husband, in youth; and sons, in old age; a woman does not deserve independence. (3)

Condemnable is the father who does not marry his daughter at the proper age: condemnable is the husband who does not visit his wife (during her menstrual period‡); and condemnable is the son who does not maintain (*lit* protect) his mother after the demise of her lord. (4)

Women should be especially protected from the slightest of corrupting influences (such as, a bad company etc.,) since an unprotected woman aggrieves the two families (*i.e.*, those of her farher and husband). (5)

---

* KULLUKA states that, the duties of married life, although not falling within the purview of the ordinary legal duties of an individual, have been dealt with in this chapter as such, because their violations are punishable by law as crimes, and the king's coutt has jurisdiction to take cognisance of cases in which the rights or obligations, which these duties entail, are sought to be established or enforced.

† The text has *Vishayeshu cha Sajyantyah*, KULLUKA explains it by *Anishiddheshvapi ruparasādi-Vishayeshu* in not condemnable objects of sight, hearing, etc.

‡ Within eight days of the cessation of her flow.

This (protection of wives) forms the highest duty of the members of all the four social orders. Even weak (*i. e.*, diseased or physically deformed) husbands should endeavour to protect their wives. (6)

By assiduously protecting his wife, a man protects (the purity of his) progeny and family, as well as his character, Self, and virtue. (7)

The husband, by entering (into the body of) the wife, takes birth as the fœtus in her womb, a wife is called Jâyâ (Jenetrix), inasmuch as the husbaed is again born in her. (8)

A wife gives birth to a child similar (in every respect) to the man who impregnates her; hence, for the purity of his progeny, one must assiduously protect his wife. (9)

Wives (*lit.*, women) cannot be kept by force; it is by the application of the following expedients that they can be kept under control. (10)

They should be employed in storing and spending money (*i.e.* in looking after the expenses of the household), in maintaining the cleanliness of their persons and of the house, and in looking after the beddings, wearing apparels, and household furniture. (11)

Imprisoned in the house and closely guarded by their male relations, (bad) women are not sufficiently protected (*i.e.* they can find opportunities to gratify their evil propensities). Women who guard themselves are said to be truly guarded (and protected). (12)

Wine-drinking, evil company, separation from the husband, idle rambling, sleep at the improper time, and residence in another's house are the six factors which tend to defile a woman. (13)

They do not care for the personal beauty or young

age; women only long for sexual intercourses with men, whether they be good-looking or bad looking. (14)

, On account of the germination of erotic fancies in their minds at the mere sight of men, and on account of the inborn absence of affection and innate fickleness of heart, women, though well protected by their husbands, make transgressions against them. (15)

Thus having known their god-given;nature (*lit.*, as created by the creator of universe, Prajapati), let a man protect his wife to the best of his endeavours. (16)

Fondness for ornaments, beds and cushions, intense erotic feelings, anger, crookedness, and scandal are natural to women in the opinion of Manu. (17)

The purificatory rites of women are (*i. e.*, must be performed) withoat the Vediac Mantras; this is the decision of the law code. And for this disqualification of Mantra-less-ness, women are like unto inorganic things. This is the conclusion. (18)

The proneness of women to infidelity has been largely sung in the *Vedas* and *Nigamas*. Now hear what has been said in the *Vedas* regarding the expiation of their incestuous sin. (19)

"Inasmuch as my mother, faithless to her lord, used to stroll about in quest of other men's (embraces,) may my father purify her ovum, defiled by her incests with others)." This (Mantra of the *Veda*) serves as an illustration (of what has been said in the preceding couplet). (20)

For the expiation of the sin which a woman commits by contemplating transgressions against her lord, however slight, this *Mantra* has been enjoined to be employed. (21)

As a river in contact with the sea becomes briny,

so a woman acquires traits of mind and character similar to those of the man she is united with. (22)

Though born of vile castes, AkshamâlÂ, united with Vas'ishtha, and S'ârangi, wedded to Mandapâla, became highly glorified. (23)

These and other women of low origin acquired excellent traits of character through contact with the auspicious mental traits of their respective husbands. (24)

Thus the rule relating to the auspicious living of men and women (husbands and wives) has been laid down; now hear me discourse on the law relating (to the right in children* which is conducive to happiness both in this world and the next. (25)

For conceiving progeny, wives, the lights of households, the repositories of bliss and auspiciousness, should be honoured with presents of apparels and ornaments). No distinction exists between the wife and the goddess of fortune in the house. (26)

Wife is the manifest source of procreation and bringing up of children, and of the performance of the duties of every day life as well.† (27)

Giving birth to children, performance of religious sacrifices *(Agni Hotra,* etc.*)*, nursing, excellent (sweetest) love, and the acquisition of heaven by one and his manes are contingent on his wife. (28)

She, who, pure and controlled in her mind, speech and body, transgresses not her lord, attains to the re-

---

* Whether the son belongs to its natural father, or to the husband of its mother? *(Kim Kshetrino'patyamuta Bijinah).—Kulluka.*

† Such as hospitality to Atithis, and feeding his friends and relations *(Atithi mitra-bhojanadeh.)—Kulluka.*

gion of the husbands *(Patiloka)* and is called chaste by the virtuous. (29)

Through transgressions against her lord, a wife becomes condemnable in this world, takes birth in the womb of a she-jackal in her next existence, and is afflicted with diseases of sin. (30)

Now hear me relate the anecdote regarding the procreation of a son which the great sages of yore had narrated for the good of the universe. (31)

The son belongs to the father, but regarding the denotation of "father" there are two contrary dicta of the *S'ruti* (*i.e.*, *Veda*). Some call the actual progenitor of the son as his father, while others aver that, the man on whose wife the son is begotten is his father. (32)

The woman is said to be like unto a field, and the man is like unto a seed; the origin of all creatures is (in) the union of the seed and the soil. (33)

In some cases the pre-eminence is of the seed,* and in others the dominance is of the soil;† commendable is the offspring where the seed and the soil are equally dominant. (34)

Of the seed and the soil the predominence is said to be of the seed, inasmuch as the births of all created

---

* The birth of Budha illustrates a case of this kind. Soma, without any appointment begat Budha on the person of Ilâ and claimed him as his son in opposition to the lawful husband of his mother.

† Procreation of children on the widows of Vichtravirya by Vyâsa, under an appointment, furnishes an exámple of the pre-eminence of the soil, where the sons of the union, (Pandu and Dhritarashtra) became the lawful sons of the deceased husband of their mother.

things are marked by the (specific) traits of their seeds. (35)

Like the seed, which is sown in a cultivated field in the proper season, is the sprout that germinates therefrom, marked by its (seed's) specific features. (36)

This earth is said to be the eternal womb of all created things; but at no stage of its development a plant is seen to partake of the specific properties of the soil. (37)

Different kinds of seeds, sown in the same field by husbandmen in the proper season, are seen to sprout up in different forms according to the specific natural variations of their species. (38)

Brihi, Salis, Mudga, sesame, kidney beans, garlics and sugar-cane sprout up according to the nature of their seeds. (39)

From the seeds of one kind sprouts of another kind (of vegetables) are not seen to germinate: like sprouts germinate from the like species of seeds. 40.

Hence, a wise, modest, man of sicience and erudition, seeking longevity, must not sow his seeds in another's field (wife). (41)

Men, learned in history, recite a verse on the subject, framed by Vâyu, which forbids men to sow their seeds in other men's wives. (42)

As an arrow, hit by one into the aperature of an arrow on the body of an animal previously shot by another, becomes futile,* so the fruit of the seed, cast by one in the wife of another, does not belong to him. (43)

Historians say that, this earth is called *Prithivi* from the fact of her first being the wife (*i.e.*, enjoyed by) king, Prithu; a field is named after the person who first clears it of the jungle, and a game belongs to him who hits it first. (Hence, a son procreated on another's wife does not belong to his progenitor.) (44)

It is only with his wife and progeny that a man becomes complete. Hence, the wise call the husband and wife as identical. (45)

By sale or separation (abandonment) the husband and wife can not be liberated (severed) from each other; we know this law to have been originally made by the creator of the universe. (46)

Only once can the partition of an estate be made, only once can a girl be given away in marriage, and only once can a thing be gifted. Each of these three things can be made only for once. (47)

As in respect of cows, mares, she-camels, female slaves, she-buffalos, she-goats and ewes the young ones do not belong to their progenitors, so sons begotten on other men's wives do not belong to their natural fathers. (48)

Seed-owners, without fields of their own, who sow their seeds in other men's fields, can never be entitled to the crops raised therefrom. (49)

Even if a bull procreates a hundred calves on another's cows, all those calves shall belong to the owner of the kine; in vain the bull has spent his seed! (50)

Similarly, the seed cast by one in another's field (wife) contributes to the benefit of the owner of the field, the caster of the seed does not obtain the fruits (offspring) thereof. (51)

In the absence of any express agreement between the owner of the field (husband of the woman) and the caster of the seed regarding the right in the fruits (offspring or issues of the union), the fruits shall manifestly belong to the former, inasmuch as in such an instance the womb has a greater preeminence than the seed. (52)

But if there be a previous compact of giving the fruit to the caster of the seed, then both the caster of the seed and the owner of the field (*i.e.*, the husband of the woman) shall be equally entitled to enjoy the fruit (offspring). (53)

If a seed, carried away by the wind or a stream of water, sprouts in another's field, the owner of the field shall have it and not the sower of the seed. (54)

This is the law relating to (the right in the) offspring of a cow, mare, female slave, she-goat, ewe and a female bird. (55)

Thus the synopsis of the law relating (to the relative pre-eminence of) the seed and the womb have been promulgated; now hear me discourse on the duties of women on the failure of issues. (56)

The wife of an elder brother is said to be like a preceptor's or superior's wife unto his younger brother, and the wife of a younger brother is said to be like unto a daughter-in-law to his elder brother. (57)

Except in the case of a failure of issues, an elder, by going unto the wife of his younger brother, or a younger brother, by going unto the wife of an elder brother, even under an appointment, becomes degraded. (58)

In the absence of a son, a woman wishing to obtain a progeny, shall lie down, under an appointment, with a younger brother, or with a *Sapinda* relation, of her husband for the procreation of a son. (59)

A man, appointed to procreate a son on a widow,

shall anoint his person with clarified butter and silently procreate a son on her in the night; but he must not procreate a second son under any circumstances whatsoever. (60)

Men, wise in the knowledge of procreation of children, aver that one with a single child must be regarded as almost sonless; hence, a man (*i.e.*, a *Sapinda* or younger brother of her husband), under an appointment, may procreate two children on a woman. (61)

After the procreation of a son on a widow (by a younger or an elder brother (of her deceased husband) he shall revere or look upon her as a preceptor's wife or a daughter-in-law as the case may be. (62)

An elder brother or a younger brother, who transgresses the rules of appointment out of amorous exuberance, commits the sin of defiling the bed of a daughter-in-law or of a preceptor's wife. (63)

Bráhmaṇas shall never allow a widow of their own to get a son procreated on her by any one under an appointment; by so engaging her one kills the eternal virtue. (64)

Procreation of children by appointment on another's wife *(Niyoga)* has nowhere been mentioned in the *Mantras* of nuptial rites, nor the marriage of a widow has ever been mentioned in the *Sástra*. (65)

This beastly custom, which first prevailed among men during the reign of king Vena, is condemned by the erudite Bráhmaṇas. (66)

That foremost of kings (Vena), having enjoyed the whole earth, with his mind clouded by erotic feelings, introduced this custom (procreation of children under appointment on another's wife) of yore among men which led to the intermixture of castes. (67)

Since that time, he, who has appointed a widow to get a son procreated on her by another man, has been condemeed by the virtuous. (68)

A girl whose betrothed husband has been dead after the betrothal her (deceased) husband's brother shall take (marry) in the following manner. (69)

He, having married her, pure in body and mind and clad in a white cloth, shall visit her once in each month during her menstrual period. (70)

Having married a girl to one, let not a wise man marry her again to another; by so doing a man commits sin. (71)

Even having formally accepted the gift of (*i.e.*, married) a girl, possessed of any inauspicious physical features, diseased, deflowered, or fraudulently given in marriage by ,suppressing a physical deformity, one may abandon her (before the rite of seven steps is gone into). (72)

If a miscreant gives away a faulty girl in marriage without giving out the nature of her defect, the gift of such a miscreant (*i.e.*, the marriage bond of the girl) may be cancelled. (73)

A man of business must go to a foreign county after first having made provisions for the maintenance of his wife; an honest wife may be compelled to take to the evil path in want of a suitable provision. (74)

In the event of her husband having made suitable provisions for her before leaving the country, let her live with the greatest propriety; in the absence of any suoh provision, let her live by plying any commendable art (such as weaving, spinning, etc.) (75)

For eight years a wife shall wait for her husband, absent in a distant country for prosecuting an object of virtue; for six years shall she bide her time for a husband, absent in a distant country for study or for achieving fame, and three years for a husband, absent on a visit to a co-wife in a distant country, (after which she shall go to her lord). (76)

A husband shall wait one year for a hostile wife; after the lapse of a year, if her hostile feelings still continue, he shall take back what he might have given her, and marry a second wife. (77)

Of a wife who slights her husband for his sickness, or for his addiction to wine or gambling, the husband must forswear the bed for three months, and she must not be allowed to use her beddings and ornaments during that period. (78)

But a wife failing to nurse an insane, degraded, sexless or seedless husband, or one afflicted with a sinful disease, is not fit to be abandoned by the husband for that hostile conduct, nor the things which he might have presented to her can be taken back from her. (79)

In the event of one's wife becoming a drunkard or faithless, hostile, invalid, extremely hot-tempered or spend-threft, one shall marry a second wife. (80)

The husband of a sterile woman shall remarry on the eighth, the husband of a wife whose children die in infancy on the tenth, and the husband of a wife who has given birth to daughters only on the eleventh year of their respective marriages, while the husband of a harsh-tongued wife may remarry without the least delay.* (81)

---

* Such a harsh tongued wife, if she has given birth to a male child, may be abandoned by the husband, but he will not be competent, in pursuance of a prohibition by A'pastambha, to marry during her life-time, inasmuch as by giving birth to a son she

If a wife of good conduct, who is attached to the good of her lord, happens to be afflicted with (an incurable) disease, let her husband marry again with her consent; but he must not insult (or neglect) her under any circumstances whatsoever. (82)

But if the first wife of a remarried husband (attempts to) leave his house out of anger, he must either keep her imprisoned (in the house) or send her to her father's family for good. (83)

The wife (of one other than a Brâhmaṇa), who, being prohibited to drink wine in a marriage-festival, drinks it, or attends a public dancing party, should be punished with a fine of six *Krishnalas*. (84)

If members of twice-born castes happen to marry wives of other castes, their precedence, honour, and dwelling-houses should be according to the superiority of their castes. (85)

A wife belonging to his own caste must attend to the physical comforts of a man having many wives and shall be his cohort in practising virtues (performing religious rites): a wife who is not of the same caste with her husband must never do these things. (86)

He, who, having a wife of his own caste, causes, out of foolishness, a wife of another caste to perform these duties, is said to be by the ancient sages like unto a *Brâhmana Chandala* (*i.e.*, a son begotten by a S'udra on a Brâhmaṇa woman). (87)

A girl, even before having attained the proper age of marriage, should be duly married to a handsome, qualified husband of her own caste, (if such an opportunity occurs). (88)

---

has acquired the privileges of a *Dharma Patni* (indefesible right of wifehood)

Rather should a girl, who has attained puberty, stay unmarried in her father's house for her whole life-time than she should be wedded to a non-eligible (*lit.* disqualified) husband, for any consideration whatsoever. (89)

A girl, who has attained puberty, shall wait (unmarried in her father's house) for three years (after the appearance of her first flow); after that, she shall take a husband of her own caste and status (without waiting for the consent of her guardians.) (90)

For taking a husband herself, a girl, not given away in marriage at the proper time by her father, acquires no demerit, nor does the man who takes her as his wife. (91)

A girl, who through her own endeavours has taken a husband, must not take away the ornaments, etc., given to her by her father, mother or brother, inasmuch as by so doing she will be guilty of theft. (92)

For having married a girl who has attained her puberty, one must not pay any money to her father, inasmuch as for having impeded conception during the menstrual period his right of fatherhood (*Juris peters*) in the girl has been extinguished. (93)

Let a man of thirty years marry an amiable girl of twelve years of age, or a man of twenty-four years marry a girl of eight years of age.* One may marry

---

* This couplet does not lay down the minimum age limit of marriage, but enjoins that the highest desparity of age allowable between the husband and wife. Under no circumstances, the age of the wife should be less than one-third of that of the husband.

earlier, if delay be detrimental to one's religious duty.* (94)

Through the ordaination of the gods one obtains a wife and never by his own willing.† Let him always maintain such a virtuous wife and (thereby) do the pleasure of the gods. (95)

Women are created to conceive pregnancies, and men are created to impregnate women. Hence, like the act of procreation, the religious duties of the husband and wife are correlated.‡ This is said in the *Veda*. (96)

If the (betrothed husband) of a girl happens to die after he has paid the price for her hand (*lit.* marriage duty) to her guardian, she should be married to a younger brother of the deceased, if she approves (of such a marriage). (97)

Even a S'udra must not take any price (*lit.* duty or pecuniary consideration) for the hands of his daughter when giving her away in marriage. Such acceptance of money constitutes a sale of the girl in disguise. (98)

Honest men of yore, never did, not the virtuous men at the present do marry a girl to another after having agreed to marry her to one. (99)

---

* As in the case of a Brâhmana who has finished his *Vedaic* study before the age of twenty-four and thus stands under the obligation of settling in life as a house-holder.—*Kulluka.*

† The gods such as Bhaga, Aryaman (the presiding deity of day) and Savita (the sun-god *lit.* impeller of the universe) of mighty intellect have given me a wife to discharge the duties of the household (*Bhagorvamà Savità Purandhi Mahyam Vadhurgàrhapatyàya*, etc., S'ruti).

‡ The wife must be the companion of the husband in doing religious sacrifices: "clad in a silk cloth, let the wife, and the husband kindle the sacred fire (*Kshaume Vasànàvagninàdadhiyàtàm*,—S'ruti).

Even in my past existences never did I hear of the disguised sale of a girl in the form of a marriage on the acceptance of money (by her father.) (001)

There should be mutual fidelity (between the husband and wife) till death. This should be known as the primary duty of the husband and wife in brief. (101)

A married man and woman should always so endeavour as not to live separate from, and make transgressions against, each other. (102)

Thus the loving duties of the husband and wife towards each other, as well as those, which are obligatory (on them) for the procreation of sons in their absence, have been formulated; now hear me discourse on the law relating to the division of paternal estates. (103)

After the demise of their father or mother, let the brothers congregate and equally partition the paternal (or maternal) estate among themselves: during his (or her) life-time they are not the lords thereof (*i.e.*, have no right therein.)* (104)

[If the brothers wish to live undivided], let the eldest one take the whole of the paternal estate, and the rest (*i.e*, the other brothers) shall depend upon (obtain from) him for their maintenance as they did on their father (before). (105)

The moment one's eldest born comes into being one becomes possessed of a son and discharges the

---

* But in a paternal estate partitioned by the father among his sons during his life-time the sons have all rights of ownership.—Cf.

If the father voluntarily makes a division of his estate, let him partition it among his sons (*Vibhâgancha pitá Kuryát ichchhayá Vibhajet Sután*).—*Yájnavalkya.*

debt to his manes (*Pitris*); hence the eldest son is entitled to receive the entire (paternal estate.) (106)

He (*i.e.*, the eldest son) on whose birth the debt (to the manes) is discharged and the father obtains immortality is called the son according to virtue (*Dharma-putra*), the rest are sons of (*i.e.*, begotten in) lust. (107)

Like a father must the eldest brother maintain his younger brothers, and the younger brothers must live in obedience to him as to their father. (108)

Inasmuch as the eldest brother can exalt the family (by his noble conduct), or bring ruin upon it (by setting a bad example to his youngers), the eldest brother is the most revered; and the virtuous younger brothers should not condemn their eldest brother. (109)

The eldest brother, who stands unto his youngers as their father or mother, is like a father or mother unto them; failing to discharge these duties, him they should respect as a friend relation). (110)

Thus they (brothers) should live undivided; or seeking the furtherance of virtue,* they should be separate and separately perform the (five great daily house-hold) sacrifices. (111)

A twentieth part of the paternal property, together with the best of articles is the portion of the eldest son, a fortieth part (of the paternal estate) forms the portion of the second son, and an eighieth part (of the

* Cf. Brihaspati—Of brothers living in commensality the rite of worshipping the manes, Brahmanas and gods should be one (and joint); living separate, each of them should perform these rites in his separate house: *Eka pákena vasatám pitridevadvijá rchanam; Ekam bhabet bibhaktánám tadeva syád grihe grihe.)*

paternal estate) forms the portion of the youngest son.* (112)

The portions which should fall to the eldest and youngest sons have been laid down; sons intermediate between them should all have the portion of the second son (*i.e.*, a fortieth part of the whole paternal estate. (113)

The eldest son† shall take the best one of the articles (left by the father), as well as the best one of each ten animals (such as, cows‡ etc.) (114)

Among sons equally discharging the ten religious duties of (*Vediac* study, etc., *i.e.*, equally qualified) the eldest one shall obtain no (preferential) excess share, but a little in excess should be given to him for his honour. (115)

After the division of the paternal state in the aforesaid manner, the brothers shall equally apportion the residue among themselves; or in the alternative, they shall partition it in the manner following. (116)

The eldest son shall take one share and one share in addition thereto (*i.e.* two shares,) the second son shall take one and a half share, and the other younger sons shall take one share each. This is the decision of Law. (117)

The brothers shall separately give quarter parts out of their respective shares to their unmarried sisters;

---

* The residue of the estate should be equally divided among them (*Avashishtam dhanam Samam Kritvà vibhajaniyam*) *Kulluka.*

† In the event of the eldest son being possessed of excellent qualifications and the other sons being devoid of them.—*Kulluka*

‡ Cf. *Dasáta Pas'unám* (the best one of each ten animals) *Gautamá.*

and failing to give them (sisters) such shares, they shall become degraded in life. (118)

A goat, a lamb, or an animal with unbi-furcated hoofs, remaing odd after the division, shall fall to the share of the eldest son. (119)

A son, begotten by a younger brother on the wife of his eldest brother under an appointment, shall have an equal share with his uncles (at the time of the division of the paternal estate among them).* This is the decision of Law. (120)

A son begotten on the wife of the eldest brother can not be lawfully called the son of the eldest brother, inasmuch as the preeminence is of the progenitor in respect of the procreation of a child. Hence, he should be discarded.† (121)

If a doubt arises as to how shall the division of the paternal estate be made, if the eldest son is begotten on the youngest wife, and the youngest son is begotten on the eldest wife of a man :— (122)

The son of the eldest wife (in such a case) shall take the best bull as his preferential share (although he is the youngest son of his father), and the sons of other co-wives, though they be his elders, shall take comparatively inferior bullocks according to the juniority of their respective mothers. (123)

The eldest son, begotten on the eldest wife, shall take fifteen cows and one bullock (as his share), and the other sons shall take according to the precedence of their respective mothers. This is the decision. (124)

---

* He must not claim an excess share under the husband of his mother, the eldest son of his grandfather.

† *i.e.* he can not claim an excess or additional share under the husband of his mother as the lawfully begotten son of the eldest brother.

The seniority among sons of co-wives of the same caste is said to be according to their births, and not according to the priority of their respective mothers. (125)

[The invocation of Indra in the Agnishtoma sacrifice] by the *Mantra*, known as *Sva brâhmana*, should be made by the eldest brother; and in respect of twin-born sons, the one, that is first delivered of the womb, should be regarded as the elder. (126)

If a sonless man marries his daughter to another on the stipulation that, "sons born of her womb shall do my *S'râddhas* and offer me oblations," that daughter is called a *Putrikâ*. (127)

In this way *Putrikâ* (compacts) were created of yore for the increase of his progeny by the patriarch (*lit*, lord of creatures) Daksha himself. (128

Decked with ornaments, ten (of his daughters) he complacently gave to Dharma (the god of virtue); thirteen to Kas'yapa; and twenty seven, to king Soma. (129)

One's Self is identical with his son, and a daughter is like unto a son: in the presence of one's (putrikâ) daughter, who is identical with his self, who else shall take his property (*lit.* wealth)? (130)

The mother's dowry shall be the portion of (her) daughter, and his daughter's son shall take the entire estate of a sonless man. (131)

(His) daughter's son shall take the entire estate of a sonless father, and he (*i.e.* daughter's son) shall offer two oblations (*Pindas*), one to his (own deceased) father, and another to (his deceased) mother's father. (132)

Virtually there exists no difference between a son's son and a daughter's son in this world, both their respective father and mother have originated from the body of one and the same man. (133)

In the event of the birth of one's son after the creation of the *Putriká* (compact), that son and the son of the *Putriká* daughter shall have equal shares in his estate, in asmuch as a female can not have the privileges of) eldest-born-ship. (134)

On the death of a sonless *Putriká* daughter, her husband shall unhesitatingly take the entire estate left by her (*i.e.*, her father shall have no right in her property on the strength of that *Putriká* compact.) (135)

By the son, whom one's daughter, whether married with or without the *Putrika* compact, gives birth to, her father becomes possessed of a son; such a daughter's son shall offer (*S'ráddha)* oblations to her (deceased, sonless), mother's father, and take (inherit) his estate. (136)

By a son one conquers the worlds, by a son's son one attains ths infinite, by the son of a son's son one attains the region of the sun. (137)

Since a son succours his father from the hell called *Put*; hence, the self-begotten one (Brahmá) has called a son, *Putra* (*lit*, deliverer from the hell of *Put*.) (138)

No distinction is found between a son's son and a daughter's son in this world, in asmuch as a daughter's son, like a son's son, can succour a man from hell. (139)

The son of a *Putriká* daughter shall first offer an oblation (*Pinda*) to his (deceased) mother, then to his mother's father, and then to her father's father. (140)

A *Dattaka* (adopted) son, possessed of all commendable qualifications, though born of another

Gotra (family), shall take the estate of his putative father.* (141)

An adopted son must not take the property or *Gotra* (family title) of his natural father. The *Pinda* follows the estate and the property, ;† hence, an adopted son must not offer *S'râddhas* unto his natural father. (142)

The son, begotten on a girl without an appointment from her guardians, and the son, begotten on a woman with a son by her husband's younger brother even under an appointment, shall have no shares (in the paternal property), inasmuchas they are bastards, and offspring of lust. (143)

A son, begotten on a woman under an appointment but not conformably to the rules, shall not be competent to inherit (his) ancestral property, inasmuchas he has been procreated by a degraded person. (144)

A son, begotten on one's wife by another under an appointment, shall take an equal share in the estate (left by him) like a son born of his own loins; in asmuch as the seed virtually belongs to the owner of the field (husband of the woman) in such a case, and the son thus begotten is his legitimate son. (145)

---

* *Ekevaurasah putrah pitrasya Vasunah prabhuh* (only the son of one's own loins, is the lord of (heir to) the whole ancestral estate. KULLUKA quotes the preceding maxim and says that, in the presence of a son of one's own loins his adapted son is not entitled to his whole property but must take a sixth part thereof as his own share like a Kshetraja son. GOVINDARAJA, on the other hand, holds that, one's adapted son is heir to the whole estate left by him even in the presence of a son of his loins, if any.

† A man obtains (is heir to) the wealth and family title (Gotra) of him unto him he offers *S'râddha* oblations *(Pindas)*.

He who maintains the estate and widow of a deceased elder brother shall procreate a son on the person of that widow and give his (deceased brother's) estate to the son, thus begotten. (146)

The son of her, who, even under an appointment from her guardians gets him procreated on herself by the younger brother of her deceased husband, or by any (of his male *Sapinda* relations) out of lust,* is called lust-begotten and invalidly procreated; such a son shall take no share in (the paternal estate). (147)

This should be understood as the law relating to the division (of the paternal property) among uterine brothers of the same caste, now hear me expound the law relating to the division (of the paternal property) among sons begotten by one and the same man on women of different castes. (148)

If a Brâhmana has had wives belonging to the four (different) castes in the order of their enumeration, the division of the estate among sons of those wives should be made conformably to the following rule. (149)

One tiller, a cow, a bull, the house (or room), ornaments and the best portion of other estates shall go to the son of the Brâhmaṇa wife as his (*Uddhâra*) preferential share. (150)

Out of the remaining estate three parts shall go to the Brâhmaṇa son, two to the Kshatriya son, one and a half part to the Vais'ya son, and one part to the S'udra son. (151)

---

* Cp. Narada *Mukhàt mukhum pariharan gátrairgàtrànyasamspris'an; Kule tadavasheshecha santánárthham na kàmata iti.* without touching her face and limbs with his face and limbs, let him procreate a son (on her) for progeny and not out of lust, etc.

[Or instead of giving a preferential share (excess) to the Brâhmaṇa son], let the-versed-in law divide the whole estate into ten (equal parts, and allot them (to the sons) in the following lawful manner :—(152)

Let the Brâhmaṇa (son) take four (such) shares ; the Kshatriya (son), three ; the Vais'ya (son), two ; and the S'udra (son), one. (153)

But let him not in consideration of virtue give more than a tenth share to his S'udra son, whether he be a good son or otherwise. (154)

The son of a Brâhmaṇ, Kshatriya, or Vais'ya by a S'udra wife is not entitled to take any share in his property ; whatever his father will give shall be the portion of (such a S'udra son).* (155)

Of sons of twice-born ones by wives of their own castes, let the younger sons give preferential shares to their (respective) eldest brothers and then equally divide the estate among themselves. (156)

A S'udra is not competent to marry any other wife than one of his own caste, and sons begotten on her, even if they number a hundred, shall take equal shares (in their paternal property). (157)

Of the twelve kinds of sons of men, as said (recognised) by the self begotten Manu, six are heirs and *Bandhus*, and six are neither heirs nor *Bandhus*. (158)

The *Aurasa* (a son of one's own loins), *Kshetreja* (a son procreated on one's wife or widow by another), *Datta* (adopted son), *Kritrima* (filiated son), *Gudhotpanna* (a son secretly procreated on one's wife) and

* This is not contradictory to provisions laid down in the preceding verses (151, 153 and 154). KULLUKA says that, this rule shall hold good in respect of sons of twice-born ones by S'udra women who are not their married wives.

Apaviddha (taken and adopted) these are the six sons who are both heirs and *Bandhus*. (159)

Six sons (such as), *Kâninah*, *Sahodah*, *Kritah*, *Paunarbhava*, *Svyamdatta*, and *S'audra* (son by a S'udra wife) are no heirs (to their paternal property), although they are *Bandhus* (*i.e.*, competent to offer libations of water etc., to their fictitious, deceased father.)* (160)

Disastrous is the result of attempting to cross over the darkness of death with the help of a bad son like unto that of sailing across a river with a badly made raft.† (161)

Though one's *Kshetraja* son and a son of his own loins are both heirs to one and the same property (*i.e.*, to the estate left by him), yet each of them shall

---

* The text has *Shadadàyàdabàndhavàh*. MEDHATITHI explains it by "*Shadadàyàd abándhavàh*" in as much as these six sons are not competent to inherit the estate of their deceased father, they are *abándhavàh*, *i. e.* not competent to offer libations of water, etc. to his spirit. Baudháyana, however, confirms our view of interpretation and asserts that, although these six sons are not heirs, they are not disqualified from offering water etc., to the spirit of their deceased father by fiction; and hence, they are *Bandhus*.

Cf. *Kâninancha Sahodancha Kritam paunarbhavam tathà; Svayamdattam Nishâdancha Gotrabàjah prachakshate*. Sons such as, *Kànina*, *Sahoda*, *Kreeta*, *Paunarbhava*, *Svyamdatta* and *Nishàda* (son of a Brahman by a S'udra wife) partake of the *gotras* of their fathers, *i.e.* they are competent to do the water-rite etc. to his spirit.

† A son of inferior status such as, a *Kshetraja* son (*i.e.* a son begotten on one's wife by another under an appointment), like a foolish or illiterate son of one's own loins, fails to do the fullest spiritual benefit to the spirit of his fictitious father.

take the estate of his own natural father, and no other.* (162)

Only the son of one's own loins is the owner of (heir to) the paternal estate; with a view to create no hardship on them, let him give maintenance to other sons (of inferior status. (163)

The son of one's own seed, while dividing the paternal estate, shall give a fifth or sixth part thereout to the *Kshetraja* son (of his father) as his share. (164)

One's *Kshetraja* and *Aurasa* (son of his own loins) sons are heirs to (*lit.* sharers of) the paternal estate; of the ten remaining (kinds of) sons (such as, the *Dattaka* etc.,) who share the *Gotra* of their father, each succeeding one shall take a share in (*i.e.*, inherit) the paternal property in the absence of one immediately preceding him in the list of enumeration. (165)

A son begotten by a man himself on a lawfully married wife of his own caste should be known as his *Aurasa* (son), the foremost of sons in respect of status or pre-eminence. (166)

A son procreated on the wife of a sick or impotent person or on the widow of a deceased individual under an appointment by another, is called a *Kshetraja* or

---

* In the light of the dictum of Yajna-Valkya, "Virtually, he is the heir, and shall offer *Pindas* to both of them," *Ubhayorapyasau rikthee pinda-dâtâcha dharmatah.*

The couplet contempletes the case where after the procreation of a son on one's wife by another under an appointment, one of his own loins is born. Both MEDHATITHI and GOVINDARAJA explain *Aurasam* in the couplet by a son procreated by one on another's wife without an appointment, which is manifestly absurd, inasmuch as such a son is not competent to take a share in his estate.

Talpaja (procreated in the bed of) son (of that sick, impotent or deceased person.) (167)

The son whom his (natural) father or mother gladly gives to one of his own caste during the distress of his son-less-ness (*i e.* gives him to be filiated by one on the failure of one's issue), by consecrating him with water, is called a *Dattaka* or *Datrima*) son. (168)

The son whom a knower of merits and demerits* takes out of his own caste and entrusts him with the duties of a son is called a *Kritrima* (*lit* artificial one. (169)

The son who is begotten on one's wife in his own house by an unknown man is called a *Gudhotpanna* (secretly born) one; as a son, he belongs to him in whose bed he is procreated. (170)

The son, who deserted by his parents, or given by either of them is adopted as such by one, is called an *apaviddha* son to the latter. (171)

The son who, is secretly procreated on one's wife before her marriage in her father's house is called his *Kânina* son, the offspring of the girl whom he has married. (172)

The man who marries a chaste wife, either with or without the patent signs of pregnancy, is said to be the father of that *Sahoda* (*lit.*, got with the marriage) son, born in the womb at the time of the marriage. (173)

The son, whom one buys for filiation from his parents, is said to be his *Kreeta* (purchased) son, whether he be of his own caste or otherwise.* (164)

---

* According to Yajnavalkya all these filiated sons must be of the same caste with their putative fathers. *(Svajâtiyeshvayam prokta stanayeshu mayà vidhih).* According to Manu, all kinds

The son, whom one's widow, or deserted wife voluntarily gets procreated on her person by her second husband, is said to be the *Paunarbhava (lit*, the son of a remarried woman) son of the latter. (175)

If that wife, with unruptured hymen, takes another husband,then let the second husband lawfully marry her again ; similarly if a wife, after having deserted the husband of her girlhood and known another man, returns to her husband of girlhood, then let that first husband lawfully marry her again. (176)

The son, who in the absence of his natural parents, or being deserted by them without any reason, gives himself up to a man as his son, is said to be the *Svayamdatta* (self-given) son of the latter. (177)

The son whom a Brâhmaṇa procreates out of lust on his S'udra wife is like unto a corpse (S'ava) even when alive (párayana,) and is accordingly called a *Párasâva* (*lit*, a living corpse). (178)

The son of a S'udra by a slave girl, or by the wife of a male slave, shall take an equal share in his estate with the sons of his married wives, if he (the father) so desires it. This is the decision of law. (179)

The sages have enumerated (recognised) these eleven kinds of sons such as, the *Kshetraja* etc., as proxies of the *aurasa* son to guard against the extinction of the rites of *Sráddha*, etc. (180)

Excepting the Kshetreja son, (sons, procreated by other men's seeds (on one's wife) and incidentally mentioned in connection herewith, should be regarded

---

of filiated sons, excepting the one called *Kreeta* (purchased), must be of the same caste with their putative fathers.

as the sons of those from whose seeds they have originated, and of no other.* (181)

If one among several uterine brothers gets a son, by that son all of them shall be possessed of a son. This is what Manu has said on the subject. (182)

Of several co-wives, if one of them gets a son, then by that son all of them will be possessed of a son. This is what Manu has said. (183)

In the absence of a son of superior status, one of the immediately inferior status shall be entitled to (the paternal property; of several sons of equal or similar status each shall have a share (in the paternal) property. (184)

Sons shall take (inherit) the property of their father, and not his (*i. e.* father's uterine) brothers or ancestors (grand-father etc.,) shall inherit his property; but the father shall take (inherit) the property of a son-less son,† and in his (father's) absence the brothers of the son shall take (his property. (185)

Let a man do the water-rite and offer oblations to his three ancestors (*i.e.* father, grand-father and great grand-father), no *Sapinda* relation-ship exists between the offerer of such oblations and his fifth ancestor (*i.e.* great great grand-father.) (186.

Of the *Sapinda*-relations, one nearest to the deceased shall inherit the property (in exclusion of one more

---

* As the wise use oil as a substitute for clarified butter, so these eleven kinds of sons are only proxies for *Aurasa* and *Putrika* ones. *Ajyam Vinà yathà tailam Sadbhi pratinidhi Kritam, Tathaikàdas'a putràstu putrikaurasayorvinà Briddha Brihaspati.*

† *i. e.* of a son, dead without leaving a wife, daughter, or a son of any kind.

remote; in the absence of one's *Sapindas* one's *Samâno-dakas* shall inherit his property, and in the absence of a *Samânodaka* his preceptor, and in the absence of a preceptor his disciple (shall inherit his property.)* (187)

---

* In the absence of a son of any of the eleven kinds the line of succession shall be as follows: widow of the deceased, in her absence the *Aputrikà* daughter, in her absence the father or mother of the deceased, in their absence the uterine brothers, in their absence their sons, in their absence the father's mother, in the absence of the sons of the grand father, then the sons of the great-grand father, in their absence Samanodakas, in their absence his disciple.

MEDHATITHI says that, a widow is disqualified from inheriting the estate of her deceased husband, but the following express provisions of the several ancient law codes will serve to conclusively demonstrate the error of his view. 187

यदाह याज्ञवल्क्यः ।

पत्नी दुहितरश्चैव पितरौ भ्रातरस्तथा ।
तत्सुतोगोत्रजोबन्धुः शिष्यः सब्रह्मचारिणः ।
एषामभावे पूर्वस्य धनभागुत्तरोत्तरः ।
स्वर्यातस्य ह्यपुत्रस्य सर्ववर्णेष्वयं विधिः ।

बृहस्पतिरप्याह ।

आम्नाये स्मृतितन्त्रे च लोकाचारे च सूरिभिः ।
शरीरार्द्धं स्मृता जाया पुण्यापुण्य फले समा ।
यस्य नोपरता भार्य्या देहार्द्धं तस्य जीवति ।
जीवत्यर्द्धशरीरे तु कथमन्यः स्वमाप्नुयात् ।
सकुल्यैर्विद्यमानैस्तु पितृमातृसनाभिभिः ।
अपुत्रस्य प्रमीतस्य पत्नी तद्भागहारिणी ।

पूर्वप्रणीताग्निहोत्रं मृते भर्त्तरि तद्धनम् ।
विन्देत् पतिव्रता नारी धर्म्म एष सनातनः ।
जङ्गमं स्थावरं हेम कुप्यं धान्यमथाम्बरम् ।
आदाय दापयेच्छ्राद्धं मासषाण्मासिकादिकम् ।
पितृव्यगुरुदौहित्रान् भर्त्तृस्वस्रीयमातुलान् ।
पूजयेत् कव्यपूर्त्ताभ्यां वृद्धानाथातिथीन् स्त्रियः ।
तत्सपिण्डाबान्धवा वा ये तस्याः परिपन्थिनः ।
हिंस्युर्धनानि तान् राजा चौरदण्डेन शासयेत् ।

वृद्धमनुः ।

अपुत्रा शयनं भर्त्तुः पालयन्ती व्रते स्थिता ।
पत्न्येव दद्यात्तत् पिण्डं कृत्स्नमर्थं लभेत च ।

Wife (widow), daughters, father, mother, brothers, their sons *Gotraja* (of the same family), *Bandhus*, disciple and Brahmacharins of the same school, each succeeding one is heir in the absence of the person immediately preceding him in the order of enumeration—This is the law in respect of the inheritence to the property of a sonless deceased person of whatsoever caste.

Jàjnavalkya

In the Vedas, Smritis, and Tantras as well as in common parlance of the world the wise men call the wife the half of her husband.

He who has left a widow surviving him has got the half of his body verily alive, and when half of his body is alive, who else shall take his property ? * * *

The king should punish as thieves, the Sapinda relations of her deceased husband, attempting to rob her inheritance, (her husband's estate) or to oust her thereof.

Brihaspati.

A chaste widow, self-controlled and preserving the sanctity of the bed of her deceased husband, shall offer him oblations and take his entire estate.

Briddha Manu

In the absence of all these relations, Brâhmaṇas, well-versed in the three *Vedas*, pure, and with their senses fully controlled, shall take (the) estate, whereby virtue will not be impaired. (188)

Unacceptable (*i.e.*, uninheritable) is the estate of a Brâhmaṇa by the king under all circumstances; on the failure of all these heirs (successors), let the king take the estate of a deceased person of whatsoever other caste. (189)

Let the widow of a deceased, sonless man get a son procreated on her person by a man of her husband's *Gotra* (*i.e.*, his younger brother, or a *Sapinda* relation), and let the entire estate of that deceased person be invested in that son. (190)

Of two sons, begotten on the same woman by two different men, contending for the paternal estate, let either of them take the property left by his own (natural) father and no other. (191)

On the death of their mother, let all the uterine brothers and their unmarried sisters equally partition the maternal estate among themselves, and let them give quarter parts of their respective shares to their married sisters.

To the (unmarried) daughters of these (married) daughters should be lovingly given out of the estate of their (deceased) grand-mother (*i e.*, mother's mother) a little as worthy of each of them. (193)

Presents given to a woman before the nuptial fire (*Adhyagni*), those given to her at the time of her going to her husband's family from her father's house (*Adhyavâhanikam*), those given to her on happy rites (*lit.* ceremonies of gladness), and those respectively given to her by her father, mother and brother form the six kinds of *Stridhanam* (*lit.* woman's property) (194)

Estates, given to her after her marriage by her parents, husband's parents, and relations (*Anvádheyam*) as well as those given to her by her husband out of love, let her sons divide among themselves, if she happens to die in the life-time of her husband. (195)

Estates received by the wife in the *Bráhma, Daiva, A'rsha, Gándharva,* or *Prájápatya* form of marriage (*i.e.*, the six kinds of *Stridhanam*) her husband shall take, if she dies sonless in his life-time. (196)

Whatever property is given to a woman in the *A'sura*, etc., forms of marriage, her mother, and (in her absence), her father shall take, if she dies sonless in her or his life-time. (197)

Any thing given to his co-wives (of different castes) by her father, the daughter of his Bráhmaṇa wife shall take ; and in her absence, her son. (198)

Out of the estate jointly belonging to many of their relations, wives shall not be competent to create their *Stridhanas*, nor out of the estates of their respective husbands without their consent ; (otherwise the estates shall not be regarded as (*Stridhanas*). (199)

The ornaments which a woman has worn during the life-time of her husband his heirs shall not take ; by so-doing they shall be degraded. (200)

A eunuch, a degraded person, a born blind or deaf man, an idiot, or those devoid of any organ, shall not take any share in the paternal property. (201)

But ample and adequate maintenances should be given to them according to the resources of the estate ; a non-giver of such maintenances shall be degraded in life. (202)

But if these eunuchs, etc., ever feel inclined to marry (*i.e.*, get rid of their sexual incapacities), sons begotten by them (on their wives) shall have shares in the paternal property. (203)

After the demise of their father, however small a property the undivided eldest brother may acquire, the educated youngest brother shall take a share therein. (204)

In the property acquired by the exertions of the illiterate younger brothers, even if that be not the paternal estate, all of them shall have equal shares. This is the decision. (205)

The wealth which one's acquires by his skill or knowledge (*Vidyâ-dhanam*),* the wealth which one obtains from his friends (*Maitrya-dhanam*), the wealth which one obtains on his marriage, and the wealth which one obtains as a present of honour on the occasion of a *Madhuparka* (offering of a cup of honey) shall be exclusively his own. (206)

If a brother, capable of earning money (*lit.* wealth) by his own skill or exertion,† does not wish to take his share in the paternal estate, then his other brothers shall give him something for his maintenance out of his

---

* *Vidyâdhanam*—Kâtyâyana explains it by the wealth which one acquires by his knowledge acquired from another by staying in the house and eating the food of the latter. The wealth which one acquires hy such knowledge can not be partitioned. *Para bhakta pradànena pràptá vidyà yadànyatah, tayà práptamcha vidhinà vidyà-pràptam taduchyate. Upanyasti cha Yallabdham Vidyayà panipurvakam Vidyà dhanantu tadvidyát vibhàgena vibhàjyate.*

† Such as by entering the king's service, etc., (*Ràjánugamanàdi Karmanà*)—*Kulluka.*

own share, make him separate, and divide the residue among themselves.* (207)

Whatever one has earned by his own labour without impairing (*lit.* destroying) the paternal estate, one may not give a share of that self-acquired property to another, if he so desires it. (208)

A son, who has managed to recover an ancestral property which his father had failed to do in his life-time, must not divide the same among his own brothers; if he does not so desire it. (209)

Divided brothers, if after having lived jointly (*i.e.* joint in food and funds) for a while, again wish to partition their estate, they shall partition it equally among themselves; in such a case there exists no preferential (excess) share for the eldest brother. (210)

Of brothers, some of whom, whether the eldest or the youngest, are absent at the time of the division of the estate, the shares of the absent brothers therein will not be extinguished for their absence. (211)

His uterine brothers shall congregate and divide such shares (of their dead, absent, or ascetic brothers), among themselves,† and the joint and undivided (step) brothers and uterine sisters shall divide such shares among them. (212)

The eldest brother, who, out of greed, deprives his younger brothers (of their paternal property) is not worthy of the honour of eldest-born-ship, has no right

---

* The sons of such a separate brother shall not claim any share in the paternal property, to which he has voluntarily relinquished his right.—*Kulluka.*

† In the absence of a son, wife, daughter, father or mother of the absent or defunct brother.

to claim the preferential (excess) share of the eldest-born, and deserves to be punished by the king. (213)

Brothers, addicted to vices, shall have no shares (in the paternal estate); the eldest brother, without giving their shares to his younger brothers, must not make any exclusive property of his own out of the paternal estate. (214)

If the brothers live undivided with their father and all earn money, then at the division of the estate the father must not give an excess share to any of them. (215)

A son born after the partition of his paternal estate shall have his share therein; if the brother live undivided, he shall obtain his share from the undivided brothers. (216)

The estate of an unmarried son, deceased without an issue, shall go to his mother; in the absence of the mother, his father's mother shall get the same. (217)

After the due division of the paternal estate, if any debt or assets of the father be found out, then let the brothers equally divide the same among themselves. (218)

Clothes, leaves, ornaments, articles of confectionary *(Kritânnam)*, slave girls, priests, and pasture grounds are said to be indivisible. (219)

Thus I have described to you (the law relating to) the division of property and the procedure of (procreating) *Kshetreja* sons, etc; now hear me discourse on the law (for the prevention of) gambling with dice (*Dyutam*). (220)

Let a king banish gambling with dice (*Dyutam*) and betting on fighting animals (*Samâhvaya*) from his realm; both these (vices) tend to destroy the kingdom of a sovereign. (221)

Gambling with dice, or betting on fighting animals is a theft, openly committed; the king should always endeavour to repress these two (crimes). (222)

Gambling with inanimate things (such as dice, rods, etc.,) is called *Dyutam*; betting on (fighting) animals is called *Samâhvaya*. (223)

All of them, who engage themselves, or cause others to engage in gambling with dice, or in betting on fighting animals, the king shall kill, as well as those *Sudras* who wear the insignias of Brâhmanas (224)

The king shall speedily banish from his realm gamblers, street-dancers and singers, men of cruel deeds, revilers of the Vedas, miscreants, and wine-brewers. (225)

By staying in the realm, these (miscreants), who are thieves in disguise, daily cheat the honest subjects of the king (of their earnings), and thus prove a source of torment to them. (226)

Gambling has been known to create great enmities of yore; hence, a wise man must not gamble with dice even out of fun or sport. (227)

On him, who shall openly or secretly gamble with dice, the king shall be competent to inflict an ample and condign punishment according to the gravity of his offence. (228)

A Kshatriya, Vais'ya, or S'udra, incapable of paying the penalty, shall pay it by the labour of his body; a Brâhmaṇa, similarly circumstanced, shall pay it off by easy instalments. (229)

Women, infants, old or insane persons, poor men, and sick folks, incapable of paying the penalty, the king shall punish with stripes of bamboo-twists, or with chords, or by binding them. (230)

Officers in the king's service, who, in consideration of bribes (*lit.* affected by the heat of wealth), have destroyed the affairs of suitors, the king shall make stript of all their possessions. (231)

Falsifiers of the king's mandates, corrupters of the king's ministers, killers of women, of infants, and of Brâhmaṇas, and men in allegiance with the enemy the king shall cause to be killed. (232)

Whatever has been lawfully adjudicated in accordance with the instructions of the *S'âstra (res judicata?)* the king shall prohibit the revival thereof (in the court.) (233)

Whatever the counsellors or judges, employed in hearing suits, shall wilfully adjudicate in the wrong way, the king shall re-adjudicate himself and shall punish them with a fine of one thousand *Panas*, each. (234)

A killer of a Brâhmaṇa, a wine-drinker, a thief, and a defiler of his preceptor's or superior's bed should be respectively known as *Mahâpatakins* (great sinners). (235)

Any one of these four kinds of *Mahâpâtakins*, failing to perform the expiatory penances, the king shall punish with fines as well as with corporeal punishments. (236)

The mark of a female generative organ should be branded on the forehead of a defiler of his preceptor's bed; that of a wine-bowl, on the forehead of a wine-drinker; that of a dog's foot, on the forehead of a gold-stealer; and that of a headless human body, on the forehead of the killer of a Bráhmaṇa. (237)

No one shall eat with them, or serve them as priests, or teach them the *Vedas*, or marry their daughters to them; they must wander miserable in this world, ousted of all forms of virtue. (238)

Their relations shall renounce these cruel miscreants, branded with the aforesaid signs and unto whom no one shall make obeisance. This is the ordination of Manu. (239)

But these (sinners), after having done the proper expiations according to their castes, shall not be branded with the aforesaid signs on their foreheads; but they shall pay a penalty of the *Uttama Sáhasa* class to the king. (240)

A Brâhmana, accidentally (*lit.* unwilfully) guilty of any of these great sins (*Mahápátakas*), shall pay a fine of the *Madhyama sâhasa* class to the king; wilfully guilty of any of these crimes, let the king banish him from the country with all his clothes and belongings. (241)

Others (*i.e.* Kshatriyas etc.), accidentally guilty of any of these great crimes, shall be dispossessed of all their possessions; wilfully guilty, they shall be banished from the country. (242)

Let not the virtuous king take the wealth of a *Mahâpâtakin*; by taking it out of greed, he is associated with that (great) sin. (243)

The fine realised from a *Mahápâtakin* (great sinner) shall be thrown into the water as an offering to *Varuna* (the god of water), or it should be given to a Brâhmana, well read in the Vedas. (244)

Varuna is the lord of punishment, he wields the rod even over kings; a Bráhmaṇa, well-versed in the *Vedas*, is the lord of the universe. (245)

In the country, where the king does not accept the wealth of the miscreants, long-lived men are born at proper times (*i.e*, no premature birth or death occurs therein). (246)

There the Vais'yas fully harvest the several crops, as they sow (during the year, children do not die in infancy, and babes are not born deformed. (247)

A S'udra, guilty of wilfully tormenting a Brâhmaṇa, let the king put to death by the painful mutilation of his limbs or organs. (248)

In respect of the impartial administration of justice (*lit.* infliction of punishment), a king commits the same crime by punishing an innocent man as he does by suffering a guilty person to go unpunished. (249)

Thus the procedure relating to suits between two litigent parties, which are divided into eigteen branches, has been fully described. (250)

Let the king, fully discharging these duties, covet the country which he has not conquered (*lit.* obtained) and protect that which he has conquered. (251)

Building forts according to the S'astra in a well-populated country and residing therein, let the king assiduously weed out the thorns (exterminate the caitiffs, etc.,) of his realm. (252)

Kings, always eager to protect their subjects, go to heaven by protecting the virtuous and punishing the wicked *lit*, by clearing the realm of thorns.) (253)

The king, who receives the revenue from his subjects without punishing the thieves (and miscreants), produces a source of terror in his realm and becomes deprived of heaven, (after death.) (254)

The kingdom of the king, under the protection of

whose strong arms the realm becomes free from terror, thrives like a tree watered, each day. (255)

The king, who sees through his spies, must detect two kinds of thieves; those who openly rob other men and those who rob them in secret. (256)

The open deceivers are those several kinds of tradesmen (who openly steal by means of false weights and exorbitant prices), while the secret thieves are those who rob people in forests, (or by boring holes in the walls of their houses.) (257)

Bribe-takers, those who extort money from others by intimidation (robbers), cheats,* deceivers,† false soothsayers, palmists, men of secret vices, trainers of elephants who train them badly or inadequately, half-educated physicians, professional artists (painters, etc.), adepts in the traffic of females, and non-aryans who use the insignias of Aryans, these should be known as the open thorns (thieves) of the realm. (258—260)

The king, by encouraging spies, stationed in many places, and ostensibly carrying on the same professions with these miscreants, shall bring them under his control. (261)

The king, by proclaiming the offences of these (open and secret thieves) in their respective trades, shall punish them according to their bodily strength and pecuniary circumstances. (262)

Since, without punishment these evil-minded ones, wandering meekly in the disguise of honest men, can

---

* *Vanchakas*, such as those who give gilded metals in exchange of gold.—*Kulluka*.

† *Kitabas*, such as those who gamble with dice, or bet upon fighting animals.—*Kulluka*.

not be dissuaded from carrying on their nefarious trades. (265)

The king shall cause public assembly-rooms, water-chambers,* cake-shops, wine shops, houses of infamy, hotels (*lit.* food-shops), crossings of roads, grounds underneath the famous trees, trysting places, places of public shows or spectacles *(Prekshanáni)*, dilapidated gardens, forests, houses of artisans, deserted rooms, orchards, artificial bowers, etc., to be searched by spies, or by stationed or moving columns of foot-soldiers for repressing the thieves. (264—266)

He (*i.e.* the king) shall detect and destroy them (*i.e.*, thieves) with the aid of skilful former thieves, who had been their abettors or accomplices, and who are fully acquainted with their practices and locations, etc. (267)

They shall decoy them out of their retreats with prospects of feasts (*lit.* food and eatables etc.,) or of seeing holy Bráhmanas, or of witnessing deeds of valour, and have them congregated (at a previously appointed place). (268)

Those (thieves), who shall not congregate there, or being warned by the spy-thieves of the king shall avoid their company, let the king forcibly attack and kill with their friends, cognates, and relations. (269)

Let not the virtuous king kill a thief caught without his booty (or implement of boring holes in the walls); caught with these, let him kill the thief (without) the least hesitation. (270)

Them also, who shall knowingly give food and shelter to thieves, or give them utensils of (daily use),

* The text has *Prapá* which literally means a chamber where water is given to the way-farers and passers by.

the king shall kill (for their indirect complicity in the crime.) (271)

Those who are entrusted with the duty of policing the realm, as well as those who guard its boundaries, if found implicated with planning thefts (or robberies), shall be punished as thieves by the king. (272)

The king shall punish the swerving of a man of virtuous living (*i.e.* Brâhmana) from the path of his duty. (273)

Them, who on hearing that a village is being looted, or a bridge is being hewd down, or a theft is being committed by thieves, do not chase them for their apprehension to the best of their might, let the king banish from the country, with all their belongings (*lit.* unstript of their cloths. (274)

Stealers of king's treasure, those who are hostile to him, as well as those who secretly contrive to advance the cause of the king's enemy, he (*i.e.* the king) shall kill by inflicting various punishments on them. (275)

Of thieves, who commit thefts in the night by borning holes (in the walls of houses), let the king cut off the hands; and after that, place them on the tops of sharp pointed pikes. (276)

Those who steal by cutting knots of clothes (*i.e.* things tied up in knots at the ends of cloths) should be punished with the mutilation of fingers on the first conviction, with the mutilation of hands and legs on the second, and with death on the third. (277)

Them, who shall knowingly give fire, food, tools or shelter to thieves, or secrete their stolen articles in their houses, let the king punish as actual thieves. (278)

He who has cut away the embankment (*lit*, destroys) a tank should be killed, or killed by being drowened in water; but in the event of his duly repairing the same and making it as before, he shall pay a fine of the *Uttama Sâhasa* class to the king. (279)

Those, who break open a royal store-house, or a treasury, or a divine temple, or an arsenal, as well as stealers of king's elephants or horses, should be punished with death without the least hesitation. (280)

He, who has destroyed the entire water of a tank, dedicated to public use, or has stopped the channel of a running water course by means of an embankment, shall be punished with a fine of the *Prathama Sàhâsa* class. (281)

One, found guilty of defecating, except in the time of distress, on the king's high way, shall be punished with a fine of two *Karshâpanas*; moreover he shall be caused to remove the feces himself. (282)

But a distressed person, an infant or an old man, found guilty of the same offence, shall be liabe to to remove the feces. This is the decision. (283)

Physicians, found guilty of making wrong medical treatments in respect of beasts and men, shall be respectively punished with fines of the first *Sáhasa* and middling *Sàhasa* class. (284)

A breaker of a flight of steps, of a banner post, or of a divine image shall be punished with a fine of five hundred *Panas*; he shall be liable to reconstruct and replace the same. (285)

For having adulterated an unadulterated article, or having bored a gem which ought not to be bored, or for having bored it at the wrong place, one shall be punished with a fine of the *Prathama Sáahasa* class. (286)

He, who sells unequally (mixed) goods to one who has paid the proper price for the superior quality, or sells articles of equal value to one for a greater and to another for a lesser value, shall be liable to pay a fine of the middling *Sáhasa* class to the king. (287)

Houses of incarceration (Prison houses) should be situated near the public high way, so that the enchained miscreants may be seen in their miserable plight by the passers by. (288)

A house-breaker, a filler of a ditch, and a breaker of a wall-door shall be instantaneously banished from the country. (289)

For having practised a fatal incantation (*i.e.* a spell practised for one's death), for having hypnotised (*lit*, subjugation of one's mind) one who is not his intimate relation,* or for having practised an incantation for the distraction of one's mind, the offender shall be punished with a fine of two hundred *Pannas*, (if death of its victim has not resulted therefrom†) (290)

For having sold devitalised seeds or bad seeds as good ones, or for having obliterated (lit demolished) the boundary marks of a village), one shall be punished with mutilation of organs (such as the nose, ears, etc). (291)

---

* The text has *Anáptai*, which means not by his own people. A wife, mother or a father is at liberty to hypnotise her husband or his or her son; but one attempting to hypnotise another with a view to make him make large gifts in his favour, or to extort money from him, is guilty of the offence, dealt with in this couplet.

† If death-results from such an incantation, its practiser shall be punished as a murderer.—*Kulluka.*

The gold smith is the worst of all thorns of the realm (*i.e.* thieves) ; hence, a gold smith, found guilty of treading the path of iniquity (*i. e.*, of stealing gold) should be put to death by cutting him to pieces with a razor. (292)

For having stolen implements of agriculture, or weapons, or medicines, the king shall punish the offender in consideration of the hardness of the time, and the motive of his crime. (293)

The soverign, the premier, the capital or palace, the kingdom, the treasury, the army, and the ally, these are the seven essentials (*Prakriti*) of government ; and (hence), a kingdom is called a seven-limbed (polity). (294)

Of these seven limbs of government, the destruction of each preceding one is more diresome (momentous) than that of the one immediately succeeding it in the order of enumeration. (295)

As there is no difference of importance among the three staves (of an ascetic bound together to form one), so these seven limbs of government, though contrary to one another in their virtues (*i. e.* ends and nature), are co-operative ; one does not excel another in respect of eminence or importance. (296)

In those works, which are effected by any particular limb of government, should be judged its specific pre eminence. (297)

By means of secret spies, by encouraging his army, and (by the ability) to institute works (of public utility) the king must judge his own strength as well as that of his enemy. (298)

In consideration of the prevalence of dreadful epidemics in his (enemy's) country or of any other distress therein, as well as of the great or small disturbance in his state polity, let the king make war or peace with his adversary. (299)

Tired of (*i.e.*, unsuccessful in) his attempting to increase his territory and conquer the kingdom of his adversary, let the king put forth new efforts (lit, undertake fresh works) to that end. The goddess of fortune embraces the man who has undertaken a work. (300)

[The different cycles of time such as] the *Kritam*, *Treta*, *Dvâpara* and *Kali* are but the undertakings of kings. (*i.e.* they consist of the incidents of royal lives). Hence, the king is called (the embodiment of) a *yuga* (cycle of time). (301)

When the king sleeps (remains idle and inoperative) he is the *Kali Yuga*, when he is awake (*i.e.*, without undertaking any sort of exploit), he is the *Dvâpara*, when he energetically undertakes an exploit he is the *Tretâ*, and when he is on the move, (fully operative and wakeful) he is the *Kritam* (golden age.) (302)

The divine energies of (the deities) Indra, Arka (the sun), Vâyu (the wind), Yama (the god of death), Varuna (the god of oceans), Chandra (the moon), and Agni (the fire), which enter into the composition of his self, the king shall call into play (in his works in life.) (303)

As Indra (the lord of rains) pours showers of rain on the earth for four months in the year, so the king, by showering gifts and riches on his subjects for four months, shall practise the vow of Indra (*i.e.*, imitate the conduct of Indra.) (304)

As the sun-god soaks up water (from the earth) with his rays during the eight months in the year, so the king shall extract the revenue from his subjects, this is what is called acting like unto the sun (*Arka Vratam.*) (305)

As the air runs through all created things, so the king shall penetrate into the hearts of all his subjects with the help of his spies. (306)

As *Yama* (the lord of death) deals impartially with all (irrespective of his votaries or revilers), so the king shall administer even-handed justice to all his subjects; this what is called *Yama Vratam* (*i.e.*, acting like unto Death.) (307)

As Varuna (the god of ocean) is seen to bind (the sinners) with his noose, so the king shall punish the miscreants (with imprisonment, etc.). This is what is called the *Varuna Vratam* (acting like unto Varuna. (308)

As men rejoice at the sight of the full moon, so the king, in whom stayeth the delight of his subjects, is called the moon-vowed one. (309)

Mighty, and full of indomitable prowess, the king, who constantly consumes the miscreants and the refractory vassals of his own, is said to act like unto the fire (*Agneya Vratam*). (310)

As the Earth supports all creatures on her (buoyant) body (in the air), so the king supports all his subjects. This is what is called his acting like unto the Earth (*Párthiva Vratam*). (311)

Always energetic and possessed of these expedients, let the king suppress the caitiffs both in his realm and in other countries. (312)

Even having obtained (*i.e.* fallen in) the direst distress, let him not enrage Brahmanas; (inasmuch as) enraged, they may instantaneously kill him with his army and riding animals. (313)

Who may not meet his doom by enraging the Brâhmaṇas, who made the fire, the eater of all things (clean and unclean), the great ocean, undrinkable, and the wasting moon, full again? (314)

Who can prosper by insulting the feelings of Brâhmaṇas, who in fits of anger can create separate worlds with their presiding deities, and undeify the gods?* (315)

Who, loving life, shall oppress Bráhmanas on whom do the worlds and deities constantly depend for their existence, and whose only treasure is Brahma?† (316)

As the fire is the great deity, whether consecrated or unconsecrated; so a great deity is the Bráhmana, whether he is erudite or unread. (317)

The mighty-prowessed fire is not defiled even in the cremation ground; but fed with libations (of clarified butter, and other offerings) in a saerifice, it becomes freshly augmented. (318)

And so, even if Bráhmanas betake to all kinds of evil acts, they should be regarded as (prototypes of) the supreme deity. (319)

The Brâhmana is capable of making full reprisals for wrongs done by an extremely spirited (arrogant) Kshatriya on Brâhmanas (by means of imprecation, etc.) The Kshatriya has originated from (the arm of) Brahma (320)

---

* *i.e.*, Can divest them of their divinities. Many deities of the Brahmanic pantheon, such as Indra, etc., are known to have been changed into mortals under imprecations of holy sages.

† KULLUKA explains *Brahma* by *Veda*.

From the water originated the fire, from Brahma emanated the Kshatriyas, and from stone originated iron; they are subdued by their respective sources of origin. (321)

The Kshatriya without the Brâhmana (*i. e.*, force without intellect) and the Brahmana without the Kshatriya can never thrive; acting in co-operation with each other they prosper in this world. (322)

Having given all money realised as fines from miscreants (other than *Mahâpâkins*) to Brâhmanas, and made over the throne to his son, let the king, (afflicted with an incurable disease), go to and die in a battle.* (323)

The king, discharging all the duties, (laid down in this chapter), shall employ all his servants for constantly doing good to his subjects. (304)

Thus all the acts and eternal duties of the king have been fully described, now hear me expound the duties of Vais'yas and S'udras in succession. (325)

A Vais'ya, initiated with the holy thread, shall marry, and daily attend to agriculture and cattle-rearing. (326)

Prajápati (consciousness embodied by the universe) created the beasts and gave them to the Vais'ya; and all the creatures he gave to the king and the Brahmaṇa. (327)

The Vais'ya must not desire to keep no beasts; if the Vais'ya desires to keep beasts (*i.e.*, to rear animals), let none else do that. (328)

Let the Vais'ya appraise (cultivate the knowledge of) the prices and qualities of gems, pearls, corals,

---

* Or to quit his life by starvation in the absence of a battle—*Sangrâmâ sambhave tvanas'anâdinâ*).—*Kulluka.*

metals, woven stuffs, scented things (such as camphor, etc.,) and salts. (329)

Likewise, he must possess the knowledge of sowing seeds, of the specific traits of the soil, of the measures of (*i.e.*, the rules of measuring) lands, and the rules of weighing articles. (330)

(As well as) defects or excellences of articles, the good or evil traits of countries, profits or losses in manufactured articles and the increase of animals (the method of rearing cattle, etc.) (331)

He must know the wages of artisans and workmen, and languages of different races of men, shall be able to forecast the increase or decrease in the prices, and amelioration or deterioration in the quality, of an article at a particular place and time, as well as the mode of selling or buying. 332

He shall constantly try to multiply his riches by honest means and give food to animals out of all creatures. (333)

Serving the renowned house-holder Brâhmaṇas, well-versed in the *Vedas*, forms the highest virtue (duty) of S'udras. (334)

Pure in body and mind, of gentle speech and demeanour, a S'udra, by living under the shelter of a Brâhmaṇa, attains a considerably higher status (*lit.* caste) among his fellow S'udras. (335)

Thus the auspicious duties of the Members of the four castes in times of peace (*i.e.*, not in times of distress), have been described; now hear me discourse on their duties in times of distress. (336)

CHAPTER X.

THE members of the three twice-born orders, attending to the specific duties of their castes, shall read (the *Vedas*), but the Brâhmaṇas alone shall teach the *Vedas*, and none else, this is the conclusion (1)

Cognisant of the modes of livelihood of all castes of men, and discharging the specific duties of his own order, let the Brâhmaṇa advise on the same to members of all (the four) castes. (2)

By the excellence of his specific duties, by the loftiness of his birth (from the face of Brahma), and by his comprehension of the *Vedas*,* the Bráhmaṇa is the lord of all the castes. (3)

The Brâhmaṇa, Kshatriya, and Vais'ya are the three twice-born castes; the S'udra is the fourth, there being no sub-castes among S'udras, and there is no fifth caste. (4)

Sons, begotten by members of the (four several) castes on lawful married wives, belonging to their respective social orders (castes) in the due order of enumeration, and with unraptured hymens (at the time of marriage), should be regarded as the best (of sons). Sons, begotten by twice-born ones on wives not belonging to their respective castes, do not bceome of the same castes with their fathers; they belong to different castes. Sons begotten by members of twice-born castes on wives belonging to their next inferior castes (in the order of enumeration) are said (by Manu) not obtain the castes of their fathers owing to the degraded castes of their mothers. (5—6)

---

* The text has *Niyamasya cha Dhâranát*. GOVINDARAJA explains it by "for his practising the vow of *Snatakas, etc.*, *Snâtaka Vratádidhârandt*.

Thus the status of sons begotten by fathers on wives respectively belonging to their next inferior castes has been described; now hear me discourse on the status of sons, begotten by men on wives belonging to the next but one, or next but two inferior castes of their own. (7)

Sons begotten by Brâhmanas on their lawfully married Vais'ya wives are called *Ambashthas*; sons begotten by Brahmanas on their S'udra wives are called *Nishâdas* or *Párâs'avas* (lit. living corpses). (8)

Sons begotten by Kshatriyas on their S'udra wives are called *Ugras*; they become cruel in deeds and temperaments owing to the natural mental traits of their respective parents. (9)

Sons begotten by Brâhmanas on wives of the next three (inferior) castes (*i.e.*, Kshatriya, Vais'ya and S'udra), those begotten by Kshatriyas on wives of the next two inferior castes, and by Vais'yas on wives of the next inferior caste (S'udra), in their order of enumeration, should be regarded as six inferior *(Apasada)* sons. (10)

A son begotten by a Kshatriya on a Brâhmana woman becomes a *Suta* by caste; sons begotten by Vais'yas on Kshatriya women are called *Mágadhas*, and sons begotten by Vais'yas on Brâhmaṇa women are called *Vaidehas*. (11)

Sons begotten by S'udras on Vais'ya women are called *Ayogavas*, those begotten on Kshatriya women by them are called *Kshattás*, and those which they beget on Brâhmaṇa women are called *Chandalas*, the most abominable creatures. Thus the mixed castes are originated. (12)

Sons begotten by men on wivies, belonging to castes next by one to those of their own, computed in the order of enumeration such as, the *Ambashtha* and *Ugra*, bear the anology with *Kshatta* and *Vaidehas*, which are begotten by fathers on wives belonging to castes next by one to those of their own, counted in the inverse order of enumeration. (13)

Sons of the twice-born ones, begotten by them on wives belonging to the next inferior castes to those of their own as described before, are called *Antar Janmás*, owing to the defects (inferior castes) of their respective mothers. (14)

Sons begotten by a Bráhmaṇa on *Ugra*, *A'mbastha* and *A'yogava* women are respectively called *Avrita*, *Abhira* and *Dhigvana*. 15)

The *Ayogava*, *Khattá* and *Chandála*, the lowest of men, inasmuch as they were begotten by S'udras on women respectively belonging to superior castes in the inverse order of enumeration, should be regarded as extremely low castes. (16)

The *Mágadha* and *Vaideha*, begotten by the *Vais'ya*, and the *Suta*, begotten by the Kshatriya, should be regarded as of vile castes, inasmuch as they have been begotten by their fathers on women (of their superior castes) reckoned in the inverse order of enumeration. (17)

A son begotten by a *Nisháda* on a S'udra woman, becomes a *Puhkasa* by caste; a son, begotten by a S'udra on a *Nisháda* woman is called a *Kukkutaka*. (18)

A son, begotten by a *Kshattá* on an *Ugra* woman, is called a *S'vapáka*; a son, begotten by a *Vaideha* on an *Ambastha* women is called a *Vena*. (19)

Sons begotten by twice-born ones on wives of their own castes, and devoid of the rites of initiation with the thread, etc., are called *Vrâtyas* (*lit.* broken vowed ones.) 20

Sons begotten by *Vràtya* Brâhmaṇas on lawfully married wives of their own castes, are called *Bhurjakantakas*; they are also known by the designations of *Avantyàs Vàtádhànas, Pushpadhas* and *S'aikhas* also. (21)

Sons begotten by *Vràtya* Kshatriyas on lawfully married wives of their own castes, are called *Jhallas, Mallas, Natas, Karanas, Khasas* and *Dravidas.* (22)

Sons begotten by *Vràtya* (uninitiated) Vais'yas on wives of their own castes, are called *Sadhanv, àcharyaya Kárusha, Vijanma, Maitrâ* and *Svatata.* (23)

Through the intermixture of castes, through intermarriages among forbidden castes, and through renunciation of their specific duties by (members of the four several) castes, that the hybrid ones are born. (24)

Now I shall describe in detail the castes of low origin which spring up from sexual intercourses among members of the four several) castes, reckoned in the usual or inverse order of enumeration. (25)

Sutás, Vaidehakas, Chandalas, the vilest of men, *Mágadhas, Kshattâs* and *Ayogavas* are the six hybrid castes, (begotten by fathers on mothers, respectively belonging to) castes, counted in the inverse order of enumeration (*Pratilomaja*). (26)

Members of these six hybrid castes beget on women respectively belonging to their superior castes, or to castes of their mothers, or to their own castes, sons who become of their own castes. (27)

As sons begotten by a Brâhmaṇa on a Vais'ya or Kshatriya wife, or on his Bráhmaṇa wife are superior to his sons by a S'udra wife, so among members of inferior castes, sons begotten by Vais'yas on Kshatriya women, or those begotten by Kshatriyas on Brâhmaṇa women are a little more honourable than sons begotten by S'udras on women, belonging to their (superior) castes, reckoned in the inverse order of enumeration. (28)

Sons begotten by members of the six hybrid castes, such as the *Ayogavas*, etc., on women belonging to their immediately superior or inferior castes, (*lit.* castes reckoned in the usual or inverse order of enumeration) should be respectively reckoned as viler, and more condemnable; and more deprived of the privilege of doing religious rites. (29)

As S'udras begot the vilest *Chandâlas* on Brâhmaṇa women, so the vile sons, begotten by members of the vile hybrid castes on women respectively belonging to the four castes, shall be regarded as extremely vile, degraded and condemnable. (30)

Sons begotten through intermarriage by the members of the six hybrid castes such as, the *Ayogavas*, etc., among their own castes, are divided into (grouped under) fifteen castes; (and) they are more degraded than their progenitors. (31)

Sons, begotten by members of the robber castes on women of the *Ayogava* caste are called *Sairindhras*; they are expert in dressing hair, and although not actually servants (*lit.* slaves, *Dâsas*), they live by service and by capturing birds and beasts. (32)

Sons begotten by *Vaidehas* on *Ayogava* women are called *Maitreyas*; they lavishly sing the eulogies of the king at dawn, and rouse him from sleep by ringing bells (in the morning). (33)

Sons, begotten by *Nishâdhas* on *Ayogava* women, are called *Mârgavas,* who live by working as boatmen : the inhabitants of *Aryavarta* call them *Kaivartas.* (34)

Of women of the *Ayogava* caste, who wear the clothes of corpses and eat the leavings of other men's food, are born the three vile castes (*Sairandhra, Maitreya* and *Mârgava*) who do not obtain the castes of their fathers. (35)

Of *Kârâvara* women by *Nishâdas* are born the *Charmakâras* (cobblers), and of *Kârâvara* and *Nishâda* women by *Vaidehâkas* are respectively born the *Andhras* and *Medas,* who live outside villages. (36)

Of *Vaidehika* women by *Chandâlas* are born *Pandapakas,* who manufacture bamboo-made articles and of *Vaideha* women by *Nishadas* are born the *Ahindakas.* (37)

Of *Pukkasa* women by *Chandalas* are born the loathsome, villainous *Sopâkas.* who live by working as public executioners (*lit.* by executing criminals punished with death.) (38)

Sons begotten by *Chandâlas* on *Nishâda* women are called *Antyâvasayins,* who live by working as attendants at cremation grounds, and they are the vilest of all vile castes. (39)

Fathers and mothers of these hybrid castes have been set forth, those of unknown parentage should be detected by their respective works. (40)

Of sons begotten by twice-born ones (Brâhmaṇas and Kshatriyas) on wives of their own castes, or on wives belonging to castes next, or next by one to those of their own, six castes (of sons) have the right of being initiated with the thread (*lit.* the privilege of twice-bornship), and the rest are S'udras, partaking of the status and privileges of S'udra. (41)

But in each cycle of time, these men (such as Vis'vâmitra, etc.) (*i.e.*, those born of parents belonging to the same caste or contrary), by dint of penitential austerities, and through the excellence of their (*Beejas*) paternal elements (such as, Rishyas'ringa, etc.) acquire higher castes, (and through contrary causes) are degraded to viler castes in life. (42)

The following Kshatriya castes, through the extinction, (non-performances) of their proper religious rites and on account of not seeing (*i.e.*, in the absence of their contact with) Bráhmaṇas, have been degraded to the S'udra caste in this world. (43)

[They are] the Paundrakas, Andhras, Dravidas, Kamvojas, Javanas, Sakas, Pârandas, Pândavas, Chinas, Kiratas, Daradas, Kashas. [Kshatriyas of these countries have become S'udras for having renounced the religious rites.] (44)

Members of castes, respectively originated from the face, arms, thighs and legs of Brahmaṇ (*i.e.*, Bráhmaṇa, Kshatriya, Vais'ya and S'udra) who have been comprised outside the pale of these four castes for the extinction of their religious rites, are all called *Dasyus*, whether they speak an Aryan or a non-Aryan (*Mlechchha*) tongue. (45)

Castes begotten by the twice-born ones on women belonging to their next inferior castes in the due order of enumeration (*Apusadas*, as well as those begotten by men on women belonging to castes, counted in the inverse order of their enumeration, shall live by doing lowly works, which the Bráhmaṇas are incapable of doing. (46)

Sutas shall live by working as charioteers; *Ambashthas*. by practising medicines; *Vaidehakas*, by guarding the harems of kings, and *Mâgadhas* by trading. (47).

Nishâdas shall live by killing fishes; *Ayogavas*, by doing carpentry; and *Medas*, *Andhras*, *Chunchus*, and *Madgus*, by killing wild beasts. (48)

Kshallas, *Ugras* and *Pukkasas* shall live by killing or capturing hole-dwelling animals; curing of leather (cobbler's work) is the profession of *Dhigvanas*, and drum-beating, etc., is that of the *Venas*. (49)

Doing their proper works, these castes shall live in the forest, or about cremation-grounds, or on hill tops, or underneath the lordly trees. (50)

Chandalas and *Svapachas* (*lit.* dog-eaters) shall live at the out-skirts of villages, they shall use no utensils; dogs and asses being their only wealth. (51)

They (*Chandalas*, etc.), shall wear the apparels of corpses, eat out of broken pots, wear ornaments of steel, and live a nomadic life. (52)

One, while doing a religious rite, must not see, or speak to them (*Chandâlas*); they shall carry on their monetary or matrimonial transactions among members of their own caste. (53)

One shall cause food to be given to them through his servants in broken saucers; and they must not be allowed to roam about in a village in the night. (54)

Stamped with the signs of king's permits on their persons, they shall enter the village on business (*i.e.*, for the sale or purchase of goods) in the day; and the decision is that, they shall remove the corpses of the friendless deceased (from villages). (55)

They shall kill, according to the rules of the *Sastra*, criminals punished by the king with death, and take the beddings and wearing apparels of the executed convicts. (56)

In respect of ascertaining the Aryan or non-Aryan origins of men of vile parentage, who stand outside the pale of the four castes, their respective works (acts or conduct) should from the criterion of judgment. (57)

Meanness, cruelty, malice, and doing improper acts (*i.e.*, improper deeds) point to the vile origin of a man. (58)

A son partakes of the nature of his father or mother or of both of them; a man of vile descent can never conceal his origin. (59)

Born in a noble family, the son of a faithless mother, bred in adultery, partakes more or less of the wicked nature of his vile progenitor. (60)

The kingdom, wherein such ruinous hybridisers of castes are born, soon perisheth with all its inmates. (61)

By voluntarily laying down their lives without any consideration of gain or reward for the good (succour) of Bráhmaṇas, kine, infants or women, these (castes) men ascend to heaven (after death). (62)

Annihilation of killing propensities (*i.e.*, compassion to all), truthfulness, non-stealing, purity and subjugation of the senses, these four, Manu described as the general duties of all the four castes. (63)

If the daughter of a Bráhmaṇa by his S'udra wife is married to a Bráhmaṇa, and the daughter of that union is again married to a Bráhmaṇa, and so on uninterruptedly up to the seventh generation in the female line, then at the seventh generation the issue of such union is divested of its *Pâras'ava* caste and becomes a Bráhmaṇa. (64)

Thus a S'udra may obtain the caste of a Brâhmaṇa and a Brâhmaṇa may obtain the caste of a S'udra; similarly, the sons of Kshatriya or Vais'ya fathers may acquire higher or lower castes. (65)

Of sons, begotten out of lust by Brâhmaṇas on non-Aryan women, and sons begotten by non-Aryans on Brâhmaṇa women, whose is the preference? (66)

Certainly the sons begotten by Aryans on non-Aryan women become possessed of the privileges (of instituting Paka-Yajnas, etc., *i.e.*, they become Aryans), while sons begotten by non-Aryans on Aryan women become non-Aryans. This is the decision. (67)

Owing to the defects (degraded nature) of their births, both these two kinds of sons (*i.e.*, sons begotten by Brâhmaṇas on non-Aryan women and sons begotten by non-Aryans on Aryan women) are divested of the rights of being initiated with the thread, etc., (*lit.* of the right of purificatory rites being done unto them.) (68)

As (from) good seeds, sown in a good soil, excellent cereals sprout up, so the son, begotten by an Aryan on an Aryan woman is worthy of (*lit.* acquires the privilege of) all purificatory rites being done unto him. (69)

Several wise men assert the pre-eminence of the soil; others, of the seed; while some there are who speak of the equal importance of both the seed and the soil. In such cases of conflicting opinions the following is the decision of law (*i.e.*, criterion of judgment.) (70)

Sown in a barren soil, a seed dies before sprouting, while a good field without seeds is but a hard fallow (*Sthandilam.*) (71)

Since through their excellent energies (potency), seeds, cast in the wombs of beasts (by the holy sages), fructified in the shapes of human beings, who became honoured and commendable Rishis* in life; the seed is commended (as of greater importance in an act of fecundation). (72)

In respect of a non-Aryan, who does the acts of (behave like) an Aryan and an Aryan who deports himself (*lit.* does the works of) like a non-Aryan, the ordainer, after deliberation, ordained the fact that, they are neither equal nor unequal. (73)

Brâhmaṇas, addicted to the contemplation of *Brahma*, who discharge the duties peculiar to their order, shall (alone) earn their livings by doing the six following acts. (74)

Study of the *Vedas*, teaching the *Vedas* (to pupils), performances of religious sacrifices, officiating as priests at sacrifices instituted by others, gift-making, and acceptance of gifts, these six are the vocations (*lit.* works) of the eldest borns of creation (*i.e.*, Brâhmaṇas). (75)

Out of these six acts, by officiating as priests at other men's sacrifices, by teaching the *Vedas*, and by accepting gifts from clean gift-makers, let the Brâhmaṇas earn their livelihood. (76)

Teaching the *Vedas*, officiating as priests at other men's sacrifices and gift-taking, which forms the third, are the three acts which shall never revert to the Kshatriya as against the Brâhmaṇa.† (77)

---

* The holy sage Rishyas'ringa was procreated by Vibhandaba in the womb of a she-deer.

† The text has *Brahmanat Kshatriyam prati, i.e.*, a Kshatriya shall never be competent to take gifts from a Brâhmana, or to teach him the *Veda*, or to officiate as a priest at a sacrifice instituted by a Bráhmana.

Similarly, these privileges (*lit.* acts) must not be claimed by the Vaiś'ya against the Brâhmaṇa, inasmuch as the lord of the universe *(Prajâpati)* did not ordain these duties (of gift-taking, etc.,) for the Vaiś'ya and the Kshatriya. This is the decision. (78)

A Kshatriya shall earn his living by wielding arms and weapons; and a Vais'ya, by trade, agriculture and cattle-rearing. For virtue (and not for a living) they can study the *Veda*, make gifts, and institute religious sacrifices. (79)

Of works stated before, the study of the *Vedas* forms the specific duty of Bráhmaṇas; protection of subjects forms the specific duty of Kshatriyas; and agriculture forms the special vocation of the Vais'ya. (80)

Failing to earn a living by his specific vocation, let a Bráhmaṇa earn his livelihood by doing the duties of a Kshatriya, since the vocation of a Kshatriya is more kindred to that of his own (than any other calling). (81)

Failing to earn his livelihood by either of these two callings, how shall a Bráhmaṇa obtain a living? Let him earn his living (in that case) by following the vocation of a Vais'ya, (*viz.*, agriculture and cattle-rearing). (82)

Failing to earn a living by following the vocation of a Vais'ya, let not a Bráhmaṇa, or a Kshatriya live by prosecuting agriculture, which is dependent (on bullocks) and entails the destruction of many (under ground) lives. (83)

Many people consider agriculture to be a commendable vocation, but, in fact, it is condemned by the virtuous, inasmuch as the iron-bound furrow penetrates into the earth and destroys many terrestrial lives. (84)

A Bráhmaṇa, or a Kshatriya, failing to earn his livelihood by his proper vocation, and thereby happening to infringe the Law, shall live by selling the uncondemnable and wealth-augmenting articles of trade out of those which are (ordinarily) sold by a Vais'ya. (85)

He must not sell edible articles of all tastes, confection made with sesame seeds, stones, salts, beasts and men (slaves). (86)

[As well as] clothes woven with red-coloured cotton twists or with hemp twists, silk-cloths, cloths made of sheep's wool, fruits and edible roots, and medicinal drugs (herbs). (87)

(As well as) water, weapon, poison, flesh, *Soma* plant, all kinds of scented things, milk, bee's wax, milk curd, clarified butter, oil, honey, treacle and *Kus'a* grass. (88)

[And] all kinds of wild beasts, the fanged ones in special, birds, wines, indigo, shellac, and all beasts with unbifurcated hoops. (89)

Having wilfully raised a crop of sesame seeds by himself cultivating the soil, let him speedily sell those holy (seeds) only for the purposes of religious sacrifices. (90)

For having sold sesame seeds for the purposes of food, unguents and gifts, he, with his manes, shall be merged (born) as worms in the excreta of dogs. (91)

By selling flesh, lac-dye, or salt, he shall be degraded on the very day of the sale; by selling milk a Bráhmaṇa shall become a S'udra in the course of three days. (92)

For having wilfully sold other articles of trade, a Bráhmaṇa, in the course of seven nights (days), shall assume the nature of a Vais'ya (*i.e.*, he shall be degraded to the status of a Vais'ya in a week). (93)

Saps (such as treacle, etc.,) may be given (or taken) in exchange of (emolient) saps such as milk,* clarified butter, etc)., but sap must not be taken in exchange of salt; similarly, raw rice may be taken in exchange of cooked rice, and sesame of paddy. (94)

Rather should a Kshatriya in distress live by following all these trades; but under no circumstances, should he embrace the vocation of a Brâhmaṇa. (95)

Him, who, though of an inferior caste, shall adopt, out of greed, the vocation of his superior caste for a living, let the king banish from the country, stript of all his belongings. (96)

It is better that one should live by doing the vile works allotted to his own caste than embrace the vocation of a superior caste for livelihood; living by adopting the vocation of another caste, one becomes degraded the very day. (97)

A Vais'ya, incapable of earning a living by doing the vocation of his caste, shall do the works of a S'udra in exclusion of the condemnable ones; when capable, let him resume the vocation of his own order. (98)

A S'udra, incapable of securing the services of Brâhmaṇas, shall live as an artisan to prevent the death of his wife and children by starvation. (99)

Let him (*i.e.*, S'udra) do such varied works of artisanship (such as painting, carpentry, etc.,) by which the Bráhmaṇas are best served (*i.e.*, those which are of daily use to Brâhmaṇas). (100)

Let a Brâhmaṇa, discharging the duties of his own order (*lit.* keeping to his proper path in life) without living by the vocation of a Vais'ya, do the (following) works (*lit.* duties for his livelihood), oppressed by the absence of any means of living. (101)

Let him successively accept gifts from all men, (condemnable, more condemnable and the most condemnable in their order of enumeration). A holy thing can never be virtually called defiled by the contact of an unclean substance.* (102)

In times of distress, Brâhmaṇas, by teaching the *Vedas* to the unworthy, or by officiating as priests at the religious sacrifices of their degraded institutors, or by accepting the gifts of the vile, are not degraded, in as much as they are like unto the water and the fire (*i.e.*, above all defilement). (103)

By taking his food at a place (however sinful or unholy), a Brâhmaṇa on the point of death, like unto the ether purging off all dust, shall not be associated with the sin. (104)

The hungry (sage) *Ajagartah*, for having attempted to kill his son (*S'unahs'ephal*) in order to appease his hunger (with his flesh), was not associated with the sin (of child killing). (105)

The famished *Vâmadevah*, the knower of sin and virtue, for having wished to eat (dog's flesh inorder to avoid death from starvation, was not associated with the sin (of eating dog's flesh. (106)

Opressed by hunger in a lonely forest, the (holy)

---

* As the water of the holy Ganges can never be defiled by the touch of running and unclean water-channels from the road, so a Brâhmana, true to his own duties, can never be degraded by accepting gifts even from the vilest of persons for his living—*Kulluka.*

Bharadvaja of great austerity, together with his son, was not associated with the sin (of taking vile gifts) for having accepted the gift of a large number of kine from *Vridhu* who was a carpenter. (107)

Oppressed by hunger, the holy *Vis'vâmitra*, the knower of merits and demerits, for having accepted the gift of the fiesh of a dog's thigh from the hand of a Chandala, was not associated with sin. (108)

[Of sins] of teaching the *Vedas* (to the unworthy), of officiating as priests (at the sacrifices of the degraded), and of accepting (vile gifts), the last named one shonld be regarded as the most degrading for a Brâhmana in his life after death. (109)

In times of distress let the Bráhmanas teach the *Vedas* to, and officiate as priests at sacrifices instituted by, the twice-born ones and accept gifts from S'udras. (110)

He gets rid of the sin of teaching the unworthy and doing sacrifices on behalf of the degraded by means of *Japas* and *Homas*, that which is incidental to his taking (vile gifts) he shall get rid of by means of penitential austerities and by renunciation (*i.e.*, by renouncing the articles of gift. (111)

A Brâhmana, living any where he pleases (*i.e.*, in a dale or a valley without living by his proper vocation), shall live by practising *S'ila* and *Uncha*; Sila (described before) is better than gift-taking, and *Uncha* (to live by picking up grains from fields or stubbles) is more meritorious than *S'ila*. (112)

Snâtaka Bráhmanas, in the absence of their proper means of livelihood, may beg for paddy, food grains, wearing stuff, or any metal, other than gold or silver, of the king; if the king refuses to make these gifts, they should not be asked the second time.* (113)

Unprepared (uncultivated) fields are less sinful (as gifts) than those prepared (cultivated by men), and of kine, goats, sheep, gold, paddy and cooked food each preceding one is less sinful (as a gift) than one immediately following it in the order of enumeration. (114)

Inheritance, presents (from friends), purchase, conquest,† accretion by interest, investment in (trade or agriculture), and taking gifts from the worthy form the seven lawful (honest or virtuous) sources of pecuniary income (*lit.* access of wealth). (115)

Teaching sciences other than the Vedas (*lit.* education,) art, service, doing other men's behests, cattle-rearing, trade, cultivation (done by one's own-self), contentment, (*i.e.*, resting content with little what is obtained), alms-begging, and money lending are the ten means of livelihood in times of distress.‡ (116)

A Bráhmana or a Kshatriya must not lend money for interest; but for the purposes of virtue he may

---

* The text has *tyágamarhati*. Both MEDHATITHI and GOVINDARAJA explain it by *tasya de'se na Vastavyam*—let them not live in his country.

† The first three should be understood as the honest sources of wealth in respect of all the four orders of society. Conquest is only lawful for a Kshatriya. Money-lending and investment in trade and agriculture are open only to Vais'yas, while gift-taking from worthy donors is lawful for Brâhmanas only.—*Kulluka.*

‡ Of these, means of living, which are unlawful for a particular caste under ordinary circumstances (*Anápadi*), may be embraced or adopted by it under emergency or in times of distress (*A'padi*).—*Kulluka.*

lend money to a miscreant at a very small rate of interest. (117)

In times of emergency, a king, fully protecting his subjects by his mighty prowess, shall not be guilty of the sin (of exacting rack rents), if he takes a quarter part of the agricultural produce from each of them. (118)

Conquest (of foreign countries) is the proper duty of the king, let him not dissuade from battle (when called upon to fight) : by protecting the Vaisyas with his arms, let him collect the proper revenue (from them.) (119)

In times of emergency, let the king receive an eighth part of the (stored up food grains and a twentieth part of each *Kârshâpanam* (of collected money) from the Vais'yas.* S'udras, artisans, and confectioners *(Karanas)* etc., should be made to work in lieu of revenue. (120)

[If by serving a Brâhmaṇa he fails to obtain an adequate living], let the Sudra take the services of a Kshatriya or of a rich Vaisya and thereby earn his livelihood. (121)

For the acquisition of heaven (after death), or both for heaven and a living, let the Sudra serve the Brâhmaṇa; the significance of the term *Jâta-Brâhmana* (*lit.* born for serving the Brâhmanas) which denotes a *Sudra,* will be thereby fully realised. (122)

Serving the Brâhmaṇas forms the *Summum bonum* (highest duty) of a Sudra's life; whatever else he does is futile. (123)

In consideration of the skilfulness of their services, their capacity of work, and the number of their

* A twelfth part of his grains should be taken from a Vais'ya is the injunction. In times of extreme emergency the king is privileged to take a fourth part.

dependants, let him (Brâhmaṇa) adequately fix the salaries of his Sudra (servants). (124)

He shall give him the leavings of his food,* his old and cast off clothes, and his old beddings and grainless paddy for his bed. (125)

A S'udra commits no sin by (eating the prohibited articles of fare, he can not be initiated with the thread, he is not privileged to institute (*Vediac*) sacrifices, nor he is precluded from doing the *(Pâka-yaynas)*. (126)

But S'udras, who are the knowers of virtue and seek to acquire virtue, commit no sin by imitating the doings of the virtuous in exclusion of the Vediac Mantras; rather they become commendable by so doing. (127)

Non-malicious Sudras proportionately acquire like commendations and elevations in this world and the next as they do comparatively better deeds in this life. (128)

A S'udra, even capable of earning money, must not accumulate wealth,-lest in pride of his riches he might oppress a Brâhmaṇa. (129)

Thus I have described to you the duties of the four social orders in times of distress, by faithfully discharging which men acquire exalted status. (130)

Thus I have fully described the duties of the four social orders, now I shall discourse on the mode of doing the auspicious, expiatory rites (*Pràyaschittam*). (131)

---

* The previous prohibition in respect of giving leavings of his food by a Bràhmana to a S'udra (*Na S'udrâya Matim dadyát nochchhishtam*, etc.), holds good only in the case of a S'udra, who is not his servant.

CHAPTER XI.

THOSE who marry only for the purpose of procreating children (*Santánikhs*), those who desire to complete religious sacrifices already instituted by them (*Yakshyaná*), itinerant Brâhmaṇas, those who have gifted away all their belongings, [as *Dakshinas* (fees) for *Vis'vajit* sacrifice], those who beg for the purposes of supporting their parents or preceptors, or for defraying the costs of their Vediac studies, sick folks (Brâhmaṇas) who beg for paying the costs of their medical treatment—these nine Snâtakas must be known as mendicants for virtue (*Dharma Vikshus*). To these indigent persons (Brâhmanas) must be made gifts* preferentially according to their eruditions. (1—2)

To those foremost of Brâhmanas should be made gifts of food (raw food-grains, etc.) and money, and to others gifts of cooked food should be made outside the sacrificial platform. (3)

Let the king make gifts of all kinds of gems as well as of fees (*Dakshinâs*) for religious sacrifices to these Brâhmanas and to those who are well versed in the *Vedas*. (4)

A married man, who marries a second wife by begging money of another, enjoys only the benefit of sexual gratification in her (*i.e.*, the second wife); sons of her womb belong to him who has paid him the expense of the marriage. (5)

But let a man give money according to his might to Veda-knowing Brâhmanas, as well as to those who

* Inasmuch as chárity (gift-making) is the primary form of expiatión for all kinds of misdeeds (*Dánená-Kárya-Karinah*), the framer of the code has thought fit to describe the nine proper recipients of gifts at the commencement of the present chapter.

have renounced the order of house-holder, whereby he shall acquire heaven, after death. (6)

He who has got three years' provisions of his family and the wages of his servants for three years, stocked and stored up in his house, is alone competent to drink the *Soma* juice (*i.e.*, to do the *Soma Yajna*. (7)

A Bráhmana, with a smaller provision, who has performed a *Soma* sacrifice, has not acquired the full merit of the performance. (8)

The gift by one, who can find means to give to other indigent persons in the presence of his own peoples suffering from penury, may seem to him sweet and virtuous for the time being, but it will be like unto poison in the end. That (gift) is but the shadow of virtue. (9)

Whatever virtue (*lit.* any thing done for his elevation in the next world) one practises by creating hardships on his dependants becomes a source of torment to him both here and hereafter. (10)

In the event of there being a king, if a part of a religious sacrifice instituted by a virtuous Kshatriya, or by a Brâhmaṇa, in special, stands unperformed for want of funds; let him for the performance thereof forcibly carry away that much money from the house a non-sacrificing Vais'ya, who, although possessed of a large number of animals, does not drink the *Soma* Juice (*i e.*, performs the *Soma Yajna.*) (11—12)

In the absence of such a Vais'ya, let him forcibly carry those articles from the house of a S'udra in the event of two or three limbs of his *Kâma Yajna* (a sacrifice instituted for the fruition of definite desire) standing unperformed: gifts shall not be taken from a S'udra for the purposes of a religious sacrifice.

(no harm there exists in forcibly taking articles from his house). (13)

Moreover, from a (Brâhmaṇa or Kshatriya) relation of his, who, although not a keeper of the sacred fire, is possessed of a hundred kine, and from a (Bráhmaṇa or Kshatriya) relation who, although a keeper of the sacred fire, does not perform the *Vediac* sacrifices, although he is possessed of a thousand kine—from these two relations, let him unhesitatingly take the articles requisite for his sacrifice. (14)

From him, who daily accumulates money by taking gifts but does not spend it in religious sacrifices or in works of public utility, let him forcibly take the articles necessary for the performance of his sacrifice, whereby his fame and virtue will be augmented. (15)

Having fasted for three days in want of food, a man in the forepart of the fourth day may steal a day's provision from the house of a miserly miscreant. (16)

He shall steal those food-grains from the thrashing floor, from the field, or from the granary (of such a miscreant), or from any other part (of his house), convenient, ; and if he interrogates him (*i.e.*, the stealer about the theft), let him speak the reason thereof. (17)

A Kshatriya (as well as a Vais'ya or a S'udra) must never steal what belongs to a Bráhmaṇa ; but from a Brâhmaṇa, who is the author of bad deeds and does not perform the *Vediac* sacrifices, a Kshatriya may steal articles necessary for the performance of a sacrifice in the event of it standing unperformed for their want. (18)

He, who having taken (stolen or extorted) money from miscreants give it to the virtuous (Bráhmaṇas), verily converts himself into a raft whereby he takes both its recipients and his own self across the ocean of misery. (19)

The wealth of those who regularly institute religious sacrifices is called the divine property by the wise, the wealth of non-sacrificers is called demoniac wealth. (20)

The virtuous king must not inflict punishment on a person who has stolen or forcibly carried away the wealth (of a non-sacrificer), since it is through the foolishness of the Kshatriya (king) that hunger overwhelms a Bráhmaṇa. (21)

Having ascertained the number of his (*i.e.*, starving Bráhmaṇa's) dependents, and the extent of his erudition and piety (*lit.* good conduct), the king must grant him a stipend from his own treasury. (22)

Having provided him with a stipend, let the king protect him in every way from thieves, for such protections the king receives a sixth part of his religious merit. (23)

For the purposes (*i.e.*, completion of) of a religious sacrifice a Brâhmaṇa must never beg money of a S'udra; for having performed a religious sacrifice with such money he shall be born as a *Chandâla* in his next incarnation.* (24)

A Brâhmaṇa, who, having obtained money by begging for the performance of a religious sacrifice, does not spend it all for that purpose, becomes a crow or a *Bhása* bird in his next birth for a hundred years. (25)

The miscreant, who, out of greed, robs the property of a god or of a Bráhmaṇa, shall live on the leavings of

---

* Only begging is prohibited; a Bráhmana is not precluded from instituting a religious sacrifice with money voluntarily given by a Sudra.—*Kulluka.*

vultures (rotten carcases) all through his life in his next birth. (26)

For expiating the sin of his not having performed the animal sacrifice or *Soma Yajna*, a Brâhmaṇa may take money from a S'udra to institute a *Vais'vânara* sacrifice therewith at the close of the year.* (27)

A Bráhmaṇa, who in the time of safety does a religious rite in the manner laid down for its performance in times of distress, shall not acquire the merit thereof in heaven. This is the decision. (28)

Vis'vedevas, Sâdhyas (an order of celestial beings), Brâhmaṇas, and the great sages have done the *Vais'vânari* sacrifice by proxies under circumstances, perilous to life. (29)

The evil-minded one, who, although capable of instituting a religious sacrifice in person (*lit.* as a principal), does it by proxy, does not obtain the merit thereof in the next world. (30)

A virtuous Brâhmaṇa must not complain of any wrong done to him to the king; he shall punish the wrong-doer by means of his own ((psychic) power. (31)

The Brâhmanic (psychic force) is stronger than the royal prowess; hence, let a Bráhmaṇa punish his enemies by means of his own (psychic) powers. (32)

Without the least compunction in his mind he shall recite the A'ngirasi S'ruti, as laid down in the *Atharvan* (*i.e.*, practise deadly incantations). Word is the weapon of a Bráhmaṇa, let him kill his enemies therewith. (33)

A Kshatriya shall get rid of his trouble by the prowess of his arm; a Vais'ya or a S'udra, by the aid

---

* According to a certain calendar the Vediac year used to commence with the light fortnight of *Chaitra*.

of his wealth; and a good Bráhmaṇa, by means of *Japas* and *Homas.* (34)

An institutor of proper religious rites,* governor of sons and disciples, expounder (of spiritual or moral truths, or of Law Codes), equally compassionate to all creatures, is called a Bráhmaṇa; a harsh or abusive language must not be used unto him (such a Bráhmaṇa. (35)

An unmarried girl, a youthful matron, an unread Bráhmaṇa, one of small learning, one afflicted with a disease, or uninitiated with the holy thread must not perform the *Agnihotra Homa*† (fire offering). (36)

For having cast such libations in the fire, these (unmarried girls, etc.) shall go to hell, together with the person on whose behalf they do such fire-offerings; hence, a Bráhmaṇa, well-versed in the *Vedas* and in the art of performing such fire-offerings, shall act as a *Hotá* (*i.e.*, offerer of the libation, or doer of the fire-offering.) (37)

He, who, having had the means to give a horse which is sacred to *Prajápati*, to the officiating priest (*Ríttvik*) as his *Dakshiná* (fee) on the occasion of first establishing (kindling) the sacred fire, does not give it to him, remains as one who has not kindled the sacred fire, and fails to obtain the merit of the rite. (38)

Let not one, believing and self-controlled, doing other religious rites, perform sacrifices by giving

---

* The text has *Vidháta* which may also mean an ordainer of laws.

† They are not competent to perform the *Homas* enjoined to be performed in the Vedas by a Bráhmana, morning and evening, each day (*S'raután Sáyam prátar homán na Kuryuh*).—*Kulluka.*

small amounts of fees *(Dakshiná)* to the officiating priests). (39)

A sacrifice, performed with a small amount of fees (paid to the priest), destroys the progeny, (domestic) animals, fame and the senses of its institutor, shortens the duration of his life, and acts as a bar against his Heaven. Hence, let no one perform a sacrifice with a small amount of money. (40)

An *Agnihotri* (performer of the *Agnihotra* fire-offering) Bráhmaṇa, who wilfully neglects to do the fire-offering, morning and evening, each day, shall do the penance of *Chándráyana* for a month, inasmuch as the sin (thereby committed) is equal to that of killing (one's own) son. (41)

They, who having obtained money from S'udras, do the *Agnihotra* fire-offerings, are condemned by the *Brahmavadins* as the priests of S'udras. (42)

Resting his feet on the heads of those foolish *Rittviks* (sacrificers) who do the fire-offerings with the help of money obtained from him, the S'udra donor (of the money) shall rise up from, and get rid of, hell. (43)

For having done improper acts and failed to do the commendable ones (rites), and for having been attached to objects of the senses, a man stands under the obligation of doing an expiatory penance. (44)

(Several) wise men assert that, atonement is possible only for sins, involuntarily committed; while others, grounding their decision on precedents [in the *Vedas*, hold that, expiation is possible even in respect of sins, deliberately committed. (45)

A sin, unwittingly committed, is atoned by reading

the *Vedas*; those, wilfully committed, require separate expiatory penances for their atonement. (46)

Having incurred the obligation of doing an expiatory penance for a sin accidentally (unwittingly) committed in this life, or for one done in his previous existence, a Bráhmana must not associate with other (pure) Bráhmaṇas before he has made the atonement. (47)

Of miscreants, some through misdeeds done in this life, and others through sins committed in their previous existences, become deformed in their persons. (48)

A gold-stealer is (born with) bad nails; a wine-drinker, with black teeth; a Bráhmanicide is afflicted with consumption; and a defiler of his preceptor's bed, with skin-troubles (*lit.* bad skin.) (49)

A true calumniator is born with fetid nostrils (*i.e.*, is afflicted with foul-smelling nasal catarrh); a false calumniator, with a bad smell in his mouth; a paddy-stealer is born with a limb in less; and a mixer (adulterer of grains, etc.), with a limb in excess. (50)

A stealer of food is (punished with) a sluggish appetite; and a stealer of words,* with dumbness; a cloth-stealer is born with leucoderma, and a horse-stealer is born maimed. (51)

A lamp (light)-stealer is born blind; an extinguisher of light, blind in the one eye; a killer of animal lives is (punished with) many diseases (in this life) and a ravisher of another's wife, with (a nervous swelling of the limbs (due to nervous disorder) (52).

Thus (through the dynamaics of) different misdeeds

---

* The text has *Vâgâpahârakah*. KULLUKA explains it by "*Ananujnàtadhyâin*," one who learns the *Veda* by hearing it recited by another without the premission of a preceptor.

men are born idiotic, deaf, dumb, blind, deformed, or possessed of limbs in less or excess, abhorred by the virtuous (53).

Thus for the purification of Self, expiating penances should be always practised; unexpiated sinners are born with condemnable bodily traits (54).

Killing a Bráhmana, wine-drinking, gold-stealing, and defiling the bed of a preceptor are said to be the great sins, the company of these sinners being the fifth (great sin). (55)

False speaking with a view to give out one's self as belonging to a superior caste, accusing one before the king of a crime punishable with death, and false allegation (calumny) in respect of one's own preceptor tantamount to killing a Bráhmaṇa (*Brahmahatyà*) (56)

Forgetting the *Vedas* through non-study (on the part of a Bráhmaṇa), reviling the *Vedas*, bearing false witness in a court of justice and eating unclean things are equal to wine-drinking (57).

Stealing an article held in trust, and stealing a man, horse, land, diamond or gem are said to be equal to gold-stealing (58)

Casting seed in one's own uterine sister (*Svayoni*), in an unmarried girl, in a Chandála woman, in one's own daughter-in-law, or in a friend's wife is equal to defiling the bed of one's own preceptor. (59)

Cow-killing, officiating as a priest at a sacrifice instituted by an unworthy person, incest with another's wife, abandoning one's own parents, preceptor, or son (*i.e.*, omission to do purificatory rites unto him), as well as renouncing the study of the *Vedas* and non-performances of fire-offerings. (60)

Marriage of a younger brother before the marriage of his elder, an unmarried elder brother suffering his younger to marry before him, giving a girl in marriage to either° of two such brothers, and officiating as a priest at such a marriage ceremony. (61)

Defiling an unmarried girl (with the finger),* living by usury, breaking the vow (of continence), and selling one's tanks, orchards, wives, and sons. (62)

Failure to initiate a child with the thread (before he is sixteen years of age), abandoning one's relations, teaching the *Vedas* for money, studying the *Vedas* under a preceptor who takes fees for his teaching, and selling things which ought not to be sold. (63)

Working in all kinds of mines (under the king's command), raising large dams or embankments, destruction of medicinal plants, living by the earnings of the prostitution of one's own wife, practising deadly incantations, and hypnotising by means of drugs. (64)

Felling down unwithered trees for fuels, cooking for one's own self (and not for the gods or manes), and eating condemnable (prohibited) articles of fare. (65).

Omission to establish the sacred fire, gold-stealing, undischarging the debts due to the gods, to the Rishis and to one's own manes, cultivation of prohibited sciences, and adopting the profession of a songster, or of a musician. (66)

Stealing paddy, animals, iron and copper etc.,† going unto a drunk woman, killing a Vais'ya, S'udra,

---

* The text has *Kanyáya-dushananchaiva* ; KULLUKA explains it by *Maithuna Varjamanguli prakshepàdinà* which would not bear translation.

† The text has *Kupyam* which signifies any metal other than gold or silver.

Kshatriya or a woman, and atheism (non-conformity to the doctrines of *Vediac* religion)—all these are called minor sins (*Upapàtakas*). (67)

[Each of the following acts such as,] assaulting a Bráhmaṇa with a club, etc., smelling wine or any other unclean substance which ought not to be smelled, crooked dealings, and committing unnatural offence on a man, constitutes cast-degrading *(Játi-Bhransa-kara)* sin.* (68)

Killing an ass, horse, camel, deer, elephant, goat, lamb, fish, snake or a buffalo constitutes *Sankari-karanam* (hybridising) sin.† (69)

Receiving money from the condemnable, trading, serving a S'udra, or speaking falsehood constitutes a sin which is known as *Apátrikaranam*.‡ (70)

Killing a worm, insect or a bird, eating food brought on the same plate with wine, stealing fruits, flowers, fuels, or feeling agitated at the slightest cause of disturbance constitutes a sin which is called *Malâvaham* or (mind-soiling sin.) (71)

These sins have been separately and specifically described, now hear me discourse on the expiatory penances which should be respectively practised for their atonement. (72)

For the purification of his self a Bráhmanicide shall stay for twelve years* in the forest, building a hut therein, living on food obtained by begging, and carry-

---

* A person guilty of any of these crimes becomes degraded from his caste.

† A person, guilty of killing any of these animals, will have a mixed caste (*Sankara Játi*) in his next existence.

‡ *Apátrikaranam i.e.*, a sin which makes one unworthy of receiving gifts.

ing the cranium of a human skeleton as the token of his (fell crime).* (73)

Or he shall voluntarily make himself the target of arrows shot by archers with unfailing aims; or he shall thrice cast himself in a burning fire with his head downward so that death may ensue. (74)

Or he shall institute any of the following *Vediac* sacrifices, *viz.*, the *As'vamedha*, the *Sarjit*, the *Gosava*, the *Vis'vajit*, the *Trivrit*, or the *Agnishtut*. (75)

For the expiation of the sin of killing a Brâhmâṇa, he, self-controlled, and sparing in his diet, shall travel a hundred *Yojanas* (*i e.*, eight hundred miles), muttering any of the *Vedas*.† (76)

Or he shall make over all his belongings to a Brâhmaṇa, well-versed in the *Vedas*, or shall give him a well-furnished house and ample wealth for his living. (77)

Or living on a vegetable diet, he shall walk along the shore of the river, Sarasvati from its source to its

---

* This is only in respect of an accidental killing of a Bráhmana. According to the Bhavishya Puranam a man (Brâhmana) of superior qualifications, having accidentally killed an unqualified (foolish and impious) Bráhmana, shall do this penance for twelve years. For having wilfully killed a member of his own caste, a Bráhmana shall do this penance for double the aforesaid period (*i.e.*, twenty-four years). A Kshatriya, a Vais'ya, or a S'udra, guilty of unwillingly killing a Brâhmana, shall respectively do this penance for twenty-four, thirty-six, and forty-eight years.

† This is the expiation for accidentally killing a man, who is merely a Bráhmana by caste, and when the killer is either a Bráhmana, Kshatriya or Vais'ya. The Bhavishyapuranam reads and interprets the passage as, if a *Veda*-knowing Bráhmana, a regular institutor of the *Agnihotra* fire-offering, accidentally kills one, who is a mere Bráhmana by caste, then this is the expiation for him.

place of junction with the sea, or observing moderation in food he shall thrice recite a *Vedaic Samhitâ*, each day. (78)

Or (at the end of the twelfth year), he, with his head cleanly shaven, and finger-nails parid off, shall live at the out-skirt of a village, or in a cow-shed, or in a hermitage, or underneath a tree, devoted to the good of kine and Bráhmaṇas. (79)

Or by laying down his life for the succour of a cow, or of a Brâhmaṇa, he shall be exonerated from the sin of killing a Brâhmaṇa; by succouring a cow or a Brâhmaṇa, (before the lapse of the twelfth year), he shall be free from the sin of an act of Brâhmaṇa killing, even if he does not die in the attempt. (80)

Or by thrice fighting with the robbers for the recovery of the goods (they have stolen from the house of a Bráhmaṇa), or by recovering the goods in a single fight, or by giving an equal amount of wealth to the robbed Bráhmaṇa attempting to kill himself for its loss, he shall be exonerated from the sin (of killing a Bráhmaṇa. (81)

Thus having practised these austere penances, and lived an absolutely continent life for twelve years, he shall be exonerated from the sin of killing a Bráhmaṇa. (82)

Or having confessed his guilt at the close of an *As'vamedha* sacrifice, instituted by the king, and performed the ceremonial ablution *(Avabhrita Snánam)* at the end of the ceremony, he shall be from the sin of Brâhmaṇa killing. (83)

The Bráhmaṇa is the root of virtue, the Kshatriya is its fore part; hence, by confessing his guilt in their assembly, a man becomes free from sin. (84)

On his very birth the Bráhmaṇa becomes the god of the gods and the authority (in matters of virtue) in this world. The *Veda* testifies to the source of his authority. (85)

Whatever three of these *Veda*-knowing Bráhmaṇas shall speak in respect of the expiation of one's sin shall be his perfect expiation; holy is the speech of the erudite (*Veda*-knowing Bráhmaṇas). (86)

The self-controlled Bráhmaṇa, with his mind fixed on God, shall impartially* practise any of these penances for the expiation of the sin of Bráhmaṇa-killing. (87)

For having unwillingly killed a fœtus in the womb, a Vais'ya or a Kshatriya engaged in performing a religious sacrifice, or a woman in her menses, one shall practise the same expiatory penance. (88)

As well as for having borne false witness, or calumnised his preceptor, or robbed an article held by him in trust, or killed a friend or a woman. (89)

Thus the penance is laid down for expiating the sin of accidentally (unwillingly) killing a Bráhmaṇa; no expiation there exists for the sin of wilful Bráhmaṇa-killing. (90)

For having drunk (*Paishti*) wine,† one shall atone his sin by drinking a cup of burning wine; he shall be

---

* Without showing any perference to any particular form of penance. Or in other words, he must not choose and observe a light penance, if his guilt requires the practice of a severe one.

† The Bhabishya-puranam interprets *Surá* by *Paikhti* wine (*i.e.*, wine made from pasted rice) and asserts that the expiatory penances laid down in respect of wine-drinking in the *Manu* apply to drinking Paishti wine alone in exclusion of other species of wine such as *Gaudi*, *Mádhvi*, etc.

Surá cha Paishti Mukhyoktá na tasyá stvitaresame, Paishtyáh páne tu chaitásám práyas'chittam nivodha me.

free from the sin after his inner organism has been burnt by that wine (*i.e.*, after death from drinking hot wine. (91)

Or he shall live on flame coloured cow-urine, water, milk, clarified butter, and cow-dung serum till death. (92)

For the expiation of the sin of wine-drinking, let him, clad in a woolen cloth, wearing clotted hair, and carrying the mark of a wine-bowl on his forehead, live for a year by eating sesame-cake or broken bits of rice, once in the night. (93)

Wine (*Surá*) is the impure essence (*lit.* refuge matter) of grains, and sinful is a refuge matter; hence, let not Bráhmaṇas, Kshatriyas and Vais'yas drink wine (*Surá*). (94)

Gaudi (treacle wine), *Paishti* (wine of pasted rice) and *Mádhvi* (wine made from the flowers of Mahua tree) are known to be the three species of wine; all of them, like any, must not be drunk by the foremost of Brâhmaṇas. (95)

Flesh, wine, and fermented saps are the food of Yakshas, Rakshas, and Pisâchas; they should not be eaten or drunk by Brâhmanas, who partake of the oblations of thé gods. (96)

An intoxicated Bráhmana may fall on an impure ground, or recite the Vediac mantras, or do any other improper acts under the influence of wine. (97)

He, in whose body the encased *Brahma* is washed with the stream of wine, stands divulged of his *Brahmâniac* energy and becomes a S'udra. (98)

Thus the excellent expiation for the sin of wine-drinking has been described; now I shall discourse on the expiation for the sin of gold-stealing. (99)

A Bráhmana, who has stolen gold, shall go to the king; and confessing his guilt, he shall say, "punish me, O King." (100)

The king, taking hold of a club, shall kill him (the gold stealer) with one blow, inasmuch as death purifies a gold-stealer ;* a Brâhmana gold-stealer shall effect his purification by dint of penitential austerities. (101)

A Brâhmana, wishing to exculpate the sin of gold stealing† by means of penitential austerities, shall, clad in rags, practise the expiating penance, laid down for an act of Brâhmana-killing, in the forest. (102)

Brâhmanas (*lit.*, twice-born ones) shall exculpiate themselves of the sin of gold-stealing by means of these penitential austerities; from the sin of defiling the beds of their preceptors they shall kikewise exonerate themselves by means of these purificatory penances. (103)

A Brâhmana, guilty of defiling the bed of his preceptor (*i.e*, of incest with his own step mother), having confessed his guilt, shall lie down in a red hot iron bed, holding in his embrace a burning female figour of iron, till death; he is purified by his death. (104)

---

* Dead, or surviving, if almost dead, he (gold-stealer) shall be purged off of his sin.—*Yajnavalkya*.

† Stealing gold weighing eighty Ratis or more constitutes the sin of *Steyam* according to Manu, and if the gold belongs to a Brahmana, theft of five *Krishnalam* or sixteen *mashas* weight, thereof would constitute the offence. The *Bhavishya Puranam*, on the other hand, increases the weight of gold in such cases to five *Nishkas* Says it—("Men belonging to) three castes, commencing with the "Kshatriya," happening to rob an amply qualified Brahmana of gold to the weight of five *Nishkas*..................shall regain his purity by immolating his body in fire.

Or after having cut off his reproductive organs and held them in the hollow of his blended palms, let him slowly go towards the south-west, until he falls down and expires. (105)

Stamped with the figure of a bedstead on his forehead, let him, clad in rags and growing a beard, practise the penance of *Krichcha-vratam* for a year in the forest, with all his senses fully brought under his control.* (106)

Or for expiating the sin of (accidentally) visiting the bed of his own step-mother (*lit.* elder's or preceptor's wife) he shall live on barley gruel, or on a *Habishya* (vegetable) diet, and parctise, self-controlled, the *Chándráyanam* penance for three months (in succession.) (107)

The sin of great sinners (*Mahápátakins*) should be expiated by practising these penances; persons, guilty of minor sins (*Upapatakins*), shall practise the following purificatory penances by way of atonement. (108)

One, who has committed the minor sin of killing a cow, shall live on barly gruel during the first month of his penance, and having cleanly shaved his head, beard and moustache, shall live in the pasture ground, clad with the skin of the cow he has killed. (109)

[During the second and third months of his penance] self-controlled, he shall eat a moderate quantity of food with (any sort of) non-alkaline salt in the evening of each second day, after having fasted on the previous one, and bathe with cow's urine. (110)

* The expiatory penance owing to its comparatively lesser austere character seems to contemplate the case in which a man visits the bed of his own step-mother, mistaking her for his own wife.—*Kulluka.*

In the day he shall follow the kine (to the pasture ground), inhale the dusts risen by their hoofs from the ground, and tend them with care; and after having made obeisance to them, he shall sit up in the night in the posture, known as the *Virâsanam** (111)

Bereft of all feelings of vexation or pride, he shall stand when the kine will remain standing, sit down when they will lie down, and follow them when they will roam about. (112)

By all means he must succour them, whether afflicted with any disease, or frightened by tigers and thieves, etc., or fallen in the mire, or in any unfavourable predicament. (113)

In heat, in rain, in cold, or when a strong wind is blowing, he must not protect his person before providing a suitable shelter for them (kine) to the best of his ability. (114)

Having seen a cow grazing on a field, or on a thrashing floor, whether of his own or of another, or having seen a cow suckling her calf, he must not speak of it to any body. (115)

A cow-killer, who follows a cow in this manner for three months in succession, becomes free from the sin of cow-killing. (116)

Having thus well-practised the purificatory penance, he shall make a gift of a bullock and ten kine to a *Veda*-knowing Brâhmaṇa; or in their absence he shall make over all his belongings to such a Brâhmaṇa. (117)

Brâhmaṇas, who have committed the minor sins (*Upapâtakins*), excepting those who have broken

* *Virâsanam*—Sitting on hams, with his right knee flexed and right foot placed on the left thigh and with left knee flexed, and left thigh placed on the right thigh.—*Vas'ishtha.*

their vows *(Avakirnis)*, shall practise the (abovesaid) penances, or the *Chàndràyanam* penance for purification. (118)

A vow-breaker shall sacrifice an ass, blind in the one eye, at a crossing of roads, to the deity, *Niriti*, in the night, by uttering the *Mantras* of the *Pákayajna*. (119)

Then having done a fire-offering (with the flesh of the immolated) ass unto the deity, *Niriti*, he shall offer libations of clarified butter unto *Vâyu*, *Indra*, *Brihaspati* and *Agni* in the fire, by muttering the *Rik*, running a (*Sama Sinchantu Maruta*, let Maruta sprinkle with water, etc.) (120)

The *Brahmavâdins*, the knowers of the Law, aver that, by violating his vow, and by wilfully casting his seed (during its observance), a *Bramachárin* (religious student) becomes guilty of the sin of vow-breaking (*Avakirni*). (121)

The Bráhmanic energy of a religious student, which has originated from his study of the Vedas, etc., ascend to (*i.e.* are merged in) the (deities) Máruta, Puruhuta (Indra), Guru (Brihaspati) and Agni, after he has broken his vow.* (122)

Having committed such a sin, let him (the vow-breaker), clad in the skin of an ass, beg alms at seven houses, confessing his guilt. (123)

For a year he shall live taking, once a day, food obtained by begging as above described, and bathe thrice, every day, whereby he shall be free from his sin. (124)

Havsng wilfully commited any of the caste-degrating (*Jâti-Bhransakara*) sins, he shall practise a

* Hence a vow-breaking Brahmachârin shall offer libations of clarified butter unto these deities.

Krichchhra Sântapanm penance; for the expiation of any of such sins involuntarily committed, he must practise a *Prâjâpatyam* penance. (125)

Having committed a sin of the hybridising (*Sankari Karanam*) or *Apâtri Karanam* group, he shall practise for a month the *Chândrâyonam* penance for its expiation; having committed a crime of the mind-soiling (*Malini Karanam*) group he shall live on barley gruel for three days in succession. (126)

For having wilfully killed a (good natured) Kshatriya, one shall practise the quarter part of the expiatory penance (*i.e.* for three years) laid down in respect of an act of Bráhmana-killing; and a sixteenth part of the same penance should be practised for the expiation of killing a sacrificing Vaisya, and a S'udra respettively. (127)

The foremost of Bráhmanas, having accidentally killed a Kshatriya, shall duly practise the expiatory penance, and make the gift of one bullock and a thousand kine to a Bráhmana (at its end.) (128)

Or self-controlled, and wearing clotted hair, he shall practise the expiatory penance laid down in respect of an act of Bráhmana-killing, living remote from the village and under a tree, (129)

For having accidentally killed a Vais'ya, engaged in performing a sacrifice, let these foremost of Bráhmanas practise the (preceding) penance for a year and make the gift of one hundred kine to a Bráhmana at its close. (130)

For having killed a S'udra, let him do the same expiatory penance for six months, and give a *Dakshiná* of one bullock and ten white kine to a Bráhmana. (131)

For having wilfully killed a cat, an ichneumon, a Châsa bird, a frog, a dog, a lizard (Godhâ), an owl, or a crow, let him do the penance, laid down for expiation of the sin of killing a S'udra. (132)

[For having accidentally killed a cat, etc.,] he shall live for three days on a milk-diet; or shall travel one *Yojanam*, each day, for three days; or shall bathe in a running stream of water for three days; or recite the (*Apohistà*, etc.) *Suktam* of the *Veda* for three nights. (133)

Having killed a snake, let the foremost of Bráhmaṇas give a sharp-pointed steel rod to a Bráhmaṇa; for having killed an impotent person, he shall make the gift of a *Bhàra* of straw, and of a *Màsha* weight of lead. (134)

For having killed a boar, he shal make the gift of a pitcher, full of clarified butter, and of a *Drona* measure of sesame; for having killed a peasant or parrot, he shall make the gift of a calf, two years old; of a calf, three year old, he shall make a gift, for having killed a heron. (135)

For having killed a crane, a swan, a duck, a peacock, a monkey, a falcon, or a Bhasá bird, he must make the gift of a cow to a Bráhmana. (136)

For having killed a horse, he must give a cloth to a Brṇhmana; and five Nila bullocks, for having killed an elephant; for having killed a goat, or a sheep, he must give a bullock to a Bráhmana; for having killed an ass he must make the gift of a calf, one year old, to a Bráhmana. (137)

For having killed a carnivorous beast, let hi n give a milch cow to a Bráhmana; for having killed a herbivorous animal, he must give a calf to a Brâhmana, and for having killed a camel, he shall make the gift of a *rati* of gold to a Bráhmana. (138)

For having killed a faithless wife, belonging to any of the four castes, a Bráhmana shall make the gift of a leather bag; a Kshatriya, of a bow; a Vais'ya, of a goat; and a S'udra, of a lamb. (139)

A Bráhmana, incapable of expiating his sin of snake-killing, etc., by means of gift, shall do a *Prájàpatya* penance for the expiation of each of such sins. (140)

For having killed one thousand of vertebrate animals, one shall do the penance for an act of S'udra-killing; the same penance should be practised for having killed a cart-load of invertebrate animals. (141)

For having killed a (small) vertebrate animal, one shall give a small Dakshinâ to a Bráhmana; having killed a small vertebrate animal, one regains his purity by doing a *Pránáyáma.* (142)

For having filled a blossoming, fruit-yielding tree, creeper, shrub or plant, one shall mutter a hundred *Rik mantras.* (143)

For killing parasites which germinate in food grains or in sweet saps (such as treacle, etc.,) or in fruits and flowers, drinking of clarified butter should be known as the expiation. (144)

For having cut down cereals, growing on a cultivated soil, as well as those which spontaneously grow in uncultivated fields, one shall regain his purity by living on a milk-diet for a day and by following the cows to the pasture-ground. (145)

By means of these penances, the sin, originated from acts of killing, should be expiated; now hear me discourse on the expiatory penances to be done for eating improper food, whether wittingly or unwittingly. (146)

Having unknowingly drunk *Várunî* wine* one must be re-initiated with the holy thread; for having knowingly drunk it, one shall atone for his sin by his life, this is the decisian. (147)

Having drunk water kept in a wine bowl, or in a cup (of that species of wine which is called) *Surá*, one shall live on milk cooked with Sankhapushpi (creeper) for five days in succession. (148)

Having touched, or given wine (to any body,) or having duly accepted a gift, or having drunk water, previously tasted by a S'udra, one shall live on the washings of *Ku'sa* grass for three nights. (149)

A Soma-drinking Bráhmana, having smelled the breath of a drunkard, shall do three *A'chamanams* and three *Pránáyámas* in water, and shall effect his purification by drinking clarified butter. (150)

Members of the three twice-born castes, having unknowingly tasted excreta or anything defiled by the touch of wine, deserve re-initiation with the thread. (151)

The shaving of the head, (wearing of) the holy girdle, carrying the staff, alms-begging, and practising the vow (of a Brahmachárin) are dispensed with in such re-initiations of the twice-born ones. (152)

Having eaten the food of those whose food ought not to be eaten, or having eaten the leavings of S'udras' or of women's food, or having eaten the flesh of prohibited animals, one shall live on barley gruel for seven nights. (153)

---

* *Várunî* is a kind of wine prepared from fermented ricerboilings. For having drunk any of the nine species of wine, mentioned by Pulastya, other than Paishti, Mádhavi, and Gaudi the expiation consists in being reinitiated with the thread.

Having taken *Suktas* (cordials which acquire an acid taste when stale) and decoctions of astringent drugs (such as Chebulic myrobalans etc.,) one shall remain impure until they are not evacuated from his bowels. (154)

Having taken the stool or urine of a domestic pig, of a bear, of an ass, of a camel, of a jackal, of a monkey, or of a crow, a Brâhmana shall do the *Chàndràyanam* penance (for his purification.) (155)

Having eaten dry meat, earth-born mushrooms, butcher's meat, or the flesh of an unknown animal, one shall do the same penance (*i.e. Chàndràyanam.*) (156)

For having eaten the flesh of a carnivorous animal, of a boer, of a camel, or of a cow, or having eaten the flesh of a man, of a crow, or of an ass, the performance of the *Tapta Krichchham* penance should be understood as (the proper) purification. (157)

A Bráhmana, who before having completed his Vediac study shall eat a monthly *S'ràddha* feast shall fast for three days, one of which he shall pass by sitting in water. (158)

A religious student who has somehow eaten flesh or has taken honey, shall complete the residue of his vow (of *Brahmacharyam*) by doing a *Krichchha Prâjàpatyam* penance. (159)

Having eaten the leavings of the food of a cat, of a crow, of a rat, of a dog, or of an ichneu-mon, as well as boiled rice infested with insects and hairs, one shall drink *Brahma subarchalá* (a kind of consecrated linseed gruel.) (160)

One, valuing the purity of his ownself, must not partake of any kind of forbidden food; having unknowingly eaten such a fare, one must immediately belch that out, or adopt any other kind of purifying measure. (161)

The varions purificatory penances for the expiation of sins, incidental to eating prohibited food, have been described; now hear me discourse on the expiatory penances to be practised for acts of gold-stealing. (162)

The foremost of Brâhmanas, having wilfully stolen paddy (food-grains), food or money from the house of member of his own caste, shall be purified by practising a *Krichchhra* penance for a year. (163)

For having stolen a man (slave), a woman, house, or a field, or the water of a tank or well the *Chàndràyonam* should be understood as the proper expiation. (164)

For having stolen an article or substance of insignificent value (such as, lead, etc.,) from the house of another, he shall make over the same to its owner, and do the *Krichchhara Sàntapanam* penance for the purificotion of his self. (165)

For stealing articles of food which are eaten by chewing, or any kind of liquid food, as well as for steating a bedding or a cushion, a vehicle, a fruit, a root, or a flower the drinking of *Panchagavyam* compound is the proper expiation. (166)

For having stolen hay, wood, trees, treacle, dry food grains, cloths, hydes, and flesh, one shall fast for three days (*lit.*, three day's fast is the expiation). (167)

For having stolen gems, pearls, corals, copper silver, iron, white copper and stones, one shall live on a gruel of particles of broken rice. (168)

For having stolen cloths made of cotton, silk or wool or an animal with bifurcated or unbifurcated hoofs birds, scents, cereals or camphor, one shall live on milk for three days. (169)

By these (expiatory) penances a Brâhman (*lit.*, twice-born one) shall purge off his sin of stealing; the sin of carnally knowing a forbidden woman should be expiated by the following ones (penances). (170)

For casting his seed in the womb of his own uterine sister, of a friend's wife, or of his daughter-in-law, or of an unmarried girl, or of a woman of vile (*Chandâla*) caste. (171)

Or for carnally knowing a daughter of one's own father's or mother's sister, or a daughter of the brother of one's own mother, one shall do a *Chándráyanam* penance. (172)

Let not the intelligent one covet any of the (preceding) three kinds of sisters for his wife, inasmuch as they are unobtainable (unmarriageable) on account of their tie of agnateship (*Jnátitvam*); by going unto such a (sister), one becomes degraded. (173)

For having cast his seed in a man, in a she-animal (other than a cow), in a woman in her menses, in any part of the (female body other than the proper channel), or in water, one shall practice a *Krichchara* (severely austere) *Sántapanam* (penance). (174)

After having carnally known a man or a woman, or after having copulated (anywhere, whether) in a bullock cart (or otherwise), a Brâhmana must bathe, with all his clothes on, in water. (175)

By carnally knowing a *Chandâla* or a vile caste woman, by partaking of their food, or by accepting gifts from them, without the knowledge of their vile caste, a Brâhmana becomes degraded; by wilfully doing all these acts, he becomes of the same cast with them. (176)

A wilfully faithless wife let the husband keep imprisoned in a chamber, divested of all her wifely duties; and let him cause her practise the penance laid down in connection with the sin of a man's carnal knowledge of another's wife. (177)

If she, solicited by a man of her own caste, suffers herself to be defiled by him, in that case the performance of a *Krichchra Chàndràyanam* penance is the proper expiation (178)

The sin which a Bráhmaṇa commits by sexually knowing a *Chandàla* woman* is expiated by his living for three years on food obtained by begging, and by muttering the sacred (*Sávitri*) mantra (during all that period) (179)

Thus the purificatory rites for the expiation of sins of the four kinds of sinners† have been described); now, hear me describe those which should be done for the expiation of sin, incidental to one's associating with the degraded (180)

By sharing the same bed, or cushion, or by riding in the same car with, or by eating in the company of a degraded person for a year, a man becomes degraded; by teaching the Vedas to such a person, or by officiating as a priest at a sacrifice instituted by him, or by

---

* The text has *Vrishali*; KULLUKA explains it by *Chandála* woman. The term may also mean a vile-caste or S'udra woman, an unmarried girl in her menses, an old woman, or a married woman in her flow.

† Killers of animal lives, eaters of prohibited articles of food, gold-stealers, and those who hold sexual intercourse with prohibited female relations or forbidden women.

contracting any marital relation with him, one becomes degraded on the same day (181)

He, who associates with a degraded person, must practise the same penance for his purification, as is laid down for the expiation of the sin through which that person has become degraded (182)

The *Sapindas* or *Bandhus* (relations) of a degraded person shall do the water-rite unto him in his life time, at the outskrit of their village, and in the presence of his cognates (Jnátis), priest and preceptor, on the evening of a condemnable day of the lunar month (such as the ninth day of the moon's wane or increase). (183)

A slave-girl of theirs shall kick off a pitcher, full of water, as if he had been dead; and after that, his *Sapindas* (and Samánodakas) shall fast and observe uncleanness for a day with his Bandhus. (184)

From thence all dealing, speaking, association, or sitting with that degraded person by others shall cease; the patrimony of such a person shall not be given to him (185).

The right of eldest-bornship, the honour due to him as such, and the right to a preferential excess share as the eldest born (of his father) shall be extinguished as far as such a degraded (eldest brother) is concerned; a more qualified younger brother shall take the share (in the paternal property) due to him (*i. e.*, degraded eldest brother) (186)

Having done (the proper) expiatory penance, he (the degraded person) in the company of his *Sapindas* and *Samànodaka* relations) shall bath in a tank and cast a new pitcher, full of water, therein. (187)

Having cast the pitcher in the water, he shall enter his house, and thence forward discharge all the duties of relationship with his cognates (*Jnàti*) (188)

All these measures should be adopted in respect of women who have become degraded; but they should be provided with food and raiments, and allowed to live close to their houses (189)

Let no one have any dealings with an unexpiated sinner, nor in any way calumnise the one who has made the proper atonement for his sin. (190)

Let no one associate with an infanticide, with a treacherous person, with a woman-killer, or with one who has killed a man taken under his protection, even after he has done the proper expiatory penance. (191)

Twice-born ones, who have not been initiated with the *Gàyatri* at their respectively proper ages (of initiation), shall first practise three *Krichchhra* penances;* thereafter they should be initiated with the holy thread. (192)

Bràhmanas, who do improper acts,† and who, though initiated with the thread, are ignorant of the *Vedas*, if they wish to do the expiatory penance, should be likewise advised to practise the same penance (*i e. Krichchhra Vratam*) (193)

The sin which a Bràhmana commits by earning money by vile means is expiated by his muttering the purifying *Mantras* and by renouncing the same. (194)

---

* Vràtyastoma penance according to Yàjnavalkya, the nature of the expiatory penance should be determined in these cases with an eye to the physical capacity of the penitent to do the same—*Kulluka*

† Such as taking gifts from S'udras, or serving them in any capatity whatsoever—*Kulluka*.

By muttering, self controlled, the *Sávitri mantra* three thousand times, by living in the pasture ground on milk only for one month, a Bráhmaṇa becomes exonerated from the sim of accepting the gift of an unworthy person (195)

Returned from the pasture ground, depleted with fasting and fully subdued, him (Bráhmaṇa) they must ask, " well, beloved do you wish to be on an equal footing with us ?* (196)

Having said " yea" to the Bráhmaṇas, he shall scatter grass before the cows; after the cows have commenced eating that fodder in that land, converted into a temporary sanctuary (on account of the cows eating there on), they (the Bráhmaṇas) shall accept that agreement (as to his future good conduct) (197)

Having officiated as a priest at a sacrifice in stituted by a *Vràtya* (a twice born one not initiated with th e thread within the proper age limit) for the expiat ion of his sin (*i.e.* at a *Vratya Stoma* sacrifice), or having attended the funeral rites of one (other than his parent or preceptor), or having practised any deadly incantation (such as *S'yena yâga*, etc); or done the *Ahina* sacrifice,† one shall be free from sin by doing three *Kṛichchra* penances (198)

A Brâhmana, who although capable, has not given protection to its seeker, or has taught the Vedas to one who should not be so taught, shall expiate his sin by eating barley corn for a year. (199

---

* *i.e.* do you promise not to accept gifts of the unworthy in future?

† *Ahina* sacrifice is a Vediac sacrifice in which fermented *Soma* juice was used to be drunk in large quantities for three days (nine according to others) in succession. To officiate as a priest at an *Ahina* sacrifice is defiling—*Sruti.*

Having been bitten by a village dog, jackal, ass, man, horse, camel, or a boar, a Brâhmana shall purify himself by doing a *Prânâyama*. (200)

For having eaten in the same row with diners, not fit to sit therein (*Upânkteyas*), for a month, one shall take food on the evening of each fourth day, fasting on the days previous, and read the *Sanhitâs* and do fire-offerings, each day, for his purification. (201)

Having wilfully riden in a carriage drawn by an ass, or by a camel, a Brâhmana shall purify himself by bathing stript of all clothes, and by practising a *Prânâyama*. (202)

A man, afflicted with a natural urging for stool or urine, having micturated or defecated without water,* or in water, shall regain his purity by bathing with all his clothes on in a running stream at the out-skirt of a village, and by touching a cow as well. (203)

For omission to perform the daily religious rites enjoined to be performed in the *Vedas*, as well as for breaking the vow of a *Snataka* (the rite of ceremonial ablution to be performed by a *Brahmacharin)* fasting for an entire day and night is the expiation. (204)

For having arrogantly ordered a Bráhmana to keep silence, or for having bethoued one's preceptor, the penitent shall bathe and fast for the day, and thereafter appease the insulted (Bráhmana or preceptor) by catching hold of his feet. (205)

For having assaulted a Brâhmana even with a straw, or for having fastened his throat with a piece of cloth, or for having defeated him in a dispute, one shall appease him by prostrating himself at his feet. (206)

---

* Having not washed himself with water after micturation or defecation.

For having raised a club (rod) with the intention of assaulting a Brâhmana, one goes to hell for a hundred years; for having assaulted him therewith he lives in hell for three thousand years. (207)

For as many thousands of years as the particles of dust which are stained by his blood, the assaulter of a Bráhmana shall live in hell. (208)

For having threatened a Brâhmana with a stick, one shall do a *Krichchhram* (*Prajápatyam*) penance, for having beaten him with a stick one shall do an *Ati-Krichchhra* penance; and for having drawn blood on his body, one shall do a *Krichchhrâti Krichchham* penance. (209)

For the expiation of sins in respect of which no purificatory measures have been specifically laid down (in this code), expiatory penances should be advised in consideration of the lightness or gravity of the sin and the capacity of the penitent to do the same. (210)

Measures, by adopting which men are exonerated from their sins and which had been embraced (of yore) by the manes and deities, I shall presently describe to you. (211)

A Bráhmana, doing a *Prajâpatyam* penance, shall eat his meals in the day (during the first three days of its term), at the evening (during the second three days), shall live on food obtained without solicitation and arrived at any part of the day (during the third three days), and fast for the (last) three days (of its term.)* (212)

---

* On the first three days he shall eat twenty-six morsels of food, each as large as a hen's egg, on the second three days he shall eat such twenty-two morsels of food in the evening, and such twenty-four morsels of food on the third three days.—*Parására.*

A *Krichchhra Sântapanam* penance is said to consist in living on a compound of cow-dung, cow's urine, cow-milk, curdled cow-milk, clarified cow-butter and the washings of *Kus'â* grass on the first day, and in observing a fast on the day following. (213)

A Brâhmana, doing an *Ati-Krichchhram* penance, shall eat one morsel of food, each day, for the first three days of its term as described before, and fast on the succeeding three days. (214)

A self-controlled Brâhmana, doing a *Tapta Krichchham* penance, shall bathe once a dy and drink hot water during the first three days, hot milk during the second three days, hot clarified butter during the third three days, and hot air during the fourth three days of its term. (215)

A *Parâka* penance, which consists in one's fasting for twelve consecutive days with his senses fully brought under his control, removes all sin. (216)

Let him bathe thrice and partake of fifteen morsels of food on the day of the full moon, diminish the number of morsels by one on each successive day, observing a fast on the day of the new moon, and thereafter increase the number of morsels by one, each day, till it again reaches fifteen on the next full moon-day. This penance is called the *Chândrâyanam*. (217)

The same rule should be followed in respect of a *Chândrâyanam* of the *Yava madhya* (barley-middled) kind with the exception that, the morsels of food should be increased by one, each day, commencing from the first day of the moon's increase, [till the number of morsels reaches fifteen on the full-moon day, and thereafter decreasing it by one, each day, during the dark fortnight, the penitent fasting on the day of the next new moon. (218)

A Brâhmana, doing a *Yati Chândrâyanam*, shall partake of eight morsels of vegetable food, each day, self-controlled, for a month. (219)

Let a self-controlled Brâhmana eat four morsels of (vegetable) food after sun-rise, and four such morsels after sun down, each day. This is what is called the *S'is'u Chândrâyanam*. (220)

He, who, self-controlled, eats thrice eighty morsels of vegetable food in the course of a month, ascends to the region of the moon-god, (*i.e.*, the region of the lunar *Pitris*.)* (221)

(Eleven) *Rudras*, (twelve) *A'dityas*, (eight) *Vasus*, *Maruts* and the holy sages, for the extinction of all discordant elements (in their souls), practised this *Chândrâyanam* penance of yore. (222)

Each day, during its performance, the penitent shall personally do the fire-offering, known as the *Mahá-Vyáhriti Homa*, and live a life of absolute simplicity, truthfulness, and non-irascibility, free from all killing propensities. (223)

[For a month] daily he shall bathe with all his clothes on, thrice in the day and thrice in the night, abjuring all talk with women, with S'udras and with the degraded. (224)

Worshipping the gods, Bráhmanas and preceptors, continent, and carrying the staff, etc., let him, day and

---

* According to the Brahmanic Cosmogony the region, whence, the soul, roused from its sleep of repose, and acted upon by the dynamics of acts of its former incarnation, is drawn towards the plane of human existence, and wherein it stays until it enters the life-energy of the creator of its organic frame on earth.

night, sit up awake; incapable of sitting up, let him lie down on the bare ground. (225)

He shall mutter the *Sávitri* and other sacred *Mantras* to the best of his ability; (Hence), muttering of these *Mantras* is commended in connection with practising all kinds of expiatory penances. (226)

Thus Bráhmanas shall purify themselves of sins which they are publickly known to have committed; sins, they have done in secret, they must expiate by means of *Homas* (fire-offerings) and *Japas* (mutterings of sacred *Mantras*). (227)

By confession, by repentance, by penitential austerities, (and) by (*Vediac*) study, a sinner is absolved of his sin; of a sin committed in time of distress one is absolved by gift making (charity.) (228)

Whenever a man confesses the sin he has himself committed, he casts it off as a snake casts off his slough. (229)

Whenever his mind censures the misdeed (he has done) his body becomes free from that sin. (230)

Having repented for his sin, he becomes absolved thereof; the mind becomes purified by the determination to desist from it in future. (231)

Having pondered in his mind on the fact that one has to suffer the effects of good or bad deeds in the next world, let him be engaged, body and soul, in doing good deeds, each day. (232)

Wishing to be free from the consequences of misdeeds, which he might have wilfully or unwilfully committed, let him refrain from doing it for the second time (in future.) (233)

If after having done an expiatory penance, one does not acquire the (desired) ease (*lit.* lightness) of spirit, he must continue to do the penance until his mind becomes fully relieved of its burden. (234)

Tapasyâ (devotional austerity and divine communion) is the root of all happiness which is to be found in heaven or on earth; in *Tapasyâ* doth it stay and in *Tapasyâ* does it merge. This has been said by the *Veda-knowing* wise. (235)

Knowledge is the *Tapas* of a Brâhmana, protection of subjects forms the *Tapas* (highest duty) of a Kshatriya, agriculture, trade and cattle rearing form the *Tapas* of a Vais'ya, and service forms the *Tapas* of a S'udra. (236)

The self-controlled Rishis, who live on fruits, roots or air, by means of *Tapasyâ* alone, behold the three regions (*i e.*, the universe) with all its inmates, both mobile and immobile. (237)

Medical knowledge, knowledge of Antidotes to poisons, knowledge of Brahma and residences in various regions of heaven are attained by means of *Tapasyâ*, *Tapasyâ* is the only instrument through which they are realised. (238)

Whatever is insurmountable, whatever is unaccessable (*lit.* unavailable), whatever is impassable, and whatever is impossible to be performed, is easy of accomplishment by *Tapasyâ* alone; verily irresistible is the prowess (energy of) *Tapasyâ*. (239)

Mahâpâtakins and other miscreants become free from sin by means of austere penitential austerities. (240)

Insects, flies, beasts and birds, and immobile things ascend to heaven through the energy of *Tapasyâ*. (241)

Sin which a man may commit by his body, mind and speech, *Tapasvins* (practisers of penitential austerities) can speedily consume by their *Tapas*. (242)

Of a Brâhman, purified by penitential austerities, the gods accept the offerings and fulfil his desires. (243)

By dint of *Tapasyá* the lord *Prajàpati* created this Sastras (framed this code) and by *Tapasya* the sages obtained the *Vedas*. (244)

The gods, observing the highest merit of *Tapasyâ* pronounces *Tapasyá* to be the greatest fortune (of man). (245)

Daily reading of the *Vedas* according to one's ability, performance of the five daily sacrifices, and forbearance tend to destroy the sin, incidental to the commission of any of the great sins (*Mahâpâtakas*.) (246)

As fire speedily consumes its fuels with its own energy, so a *Veda*-knowing (Bráhmana) consumes all his sins with the fire of knowledge. (247)

Thus I have described conformably to the Regulation the expiatory penances in respect of sins; now hear me describe the purificatory penances for the expiation of sins committed in secret. (248)

By practising sixteen *Prânâyâmas*, each day, accompanied by the *Gyâtri S'ira Mantra* coupled with *Pranava* and *Vyâhritis*, one becomes absolved even of the sin of killing a Brahmana in the course of a month. (249)

By muttering sixteen times, each day, for a month the *Mantra* running as *A'pa na S'os'uchad*, etc.,* first sung by *Kutsa*, or the *Mantra Pratistomehi rushasam*, etc., first sung by Vasistha, the *Máhitram*† or the *S'uddhavatya*‡ Rik, a wine-drinker becomes free from his sin. (250)

* *A'po na S'os'uchadagham*, etc.

† *Mahitreenámadho'-stri*, etc.

‡ *S'uddhavatya etànindram Stavamahe.*

By once muttering the Vediac Suktam, *Vamiyam** etc., or the *S'ivasamkalpa*† *Mantra*, a gold stealer becomes speedily free from his sin. (251)

By muttering for a month the *Mantra*, *Havishanta*, etc., or *Natamaniho*, or the *Purusha Suktam*, a defiler of his preceptor's bed becomes free from his sin. (252)

A great sinner (*Mahâpâtakin*), seeking absolution from his sin, shall mutter, for a year, any of the following Suktas, *viz*-, *Avati Helo Varunayo*, etc., or *Yatkimchid Varanadevo* etc., or *Iti me manah*, etc. (253)

Having accepted a gift from a vile or degraded person, one shall mutter for three days the (four) Riks, running as *tarat Samandu dhâvati*, etc., whereby he shall be purified. (254)

By bathing in a running stream and by muttering for a month the Rik, running as *Soma Rudrâ*, atc., or the (three) Riks, running as *A'ryayamanam Varunam Mitrancha*, etc., one becomes free from varied sins. (255)

By muttering for six months the seven Richas commencing with *Indra Mitram Varuna*, etc., a penitent becomes free from all sin; by living on food obtained by begging for a moth after having evacuated the excreta of of his body in water, a man becomes sinless. (256)

By making fire-offerings with libations of clarified butter accompanied by the recitation of the *S'âkala Mantra* (running as *Daivakritsyainasa*) for a whole year, or by muttering for a year the *Mantra*, *Nama Indras'cha*, etc., one becomes free from a *Mahâpâtakam*. (257)

---

* *Asya Vâmiyamasya Vâmasya patitasya etat*, etc.

† *Yajjàgrato du'ram*, etc.

A great sinner (*Mahâpâtakin*) shall live on food obtained by begging, and follow the kine to the pasture ground, reciting the *Pavamâni Mantra*, each day, for a year, whereby he shall be freed from his sin. (258)

Or by practising three *Paràka* penances, and by thrice reciting, self-controlled, any of the *Vediac Samhitàs*, he becomes free from all sin. (256)

Let him fast for three days, thrice bathe each day and recite the *Aghamarshanam Suktam*, at morning, noon, and evening, whereby he shall be free from all sin. (260)

As the *As'vamedha,* the king of religious sacrifices, tends to absolve all sin, so the recitation of the *Aghamarshanam Suktam* is sin-absolving in its effect. (261)

Sin toucheth not a Bráhmana who well remembers his *Vedaic Mantras* even if he destroys the three regions, or eats his food at unclean places (*lit.* here, there and any where.) (262)

By reading the *Rik*, *Yajus* or *Sâma* Samhita together with the Upanishads, a Brâhmana, self-controlled, becomes free from all sin. (263)

As a brick-bat, thrown into a large lake, soon sinks into its bottom, so all sins are merged in the three-fold *(Trivrit) Veda*. (264)

The *Rik Veda*, the *Yujur Veda* and other various kinds of *Sama Mantras* are collectively called the three-fold *Veda* (*Trivrit Veda*); a Brâhmana who knows this is called a *Veda*-knowing one. (265)

The *Mystic Pranava Mantra* (Om), the beginning of all the *Vedas*, as well as their stay, which consists of three letters, is also called the *Trivrit Veda*; he who knows it well, is also called a *Veda*-knowing one. (266)

CHAPTER XII.

O THOU sinless one, you have discoursed on the duties of members of four social orders, now truly describe to us the effects of acts, done by men in their former births. (1)

Unto them, Bhrigo of virtuous soul said, hear me (describe) the true effects of all such acts. (2)

It is the auspicious or inauspicious effects of acts, born of mind, speech and body, which impart to men superior, middling, or inferior status, according to their respective natures. (3)

The mind should be understood as the impellor of these three-fold (superior, middling or inferior) and three-located (*i. e.*, born of speech, mind and body) acts of an embodied self, which are possessed of the ten following attributes. (4)

Coveting other men's goods, planning evil to others, and false* notion (as to the next life, etc.) are the three inauspicious mental acts. (5)

Harsh speaking, false speaking, speaking ill of another at his back, and idle gossiping are the four inauspicious lingual acts. (6)

Receiving what has not been given, killing animal life (not according to the Regulation) and incest with another's wife are the three inauspicious bodily acts. (7)

A man enjoys through his mind, speech and body the effects of acts he had done by his mind, speech and body respectively in (his former existence). (8)

Through the dynamics of his (inauspicious) bodily

---

* The text has *Vitathábhi nivesáh* :—KULLUKA explains it by "*Na'sti Paralokah, deha eva a'tiná, eti,*" is such notions as there is no next life, the body is self, etc.

acts a man takes birth as an insensate thing; through the dynamics of his inauspicious lingual acts, he shall be born as a beast or bird, and it is through the dynamics of his inauspicious mental acts that he shall be born as a man of vile caste in this world. (9)

He who has conquered his body, mind and speech and has the faculty in his intellect of keeping them under restraint is said to be the man of three restraints (Tridandin). (10)

Controlling his lust and anger, he who can exercise these three kinds of rods (restraints) in respect of all creatures, obtains emancipation. (11)

He who causes the body to be operative is called *Kshetrajna* (individualised self) and the body which performs these acts is called *Bhutámá* (material organism) by the wise. (12)

Another self there is who takes birth with each individual creature, and through the angency of whom pain and pleasure are perceived (by them) in their (successive) re-births. (13)

This *Kshetrajna* (individualised self) and *Mahat* (Soul as distinct from the body and the individualised consciousness) are intimitaly associated with the five material elements, and ensconced in the bodies of all creatures, high and low, they depend upon the Supreme Soul for their existence. (14)

Innumerable (subtle) embodied Selves (*Kshetrajnas*), which fall off like sparks from the eternal body of this Supreme Soul, make the bodies of all creatures, high and low, animative and operative. (15)

Truly out of the subtile essences of the five kinds of material elements subtile bodies are formed with which the selves of miscreants are clothed, after death, for the purpose of suffering pain. (16)

Lying merged in the subtile essences of the five elements of their gross material frames, after death, they (miscreant selves) suffer the pangs which the great Law (*Yama*) has ordained for them. (17)

Having suffered pangs for its attachment to forbidden pleasures of sight, taste, touch, etc., in life, the Self (encased in the gross, subtile and causal bodies)* becomes purified again and attaches itself) (*i.e.*, becomes merged in) to the *Mahat* and *Kshetrajna*. (18)

These two (*Mahat* and *Kshetrajna*) with sleepless eyes witness the good or bad deeds of the individual, through the effects of which he enjoys pleasure, or suffers pain, after death. (19)

If he had done greater good than evil in life, he should enjoy the pleasures of Paradise, clothed with those material elements, (*i.e.*, with a material frame) after death. (20)

If he had done greater evil than good in his life, he, forsaken by those elements (devoid of a material body), should suffer the pangs which the Law has ordained for him.† (21)

---

* According to the Vedanta each individual has three kinds of bodies, *viz.*, *Bhuta* (gross material frame), *Sukshma* (made of the subtile essences of the five elements of the gross body) and *Linga* (causal). After the destruction of his gross body, the self of a man continues in his subtile and causal bodies. KULLUKA explains its by *Bhuta-Sukshma-Linga-S'arirávachchhinna*.

† The text has *Yámistá Yãtanáh* : which is usually translated as pangs inflicted by Yama, the lord of Death. We have thought fit to interpret Yama by Niyama, the Law, the ordanier. In the Pauranic literature this Law has been deified and invested with a body perhaps to bring home to the minds of its readers the

Free from sin, for having undergone those pangs of existence, after death, the individual Self again attaches itself to the five material elements. (22)

Pondering over these pangs or pleasures of the individualised self through sin or virtue, let him engage his mind in the performance of virtue. (23)

The *Sattva* (manifestation), *Rajas* (desire) and *Tamas* (nescience) are the three qualities of Self, with which *Mahat* (Consciousness converted into intellection), covering all becomings (created things), exists. (24)

Out of these, the quality which predominates in an individual imparts its characteristic virtue to his self (character). (25)

Sattva is knowledge, *Rajas* is attachment and aversion, and *Tamas* is nescience ; these qualities permeate the bodies of all created things. (26)

The pure, illuminating peace in the soul should be understood as the *Sattva*. (27)

That, which is assoiciated with misery, is unpleasant to the soul, and creates in embodied creatures an attachment to the objects of the senses, should be understood as the irresistible *Rajas*. (28)

That, which is unmanifest, devoid of the discrimination of good and evil, creates an attachment to the objects of the senses, unknowable and unscrutinisable, should be understood as *Tamas*. (29)

Now I shall fully describe the superior, middling and inferior effects of these (three kinds of) qualities. (30)

Studying the *Vedas*, practising penitential austerities, cultivating knowledge (of the *Sàstras*), purity, subjugation of the senses, performances of religious rites,

---

Vedantic Law of Karma in a concrete and comprehensible form. —*Translator*.

and contemplation of Self are the indications of the quality of *Sattva* (manifestation. (31)

Undertaking acts (for the fruition of a definite desire), impatience, performance of forbidden acts, and a constant enjoyment of the objects of the senses, are indications of the quality of *Rajas* (desire). (32)

Greed, somnolence, want of fortitude, cruelty, Godlessness, embracing forbidden vocations, beggary, and folly are the indications of the quality of *Tamas* (nescience.) (33)

Of these three qualities, which exist through all eternity, past, present and future, the following should be understood as the collective indications of attributes. (34)

An act, having done, or doing, or intending to do which a man becomes ashamed of himself, is called as marked by the properties of the quality of *Tamas* (darkness or nescience) by the wise. (35)

An act, by doing which one acquires a high renown in this world, and on the failure to complete which he does not feel any grief, should be understood as marked by the quality of *Rajas*. (36)

An act, about which every one wishes to know, and by doing which one does not feel any shame and the inner-self feels complacent, is said to emanate from the quality of *Sattva*. (37)

Lust is the effect of *Tamas*, wealth is the object of *Rajas*, and virtue is the indication of *Sattva*; of these each succeeding (quality) is higher than the preceding one in respect of merit. (38)

Now I shall briefly describe in due order the status which a man acquires through the working of each of these three qualities. (39)

Beings, possessed of the quality of *Sattva*, acquire divinity, those marked by the quality of *Rajas* take births as men, and those marked by the quality of *Tamas* are born as beasts. Thus the three fold existence (through the dynamics of these qualities) is described. (40)

This three-fold existence admits of a (further) secondary, three-fold division such as, superior, middling and inferior, according to the acts and knowledge, etc., of beings (respectively marked by these qualities.) (41)

Births as immobile things (trees, etc.), worms, insects, fishes, snakes, tortoises, beasts and deer are the effects of the inferior or worst kind of *Tamas*. (42)

Births as elephants, horses, S'udras, condemnable Mlechchhas, lions, tigers, and boars, are the effects of the middling kind of *Tamas*. (43)

Births as dancers, arrogant men (black legs), *Râkshasas*, and Pis'âchas are the effects of the superior (most refined) kind of *Tamas*. (44)

Births as *Jhallas* (clubs-men), *Mallas* (wrestlers), actors, arms-men, gamblers, and drunkards are the effects of the inferior kind of *Rajas*. (45)

Births as anointed kings of countries, priests of kings, and wrestlers are the effects of the middling kind of Rajas. (46)

Births as *Gandharvas*, *Guhyakas*, *Yakshas*, attendants of the gods, and *Apsarasas* are the effects of the superior kind of *Rajas*. (47)

Births as *Tàpasas* (practisers of penitential austerities), Yatis, Bráhmanas, the scalers of heaven, stars and *Daítyas* are the effects of inferior *Sattva*. (48)

Births as celebrants of religious sacrifices, (sages)

Vediac gods, embodied deities, stars such as the pole star, etc, years, *Pitris* and *Sàdhyas* are the effects of the middling kind of *Sattva*. (49)

Births as Brahmá, Marichi, Prajâpati, the embodied virtue, tne embodied principle of intellection (Mahat), or the unmanifest Nature are the effects of the superior kind of *Sattwa*. (50)

Thus I have fully described the kinds of acts (such as, mental, lingual and bodily) and the three kinds of existences which originate from them, (marked by the qualities of *Sattwa Rajas* and *Tamas*), and the existences (in detail which all creatures obtain according to their three-fold character (superior, middling and inferior). (51)

By indulging in pleasures of the senses, by not instituting the religious rites (such as, the rites of purification, etc.) the foolish miscreants obtain sinful existences. (52)

Now hear me describe the wombs in which the individealised Self is constrained to take its successive births in this world and the acts through which it gets such existences. (53)

For many years having suffered pangs in hell, the souls of *Mahàpatakins* (great sinners) are born in the following wombs in this world. (54)

A Bráhmana-killer is born in the womb of a bitch, sow, she-ass, she-camel, cow, ewe, she-dear, hen bird, Chandála woman and Pukkasa woman. (55)

A wine-drining Bráhmana is born in the wombs of worms, insects, filth-eating birds and ferocious beasts of the forest. (56)

For a thousand times a gold-stealer Brâhmana is

born in the wombs of spiders, snakes, lizards, crocodiles and malignat *Pis'áchas.* (57)

For a hundred incarnations a defiler of his preceptor's bed is born as a weed, a bush, a creeper, as a flesh-eating and ferocious beast, and a fanged beast of the forest, given to killing (such as, a lion or tiger. (58)

Killers of animal lives are re-born as beasts that eat raw flesh; eaters of forbidden food are re-born as vile worms; thieves are re-born as beasts that eat each other's flesh; and those who go unto vile-caste women, are re born as *Pretas* (ghosts). (59)

By keeping the company of the degraded, by carnally knowing another's wife, by stealing a Bráhmana's property, one is re-born as a *Brahma-Ràkshasa.* (60)

For having stolen jems, pearls, corals and various kinds of gems out of greed, one shall take birth in the womb of a gold-smith's wife. (61)

For having stolen paddy (food grains), one shall be reborn as a mouse; for having stolen white brass, he shall be reborn as a diving bird; for having stolen honey, he shall be reborn as a stinged flee; for having stolen milk, he shall be reborn as a crow; for having stolen any kind of sweet sap, he shall be reborn as a dog; and for having stolen clarified butter, he shall be reborn as an ichneumon. (62)

For having stolen flesh, he shall become a vulture; for having stolen lard, a diving crane; for having stolen oil, a cockroach; for having stolen salt, a *Chirivàk* insect; and for having stolen milk-curd, a small heron. (63)

For having stolen a silk cloth he shall become a *Titteri* bird; for having stolen a cloth of vegetable fibres, a frog; for having stolen a cotton cloth, a heron;

for having stolen a cow, a lizard (Godhâ); and for having stolen treacle, a bat. (64)

For having stolen, scents he shall become a mole; for having stolen edible leaves, a peacock; for having stolen confection, a porcupine; and for having stolen an uncooked article of food, a *S'alyaka*. (65)

For having stolen fire, he shall become a heron; for having stolen a household impliment (such as a winnow, etc.), a *Grihakàri* bird, (a species of bird which builds its nest with clay, weeds, etc.); and for having stolen a red cloth, a *Chakora* bird. (66)

For having stolen a deer or an elephant, he shall become a wolf; for having stolen a horse, a tiger; for having stolen fruit or roots, a monkey; for having stolen a woman, a bear; for having stolen drinking water, a *Chátaka* bird; for having stolen a cart, a camel; and for having stolen any other kind of beast, a goat. (67)

For having forcibly stolen any thing, belonging to another, or clarified butter not offered as a libation, he must needs takes birth as a beast. (68)

For having stolen these things, women also acquire demerit and are reborn as wives of the aforesaid beasts. (69)

For not having discharged the proper duties of their respective orders, in times of peace (*lit.* undistress), members of the four social orders take births in the wombs of the following beasts and become servants of their enemies in their next births. (70)

A Bráhmana, who has swerved from his duty in life, shall become a ghost, living on egesta, and vomiting flames of fire; a Kshatriya, for the same offence, shall live in the hell of *Kutaputana*, eating excreta and putrid carcasses. (71)

A Vaishya (for the same offence) shall become a *Maitràksha-Joyotika* (anus-mouthed) Ghost, (*lit.* eating, the vermins, lice, etc., of worn cloths. (72)

The senses, through which sensuous men most enjoy the sensual pleasures, become the keenest, after death, and prove a source of torment to them. (73)

By dint of practising those acts, (souls of foolish men suffer) pangs in this world and are re-born in those wombs. (74)

They suffer torments in the hell of darkness, in the hell of the forest of sword-leaves, and in the joint-splitting hell. (75)

They suffer various kinds of torments, are devoured by crows and owls, are made to walk on hot sand banks, and are whirled in the whirling torrents of the hell of *Kumbhipâka*. (76)

They take births in the wombs of beasts and constantly suffer the pangs of those miserable existences, subjected to the torments of heat and cold, and seeing many frightful visions. (77)

Frequent residences in wombs, frequent painful births, pains of incarceration (as beasts), and servitude of others they are constrained to suffer. (78)

Separation from friends and dear ones, association with the miscreants, acquisition or loss of things, and creation of friends and enemies (torment them). (79)

Helpless old age(imbecility), affliction with diseases, various kinds of pain (such as hunger, thirst, etc.,) and the unconquerable death (add to their torments in life). (80)

The feeling, with which a man does an act in life, imparts to his self a suitable body for the enjoyment of the fruit thereof in the next world, and the nature of which is determined by the nature of that feeling. (81)

Thus all the dynamical energies of acts have been fully described; now hear me discourse on those duties of Bráhmanas, by doing which they can attain the highest good (emancipation). (82)

Studying the *Vedas*, practising penitential austerities (divine contemplation and realising one's oneness with the Supreme Self), knowledge, subjugation of the senses annihilation of all killing propensities, and serving the elders are the acts which lead to the highest good. (83)

Of all these auspicious acts, which one brings the highest good to the individual? (84)

Ot these, the knowledge of self is the highest duty, that is the foremost of all knowledge, since through it one attains immortality. (85)

Of the six (aforesaid) acts, the institution of Vediac rites should be understood as the most benificial in this life and the next. (86)

All those acts are intimately connected with the institution of Vediac rites (*i.e.* they lead to self-knowledge. (87)

Vediac acts may be divided unto two classes, such as the *Pravrittam* and *Nivrittam*; by *Pravrittam* acts one enjoys happiness and prosperity (elevation), by *Nivrittam* acts one acquires emancipation. (88)

An act or rite, done or instituted for the fruition of a definite object either in this life or in the next, is called *Pravrittam*; an acts voluntarily done without any prospect of gain or reward, is called a *Nivrittam* one, (89)

By doing *Pravrittam* acts, one attains equality with the gods; and by doing *Nivrittam* acts one gets control over the material elements. (90)

Seeing his Self equally in all things, and all things in his Self, a celebrant of the Sacrifice of Self attains the kingdom of self (emancipation). (91)

The foremost of Bráhmanas, by abjuring all acts enjoined to be performed in the Sastra, shall strive to subjugate his senses, to study the Vedas, and to acquire the knowledge of Self. (92)

This is the highest success in the life of a Bráhmana in special, achievement of any other kind of success is not his success in life. (93)

The *Vedas* are the eternal eyes of the gods, manes, and men; the *Vedas* have no human authors and are independent of all logic or argument. This is the decision. (94)

Smritis which are not based on the *Vedas*, and S'âstras which are hostile to the Vedas and are founded on sophistry, are worthless in respect of the next life. They emanate from the quality of *Tamas.* (95)

S'ástras, which are not founded on the *Vedas* and are framed by men, are coming into being and vanishing. They are false and worthless. (96)

The four castes, the three regions, the four orders of house holder, etc.) the past, present ,and future are founded on the *Vedas.* (97)

Sound, touch, sight, taste, and smell, which is the fifth, have originated from the *Vedas*; the *Veda* has given birth to every thing according to its nature and function. (98)

The eternal *Vedah* embraces all created things; hence, the wise call it the greatest instrument of realising the highest good of human life (emancipation.) (99)

A *Veda*-knowing man is fit to be entrusted with generalship, sovereignty, or the highest judgeship of the land; nay, with the over-lordship of all the regions. (100)

As a fully kindled fire consumes even the moist trees, so a *Veda*-knowing man by dint of his right knowledge burns all the demerit, born of his acts. (101)

A Brâhmana, a knower of the true imports of the *Vedas*, in whichsover order of life he may be staying, happens to be one with Brahmâ, even in this life. (102)

A reader of books is greater than an illiterate one; one who has got those books by his heart is better than a mere reader; one who has got a true knowledge of their contents is greater than one who remembers them, and one who acts according to that knowledge is greater than one who has merely gained a knowledge of their contents. (103)

Tapasyá and self-knowledge are the highest good of a Brâhmana. *Tapasyá* consumeth sin, self-knowledge giveth him immortal life. (104)

He who wishes to know the true principle of virtue must know all the sciences which are based on positive observation, inference and the teachings of the *Vedas*. (105)

He, who discusses the ethical teachings of the *Vedas* and of the veda-based *Smritis* with processes of reasoning not hostile to their tenets is alone enabled to know the right principle of virtue and no one else. (106)

Now, all expedients by which self emancipation is obtained have been described; now hear me expound the secret teachings of the Institutes of Manu. (107)

Laws, not specifically laid down is this code, should be unhesitatingly accepted, as virtuous (qualified) Brâhmanas would lay down and interpret. (108)

Those who have thoroughly studied the Dharma S'ástras, are well-versed in the *Vedas* and *Vedangas*, and lead the life of a *Brahmacharin* and are the living muniments of the texts of the *Sruti* should be judged as duly qualified (lawgivers). (109)

Whatever a council of ten, or of three qualified Brâhmanas, faithful to their duties, shall lay down as the law, must be accepted as such. (110)

Such a council must consist of at least ten Brâhmanas, who have studied the three *Vedas*, are acquainted with rules of reasoning and inference, and are well versed in the *Nirukta* and law codes. (111)

In respect of determing a doubtful point of law, the council must consist of at least three Bráhmanas, well versed in the Rik, Yajush and Sam Vedas. (112)

Even whatever a single Veda-knowing Brâhmana shall determine as the law shall be accepted as such in exclusion of what has been said by ten thousand ignorant Brâhmanas. (113)

A council, consisting of thousands of assembled Brâhmanas, who are devoid of penances (vratas) and Vediac knawledge and live by the emblem of their caste, can never acquire the status of a true council. (114)

The sin of that false law, which foolish Brâhmanas, unread in the law codes, and full of the quality of

Tamas, shall lay down, shall be increased hundred fold and attach itself to its speakers. (115)

Thus I have described to you all that confer the highest good on man; those who swerve not from these duties become emancipated. (116)

Thus the lord (*i.e.* Manu), for the good of the universe, has disclosed to me all the sacred principles of virtue (Law.) (117)

Self-controlled, let him see all things, whether real or unreal, as located in the Supreme Self; the mind of him who sees all things located in Self never turns to evil. (118)

The Self is all the deities, all things are located in Self; it is Self that leads the embodied beings to action. (119)

By thought let him realise the identity of the external ether with the ether in his mind, of the external air with the bodily air which is the cause of its movements and functions, of the external fire with the fire which burns in his eyes and digests the food in his stomach, of the external water with watery parts of his body, and of the external earth with the earthly constituents of his frame. (120)

Let him realise the identity of the moon-god with his mind, of the quarters with his ear, of Vishnu with his faculty of locomotion, of Hara with his strength, of fire with his speech, of Mitra with the evacuating faculty of his body and of Prajápati with his faculty of procreation. (121)

The governor of all these deities, minuter than the minutest atom, the effulgent, great Self, which is comprehensible only in a trance, let him meditate upon. (122)

Some call this supreme Self fire, others Manu; some call it Prajâpati, others senses. Some call it life; others, the eternal *Brahma* (123).

It is this supreme Self, which, covering all the creatures with his five material aspects of earth, etc., is revolving this wheel of existence by means of growth and decay. (124)

Thus he, who surveys his Self in all things by his Self, realises his identity with all and attains the supreme status of *Brahma*. (125)

By reading these institutes of Manu as narrated by Bhrigu, one becomes of good conduct and is enabled to acquire any kind of exalted existence he likes. (126)

FINISH.

TABLE OF CONTENTS.

Manu Samhita.

SUBJECTS. PAGE.